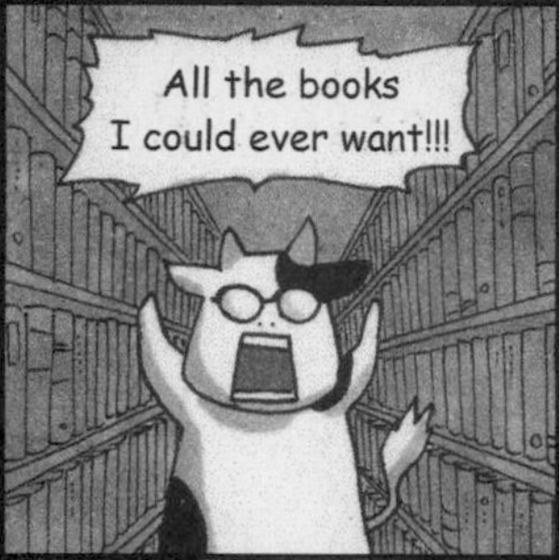

All the books I could ever want!!!

If God told me, "I will grant you anything in the world that you desire—just ask for it," I would answer without hesitation, "I want Japan's National Diet Library."

—*Hiromu Arakawa, 2008*

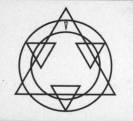

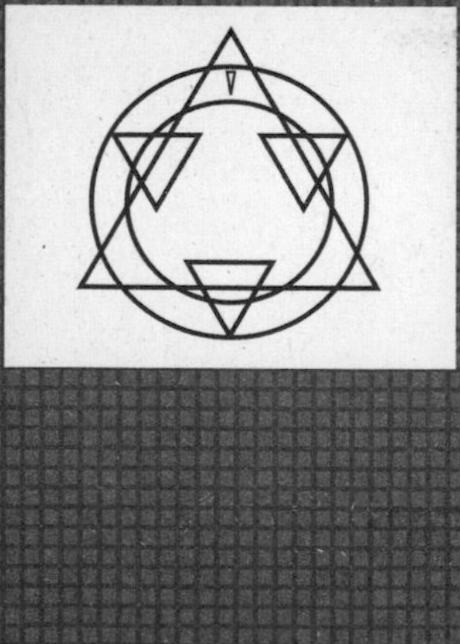

Born in Hokkaido (northern Japan), Hiromu Arakawa first attracted national attention in 1999 with her award-winning manga *Stray Dog*. Her series *Fullmetal Alchemist* debuted in 2001 in Square Enix's monthly manga anthology *Shonen Gangan*.

FULLMETAL ALCHEMIST
VOL. 19

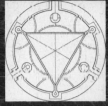

Story and Art by Hiromu Arakawa

Translation/Akira Watanabe
English Adaptation/Jake Forbes
Touch-up Art & Lettering/Wayne Truman
Design/Julie Behn
Editor/Annette Roman

Editor in Chief, Books/Alvin Lu
Editor in Chief, Magazines/Marc Weidenbaum
VP, Publishing Licensing/Rika Inouye
VP, Sales & Product Marketing/Gonzalo Ferreyra
VP, Creative/Linda Espinosa
Publisher/Hyoe Narita

Hagane no RenkinJutsushi vol. 19 © 2008 Hiromu Arakawa/SQUARE ENIX. First published in Japan in 2008 by SQUARE ENIX CO., LTD. English translation rights arranged with SQUARE ENIX CO., LTD. and VIZ Media, LLC. The stories, characters and incidents mentioned in this publication are entirely fictional.

The rights of the author(s) of the work(s) in this publication to be so identified have been asserted in accordance with the Copyright, Designs and Patents Act 1988. A CIP catalogue record for this book is available from the British Library.

Printed in the U.S.A.

Published by VIZ Media, LLC
P.O. Box 77010
San Francisco, CA 94107

10 9 8 7 6 5 4 3 2 1
First printing, July 2009

www.viz.com

RATED

PARENTAL ADVISORY
FULLMETAL ALCHEMIST is rated T for Teen and is recommended for ages 13 and up. Contains mildly strong language, tobacco/alcohol use and fantasy violence.

ratings.viz.com

store.viz.com

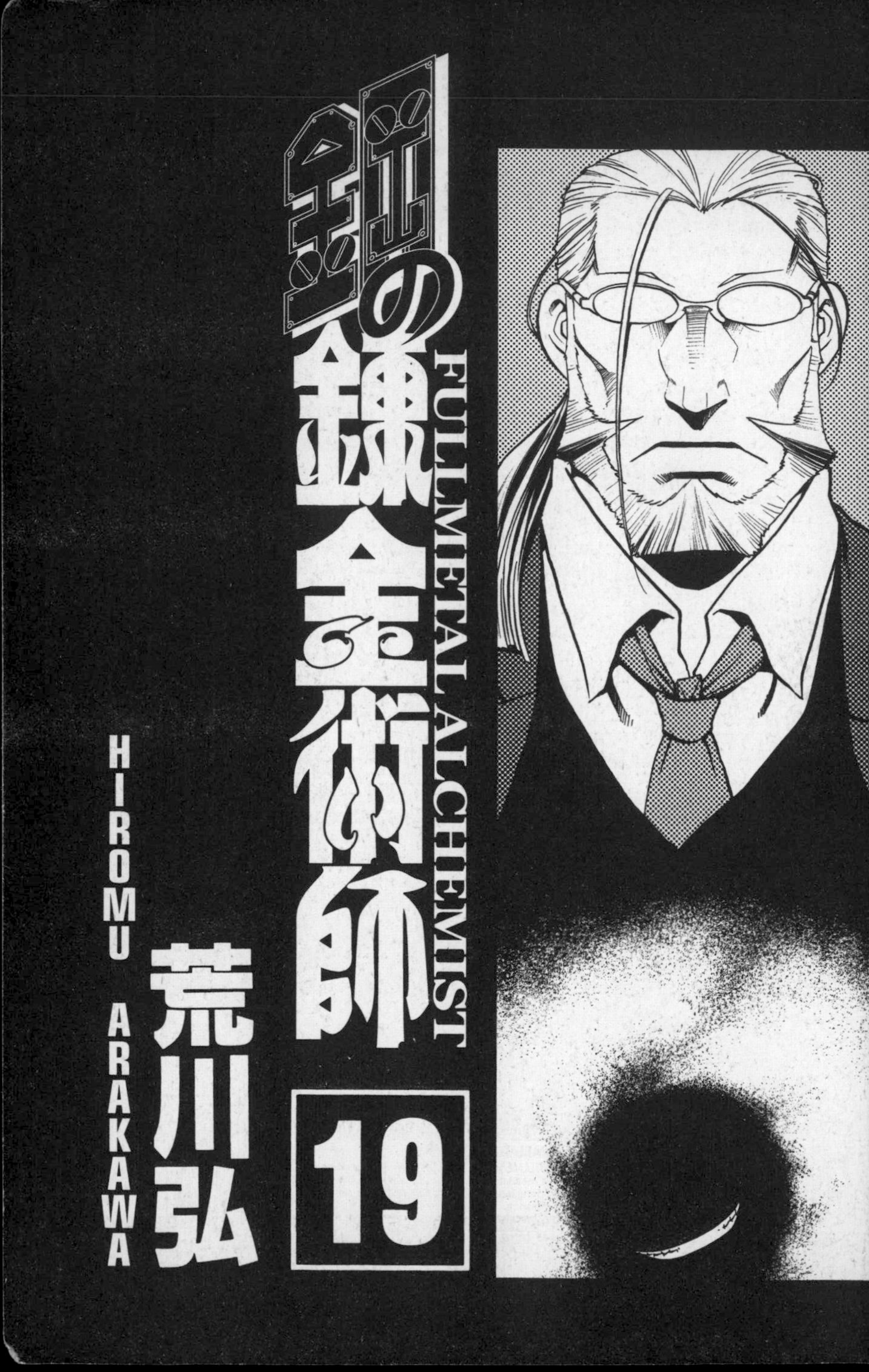

鋼の錬金術師

FULLMETAL ALCHEMIST

19

荒川弘

HIROMU ARAKAWA

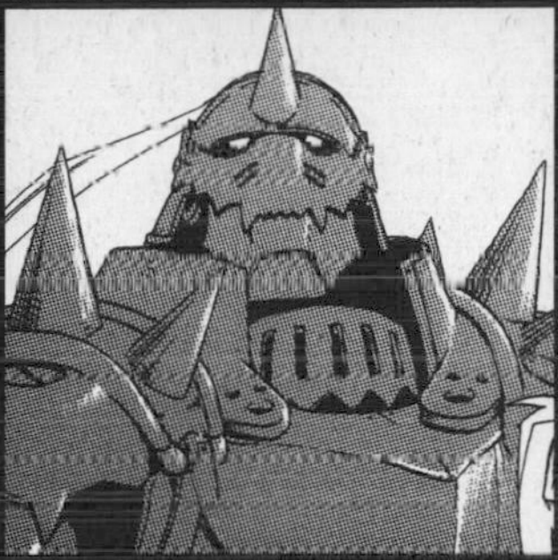

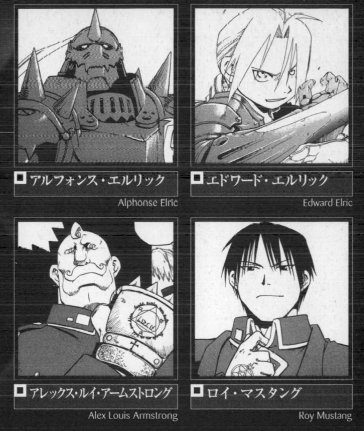

アルフォンス・エルリック

Alphonse Elric

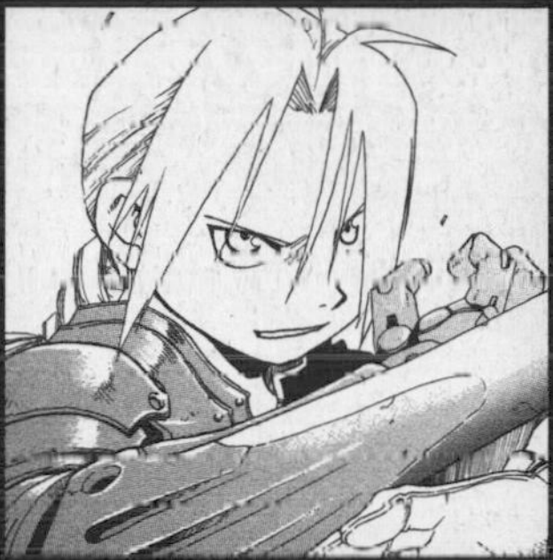

エドワード・エルリック

Edward Elric

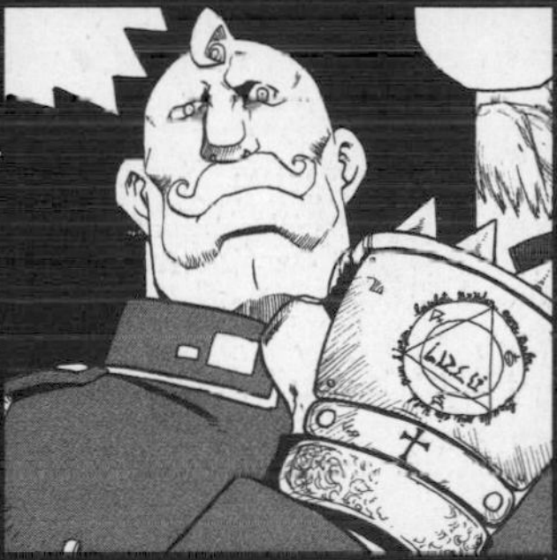

アレックス・ルイ・アームストロング

Alex Louis Armstrong

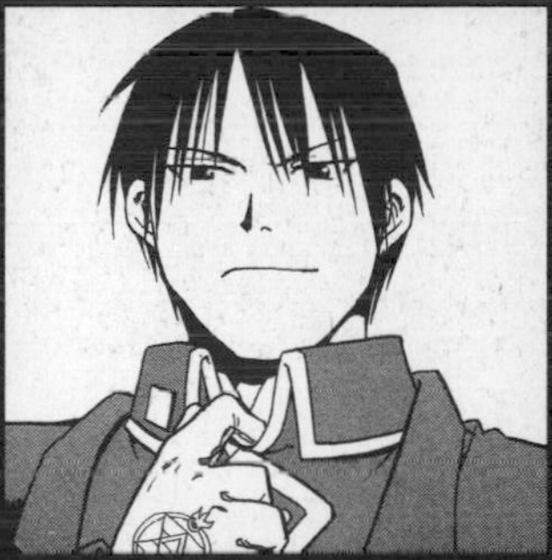

ロイ・マスタング

Roy Mustang

OUTLINE

FULLMETAL ALCHEMIST

Using a forbidden alchemical ritual, the Elric brothers attempted to bring their dead mother back to life. But the ritual went wrong, consuming Edward Elric's leg and Alphonse Elric's entire body. At the cost of his arm, Edward was able to graft his brother's soul into a suit of armor. Equipped with mechanical "auto-mail" to replace his missing limbs, Edward becomes a state alchemist in hopes of finding a way to restore their bodies. Their search embroils them in a deadly conspiracy that threatens to take the innocence, if not the lives, of everyone involved.

Since their shocking discovery of the military's ties to the Homunculi, Ed and Al have been kept on a short leash, with Winry held hostage to buy their silence. In the snowbound Mountains of Briggs, the brothers, in a tenuous alliance with Scar, come up with a plan to get Winry out of the enemy's clutches by faking her death. But all their plotting could be for naught. Major General Armstrong, their ally at Fort Briggs, has been summoned to Central Command. Now, with the murderous alchemist Kimblee hot on their trail, Ed desperately plots their next move...

鋼の錬金術師

FULLMETAL ALCHEMIST

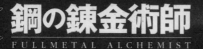

CHARACTERS

FULLMETAL ALCHEMIST

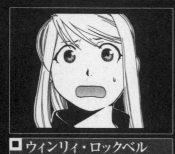

ウィンリィ・ロックベル

Winry Rockbell

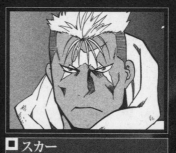

スカー

Scar

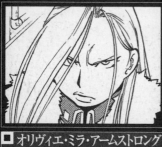

オリヴィエ・ミラ・アームストロング

Olivier Mira Armstrong

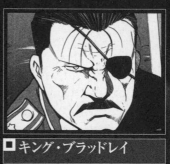

キング・ブラッドレイ

King Bradley

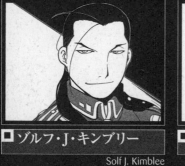

ゾルフ・J・キンブリー

Solf J. Kimblee

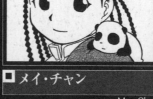

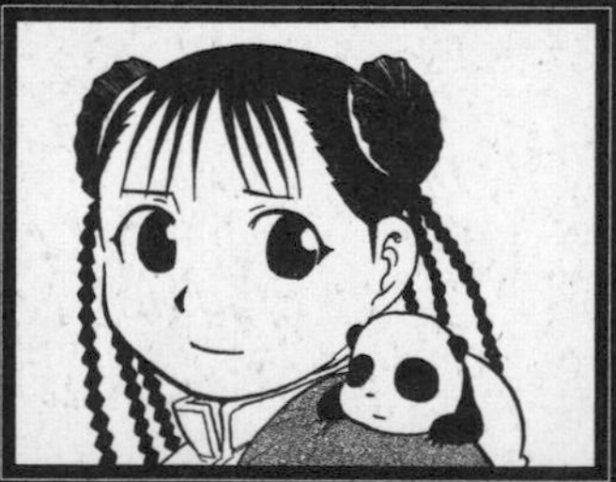

メイ・チャン

May Chang

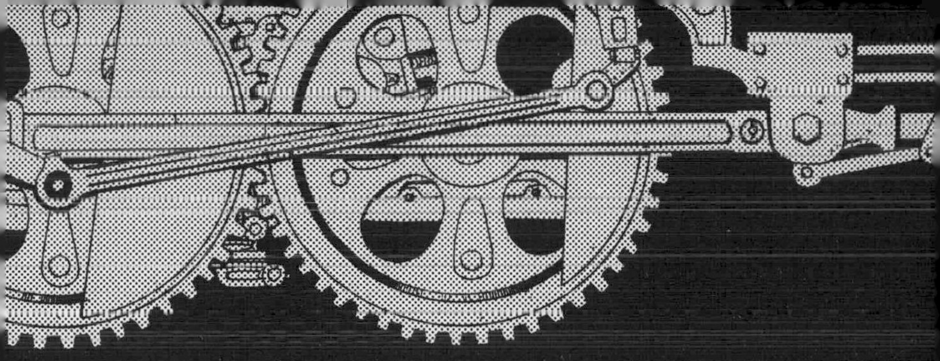

CONTENTS

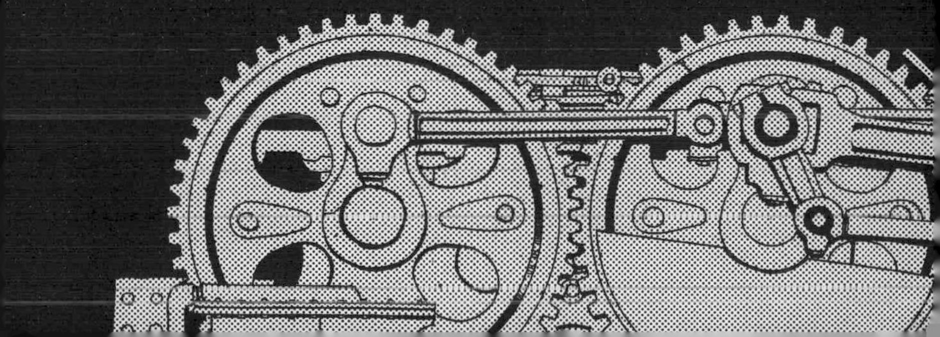

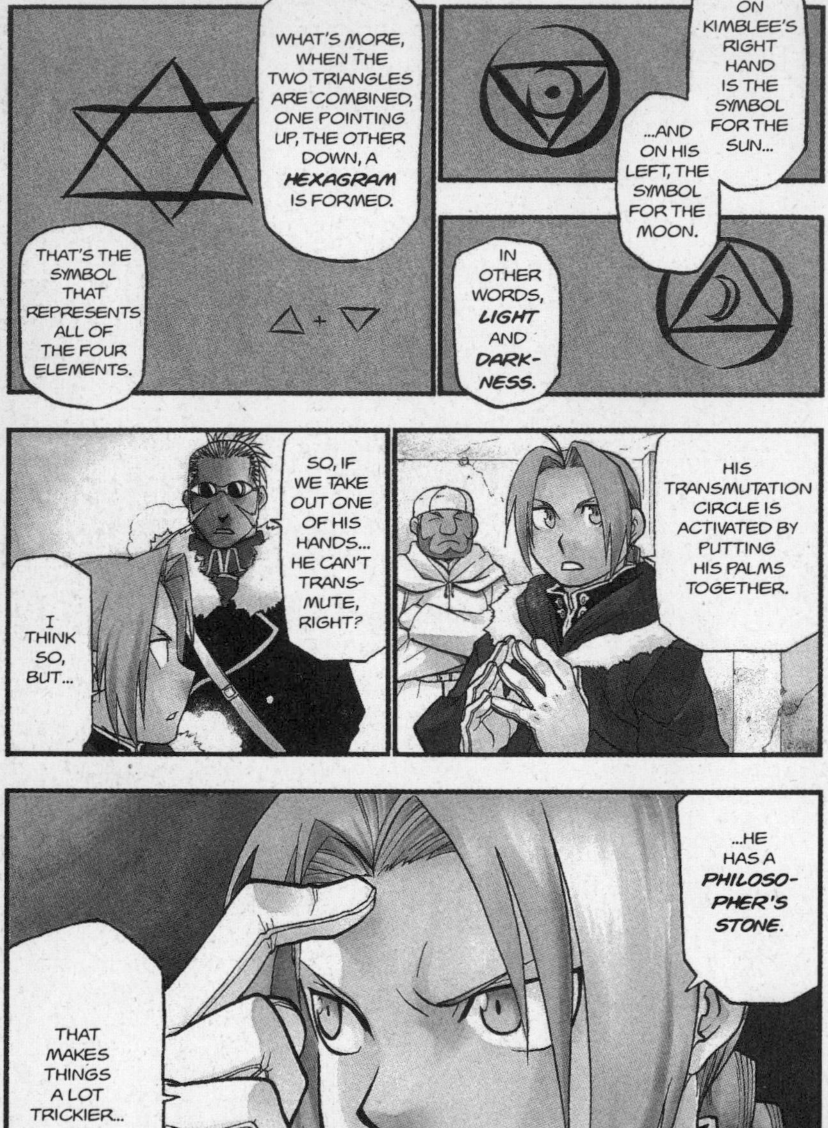
ON KIMBLEE'S RIGHT HAND IS THE SYMBOL FOR THE SUN...
...AND ON HIS LEFT, THE SYMBOL FOR THE MOON.
IN OTHER WORDS, LIGHT AND DARKNESS.
WHAT'S MORE, WHEN THE TWO TRIANGLES ARE COMBINED, ONE POINTING UP, THE OTHER DOWN, A HEXAGRAM IS FORMED.
THAT'S THE SYMBOL THAT REPRESENTS ALL OF THE FOUR ELEMENTS.
HIS TRANSMUTATION CIRCLE IS ACTIVATED BY PUTTING HIS PALMS TOGETHER.
SO, IF WE TAKE OUT ONE OF HIS HANDS... HE CAN'T TRANSMUTE, RIGHT?
I THINK SO, BUT...
...HE HAS A PHILOSOPHER'S STONE.
THAT MAKES THINGS A LOT TRICKIER...

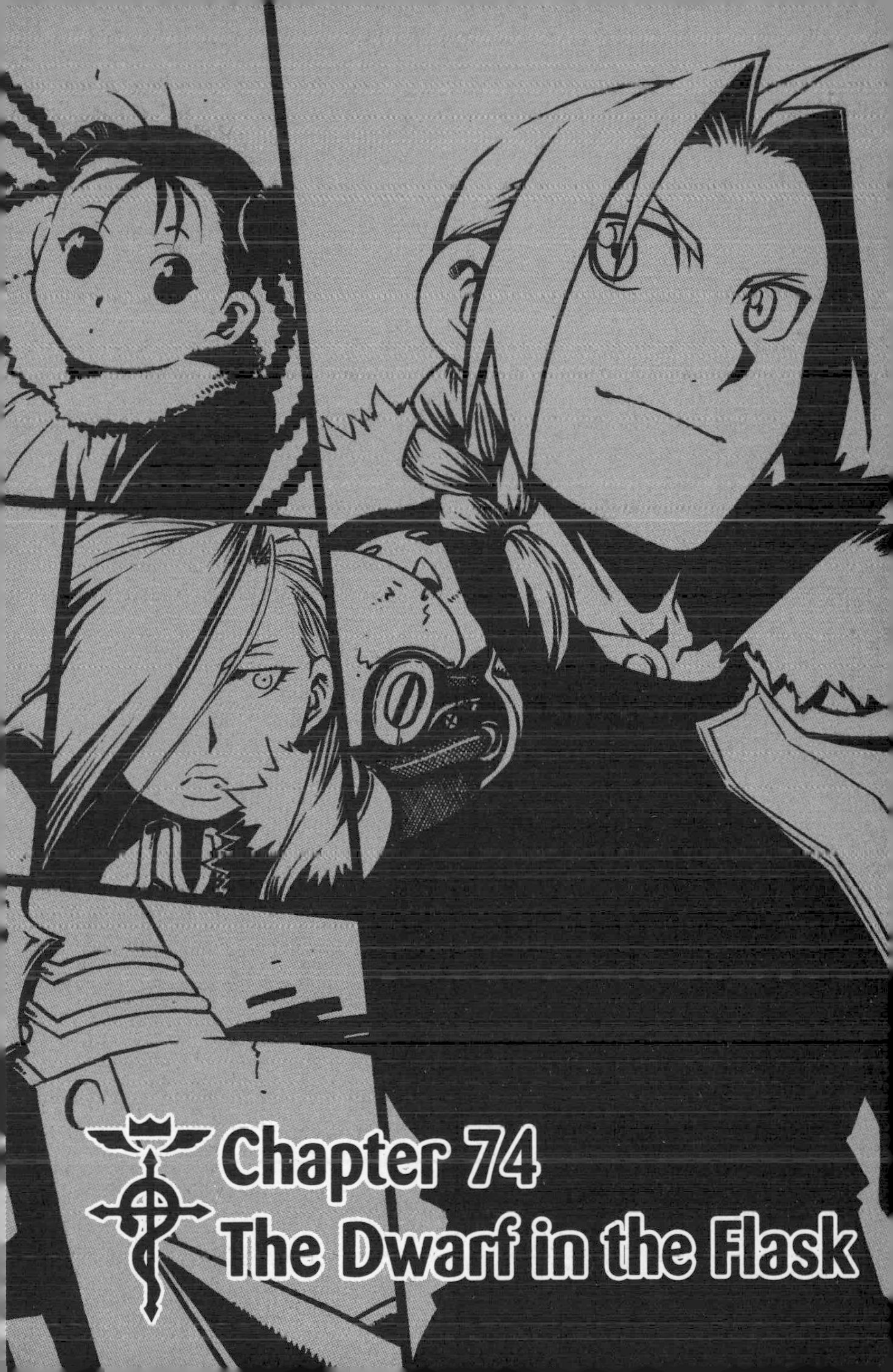

Chapter 74
The Dwarf in the Flask

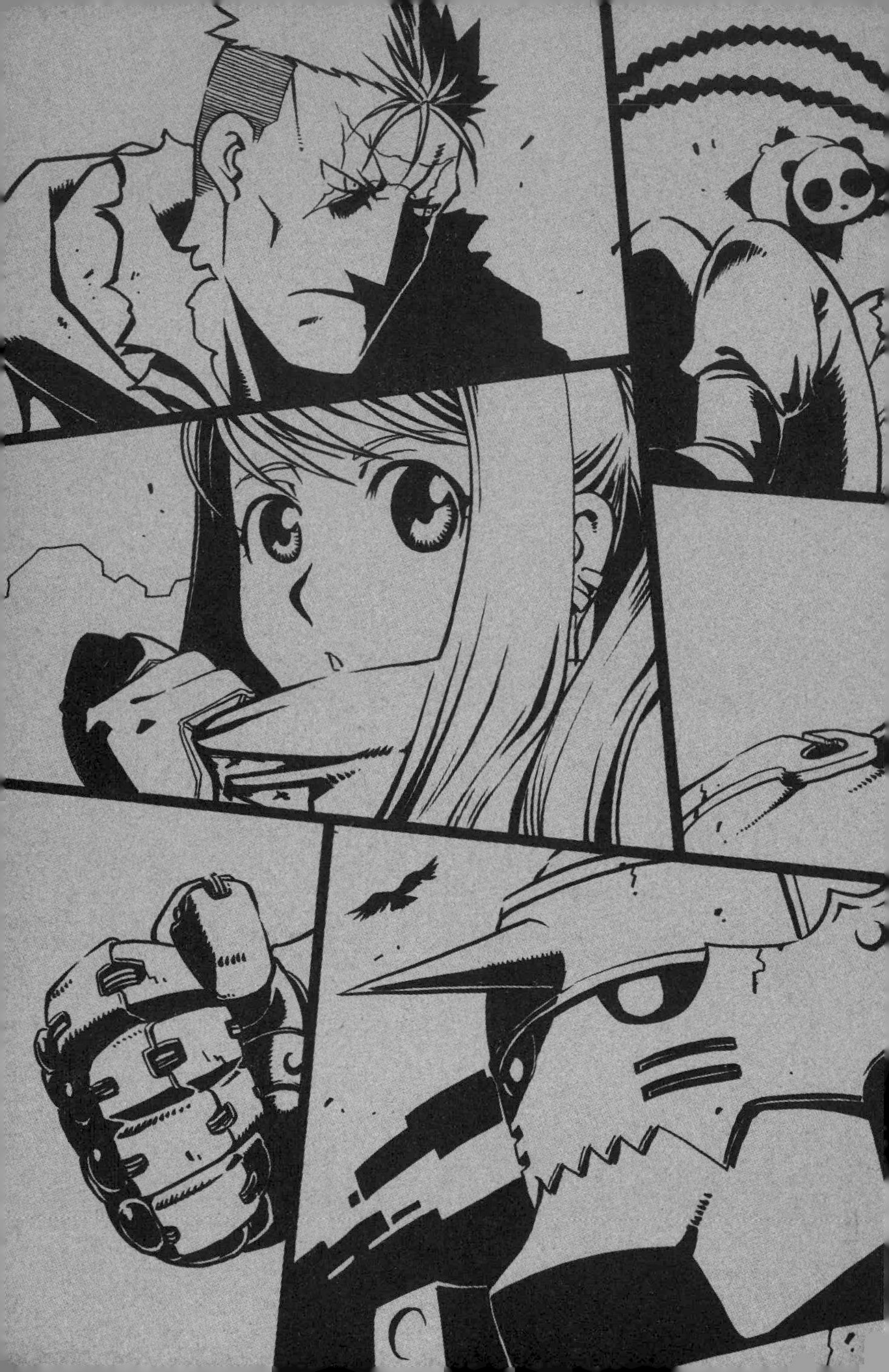

FULLMETAL
ALCHEMIST

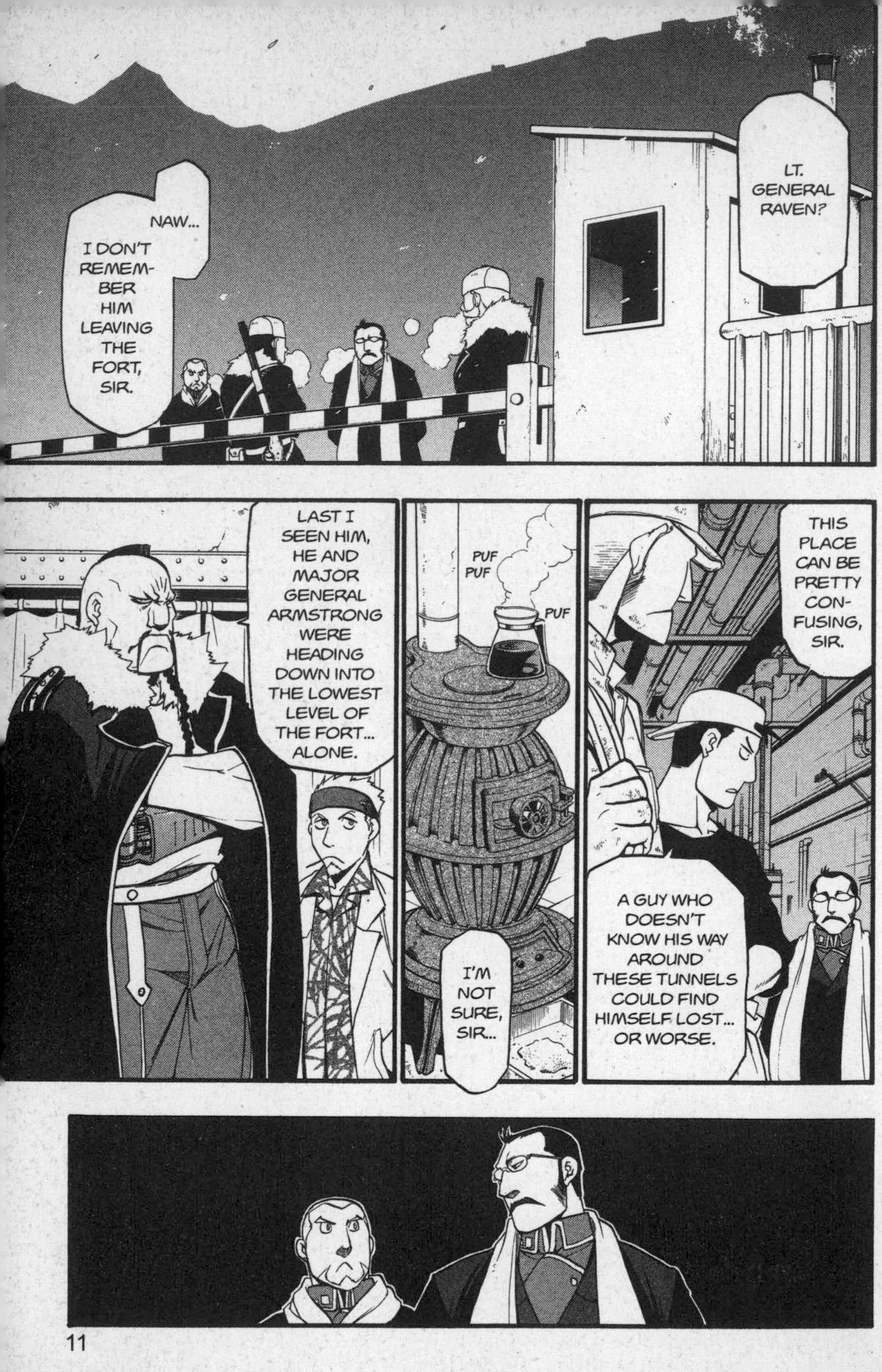
LT. GENERAL RAVEN?
NAW... I DON'T REMEMBER HIM LEAVING THE FORT, SIR.
THIS PLACE CAN BE PRETTY CONFUSING, SIR.
A GUY WHO DOESN'T KNOW HIS WAY AROUND THESE TUNNELS COULD FIND HIMSELF LOST... OR WORSE.
PUF PUF
PUF
I'M NOT SURE, SIR...
LAST I SEEN HIM, HE AND MAJOR GENERAL ARMSTRONG WERE HEADING DOWN INTO THE LOWEST LEVEL OF THE FORT... ALONE.

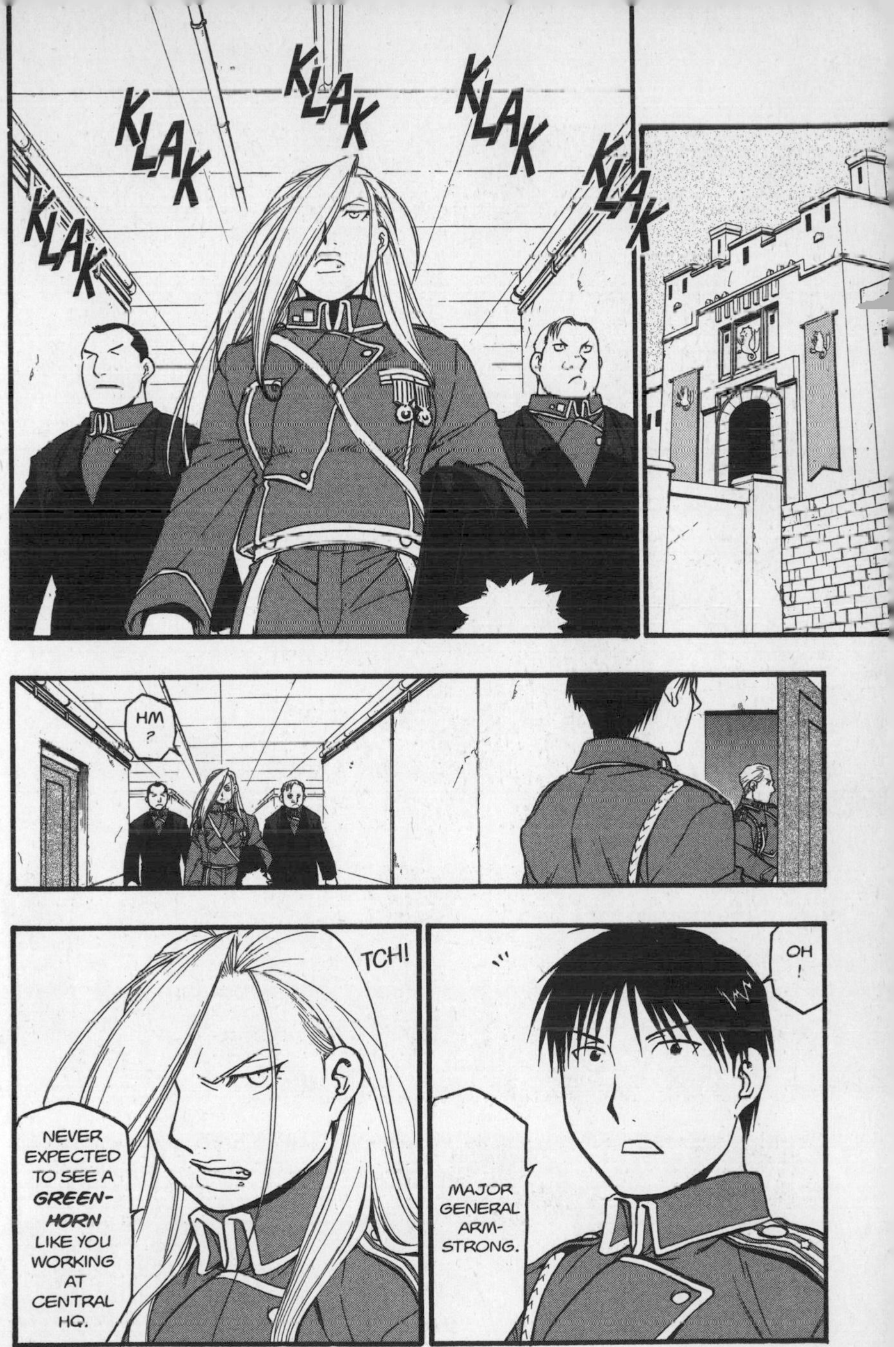
KLAK
KLAK
KLAK
KLAK
KLAK
HM ?
OH !
MAJOR GENERAL ARM-STRONG.
TCH!
NEVER EXPECTED TO SEE A GREEN-HORN LIKE YOU WORKING AT CENTRAL HQ.

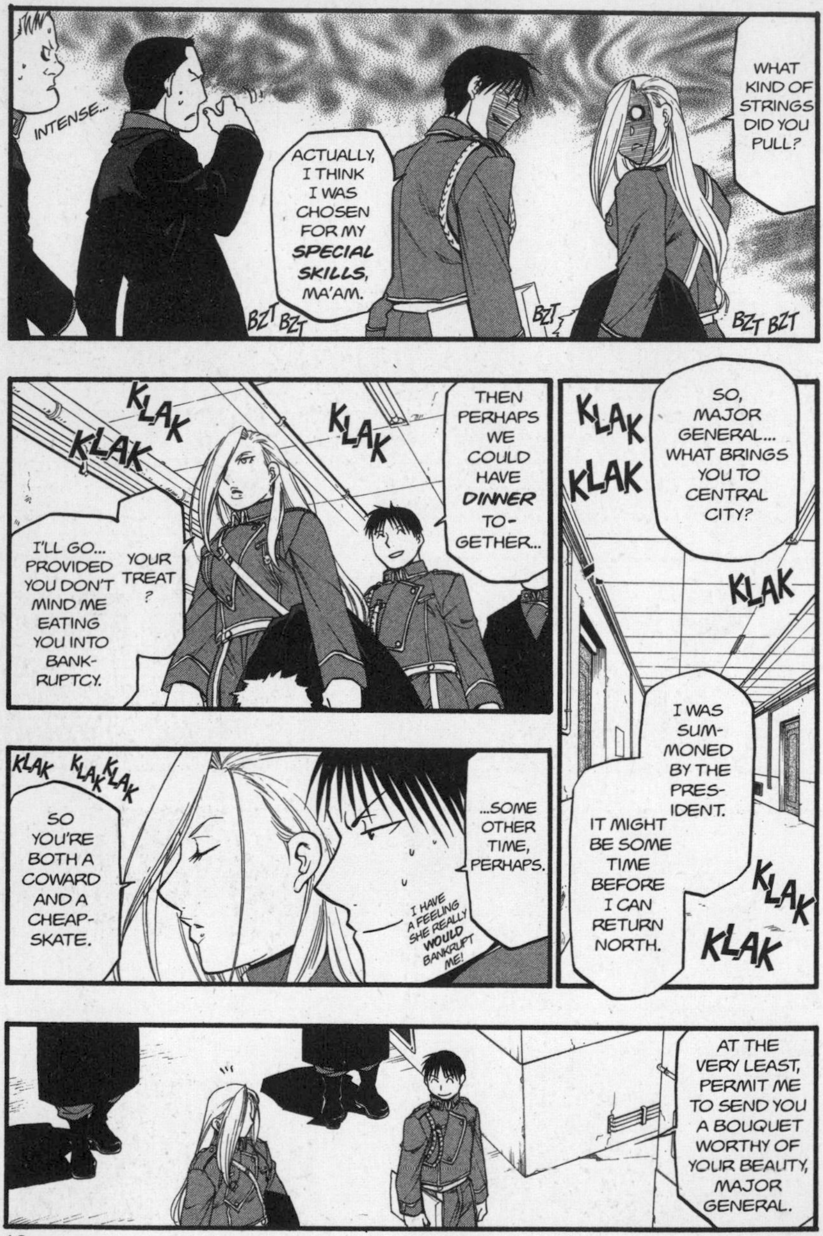
WHAT KIND OF STRINGS DID YOU PULL?
ACTUALLY, I THINK I WAS CHOSEN FOR MY SPECIAL SKILLS, MA'AM.
BZT BZT
BZT
BZT BZT
INTENSE...
SO, MAJOR GENERAL... WHAT BRINGS YOU TO CENTRAL CITY?
KLAK
KLAK
KLAK
I WAS SUMMONED BY THE PRESIDENT.
IT MIGHT BE SOME TIME BEFORE I CAN RETURN NORTH.
KLAK
KLAK
THEN PERHAPS WE COULD HAVE DINNER TOGETHER...
KLAK
KLAK
KLAK
YOUR TREAT?
I'LL GO... PROVIDED YOU DON'T MIND ME EATING YOU INTO BANKRUPTCY.
...SOME OTHER TIME, PERHAPS.
I HAVE A FEELING SHE REALLY WOULD BANKRUPT ME!
KLAK KLAK KLAK
KLAK
SO YOU'RE BOTH A COWARD AND A CHEAPSKATE.
AT THE VERY LEAST, PERMIT ME TO SEND YOU A BOUQUET WORTHY OF YOUR BEAUTY, MAJOR GENERAL.

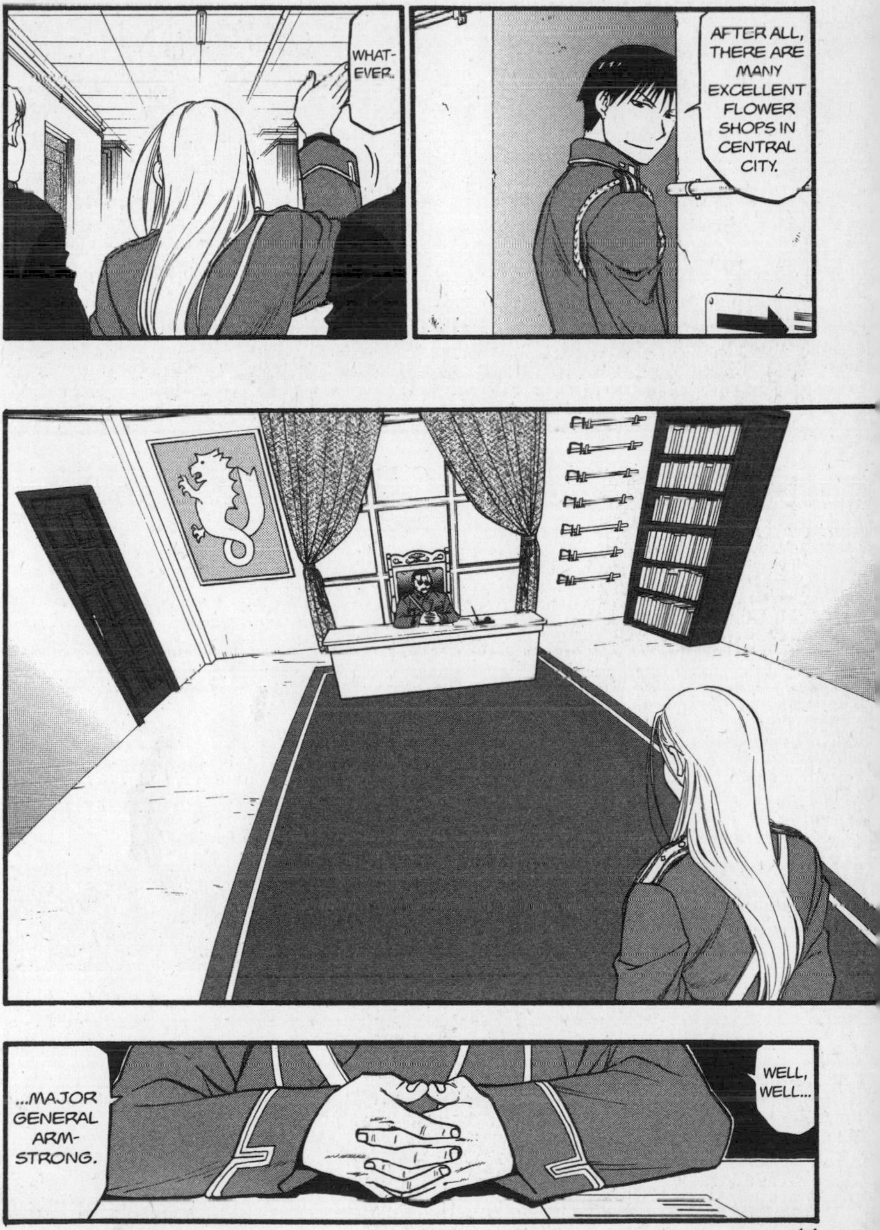
AFTER ALL, THERE ARE MANY EXCELLENT FLOWER SHOPS IN CENTRAL CITY.
WHAT-EVER..
WELL, WELL...
...MAJOR GENERAL ARM-STRONG.

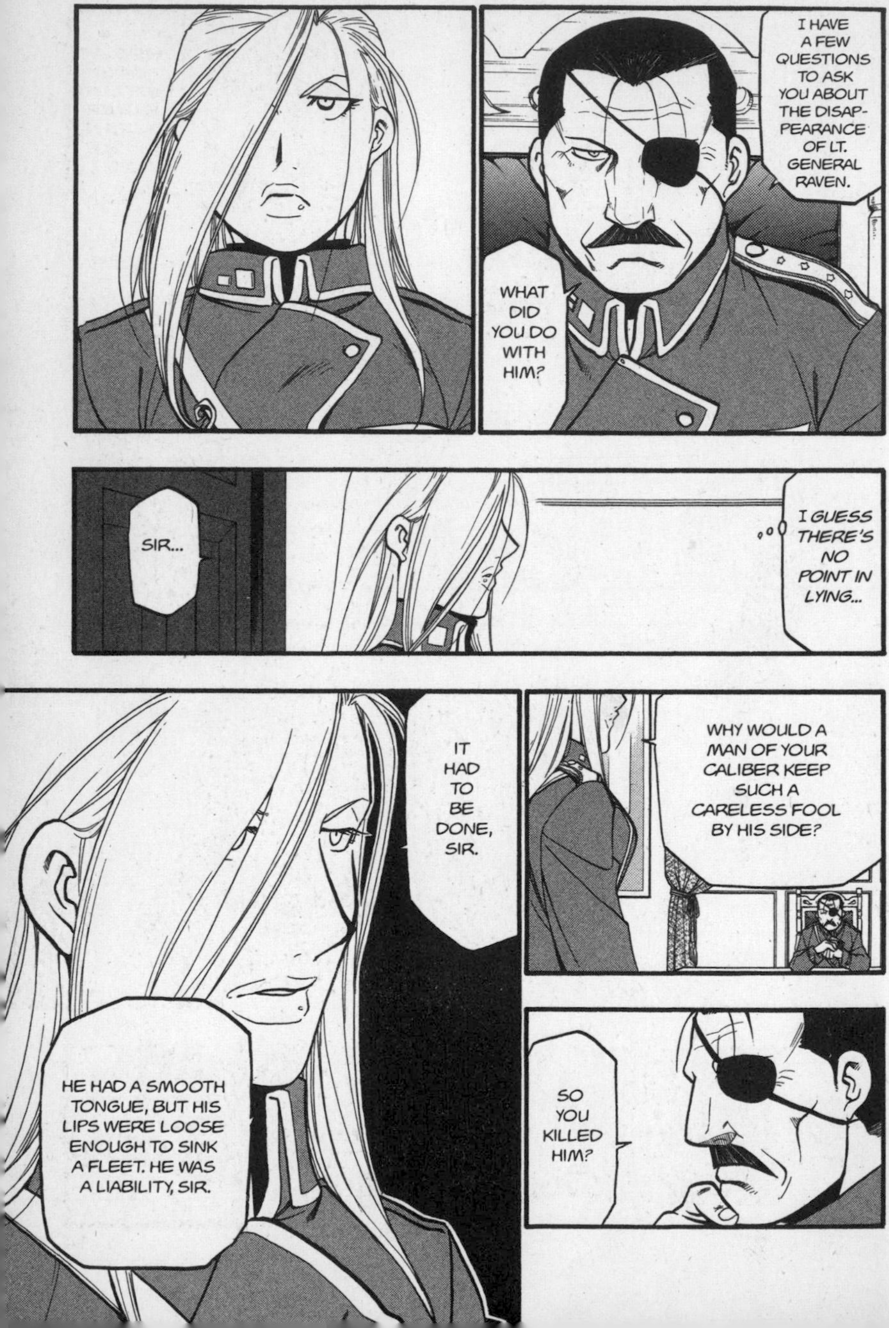
I HAVE A FEW QUESTIONS TO ASK YOU ABOUT THE DISAPPEARANCE OF LT. GENERAL RAVEN.
WHAT DID YOU DO WITH HIM?
I GUESS THERE'S NO POINT IN LYING...
SIR...
WHY WOULD A MAN OF YOUR CALIBER KEEP SUCH A CARELESS FOOL BY HIS SIDE?
SO YOU KILLED HIM?
IT HAD TO BE DONE, SIR.
HE HAD A SMOOTH TONGUE, BUT HIS LIPS WERE LOOSE ENOUGH TO SINK A FLEET. HE WAS A LIABILITY, SIR.

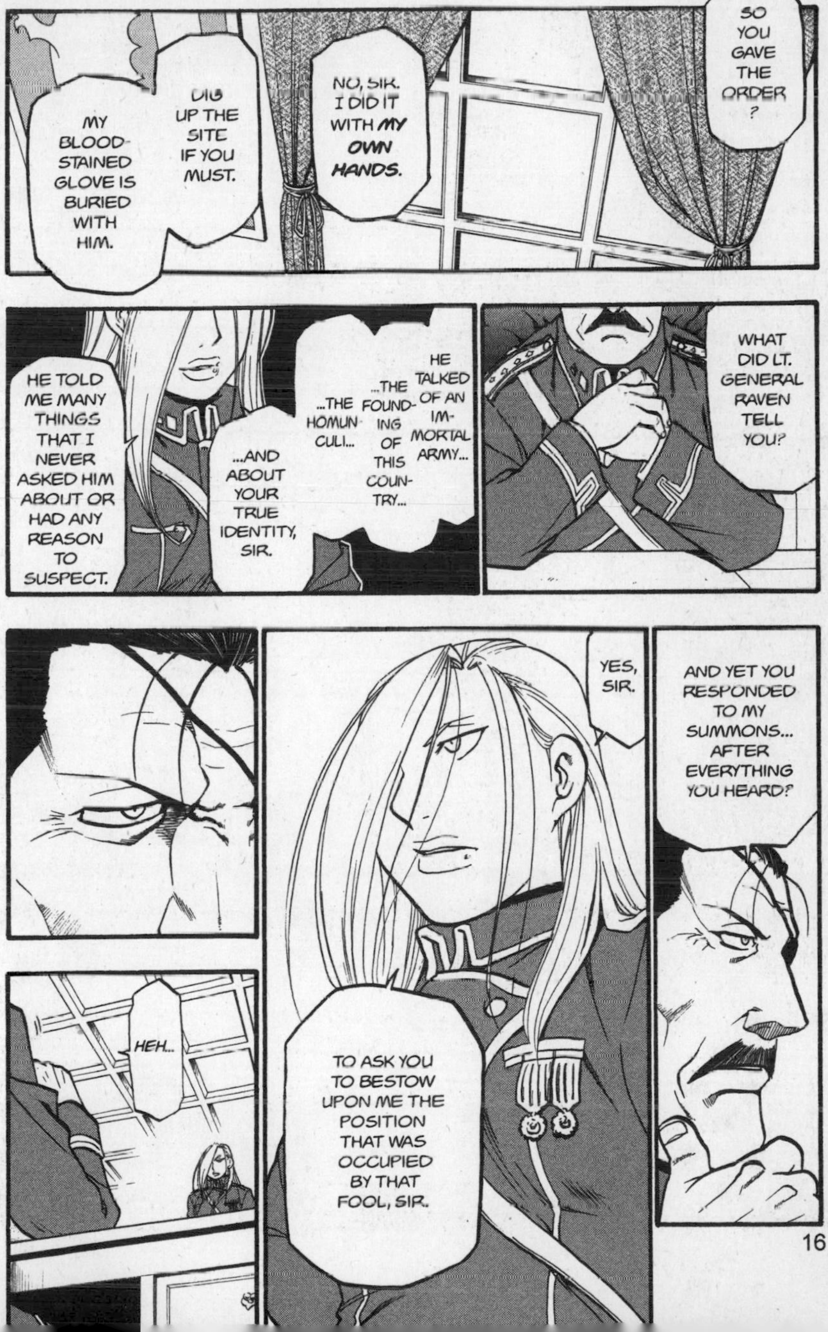
SO YOU GAVE THE ORDER?
NO, SIR. I DID IT WITH MY OWN HANDS.
DIG UP THE SITE IF YOU MUST.
MY BLOOD-STAINED GLOVE IS BURIED WITH HIM.
WHAT DID LT. GENERAL RAVEN TELL YOU?
HE TALKED OF AN IMMORTAL ARMY...
...THE FOUNDING OF THIS COUNTRY...
...THE HOMUNCULI...
...AND ABOUT YOUR TRUE IDENTITY, SIR.
HE TOLD ME MANY THINGS THAT I NEVER ASKED HIM ABOUT OR HAD ANY REASON TO SUSPECT.
AND YET YOU RESPONDED TO MY SUMMONS... AFTER EVERYTHING YOU HEARD?
YES, SIR.
TO ASK YOU TO BESTOW UPON ME THE POSITION THAT WAS OCCUPIED BY THAT FOOL, SIR.
HEH...

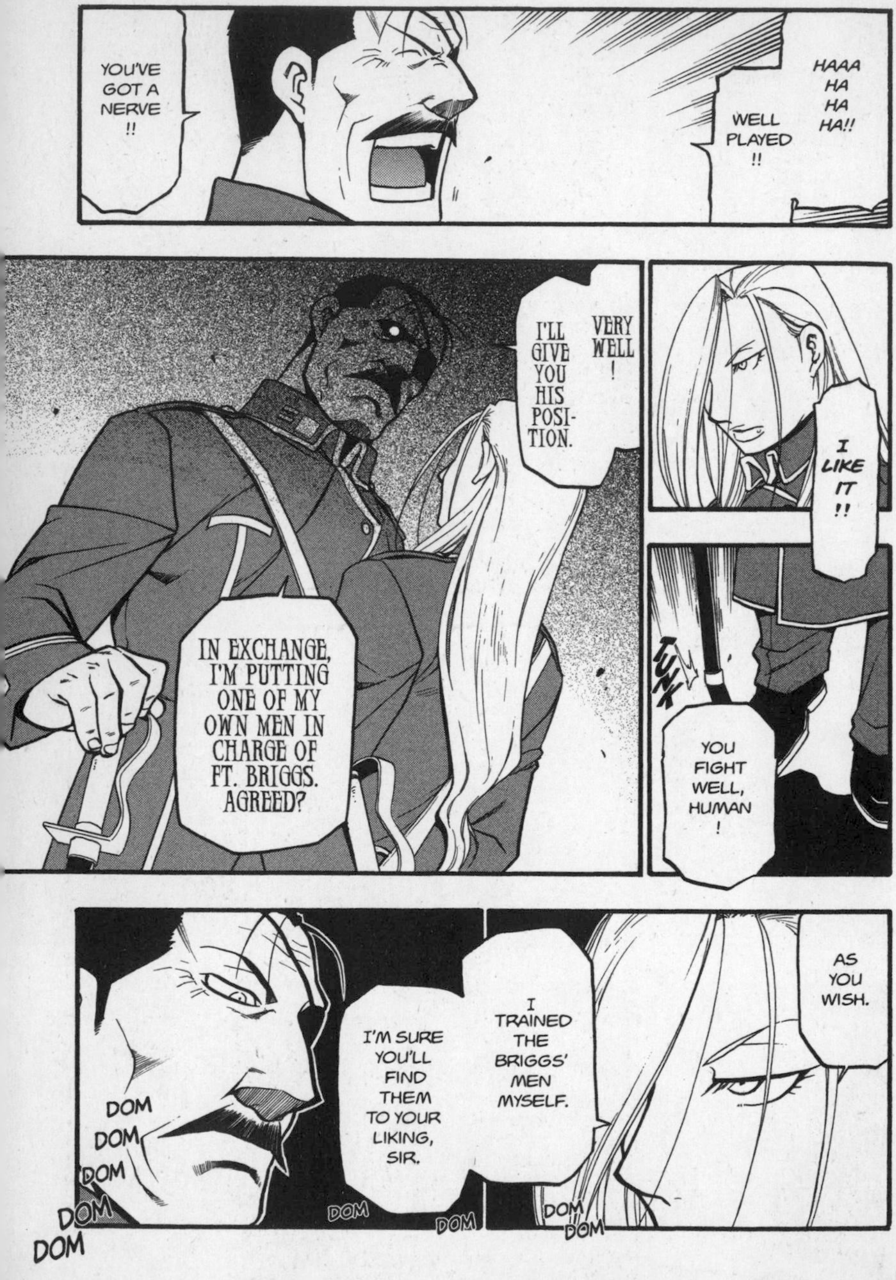

HAAAA HA HA HA!!
WELL PLAYED !!
YOU'VE GOT A NERVE !!
I LIKE IT !!
TUNK
YOU FIGHT WELL, HUMAN !
VERY WELL !
I'LL GIVE YOU HIS POSITION.
IN EXCHANGE, I'M PUTTING ONE OF MY OWN MEN IN CHARGE OF FT. BRIGGS. AGREED?
AS YOU WISH.
I TRAINED THE BRIGGS' MEN MYSELF.
I'M SURE YOU'LL FIND THEM TO YOUR LIKING, SIR.
DOM DOM
DOM
DOM
DOM DOM DOM DOM DOM DOM

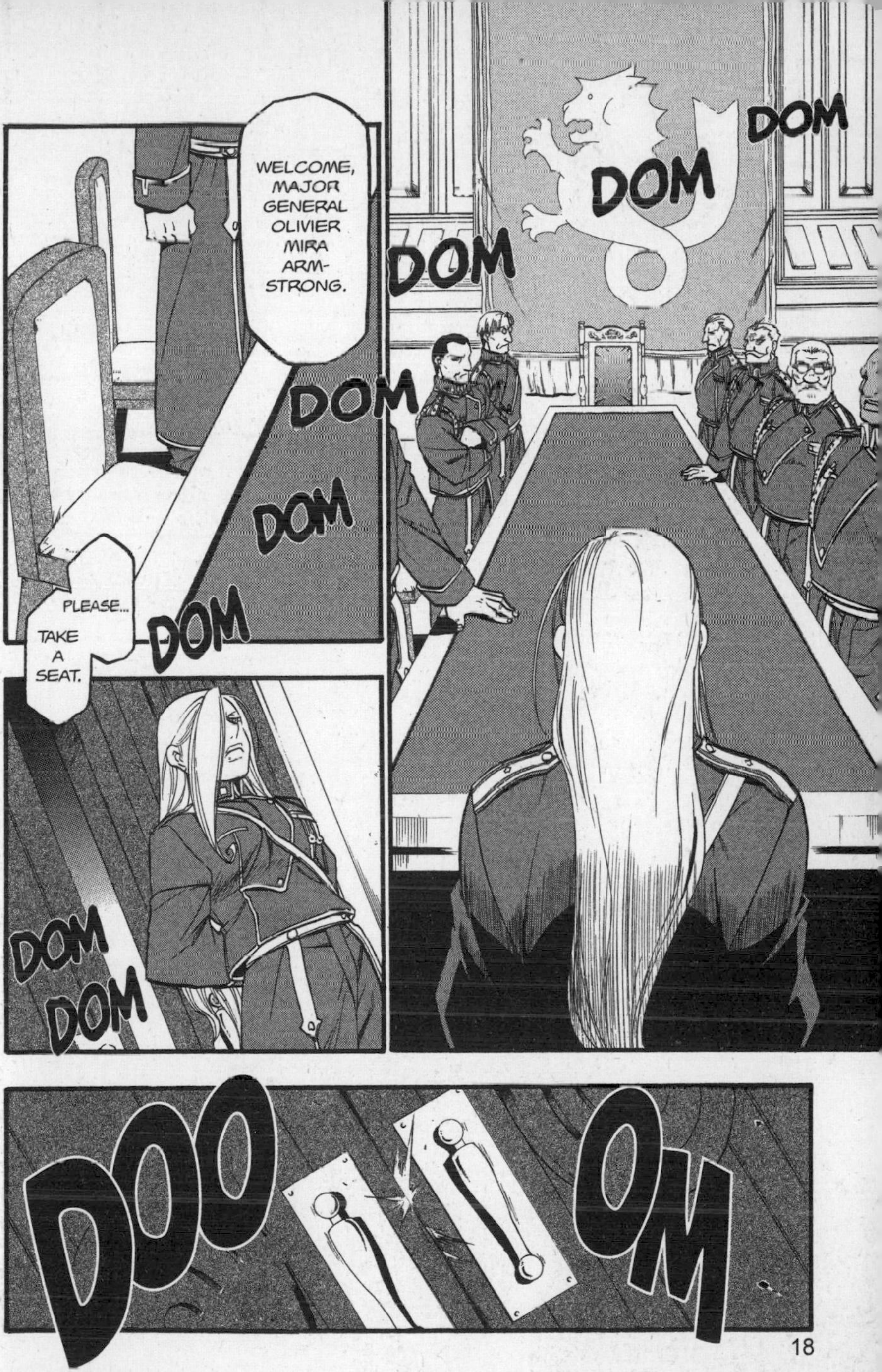
DOM
DOM
DOM
WELCOME, MAJOR GENERAL OLIVIER MIRA ARM-STRONG.
DOM
DOM
PLEASE...
TAKE A SEAT.
DOM
DOM
DOM
DOOOM

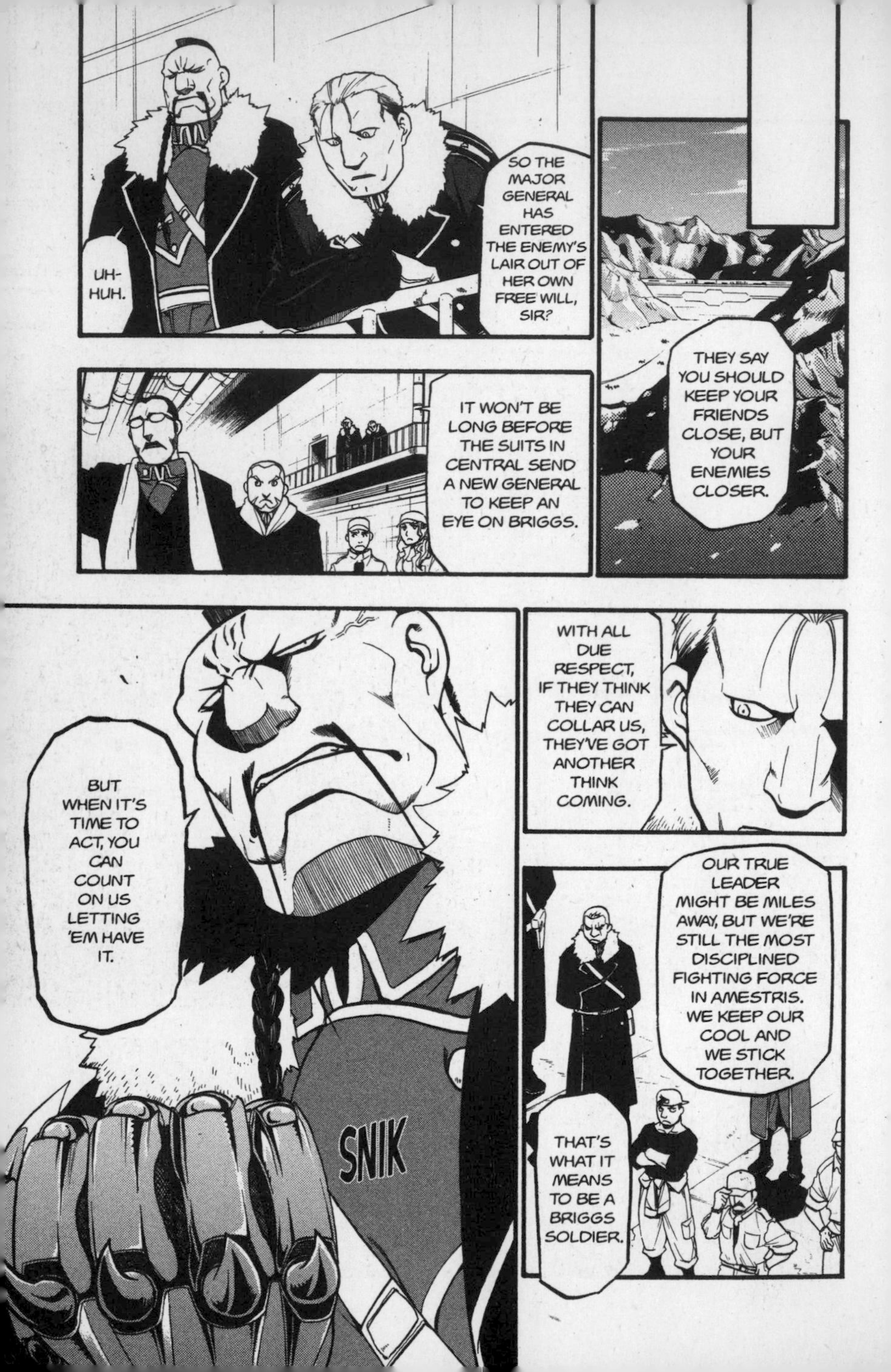
THEY SAY YOU SHOULD KEEP YOUR FRIENDS CLOSE, BUT YOUR ENEMIES CLOSER.
SO THE MAJOR GENERAL HAS ENTERED THE ENEMY'S LAIR OUT OF HER OWN FREE WILL, SIR?
UH-HUH.
IT WON'T BE LONG BEFORE THE SUITS IN CENTRAL SEND A NEW GENERAL TO KEEP AN EYE ON BRIGGS.
WITH ALL DUE RESPECT, IF THEY THINK THEY CAN COLLAR US, THEY'VE GOT ANOTHER THINK COMING.
OUR TRUE LEADER MIGHT BE MILES AWAY, BUT WE'RE STILL THE MOST DISCIPLINED FIGHTING FORCE IN AMESTRIS. WE KEEP OUR COOL AND WE STICK TOGETHER.
THAT'S WHAT IT MEANS TO BE A BRIGGS SOLDIER.
BUT WHEN IT'S TIME TO ACT, YOU CAN COUNT ON US LETTING 'EM HAVE IT.
SNIK

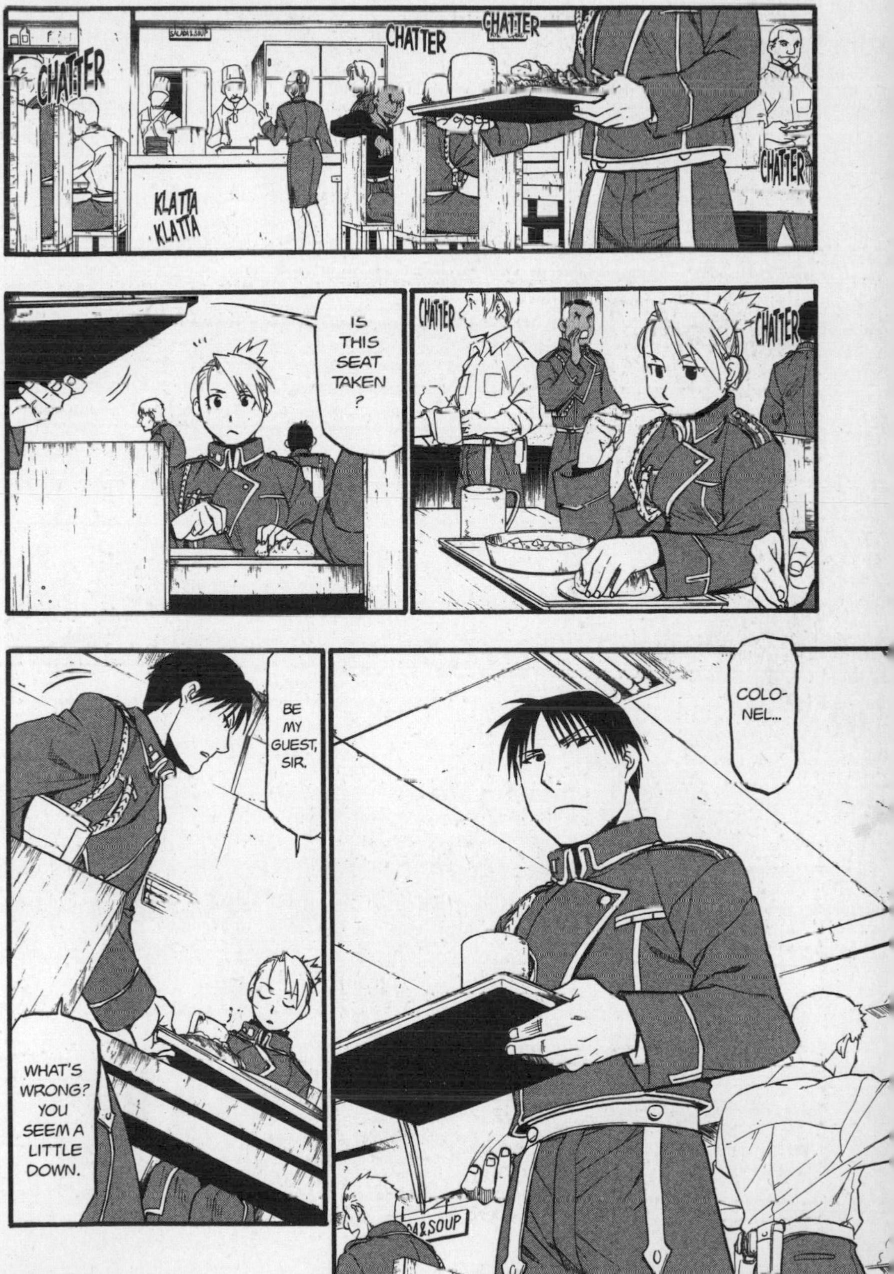
CHATTER
CHATTER
CHATTER
CHATTER
KLATTA KLATTA
CHATTER
CHATTER
IS THIS SEAT TAKEN?
COLONEL...
BE MY GUEST, SIR.
WHAT'S WRONG? YOU SEEM A LITTLE DOWN.

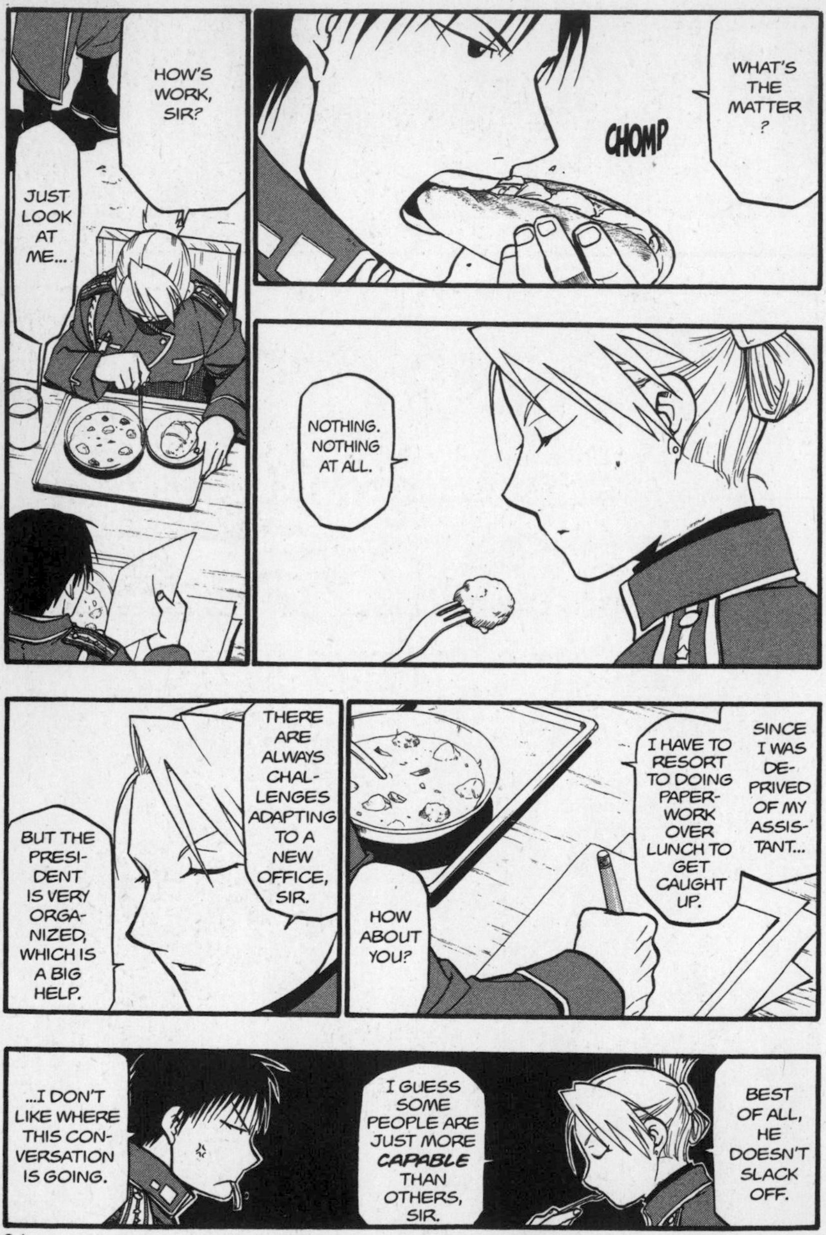
WHAT'S THE MATTER?
CHOMP
NOTHING. NOTHING AT ALL.
HOW'S WORK, SIR?
JUST LOOK AT ME...
SINCE I WAS DE-PRIVED OF MY ASSIS-TANT...
I HAVE TO RESORT TO DOING PAPER-WORK OVER LUNCH TO GET CAUGHT UP.
HOW ABOUT YOU?
THERE ARE ALWAYS CHAL-LENGES ADAPTING TO A NEW OFFICE, SIR.
BUT THE PRESI-DENT IS VERY ORGA-NIZED, WHICH IS A BIG HELP.
BEST OF ALL, HE DOESN'T SLACK OFF.
I GUESS SOME PEOPLE ARE JUST MORE ***CAPABLE*** THAN OTHERS, SIR.
...I DON'T LIKE WHERE THIS CON-VERSATION IS GOING.

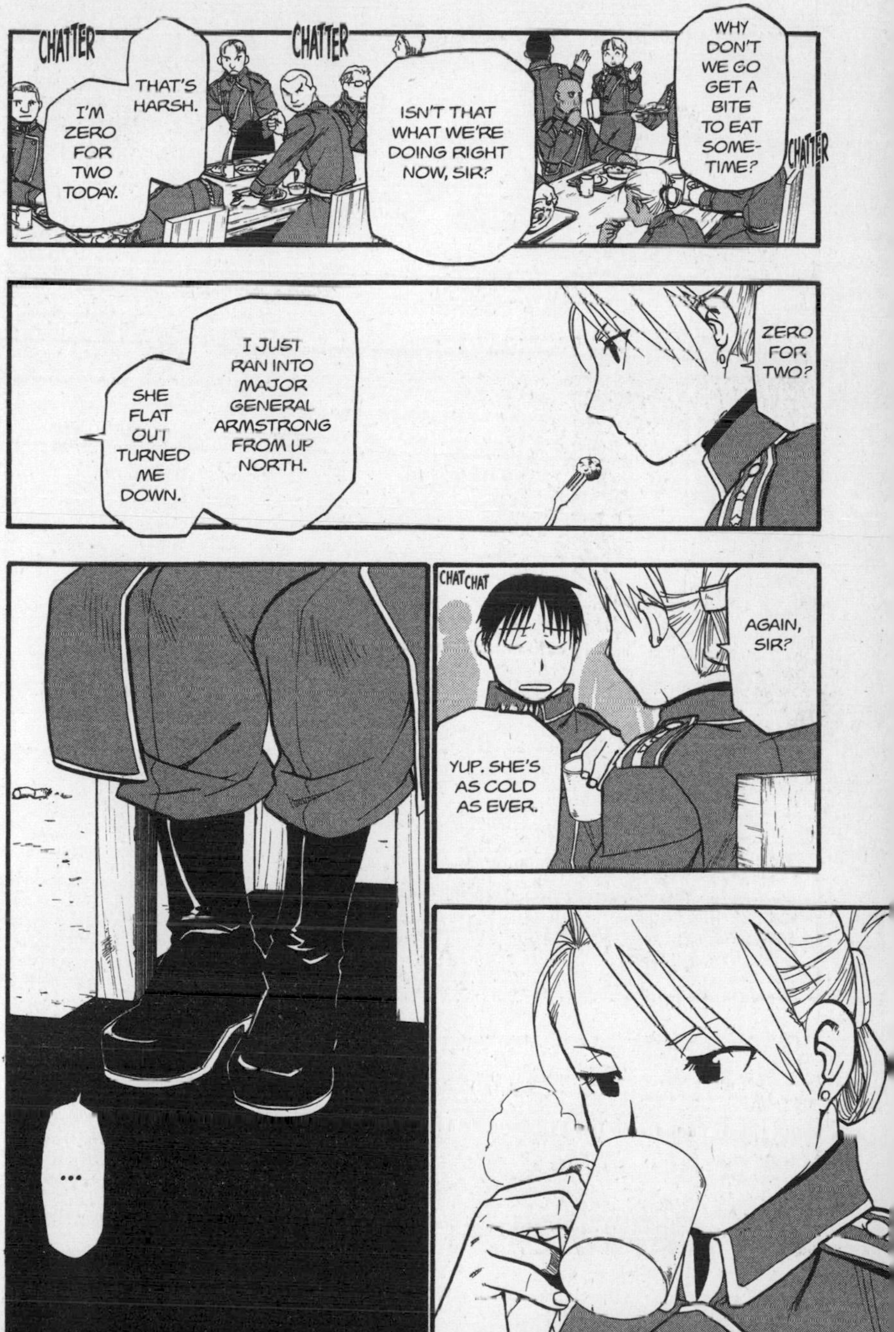
WHY DON'T WE GO GET A BITE TO EAT SOME-TIME?
CHATTER
ISN'T THAT WHAT WE'RE DOING RIGHT NOW, SIR?
CHATTER
THAT'S HARSH.
I'M ZERO FOR TWO TODAY.
CHATTER
ZERO FOR TWO?
I JUST RAN INTO MAJOR GENERAL ARMSTRONG FROM UP NORTH.
SHE FLAT OUT TURNED ME DOWN.
CHAT CHAT
AGAIN, SIR?
YUP. SHE'S AS COLD AS EVER.
...

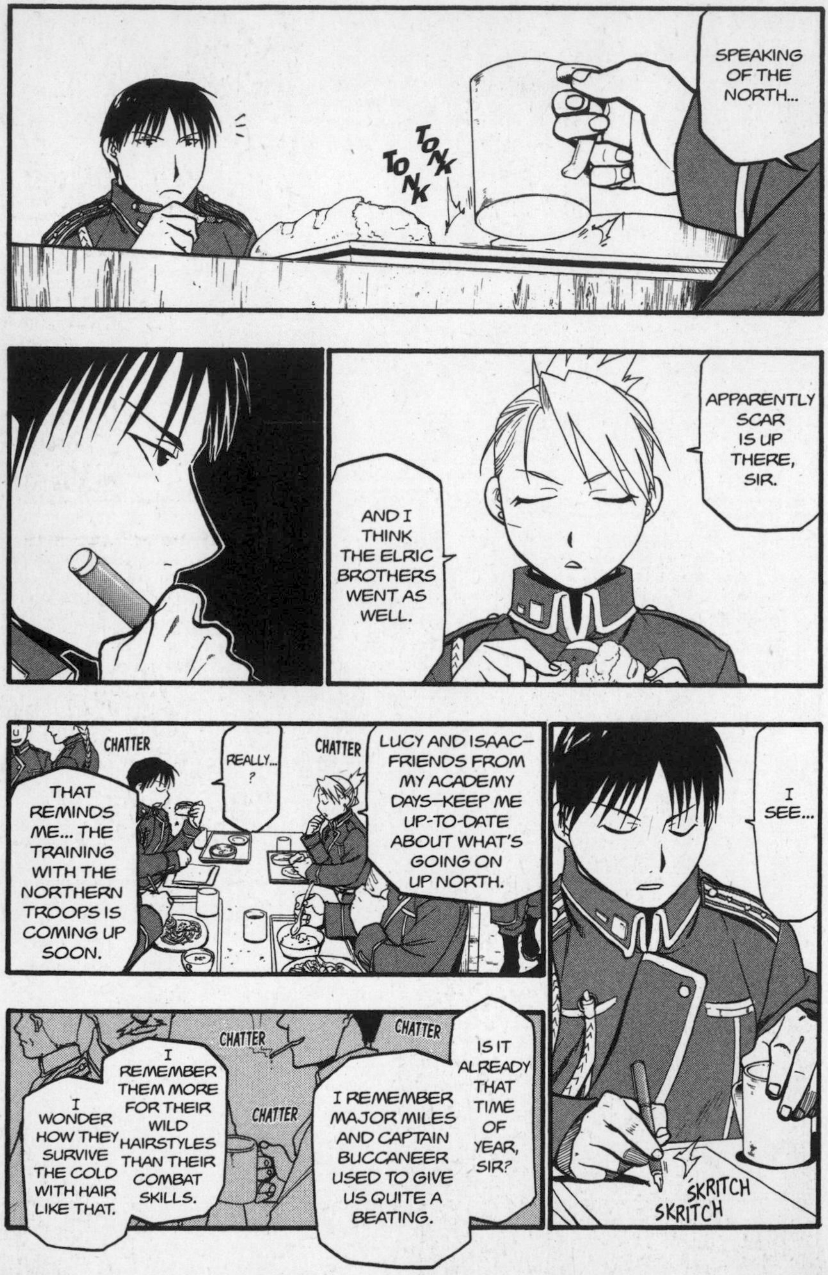
SPEAKING OF THE NORTH...
TONK TONK
APPARENTLY SCAR IS UP THERE, SIR.
AND I THINK THE ELRIC BROTHERS WENT AS WELL.
I SEE...
SKRITCH SKRITCH
LUCY AND ISAAC—FRIENDS FROM MY ACADEMY DAYS—KEEP ME UP-TO-DATE ABOUT WHAT'S GOING ON UP NORTH.
CHATTER
REALLY...?
CHATTER
THAT REMINDS ME... THE TRAINING WITH THE NORTHERN TROOPS IS COMING UP SOON.
IS IT ALREADY THAT TIME OF YEAR, SIR?
CHATTER
I REMEMBER MAJOR MILES AND CAPTAIN BUCCANEER USED TO GIVE US QUITE A BEATING.
CHATTER
CHATTER
I REMEMBER THEM MORE FOR THEIR WILD HAIRSTYLES THAN THEIR COMBAT SKILLS.
I WONDER HOW THEY SURVIVE THE COLD WITH HAIR LIKE THAT.

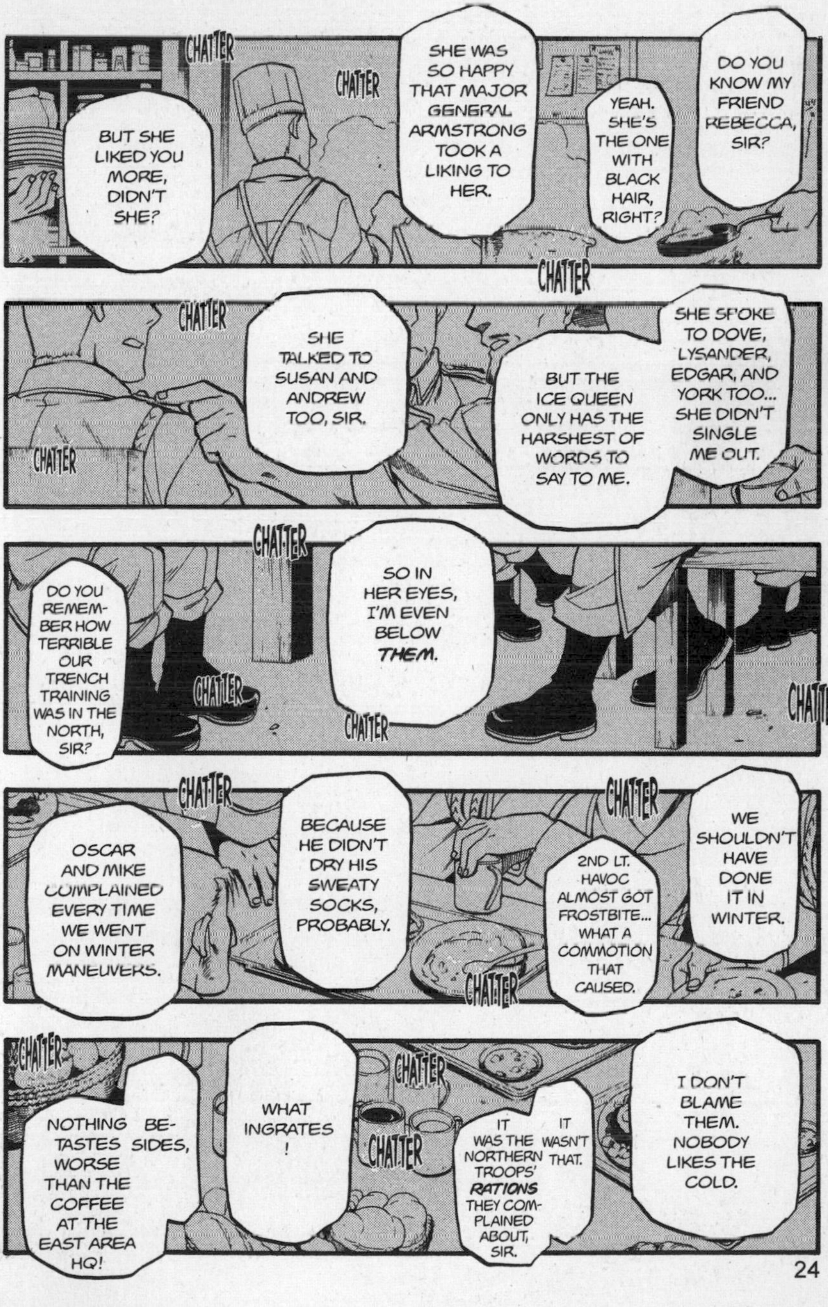
CHATTER
DO YOU KNOW MY FRIEND REBECCA, SIR?
YEAH. SHE'S THE ONE WITH BLACK HAIR, RIGHT?
SHE WAS SO HAPPY THAT MAJOR GENERAL ARMSTRONG TOOK A LIKING TO HER.
CHATTER
CHATTER
BUT SHE LIKED YOU MORE, DIDN'T SHE?
SHE SPOKE TO DOVE, LYSANDER, EDGAR, AND YORK TOO... SHE DIDN'T SINGLE ME OUT.
BUT THE ICE QUEEN ONLY HAS THE HARSHEST OF WORDS TO SAY TO ME.
SHE TALKED TO SUSAN AND ANDREW TOO, SIR.
CHATTER
CHATTER
CHATTER
SO IN HER EYES, I'M EVEN BELOW *THEM*.
CHATTER
CHATTER
CHATTER
DO YOU REMEMBER HOW TERRIBLE OUR TRENCH TRAINING WAS IN THE NORTH, SIR?
WE SHOULDN'T HAVE DONE IT IN WINTER.
CHATTER
2ND LT. HAVOC ALMOST GOT FROSTBITE... WHAT A COMMOTION THAT CAUSED.
CHATTER
BECAUSE HE DIDN'T DRY HIS SWEATY SOCKS, PROBABLY.
CHATTER
OSCAR AND MIKE COMPLAINED EVERY TIME WE WENT ON WINTER MANEUVERS.
I DON'T BLAME THEM. NOBODY LIKES THE COLD.
IT WASN'T THAT.
IT WAS THE NORTHERN TROOPS' *RATIONS* THEY COMPLAINED ABOUT, SIR.
CHATTER
CHATTER
WHAT INGRATES!
BESIDES, NOTHING TASTES WORSE THAN THE COFFEE AT THE EAST AREA HQ!
CHATTER

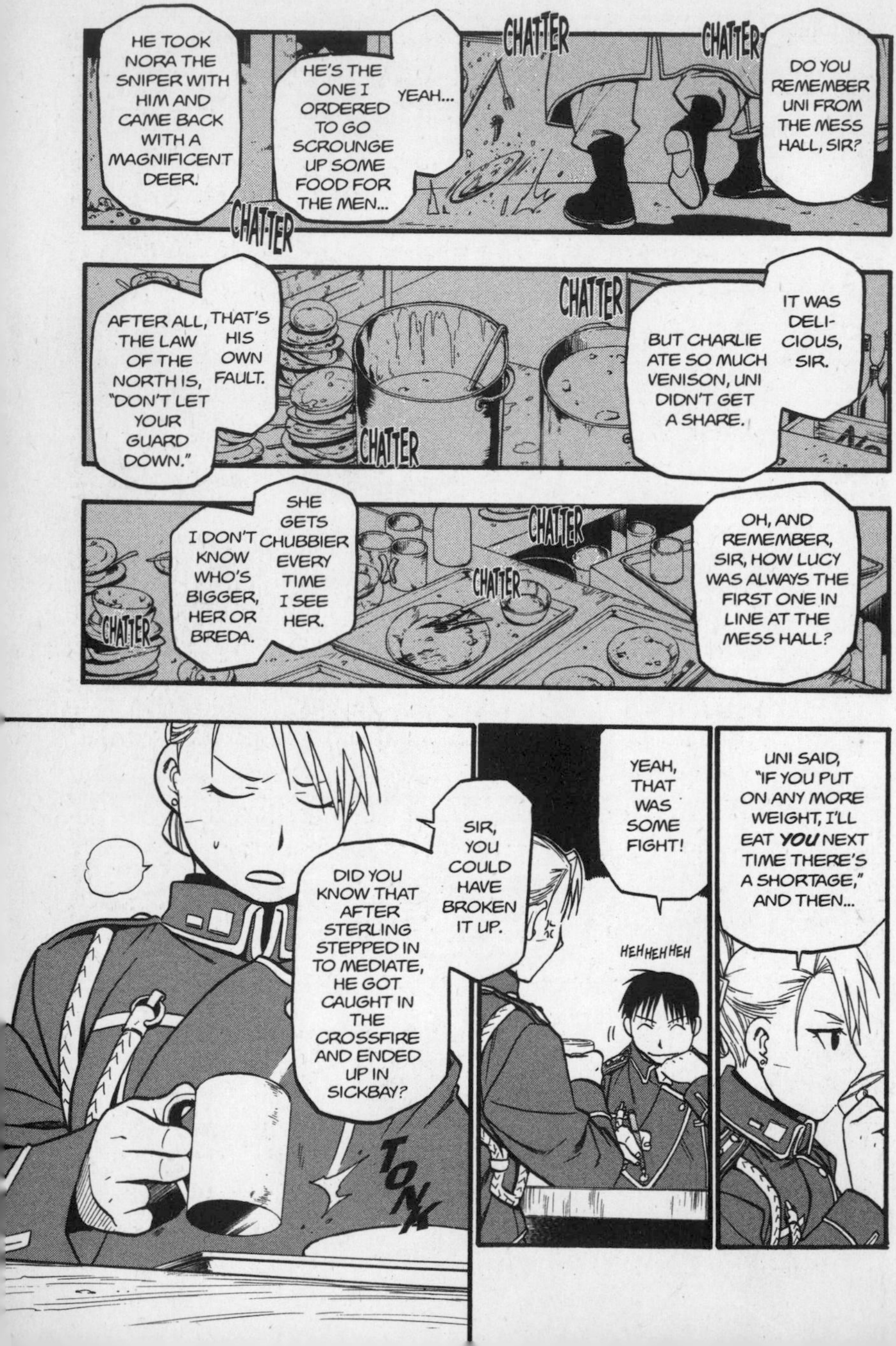
DO YOU REMEMBER UNI FROM THE MESS HALL, SIR?
CHATTER
CHATTER
YEAH...
HE'S THE ONE I ORDERED TO GO SCROUNGE UP SOME FOOD FOR THE MEN...
HE TOOK NORA THE SNIPER WITH HIM AND CAME BACK WITH A MAGNIFICENT DEER.
CHATTER
IT WAS DELICIOUS, SIR.
BUT CHARLIE ATE SO MUCH VENISON, UNI DIDN'T GET A SHARE.
CHATTER
THAT'S HIS OWN FAULT.
AFTER ALL, THE LAW OF THE NORTH IS, "DON'T LET YOUR GUARD DOWN."
CHATTER
OH, AND REMEMBER, SIR, HOW LUCY WAS ALWAYS THE FIRST ONE IN LINE AT THE MESS HALL?
CHATTER
CHATTER
SHE GETS CHUBBIER EVERY TIME I SEE HER.
I DON'T KNOW WHO'S BIGGER, HER OR BREDA.
CHATTER
UNI SAID, "IF YOU PUT ON ANY MORE WEIGHT, I'LL EAT *YOU* NEXT TIME THERE'S A SHORTAGE," AND THEN...
YEAH, THAT WAS SOME FIGHT!
HEH HEH HEH
SIR, YOU COULD HAVE BROKEN IT UP.
DID YOU KNOW THAT AFTER STERLING STEPPED IN TO MEDIATE, HE GOT CAUGHT IN THE CROSSFIRE AND ENDED UP IN SICKBAY?
TONK

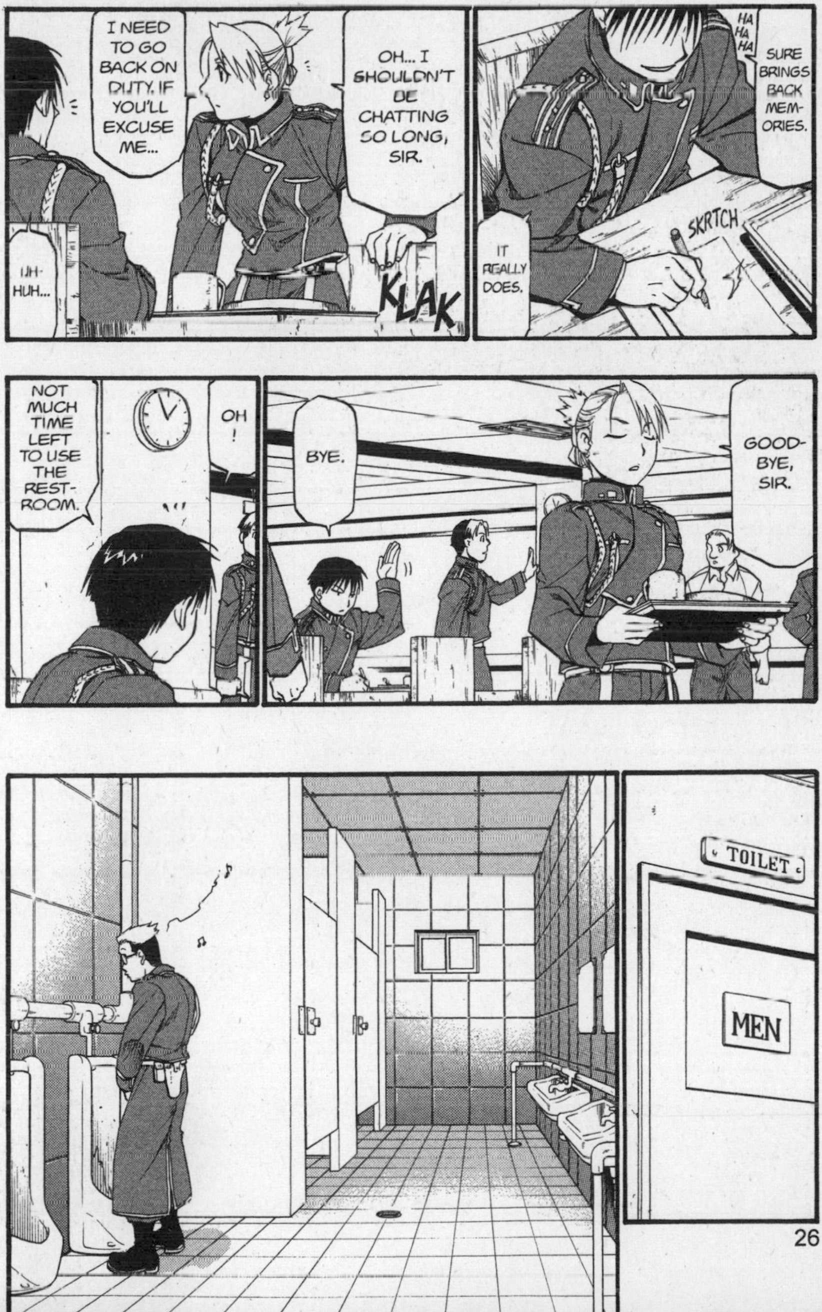
HA HA HA
SURE BRINGS BACK MEMORIES.
SKRTCH
IT REALLY DOES.
OH... I SHOULDN'T BE CHATTING SO LONG, SIR.
I NEED TO GO BACK ON DUTY. IF YOU'LL EXCUSE ME...
KLAK
UH-HUH...
GOOD-BYE, SIR.
BYE.
OH !
NOT MUCH TIME LEFT TO USE THE REST-ROOM.
TOILET
MEN

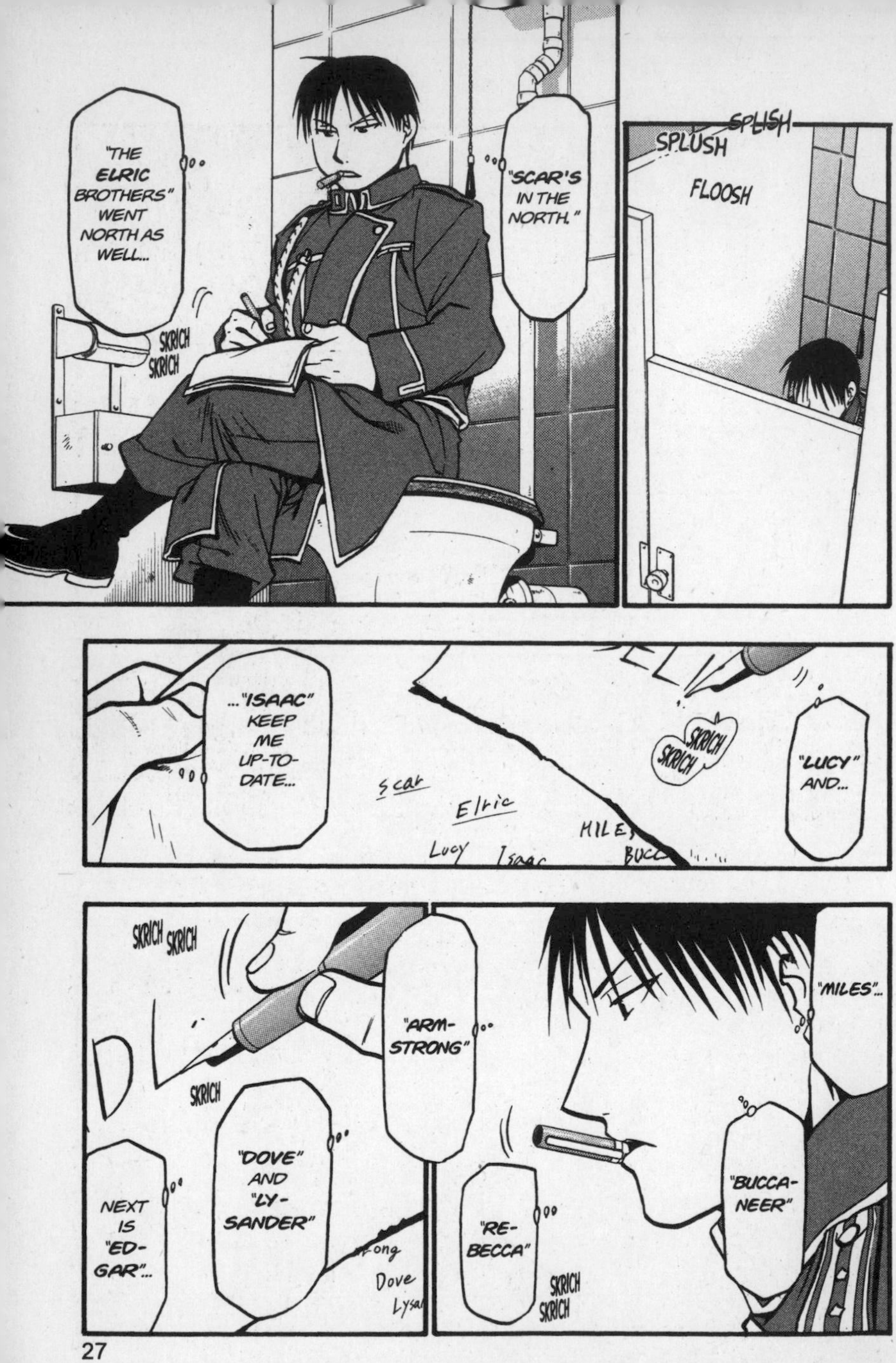
SPLISH
SPLUSH
FLOOSH
"SCAR'S IN THE NORTH."
"THE ELRIC BROTHERS" WENT NORTH AS WELL...
SKRICH SKRICH
"LUCY" AND...
SKRICH SKRICH
..."ISAAC" KEEP ME UP-TO-DATE...
Scar
Elric
Lucy
Isaac
"MILES"...
"BUCCA-NEER"
"RE-BECCA"
SKRICH SKRICH
"ARM-STRONG"
SKRICH SKRICH
SKRICH
"DOVE" AND "LY-SANDER"
NEXT IS "ED-GAR"...
Dove

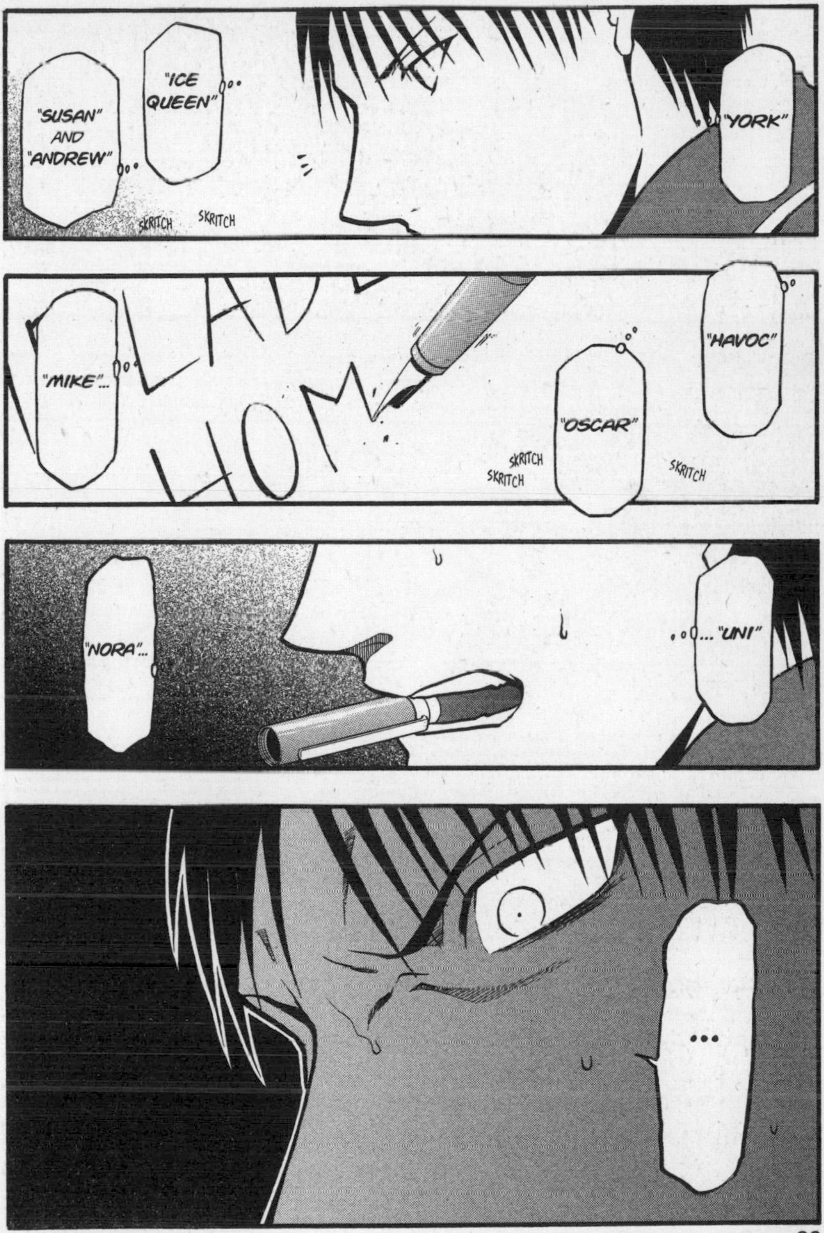
"YORK"
"ICE QUEEN"
"SUSAN" AND "ANDREW"
SKRITCH
SKRITCH
"HAVOC"
"OSCAR"
SKRITCH
SKRITCH
SKRITCH
"MIKE"...
..."UNI"
"NORA"...
...

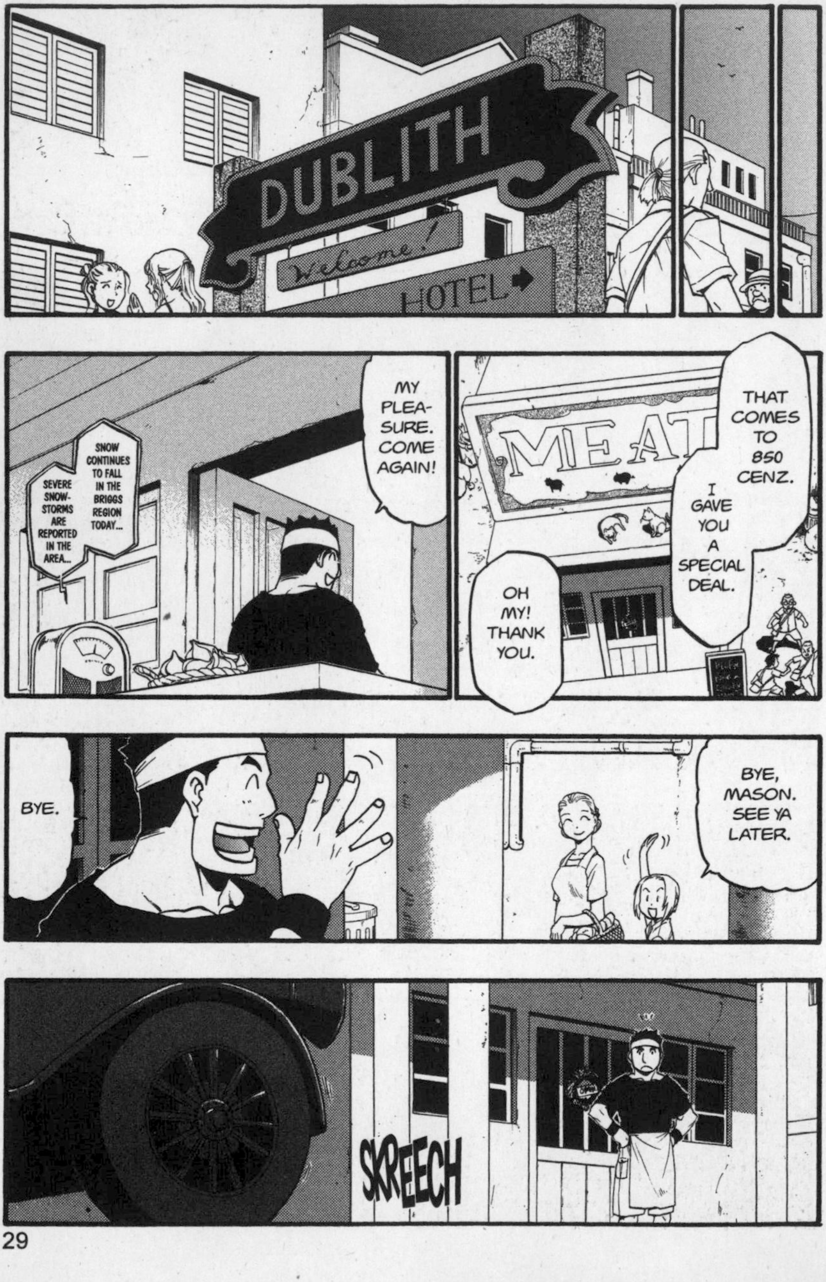
DUBLITH
Welcome!
HOTEL
THAT COMES TO 850 CENZ.
I GAVE YOU A SPECIAL DEAL.
MEAT
OH MY! THANK YOU.
MY PLEASURE. COME AGAIN!
SNOW CONTINUES TO FALL IN THE BRIGGS REGION TODAY...
SEVERE SNOW-STORMS ARE REPORTED IN THE AREA...
BYE, MASON. SEE YA LATER.
BYE.
SKREECH

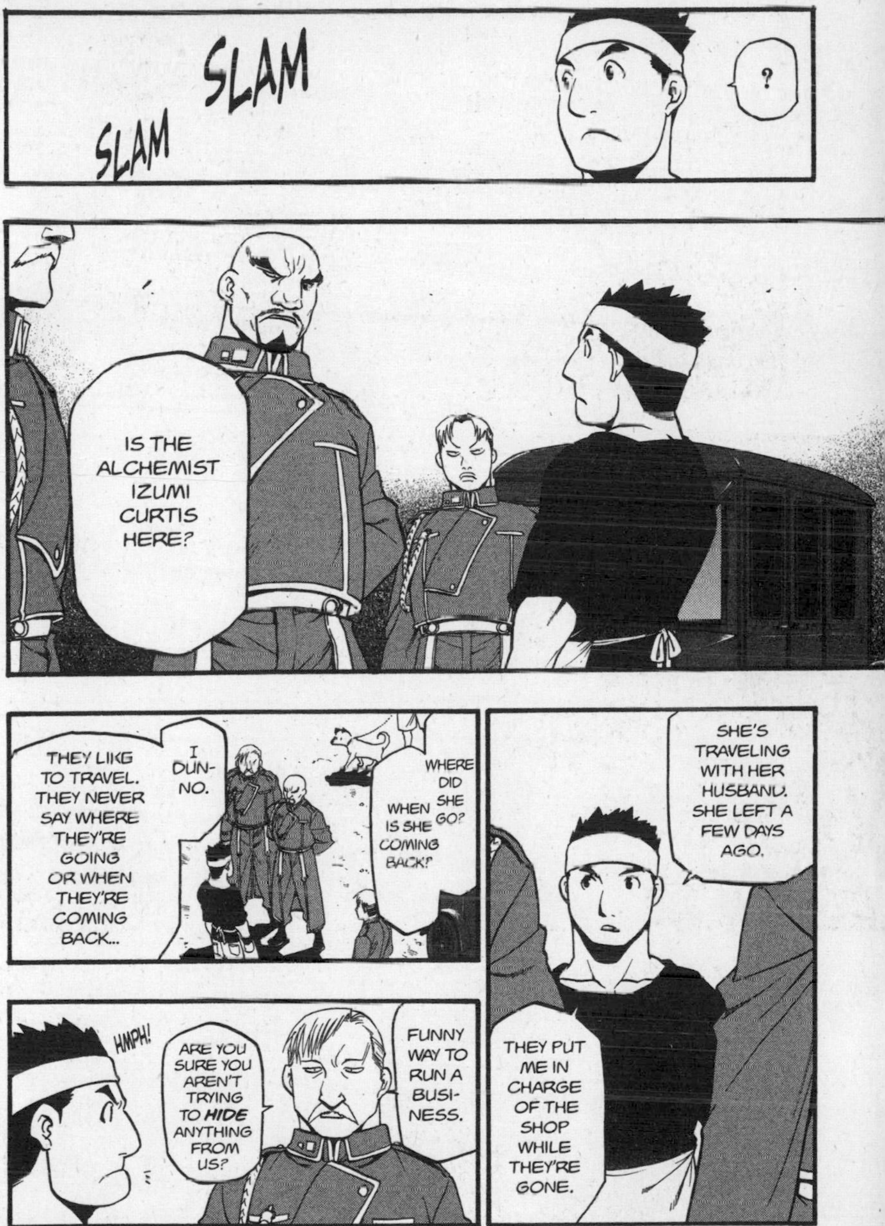
?
SLAM
SLAM
IS THE ALCHEMIST IZUMI CURTIS HERE?
SHE'S TRAVELING WITH HER HUSBAND. SHE LEFT A FEW DAYS AGO.
THEY PUT ME IN CHARGE OF THE SHOP WHILE THEY'RE GONE.
WHERE DID SHE GO?
WHEN IS SHE COMING BACK?
I DUNNO.
THEY LIKE TO TRAVEL. THEY NEVER SAY WHERE THEY'RE GOING OR WHEN THEY'RE COMING BACK...
FUNNY WAY TO RUN A BUSINESS.
ARE YOU SURE YOU AREN'T TRYING TO ***HIDE*** ANYTHING FROM US?
HMPH!

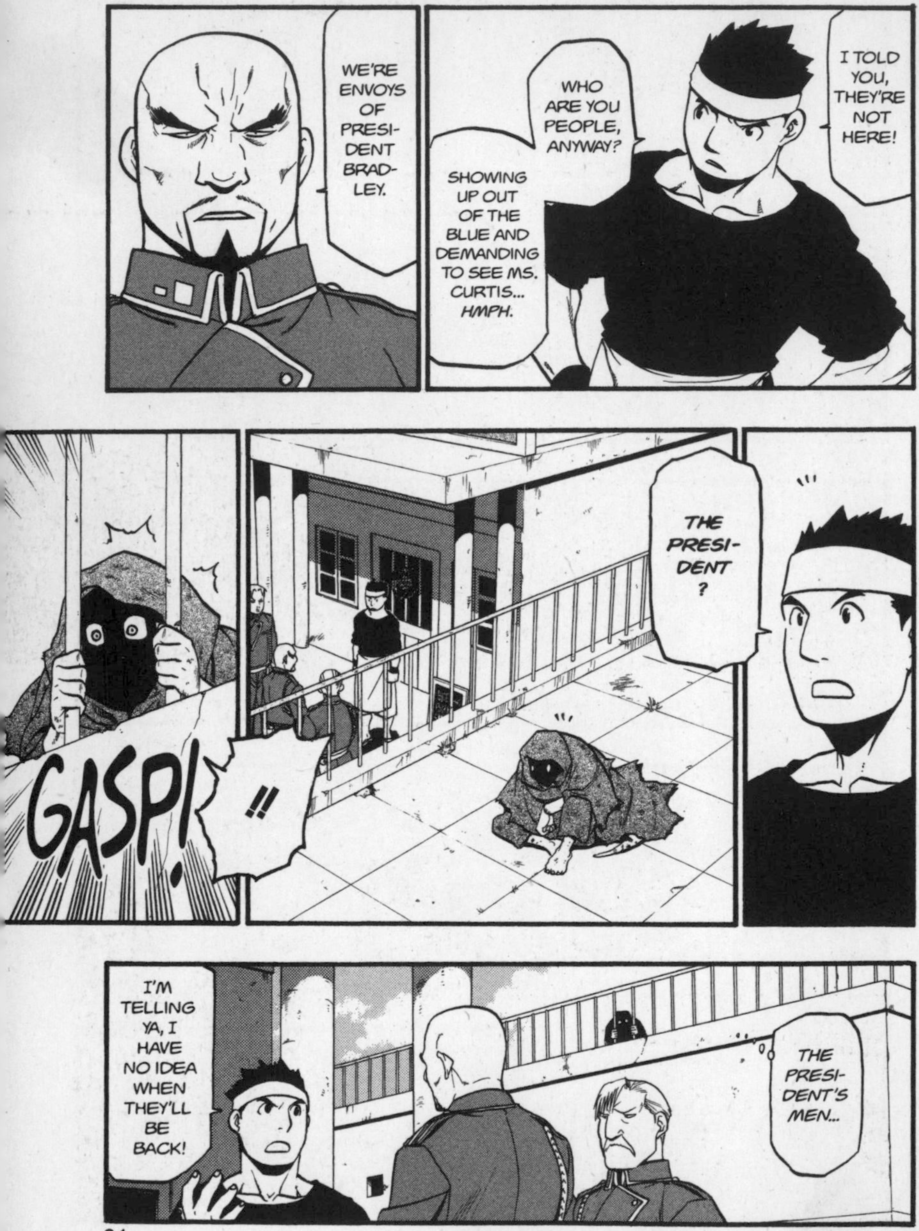
I TOLD YOU, THEY'RE NOT HERE!
WHO ARE YOU PEOPLE, ANYWAY?
SHOWING UP OUT OF THE BLUE AND DEMANDING TO SEE MS. CURTIS... HMPH.
WE'RE ENVOYS OF PRESIDENT BRADLEY.
THE PRESIDENT?
GASP!
!!
THE PRESIDENT'S MEN...
I'M TELLING YA, I HAVE NO IDEA WHEN THEY'LL BE BACK!

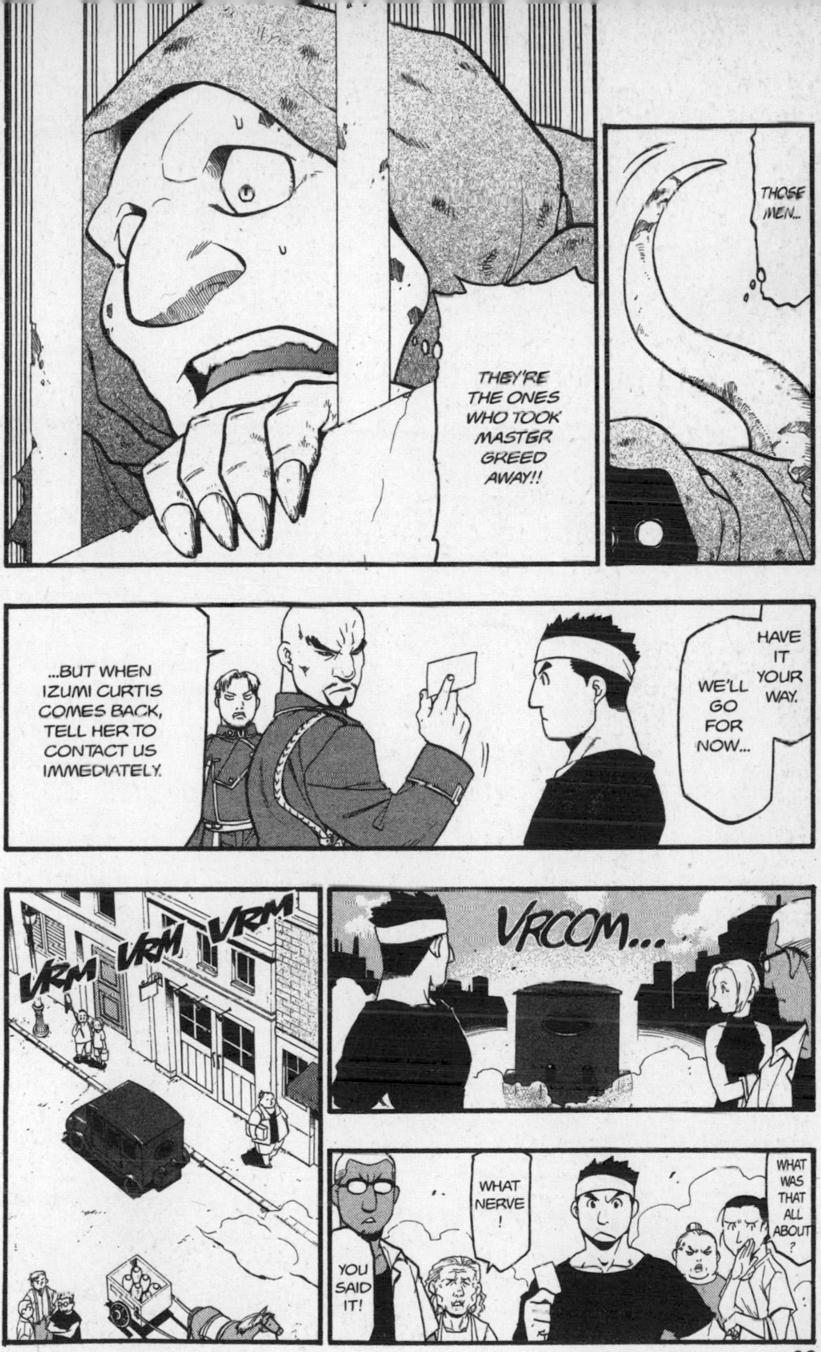
THOSE MEN...
THEY'RE THE ONES WHO TOOK MASTER GREED AWAY!!
HAVE IT YOUR WAY.
WE'LL GO FOR NOW...
...BUT WHEN IZUMI CURTIS COMES BACK, TELL HER TO CONTACT US IMMEDIATELY.
VRCOM...
WHAT WAS THAT ALL ABOUT?
WHAT NERVE!
YOU SAID IT!
VRM VRM VRM

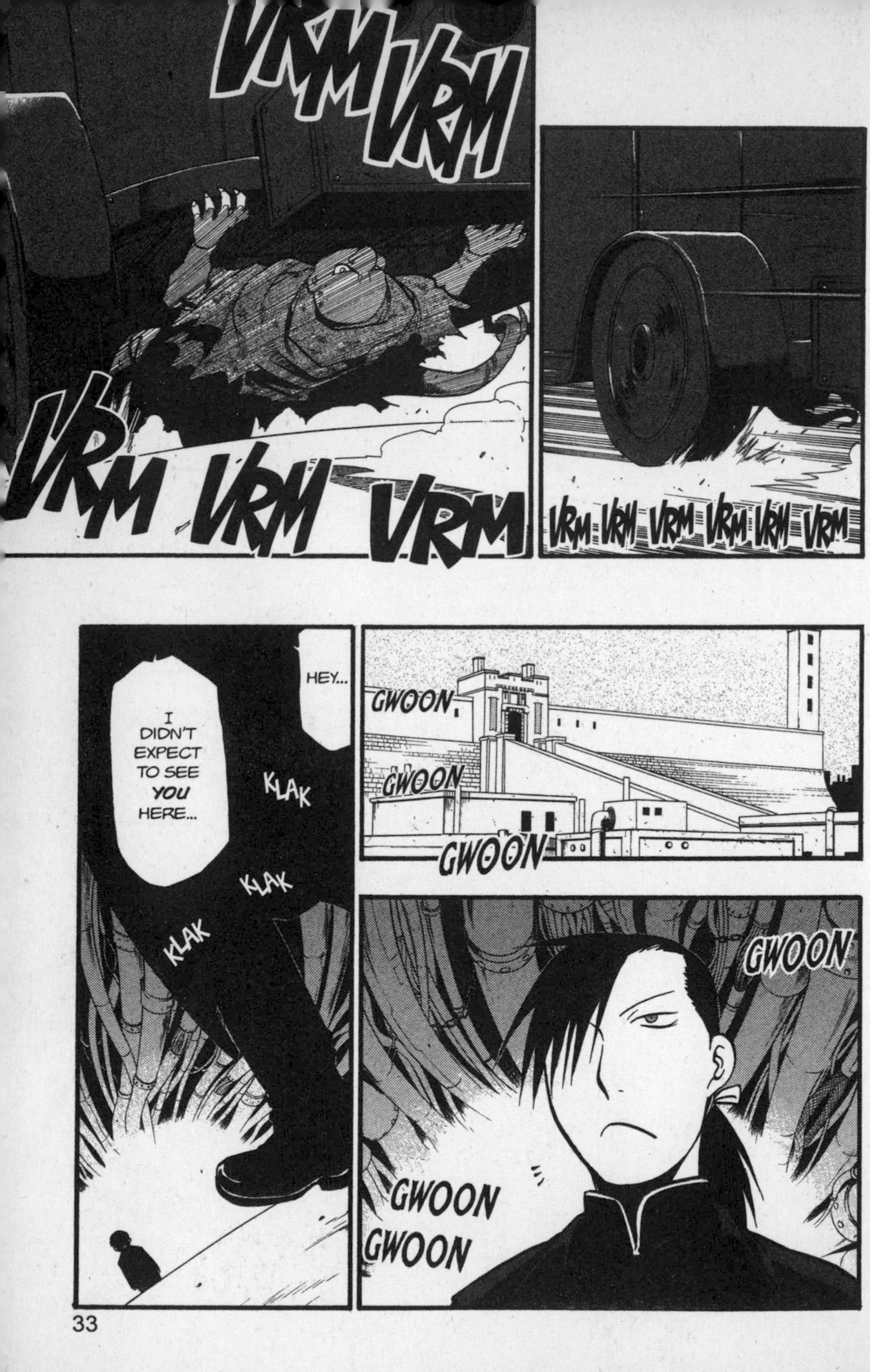

VRM VRM VRM VRM VRM VRM
VRM VRM
VRM VRM VRM
GWOON
GWOON
GWOON
GWOON
GWOON
GWOON
HEY...
I DIDN'T EXPECT TO SEE *YOU* HERE...
KLAK
KLAK
KLAK

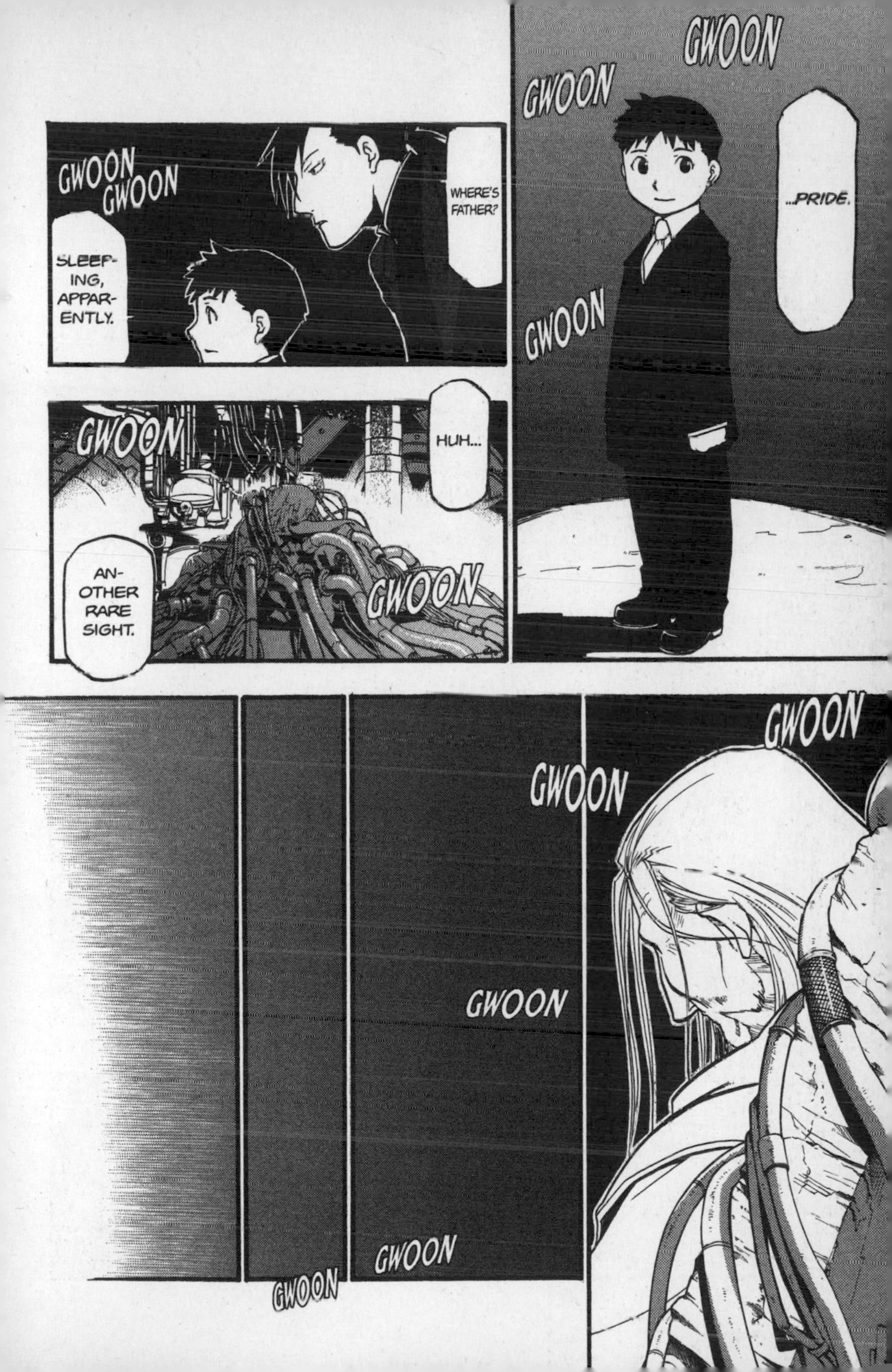
GWOON
GWOON
...PRIDE.
GWOON
GWOON
GWOON
WHERE'S FATHER?
SLEEPING, APPARENTLY.
GWOON
HUH...
ANOTHER RARE SIGHT.
GWOON
GWOON
GWOON
GWOON
GWOON
GWOON

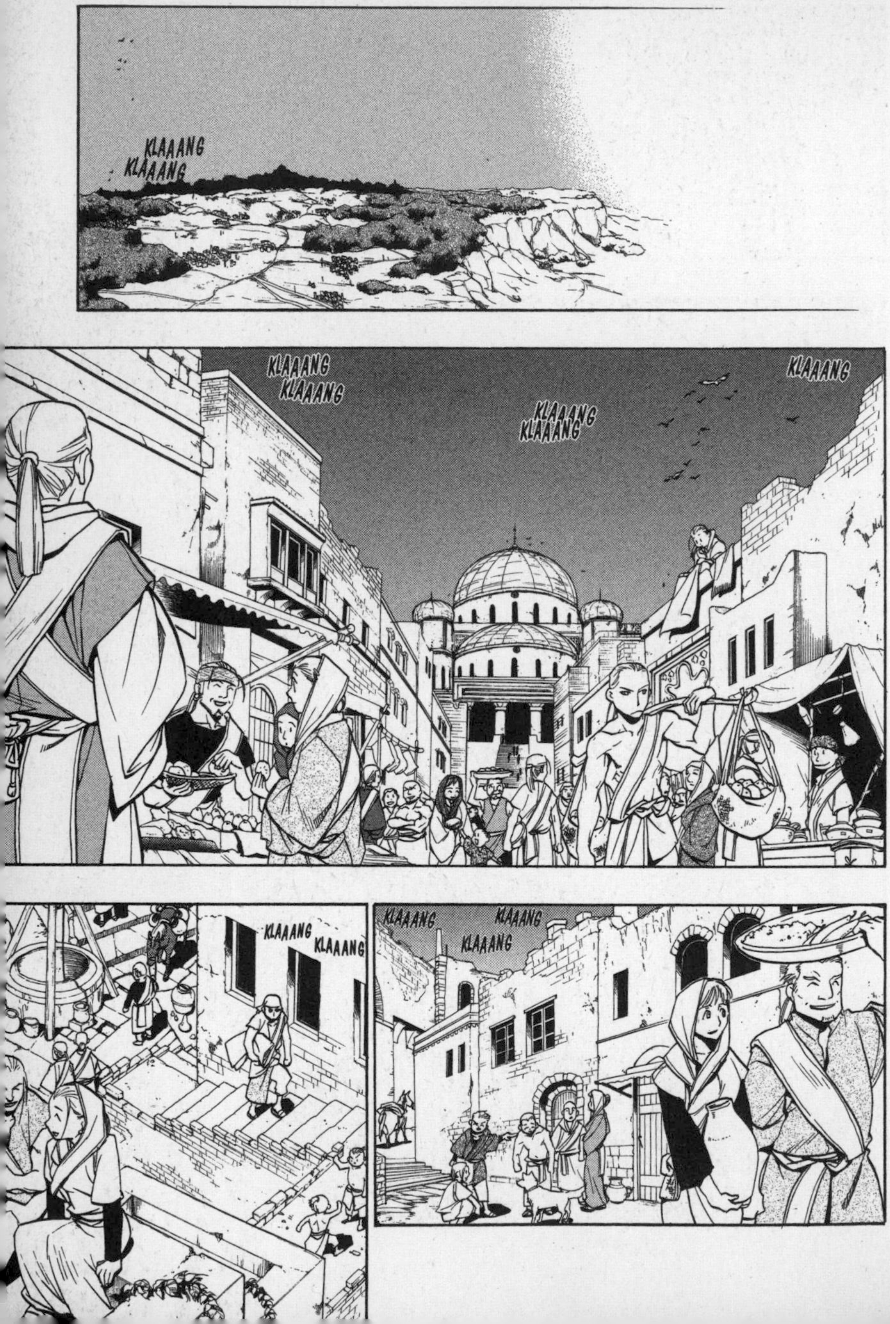
KLAAANG
KLAAANG
KLAAANG
KLAAANG
KLAAANG
KLAAANG
KLAAANG
KLAAANG
KLAAANG
KLAAANG
KLAAANG
KLAAANG

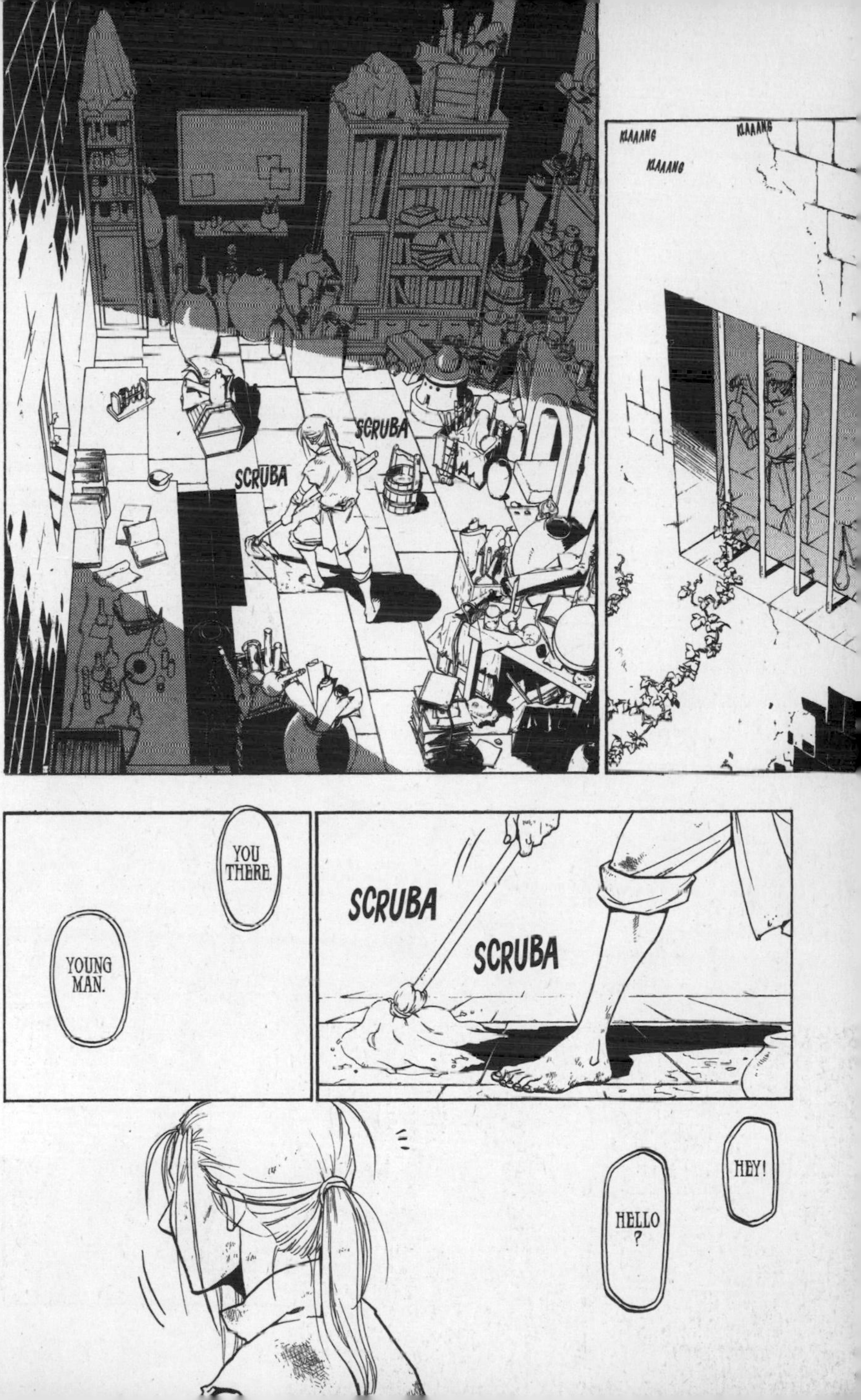
KLAAANG
KLAAANG
KLAAANG
SCRUBA
SCRUBA
SCRUBA
SCRUBA
YOU THERE.
YOUNG MAN.
HEY!
HELLO?

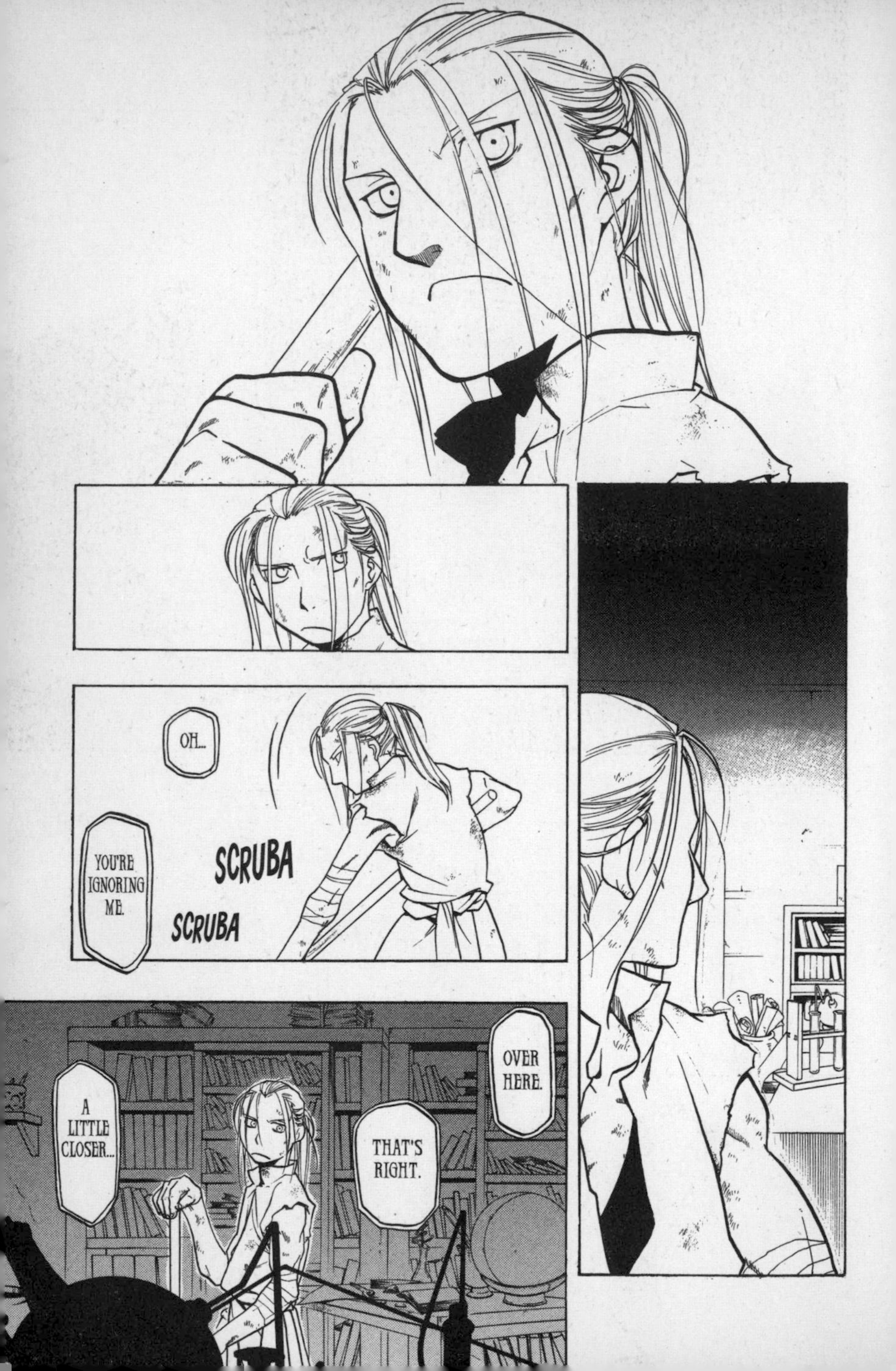
OH..
SCRUBA
YOU'RE IGNORING ME.
SCRUBA
OVER HERE.
THAT'S RIGHT.
A LITTLE CLOSER...

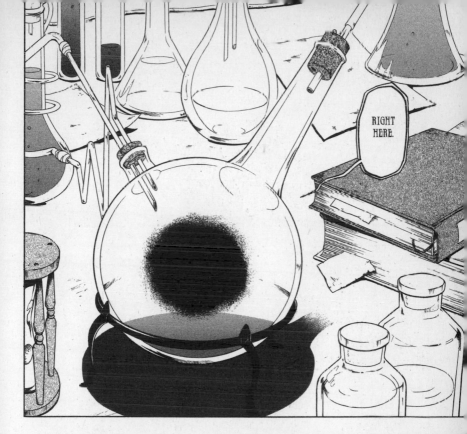

RIGHT HERE.
I'M BUSY. TALK TO ME LATER.
WHAT?
DOESN'T MY APPEARANCE SHOCK YOU?
YOU WANT ME TO ACT SHOCKED? WHAT'S IT WORTH TO YOU?
SLOOSH SLOOSH

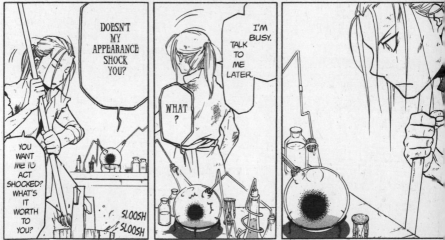

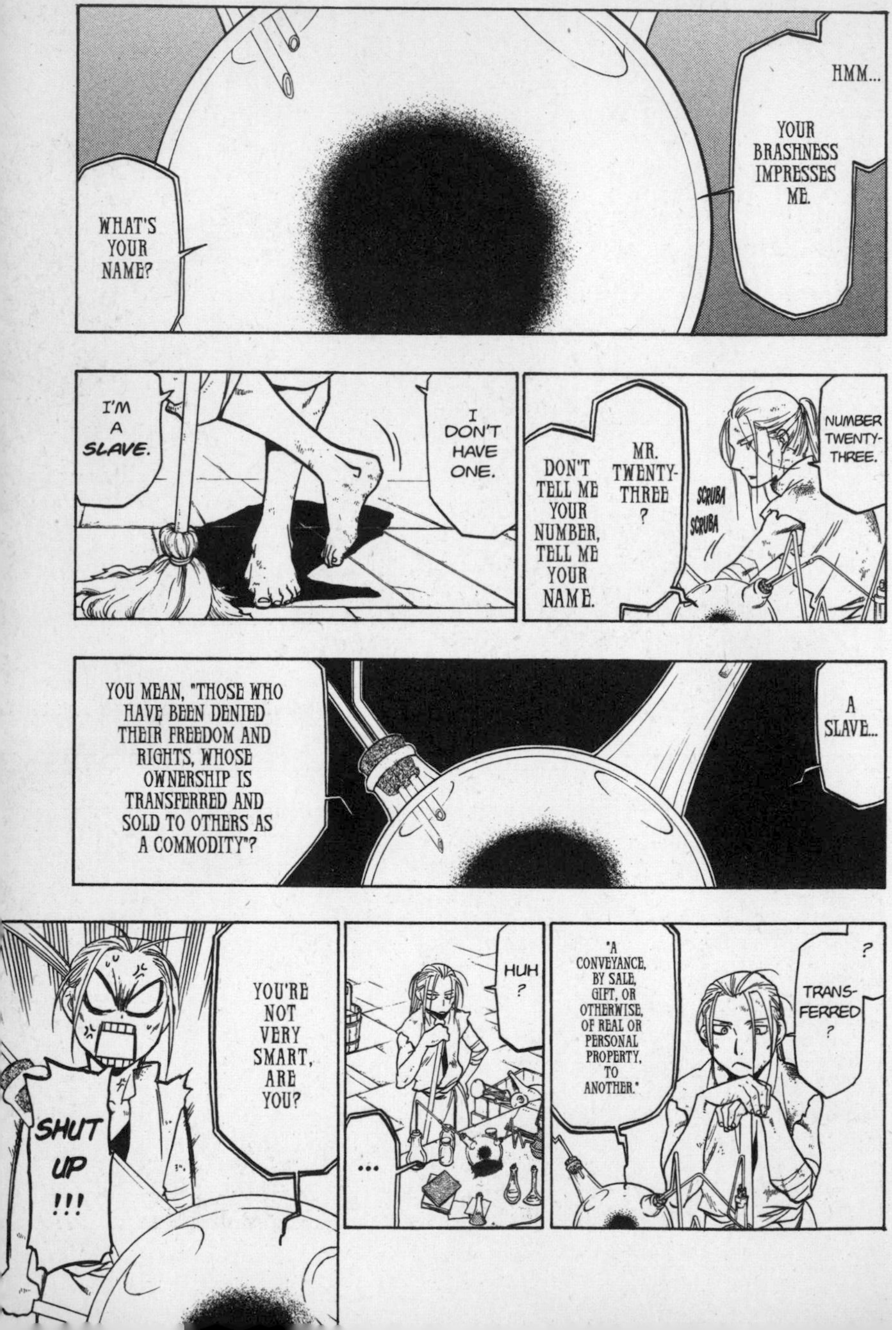
HMM...
YOUR BRASHNESS IMPRESSES ME.
WHAT'S YOUR NAME?
NUMBER TWENTY-THREE.
SCRUBA SCRUBA
MR. TWENTY-THREE?
DON'T TELL ME YOUR NUMBER, TELL ME YOUR NAME.
I DON'T HAVE ONE.
I'M A SLAVE.
A SLAVE...
YOU MEAN, "THOSE WHO HAVE BEEN DENIED THEIR FREEDOM AND RIGHTS, WHOSE OWNERSHIP IS TRANSFERRED AND SOLD TO OTHERS AS A COMMODITY"?
?
TRANSFERRED?
"A CONVEYANCE, BY SALE, GIFT, OR OTHERWISE, OF REAL OR PERSONAL PROPERTY, TO ANOTHER."
HUH?
...
YOU'RE NOT VERY SMART, ARE YOU?
SHUT UP!!!

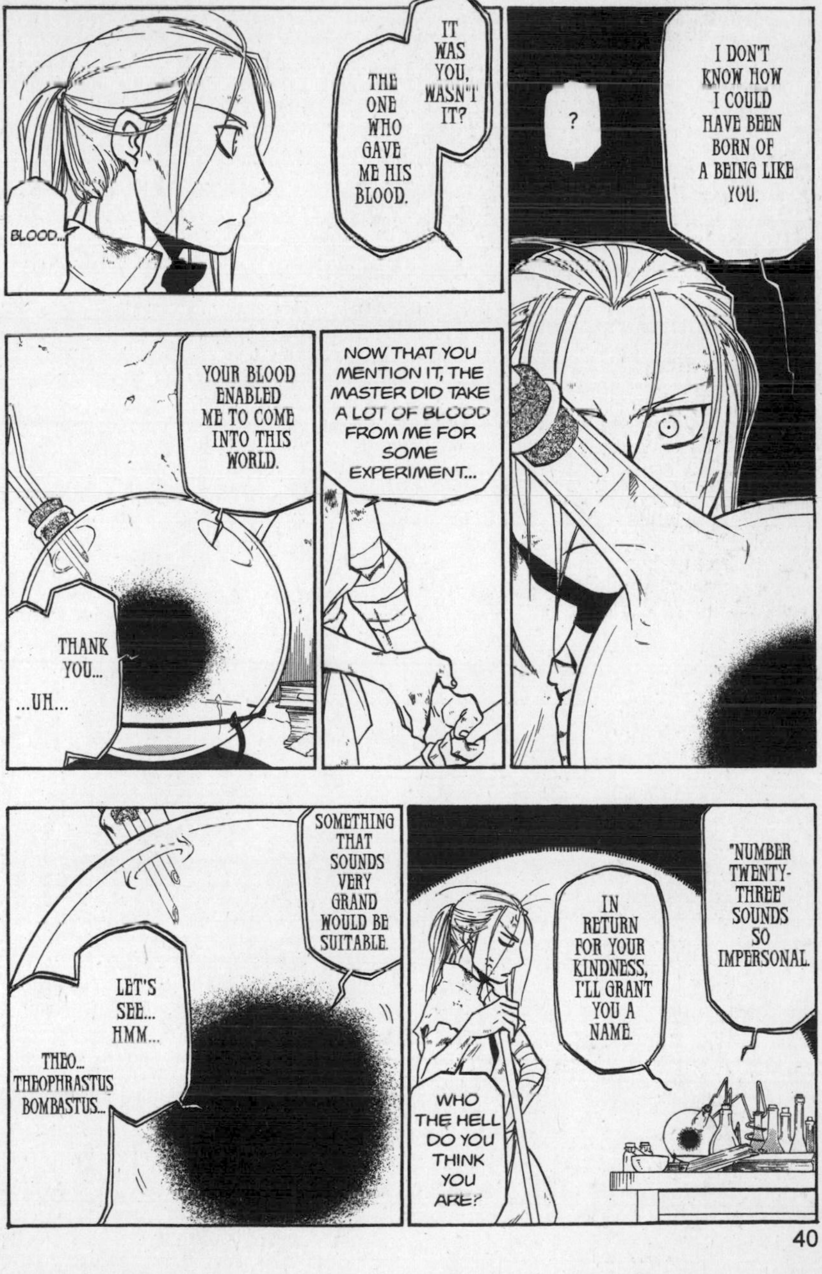
I DON'T KNOW HOW I COULD HAVE BEEN BORN OF A BEING LIKE YOU.
?
IT WAS YOU, WASN'T IT?
THE ONE WHO GAVE ME HIS BLOOD.
BLOOD...
NOW THAT YOU MENTION IT, THE MASTER DID TAKE A LOT OF BLOOD FROM ME FOR SOME EXPERIMENT...
YOUR BLOOD ENABLED ME TO COME INTO THIS WORLD.
THANK YOU...
...UH...
"NUMBER TWENTY-THREE" SOUNDS SO IMPERSONAL.
IN RETURN FOR YOUR KINDNESS, I'LL GRANT YOU A NAME.
WHO THE HELL DO YOU THINK YOU ARE?
SOMETHING THAT SOUNDS VERY GRAND WOULD BE SUITABLE.
LET'S SEE... HMM...
THEO... THEOPHRASTUS BOMBASTUS...

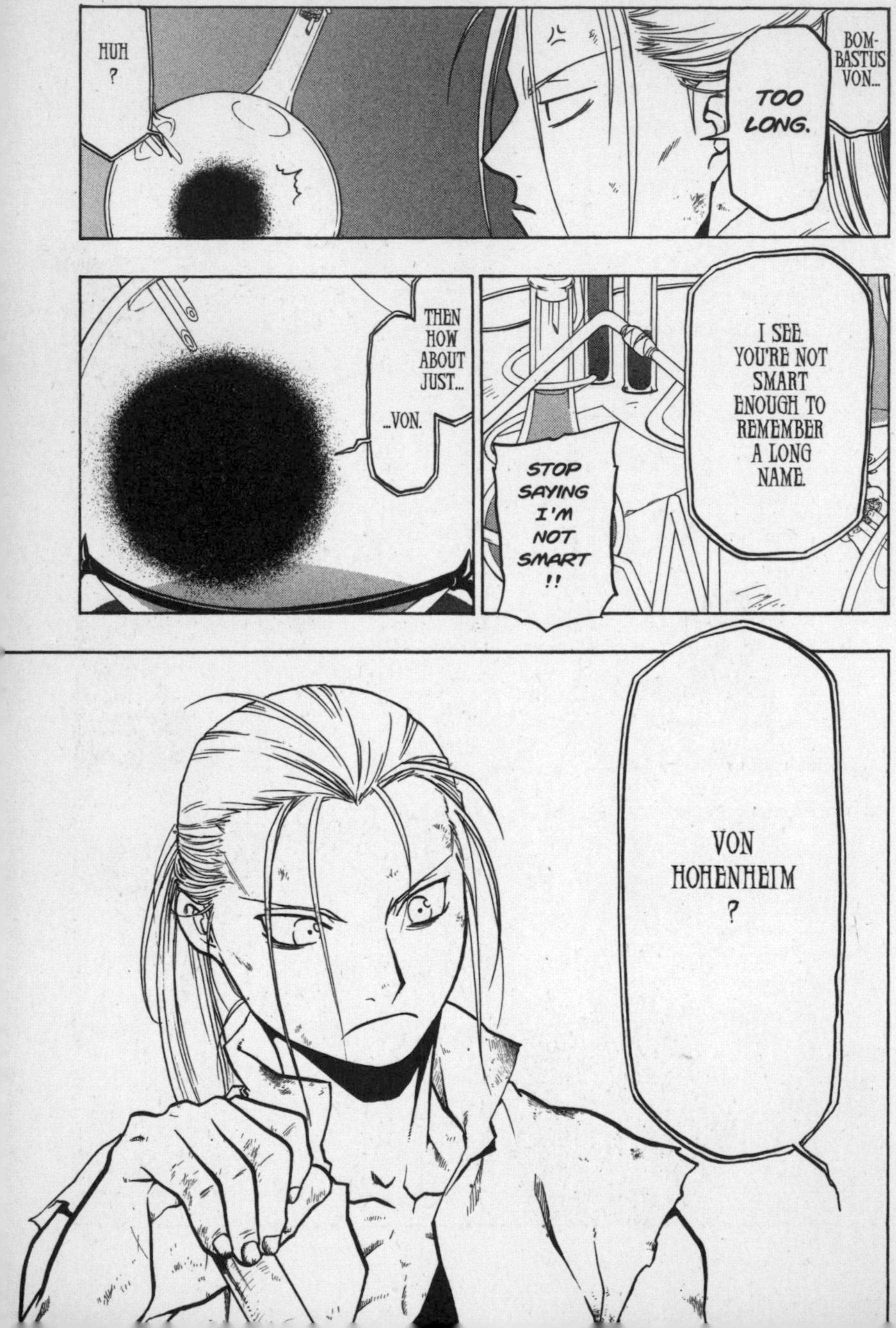
BOM-BASTUS VON...
TOO LONG.
HUH ?
I SEE. YOU'RE NOT SMART ENOUGH TO REMEMBER A LONG NAME.
STOP SAYING I'M NOT SMART !!
THEN HOW ABOUT JUST...
...VON.
VON HOHENHEIM ?

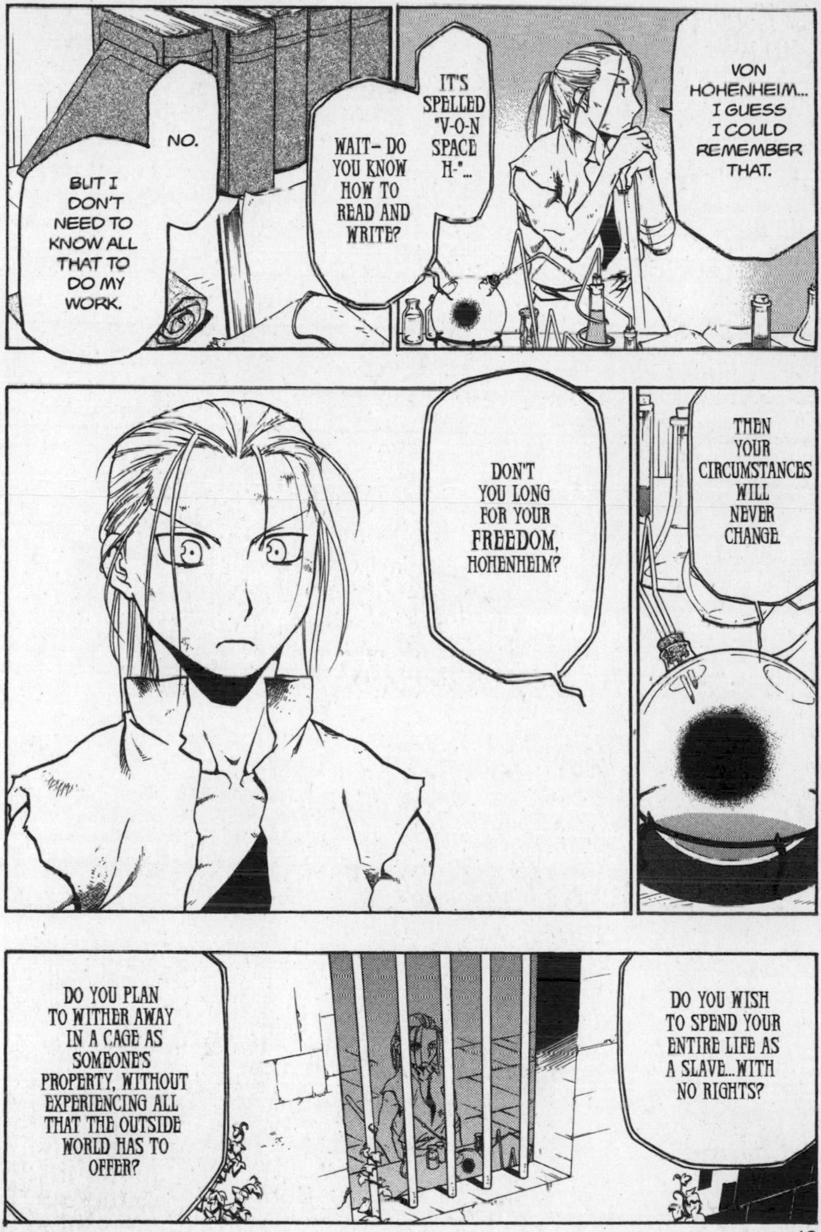
VON HOHENHEIM... I GUESS I COULD REMEMBER THAT.
IT'S SPELLED "V-O-N SPACE H-"...
WAIT- DO YOU KNOW HOW TO READ AND WRITE?
NO.
BUT I DON'T NEED TO KNOW ALL THAT TO DO MY WORK.
THEN YOUR CIRCUMSTANCES WILL NEVER CHANGE.
DON'T YOU LONG FOR YOUR FREEDOM, HOHENHEIM?
DO YOU WISH TO SPEND YOUR ENTIRE LIFE AS A SLAVE...WITH NO RIGHTS?
DO YOU PLAN TO WITHER AWAY IN A CAGE AS SOMEONE'S PROPERTY, WITHOUT EXPERIENCING ALL THAT THE OUTSIDE WORLD HAS TO OFFER?

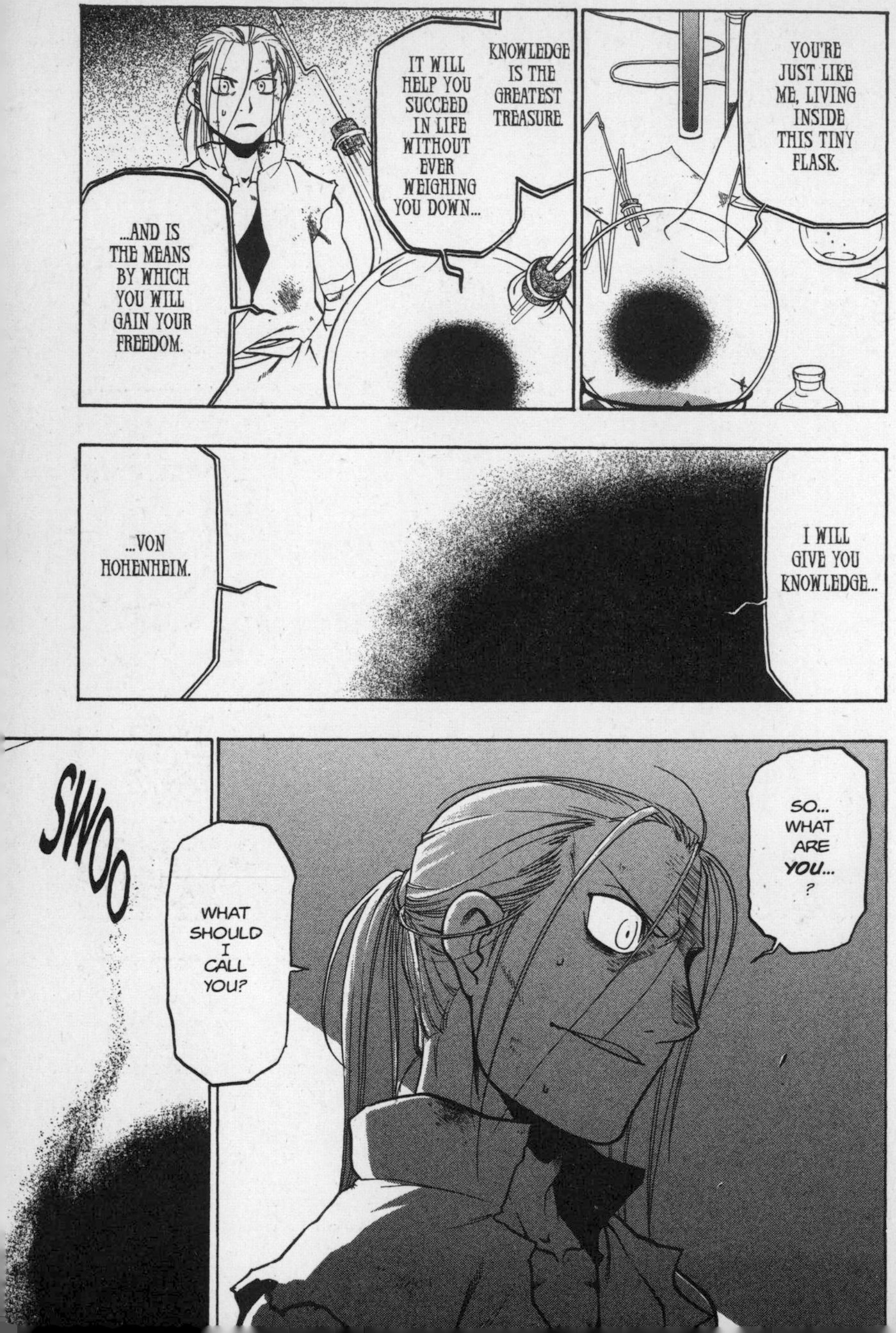
YOU'RE JUST LIKE ME, LIVING INSIDE THIS TINY FLASK.
KNOWLEDGE IS THE GREATEST TREASURE.
IT WILL HELP YOU SUCCEED IN LIFE WITHOUT EVER WEIGHING YOU DOWN...
...AND IS THE MEANS BY WHICH YOU WILL GAIN YOUR FREEDOM.
I WILL GIVE YOU KNOWLEDGE...
...VON HOHENHEIM.
SO... WHAT ARE YOU...?
WHAT SHOULD I CALL YOU?
SWOO

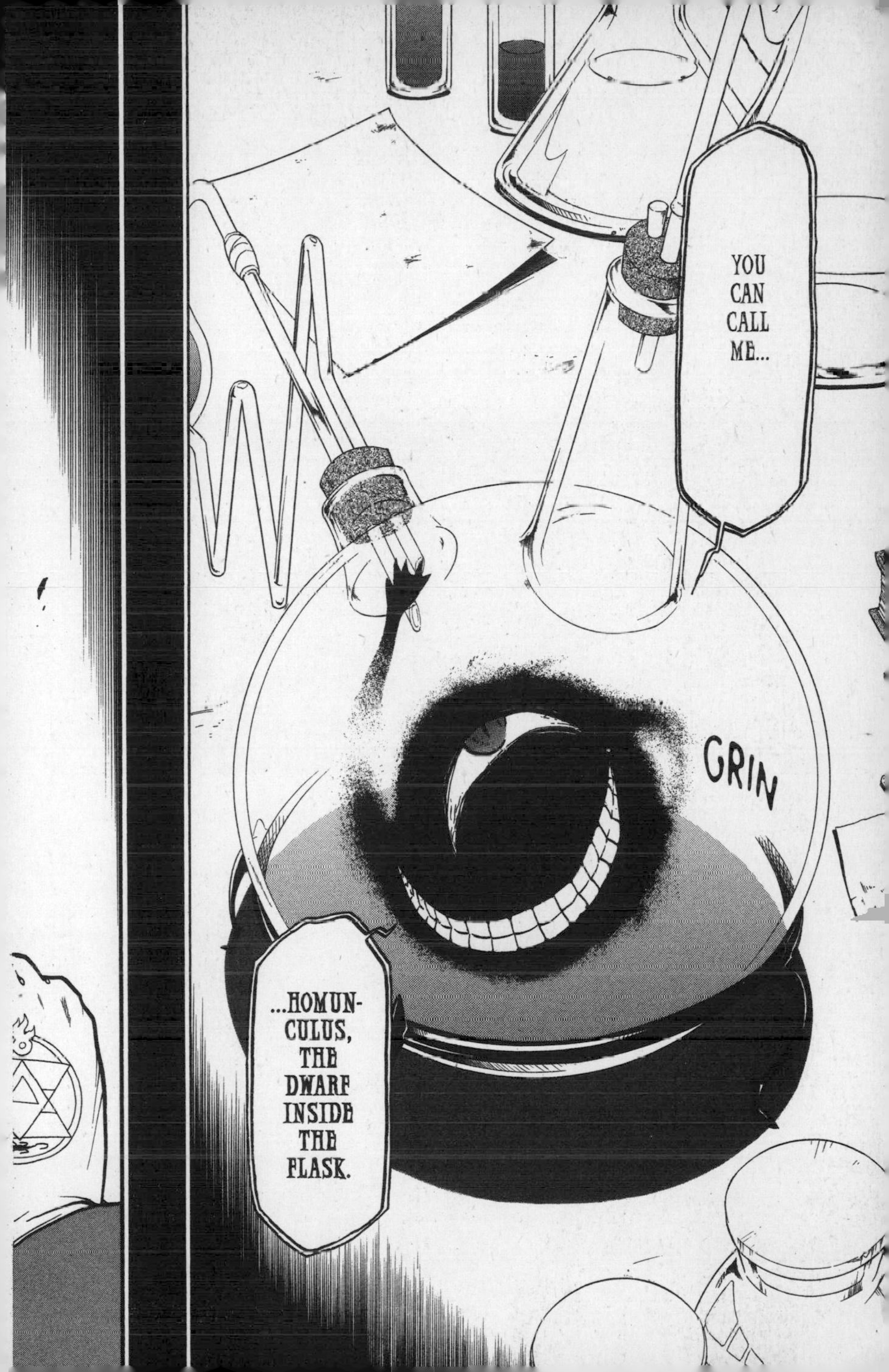
YOU CAN CALL ME...
GRIN
...HOMUN-CULUS, THE DWARF INSIDE THE FLASK.

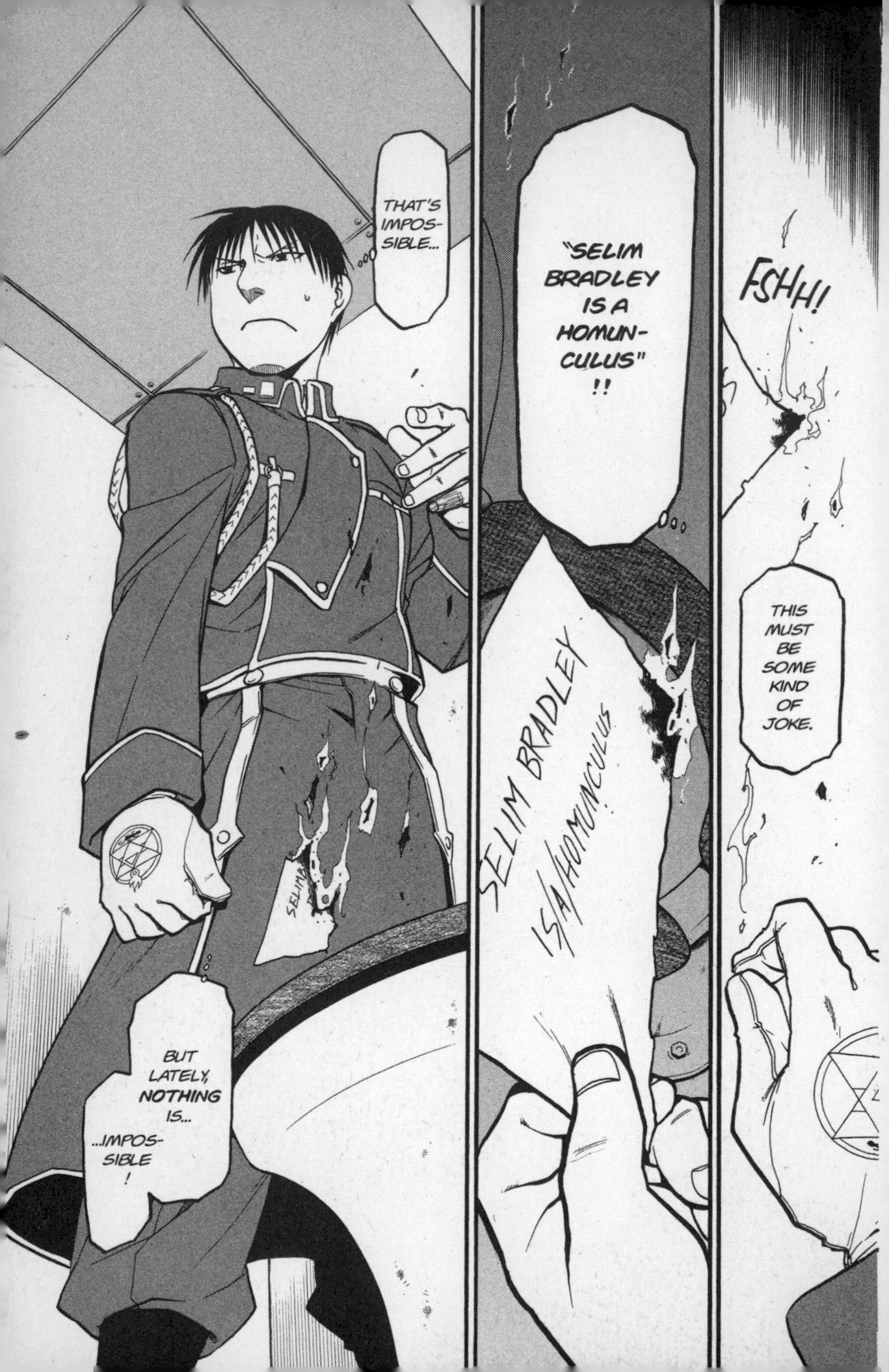
FSHH!
THIS MUST BE SOME KIND OF JOKE.
"SELIM BRADLEY IS A HOMUNCULUS"!!
SELIM BRADLEY IS/A/HOMUNCULUS
THAT'S IMPOSSIBLE...
SELIM
BUT LATELY, **NOTHING** IS... ...IMPOSSIBLE!

FULLMETAL
ALCHEMIST

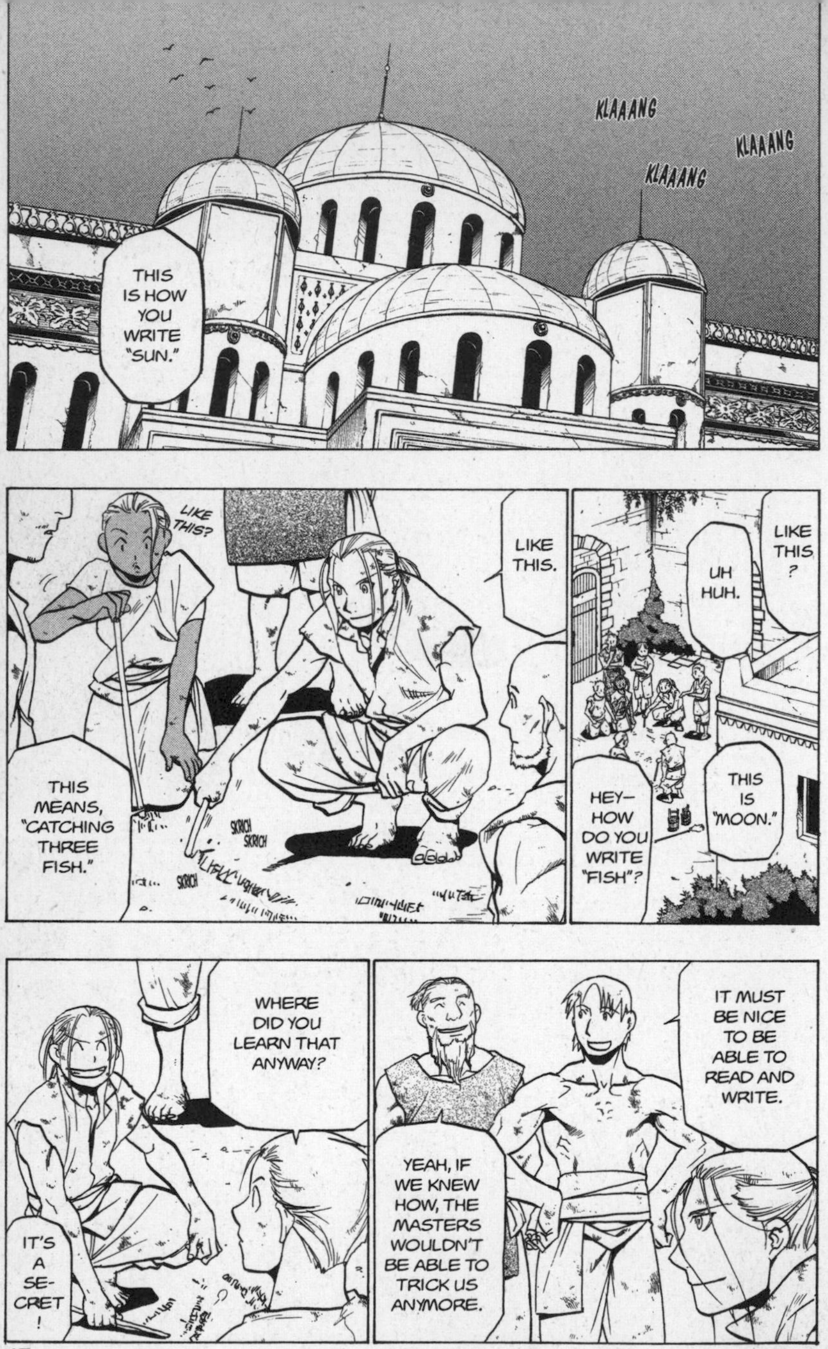
KLAAANG
KLAAANG
KLAAANG
THIS IS HOW YOU WRITE "SUN."
LIKE THIS?
UH HUH.
THIS IS "MOON."
HEY—HOW DO YOU WRITE "FISH"?
LIKE THIS.
LIKE THIS?
SKRICH SKRICH
SKRICH
THIS MEANS, "CATCHING THREE FISH."
IT MUST BE NICE TO BE ABLE TO READ AND WRITE.
YEAH, IF WE KNEW HOW, THE MASTERS WOULDN'T BE ABLE TO TRICK US ANYMORE.
WHERE DID YOU LEARN THAT ANYWAY?
IT'S A SECRET!

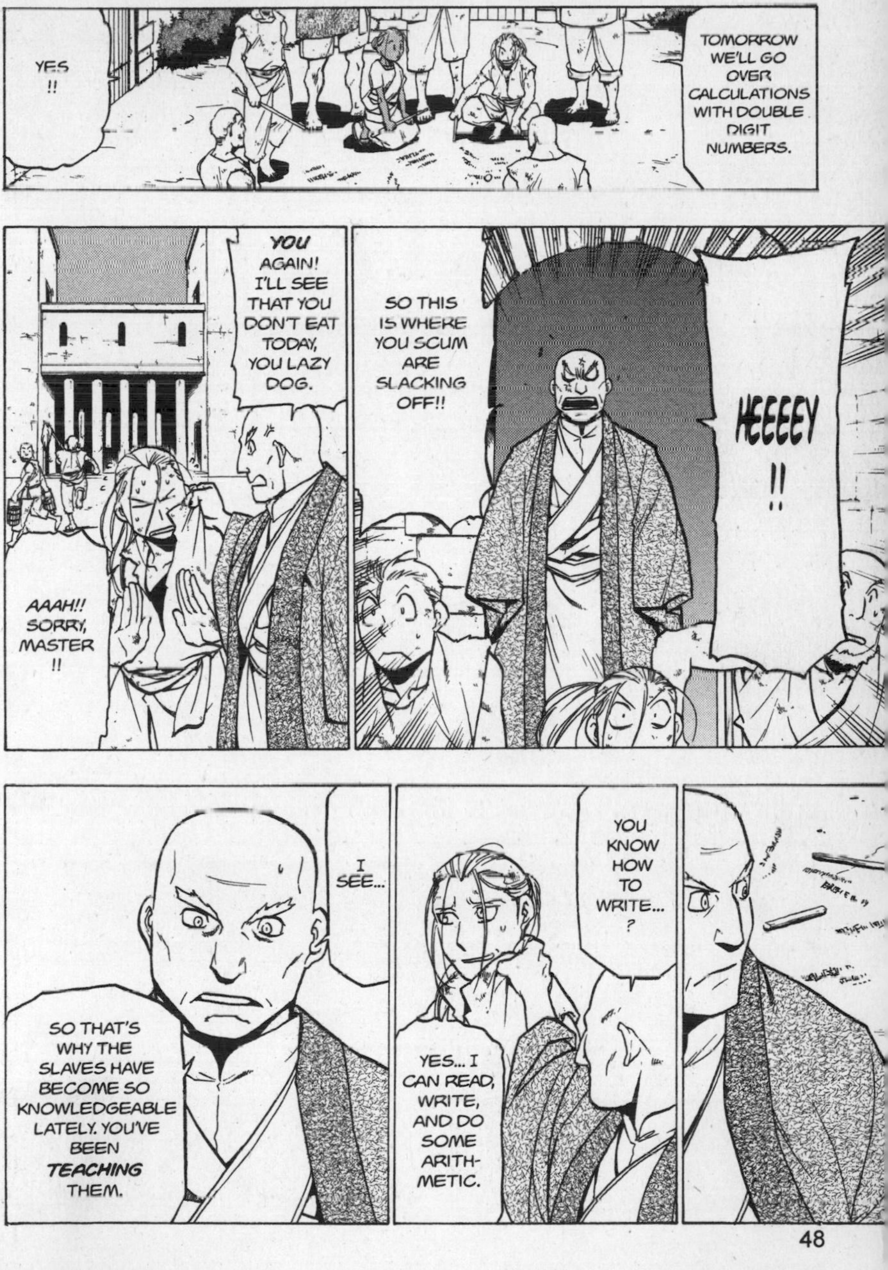
TOMORROW WE'LL GO OVER CALCULATIONS WITH DOUBLE DIGIT NUMBERS.
YES !!
HEEEEY !!
SO THIS IS WHERE YOU SCUM ARE SLACKING OFF!!
YOU AGAIN! I'LL SEE THAT YOU DON'T EAT TODAY, YOU LAZY DOG.
AAAH!! SORRY, MASTER !!
YOU KNOW HOW TO WRITE... ?
YES... I CAN READ, WRITE, AND DO SOME ARITH-METIC.
I SEE...
SO THAT'S WHY THE SLAVES HAVE BECOME SO KNOWLEDGEABLE LATELY. YOU'VE BEEN TEACHING THEM.

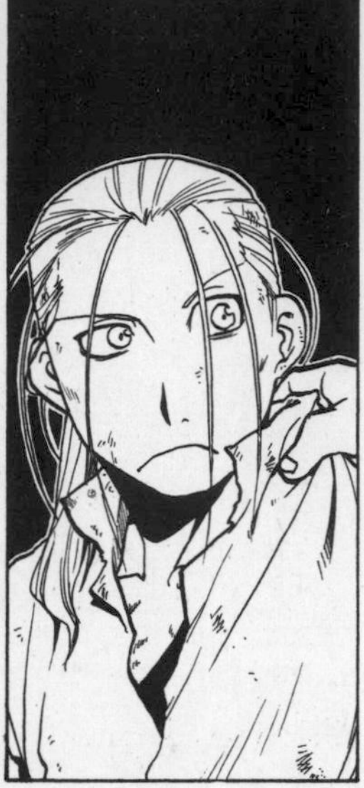

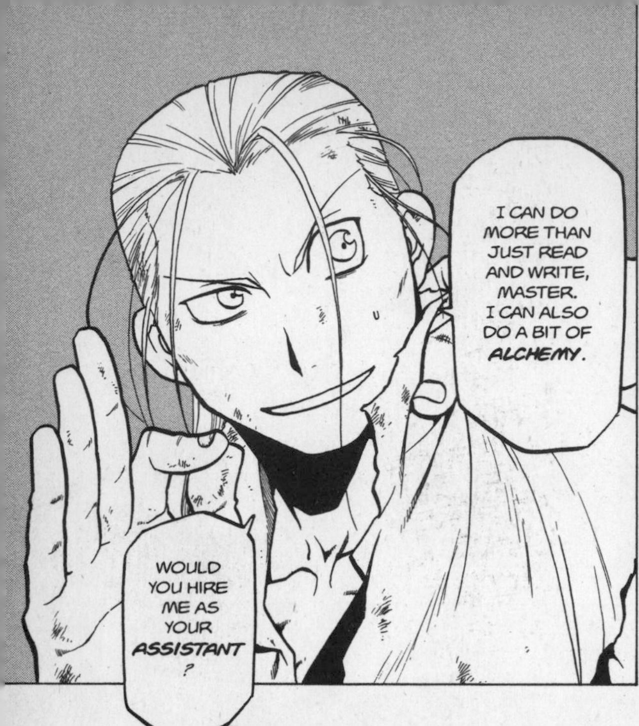
I CAN DO MORE THAN JUST READ AND WRITE, MASTER. I CAN ALSO DO A BIT OF ALCHEMY.
WOULD YOU HIRE ME AS YOUR ASSISTANT?

Chapter 75
The Last Days of Cselkcess

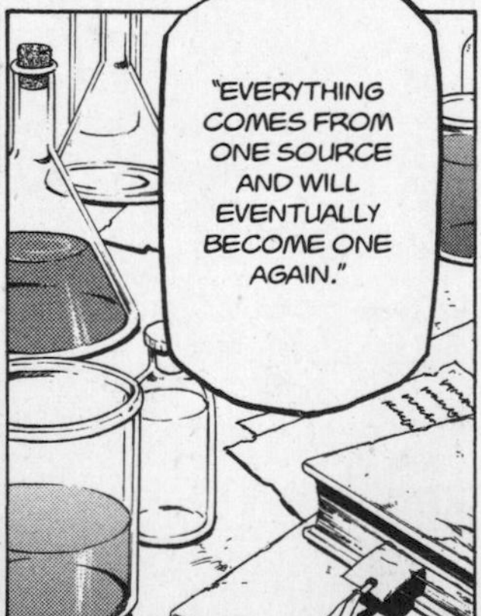
"EVERYTHING COMES FROM ONE SOURCE AND WILL EVENTUALLY BECOME ONE AGAIN."

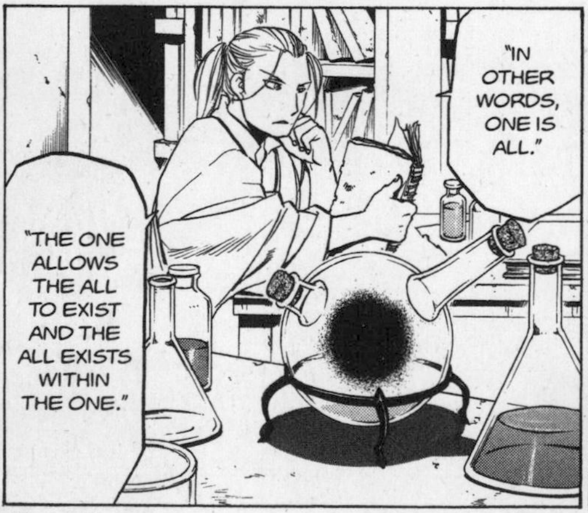
"IN OTHER WORDS, ONE IS ALL."
"THE ONE ALLOWS THE ALL TO EXIST AND THE ALL EXISTS WITHIN THE ONE."

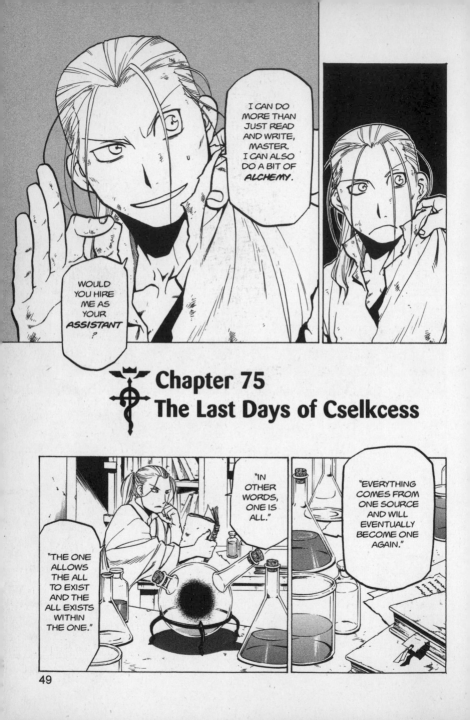

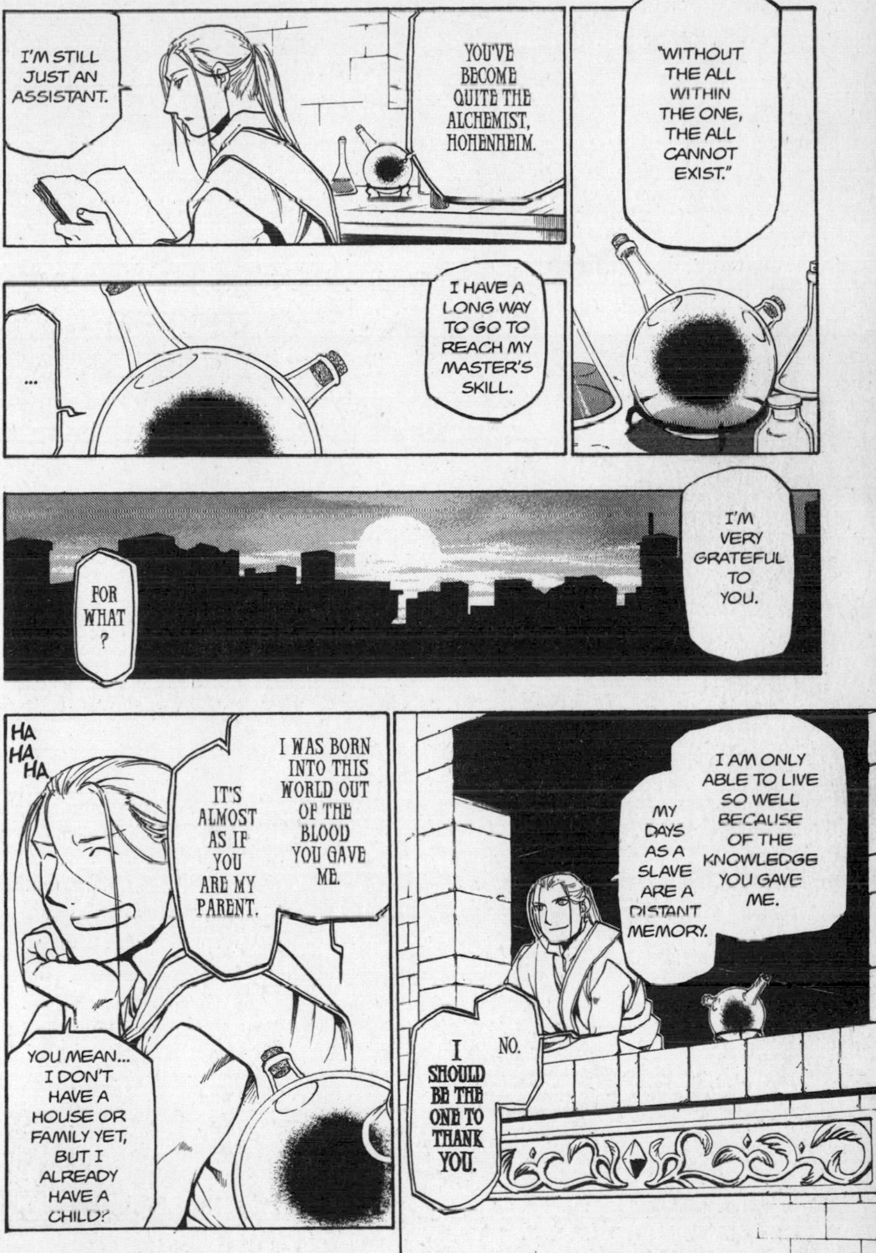
"WITHOUT THE ALL WITHIN THE ONE, THE ALL CANNOT EXIST."
YOU'VE BECOME QUITE THE ALCHEMIST, HOHENHEIM.
I'M STILL JUST AN ASSISTANT.
I HAVE A LONG WAY TO GO TO REACH MY MASTER'S SKILL.
...
I'M VERY GRATEFUL TO YOU.
FOR WHAT?
I AM ONLY ABLE TO LIVE SO WELL BECAUSE OF THE KNOWLEDGE YOU GAVE ME.
MY DAYS AS A SLAVE ARE A DISTANT MEMORY.
NO.
I SHOULD BE THE ONE TO THANK YOU.
I WAS BORN INTO THIS WORLD OUT OF THE BLOOD YOU GAVE ME.
IT'S ALMOST AS IF YOU ARE MY PARENT.
HA HA HA
YOU MEAN... I DON'T HAVE A HOUSE OR FAMILY YET, BUT I ALREADY HAVE A CHILD?

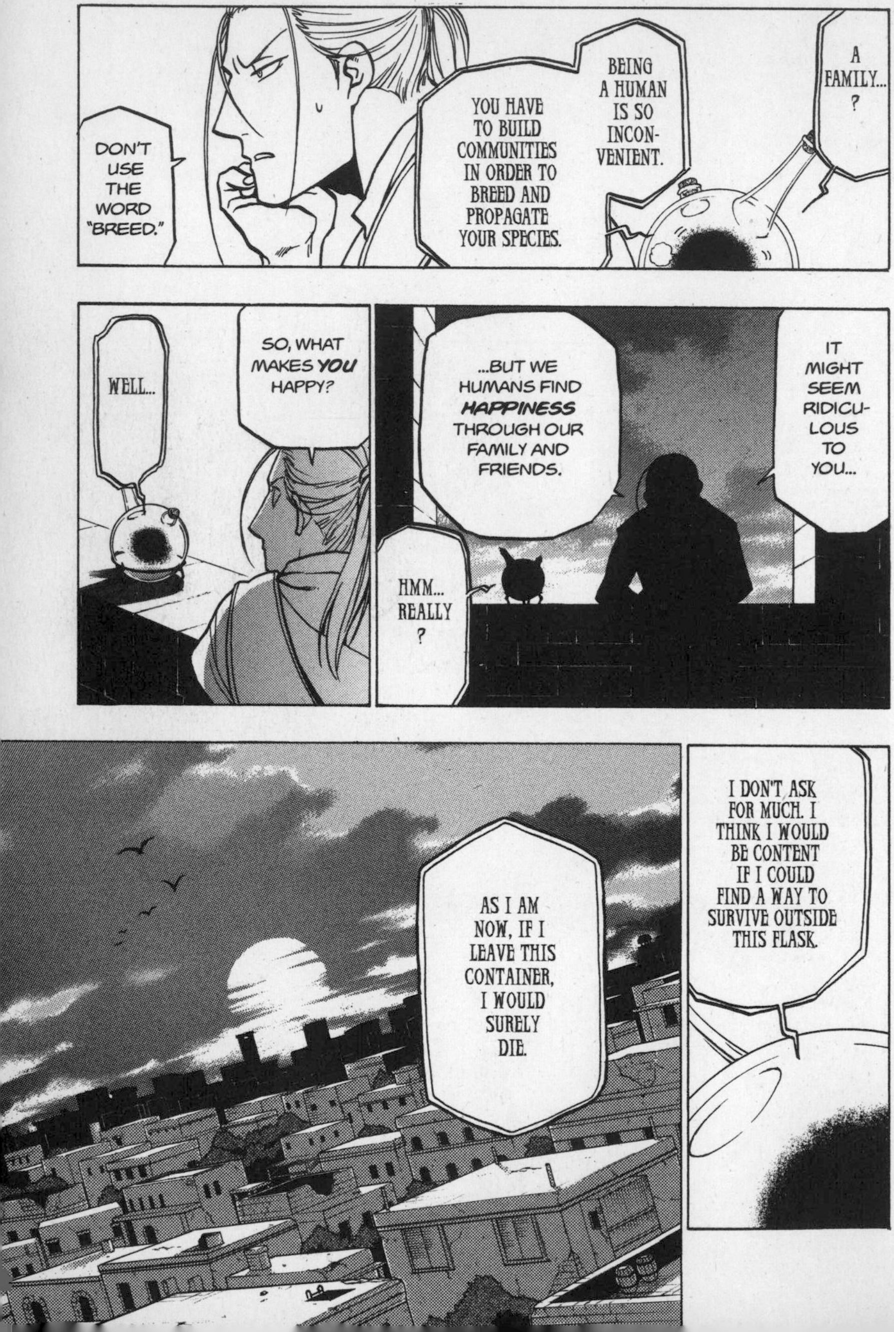
A FAMILY...?
BEING A HUMAN IS SO INCONVENIENT.
YOU HAVE TO BUILD COMMUNITIES IN ORDER TO BREED AND PROPAGATE YOUR SPECIES.
DON'T USE THE WORD "BREED."
IT MIGHT SEEM RIDICULOUS TO YOU...
...BUT WE HUMANS FIND **HAPPINESS** THROUGH OUR FAMILY AND FRIENDS.
HMM... REALLY?
SO, WHAT MAKES **YOU** HAPPY?
WELL...
I DON'T ASK FOR MUCH. I THINK I WOULD BE CONTENT IF I COULD FIND A WAY TO SURVIVE OUTSIDE THIS FLASK.
AS I AM NOW, IF I LEAVE THIS CONTAINER, I WOULD SURELY DIE.

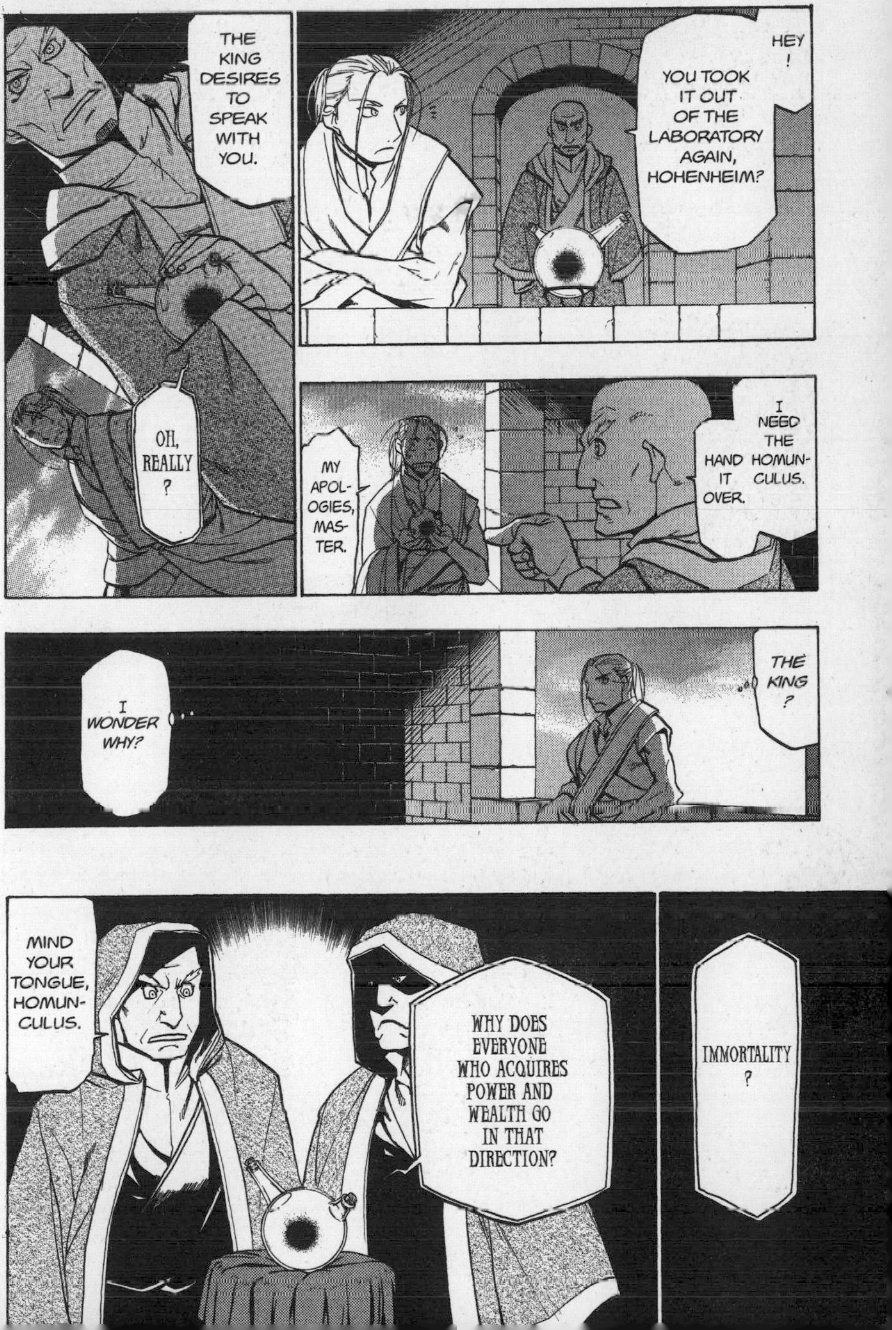
HEY!
YOU TOOK IT OUT OF THE LABORATORY AGAIN, HOHENHEIM?
I NEED THE HOMUNCULUS. HAND IT OVER.
MY APOLOGIES, MASTER.
THE KING DESIRES TO SPEAK WITH YOU.
OH, REALLY?
THE KING?
I WONDER WHY?
IMMORTALITY?
WHY DOES EVERYONE WHO ACQUIRES POWER AND WEALTH GO IN THAT DIRECTION?
MIND YOUR TONGUE, HOMUNCULUS.

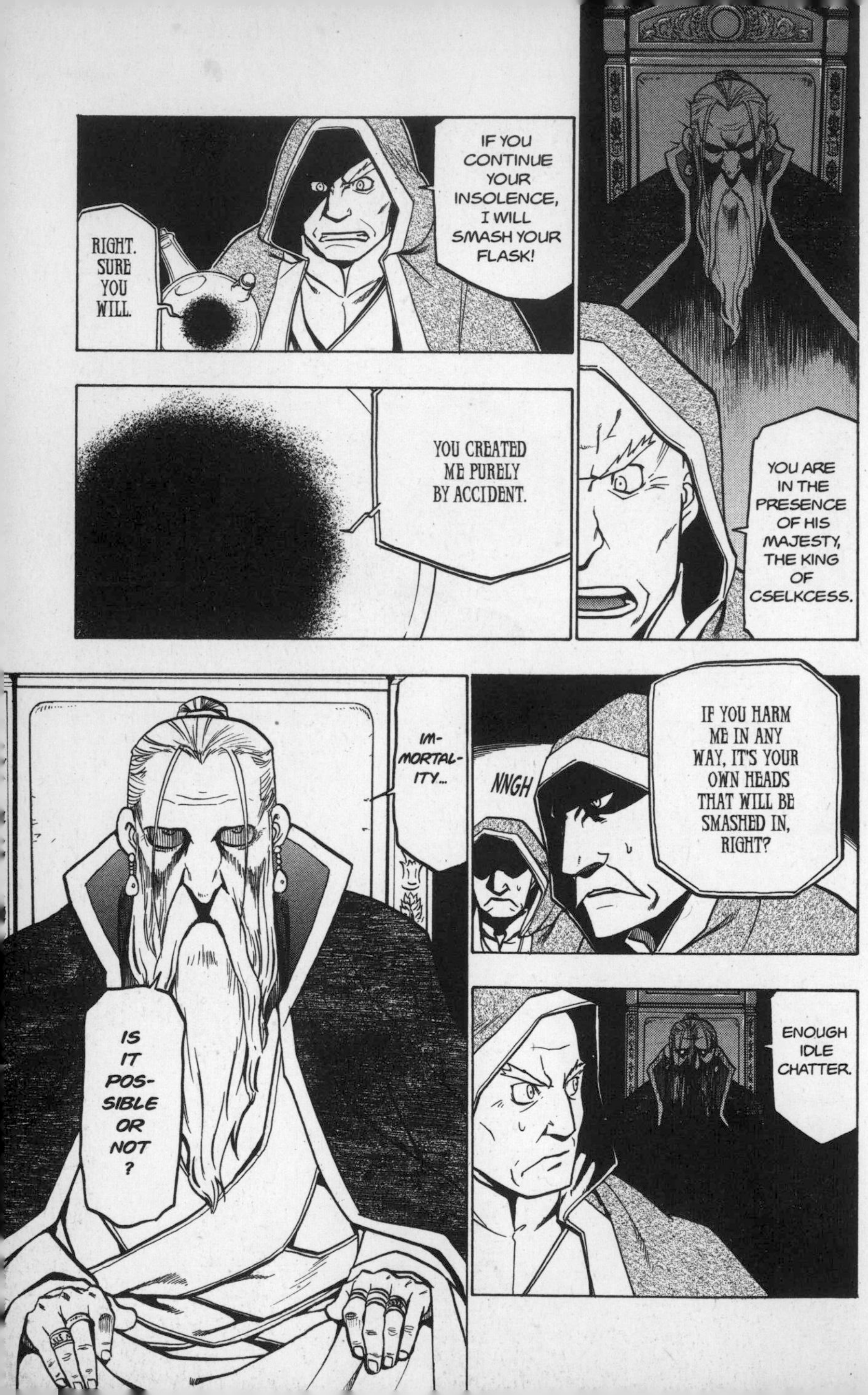
YOU ARE IN THE PRESENCE OF HIS MAJESTY, THE KING OF CSELKCESS.
IF YOU CONTINUE YOUR INSOLENCE, I WILL SMASH YOUR FLASK!
RIGHT. SURE YOU WILL.
YOU CREATED ME PURELY BY ACCIDENT.
IF YOU HARM ME IN ANY WAY, IT'S YOUR OWN HEADS THAT WILL BE SMASHED IN, RIGHT?
NNGH
ENOUGH IDLE CHATTER.
IM-MORTAL-ITY...
IS IT POS-SIBLE OR NOT?

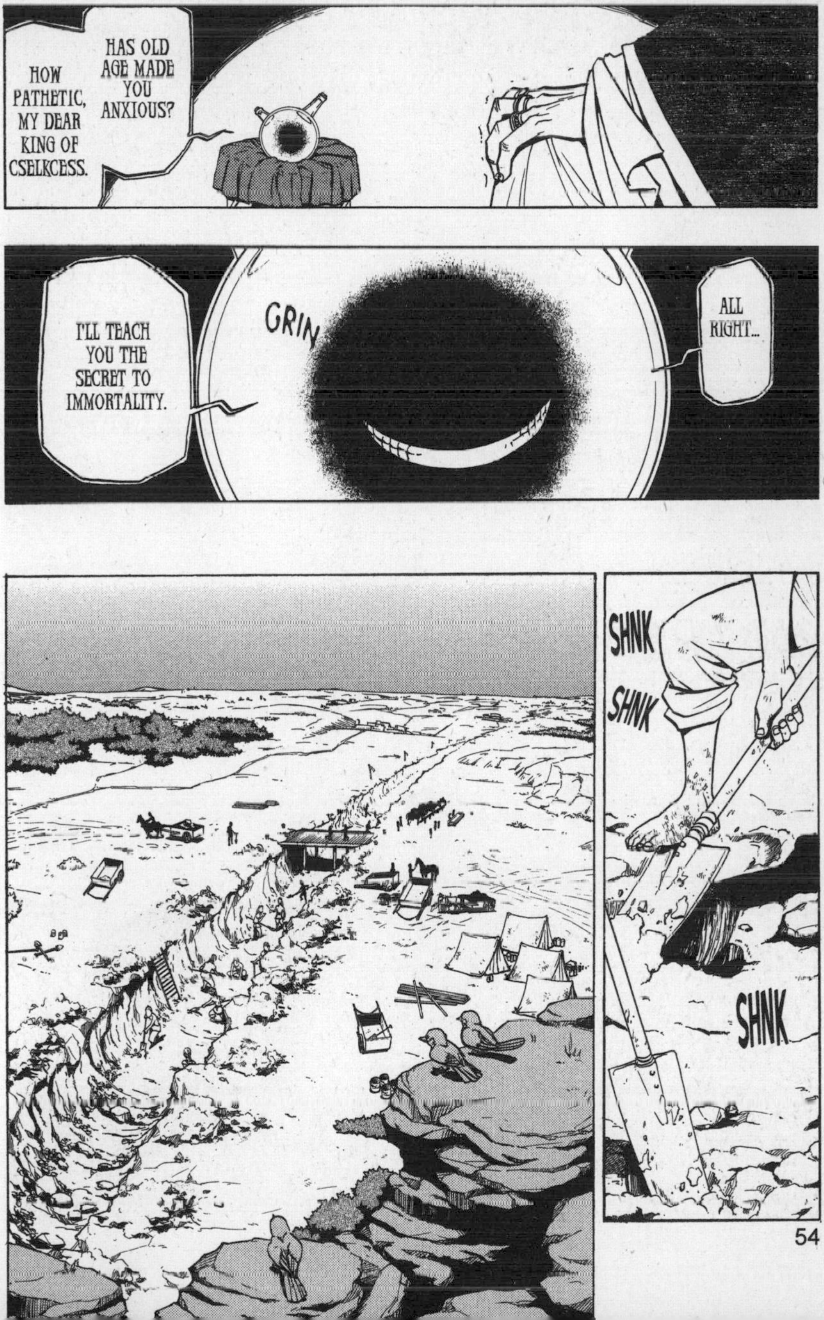
HAS OLD AGE MADE YOU ANXIOUS?
HOW PATHETIC, MY DEAR KING OF CSELKCESS.
ALL RIGHT...
GRIN
I'LL TEACH YOU THE SECRET TO IMMORTALITY.
SHNK
SHNK
SHNK

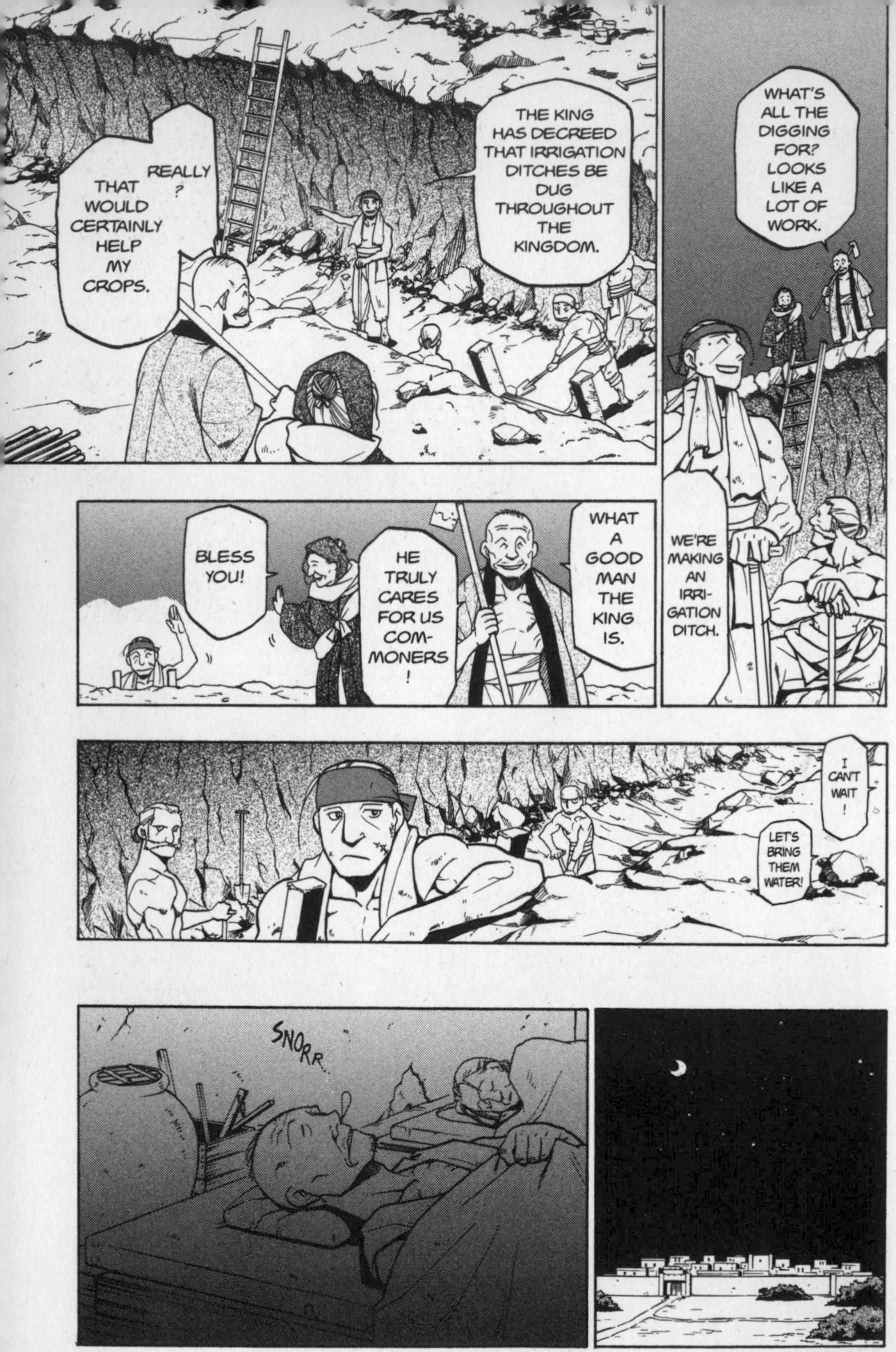
WHAT'S ALL THE DIGGING FOR? LOOKS LIKE A LOT OF WORK.
WE'RE MAKING AN IRRI-GATION DITCH.
THE KING HAS DECREED THAT IRRIGATION DITCHES BE DUG THROUGHOUT THE KINGDOM.
REALLY? THAT WOULD CERTAINLY HELP MY CROPS.
WHAT A GOOD MAN THE KING IS.
HE TRULY CARES FOR US COM-MONERS!
BLESS YOU!
I CAN'T WAIT!
LET'S BRING THEM WATER!
SNORR...

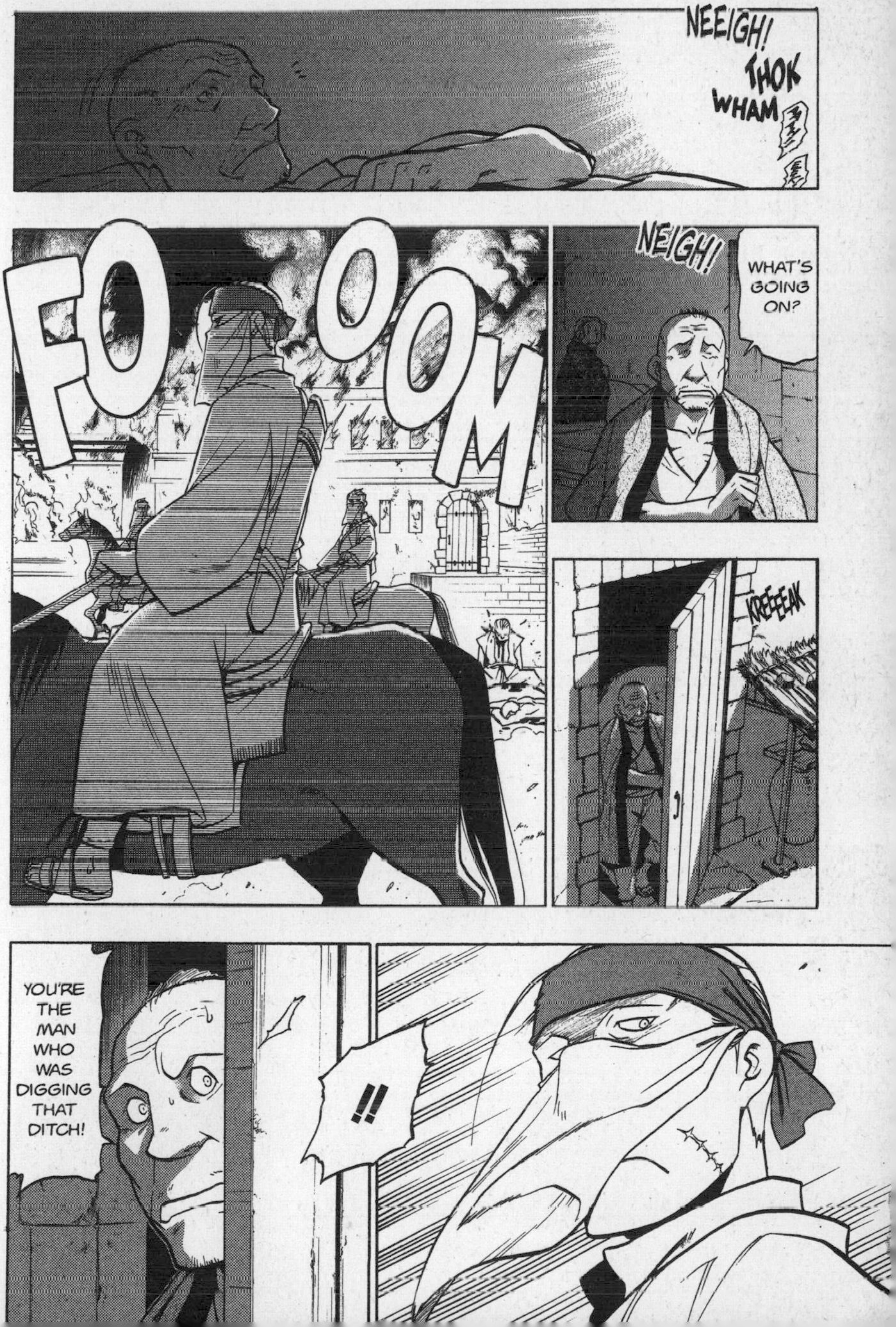
NEEIGH!
THOK
WHAM
NEIGH!
WHAT'S GOING ON?
KREEEEAK
FOOOM
!!
YOU'RE THE MAN WHO WAS DIGGING THAT DITCH!

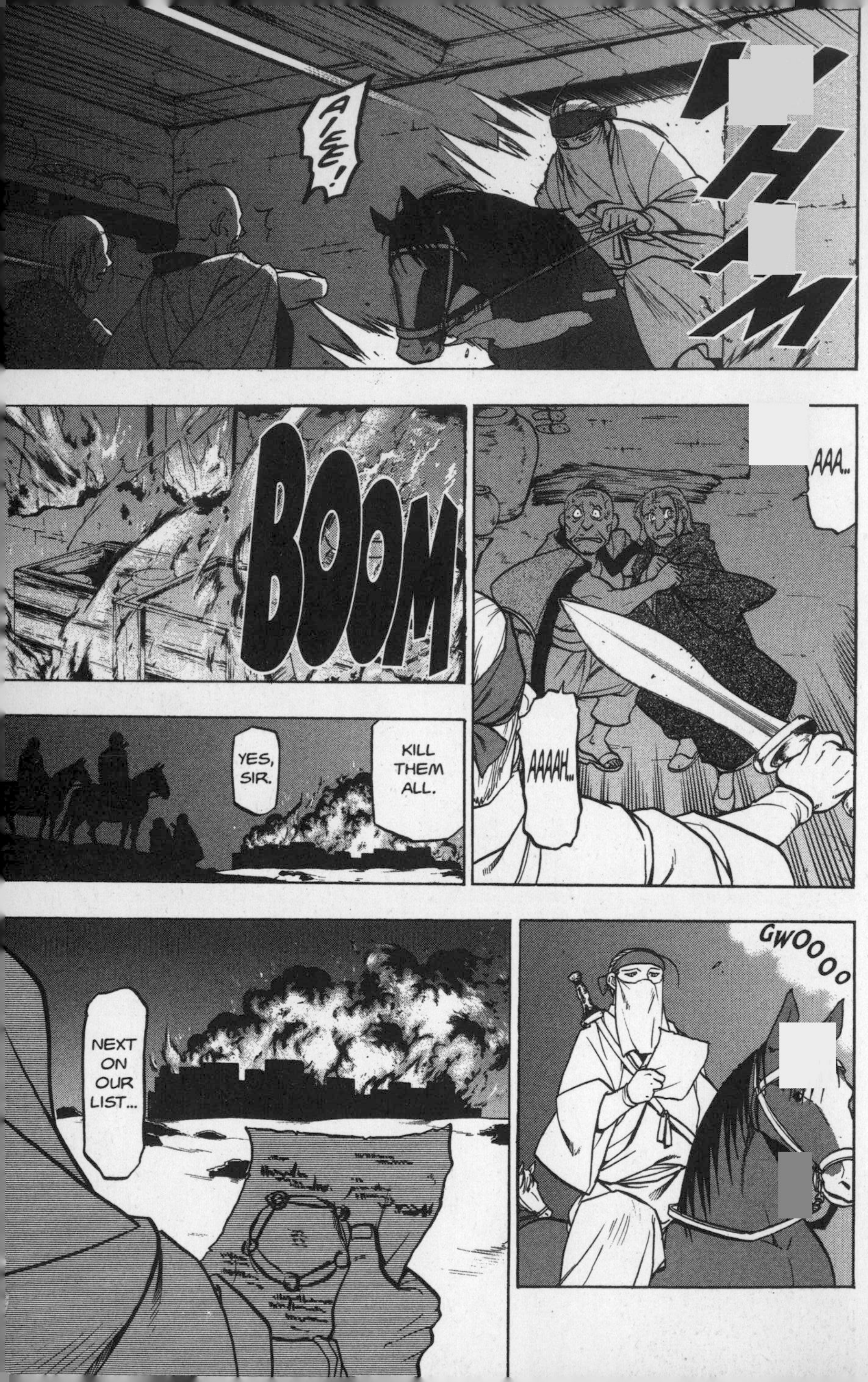
AIEE!
AAA...
AAAAH...
BOOM
KILL THEM ALL.
YES, SIR.
GWOOOOO
NEXT ON OUR LIST...

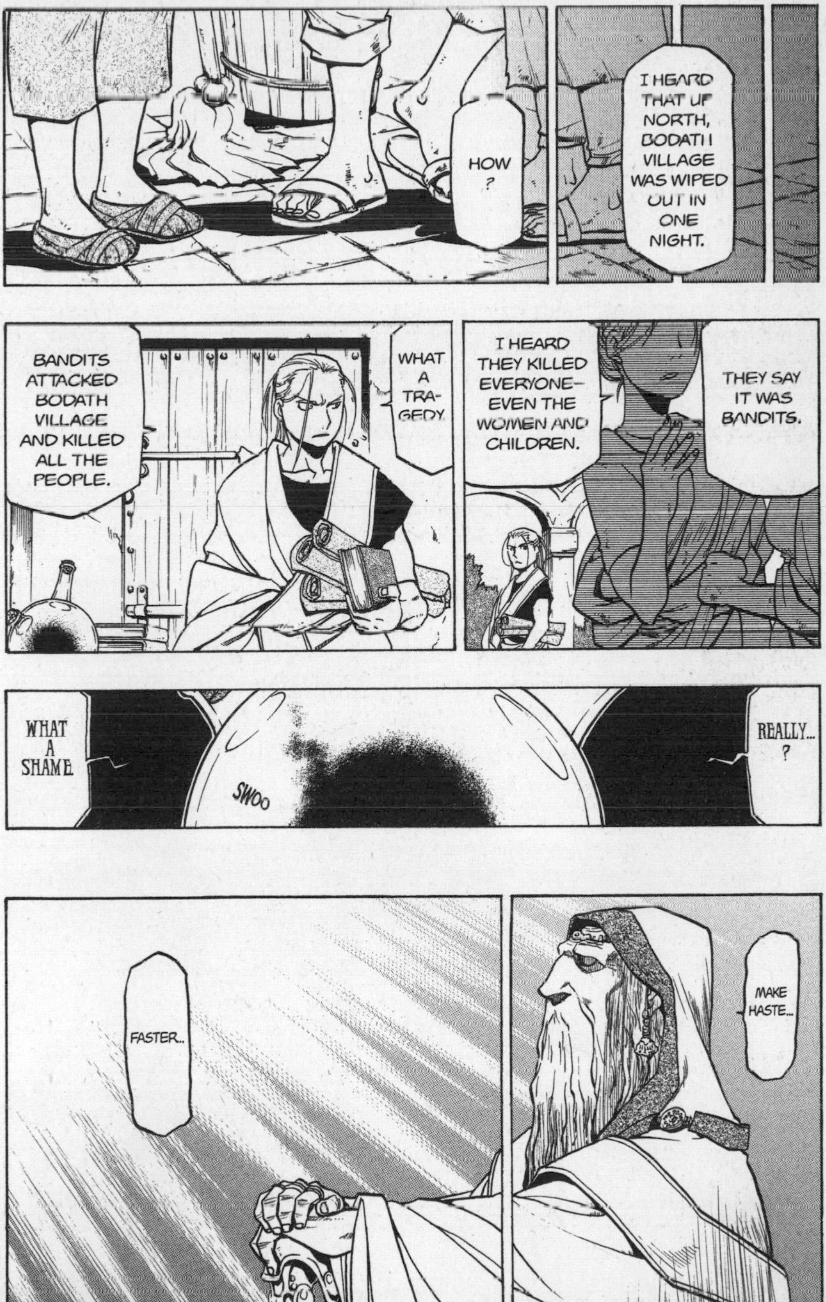
I HEARD THAT UP NORTH, BODATH VILLAGE WAS WIPED OUT IN ONE NIGHT.
HOW?
THEY SAY IT WAS BANDITS.
I HEARD THEY KILLED EVERYONE— EVEN THE WOMEN AND CHILDREN.
WHAT A TRA-GEDY.
BANDITS ATTACKED BODATH VILLAGE AND KILLED ALL THE PEOPLE.
REALLY...?
SWOO
WHAT A SHAME
MAKE HASTE...
FASTER..

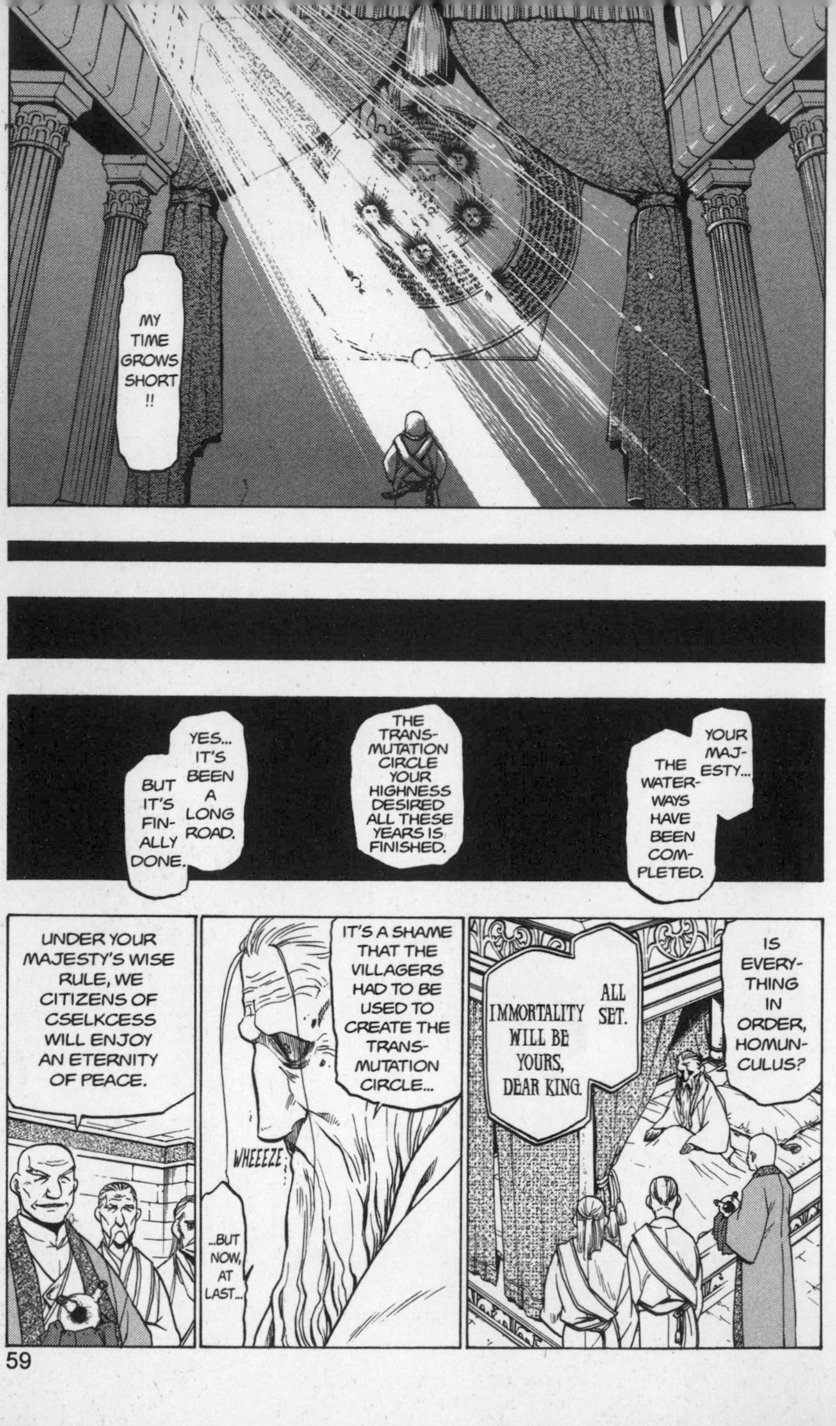
MY TIME GROWS SHORT!!
YOUR MAJESTY...
THE WATERWAYS HAVE BEEN COMPLETED.
THE TRANSMUTATION CIRCLE YOUR HIGHNESS DESIRED ALL THESE YEARS IS FINISHED.
YES... IT'S BEEN A LONG ROAD.
BUT IT'S FINALLY DONE.
IS EVERYTHING IN ORDER, HOMUNCULUS?
ALL SET.
IMMORTALITY WILL BE YOURS, DEAR KING.
IT'S A SHAME THAT THE VILLAGERS HAD TO BE USED TO CREATE THE TRANSMUTATION CIRCLE...
WHEEEZE
...BUT NOW, AT LAST...
UNDER YOUR MAJESTY'S WISE RULE, WE CITIZENS OF CSELKCESS WILL ENJOY AN ETERNITY OF PEACE.

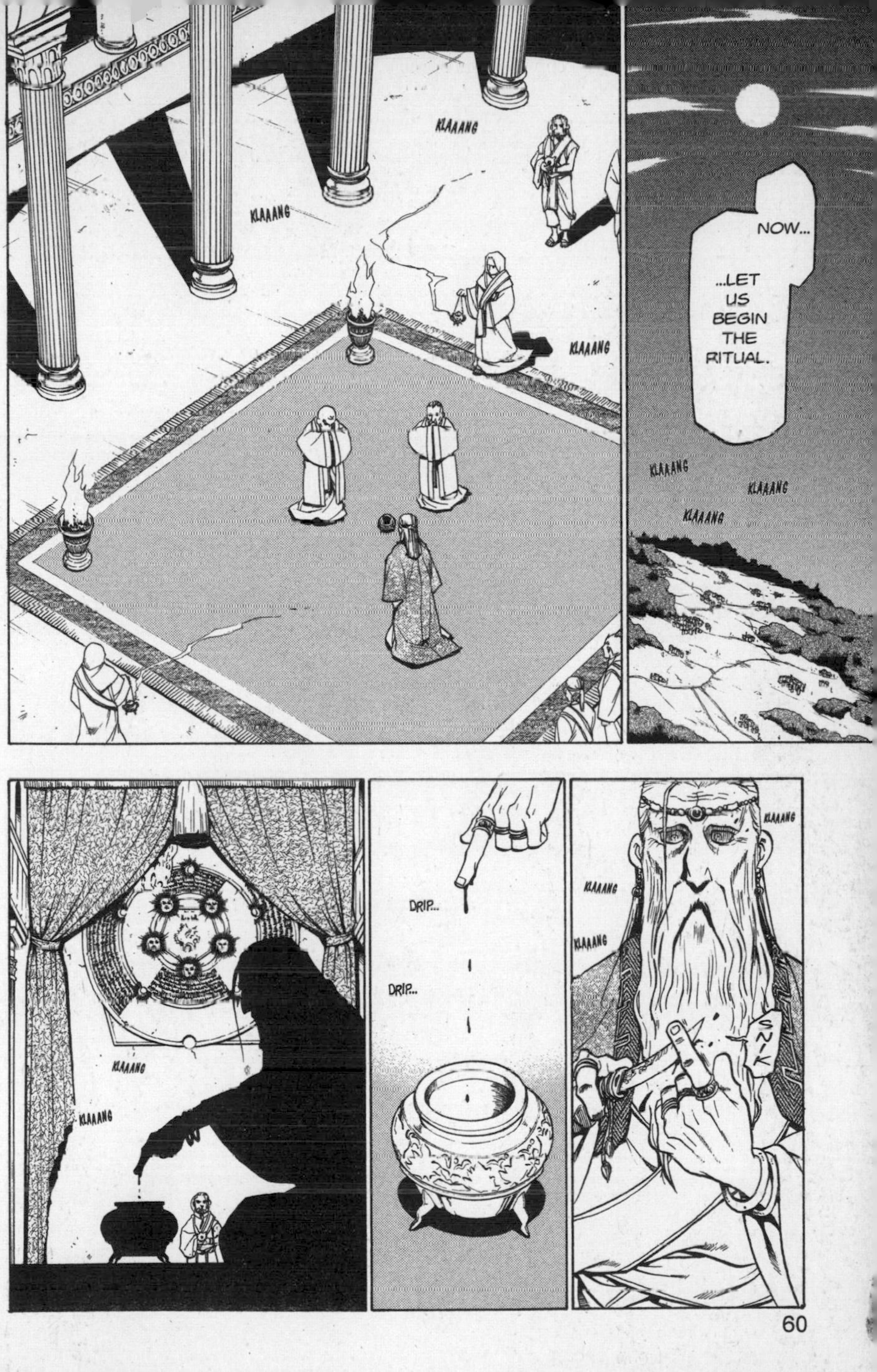
NOW...
...LET US BEGIN THE RITUAL.
KLAAANG
KLAAANG
KLAAANG
KLAAANG
KLAAANG
KLAAANG
KLAAANG
KLAAANG
KLAAANG
KLAAANG
SNIK
DRIP...
DRIP...
KLAAANG
KLAAANG

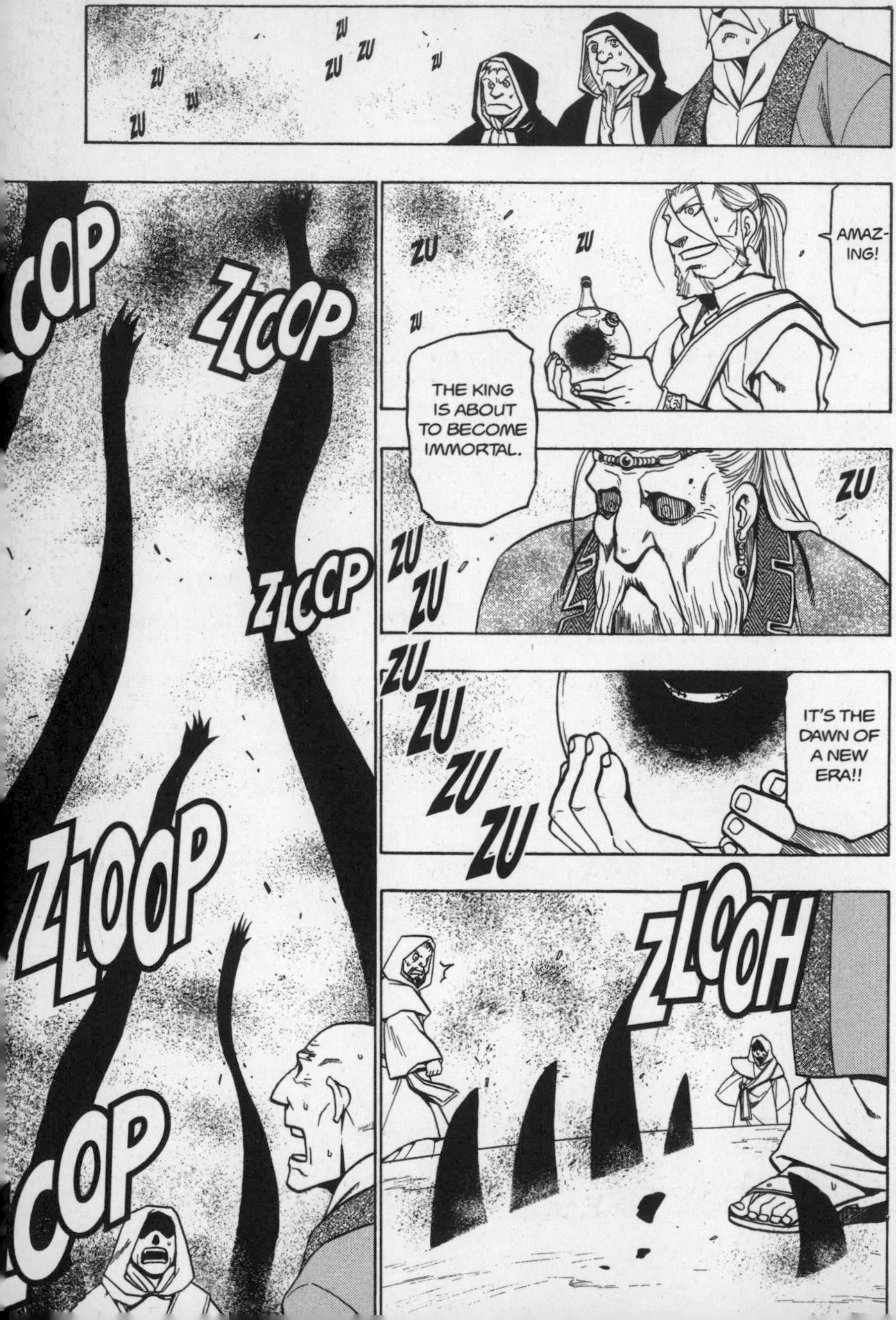

ZU
ZU
ZU
ZU
ZU
ZU
ZU
AMAZ-ING!
ZU
ZU
ZU
THE KING IS ABOUT TO BECOME IMMORTAL.
ZU
ZU
ZU
IT'S THE DAWN OF A NEW ERA!!
ZU
ZU
ZU
ZU
ZLOOOH
ZLCOP
COP
ZLCOP
ZLOOP
COP

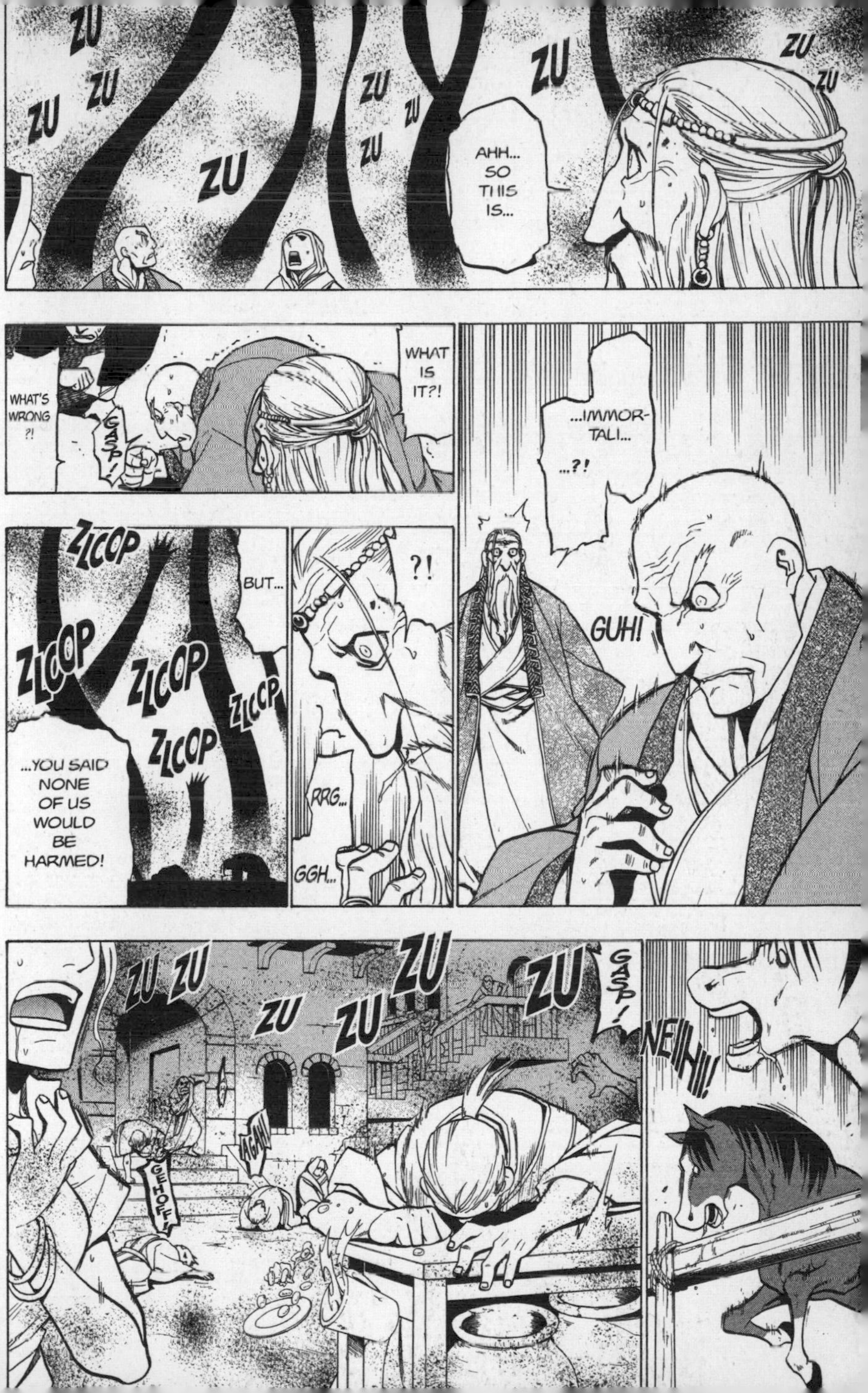
ZU
ZU
ZU
ZU
ZU
ZU
ZU
ZU
ZU
ZU
AHH... SO THIS IS...
...IMMORTALI...
...?!
GUH!
WHAT IS IT?!
WHAT'S WRONG ?!
GASP!
?!
RRG...
GGH...
BUT...
...YOU SAID NONE OF US WOULD BE HARMED!
ZLCOP
ZLCOP
ZLCOP
ZLCOP
ZLCOP
GASP!
NEIIHI!
ZU
ZU
ZU
ZU
ZU
ZU
AGAH!
GEHOFF!

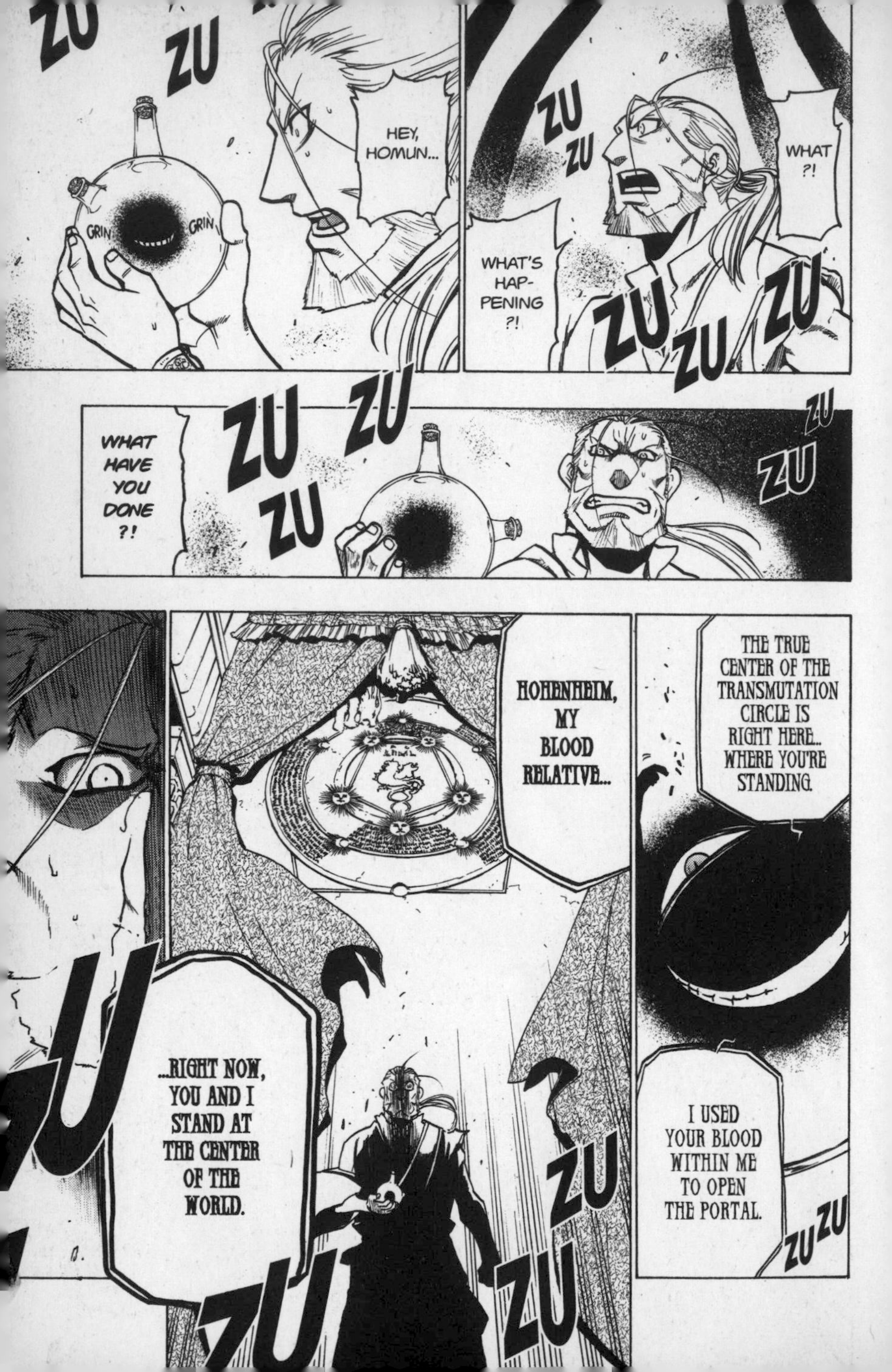
WHAT ?!
ZU
ZU
WHAT'S HAP-PENING ?!
ZU
ZU
ZU
HEY, HOMUN...
ZU
ZU
GRIN
GRIN
ZU
ZU
WHAT HAVE YOU DONE ?!
ZU
ZU
ZU
THE TRUE CENTER OF THE TRANSMUTATION CIRCLE IS RIGHT HERE.. WHERE YOU'RE STANDING.
I USED YOUR BLOOD WITHIN ME TO OPEN THE PORTAL.
ZU ZU
HOHENHEIM, MY BLOOD RELATIVE...
...RIGHT NOW, YOU AND I STAND AT THE CENTER OF THE WORLD.
ZU
ZU
ZU
ZU

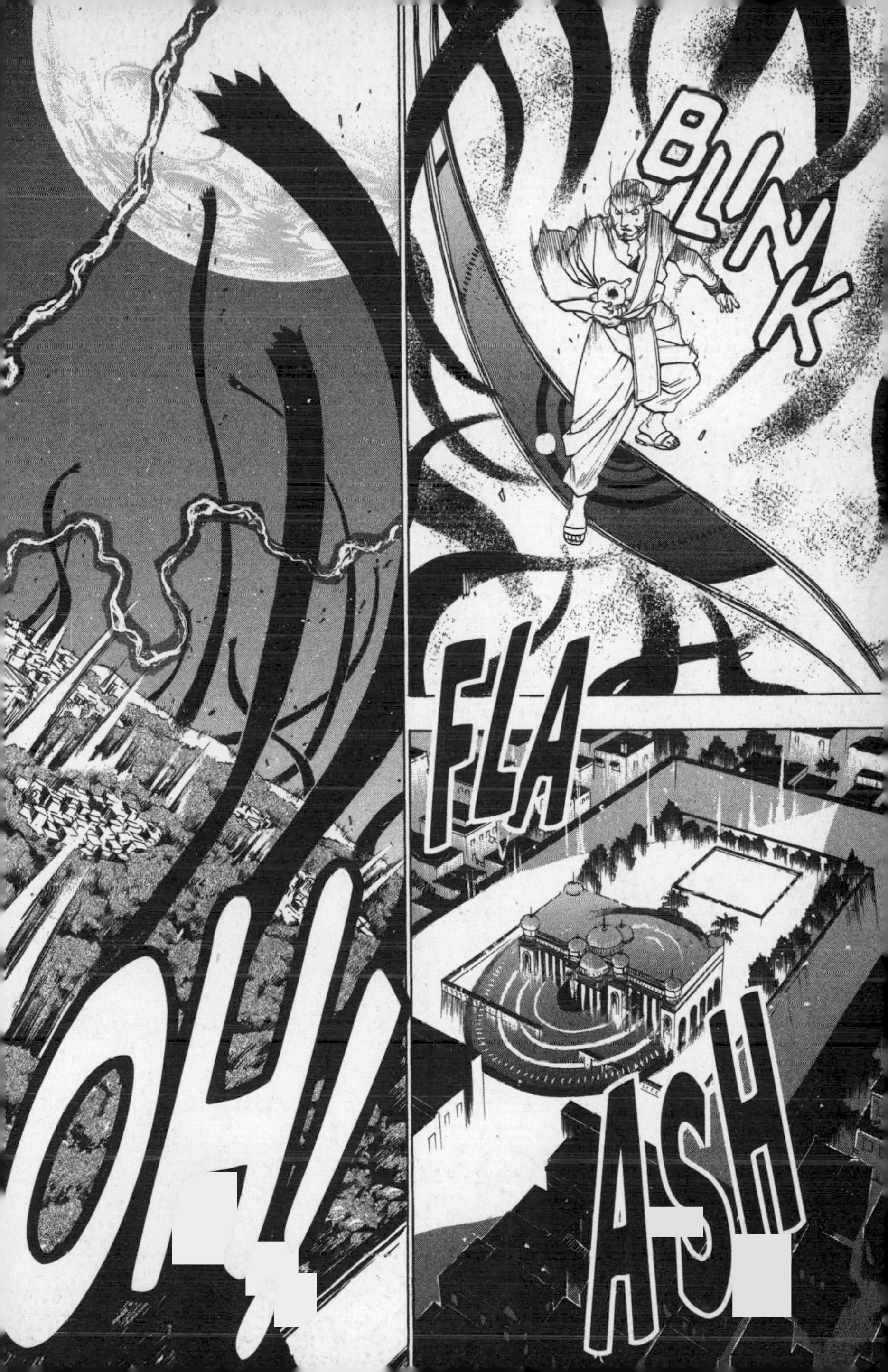
BLINK
FLA
ASH
OH

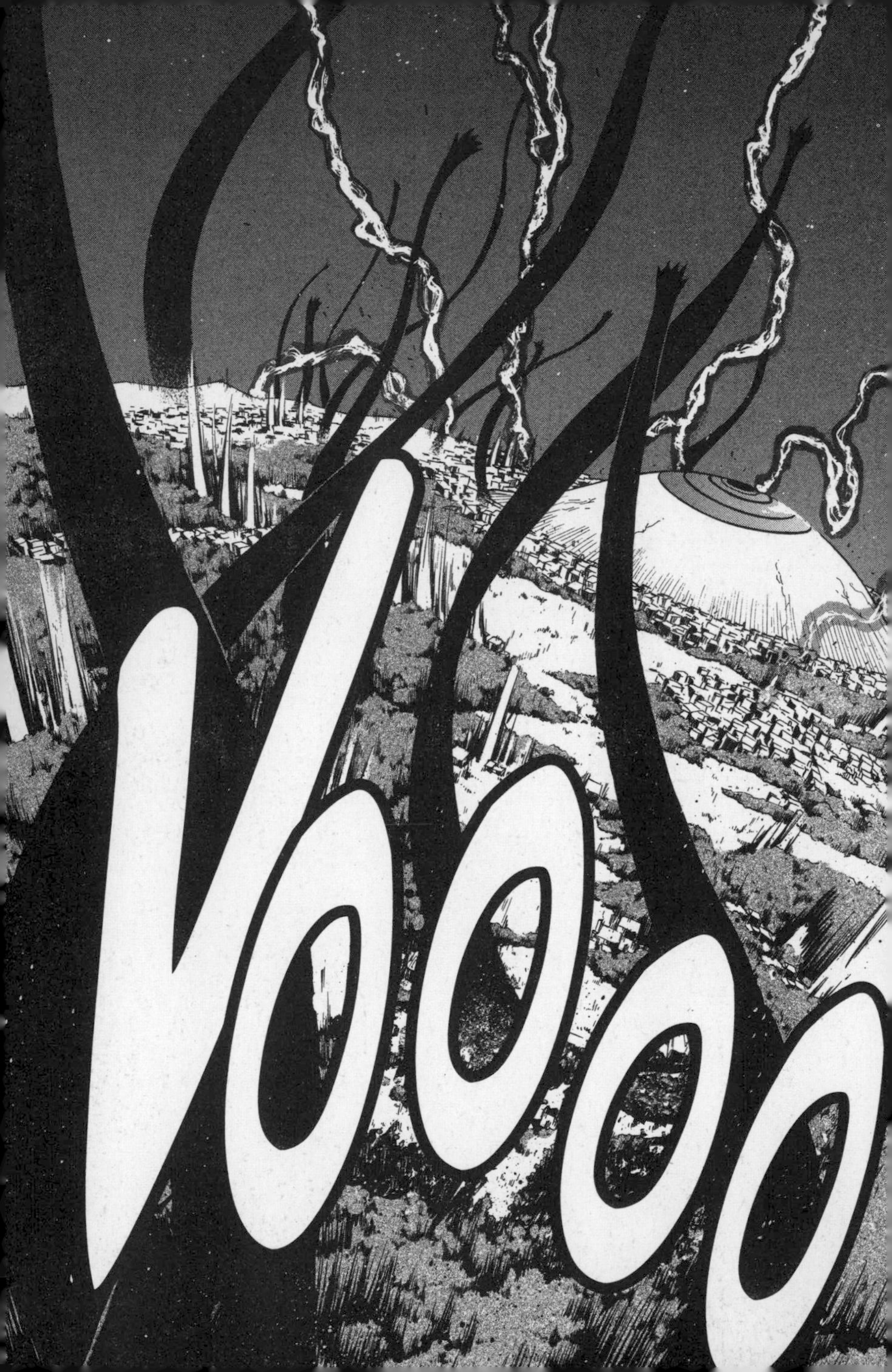
VOOOO

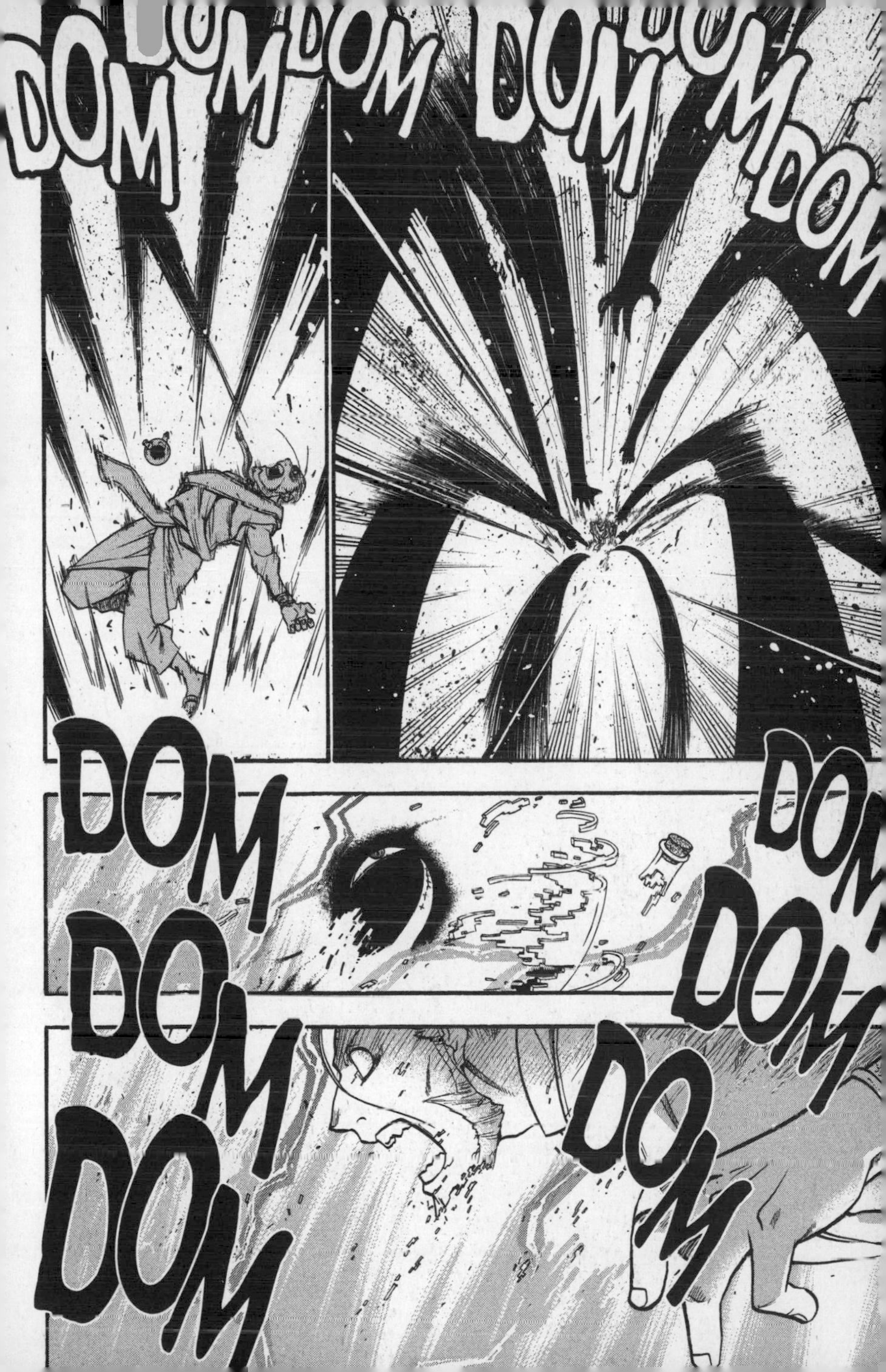
DOM DOM DOM DOM
DOM DOM DOM DOM
DOM DOM DOM
DOM DOM DOM

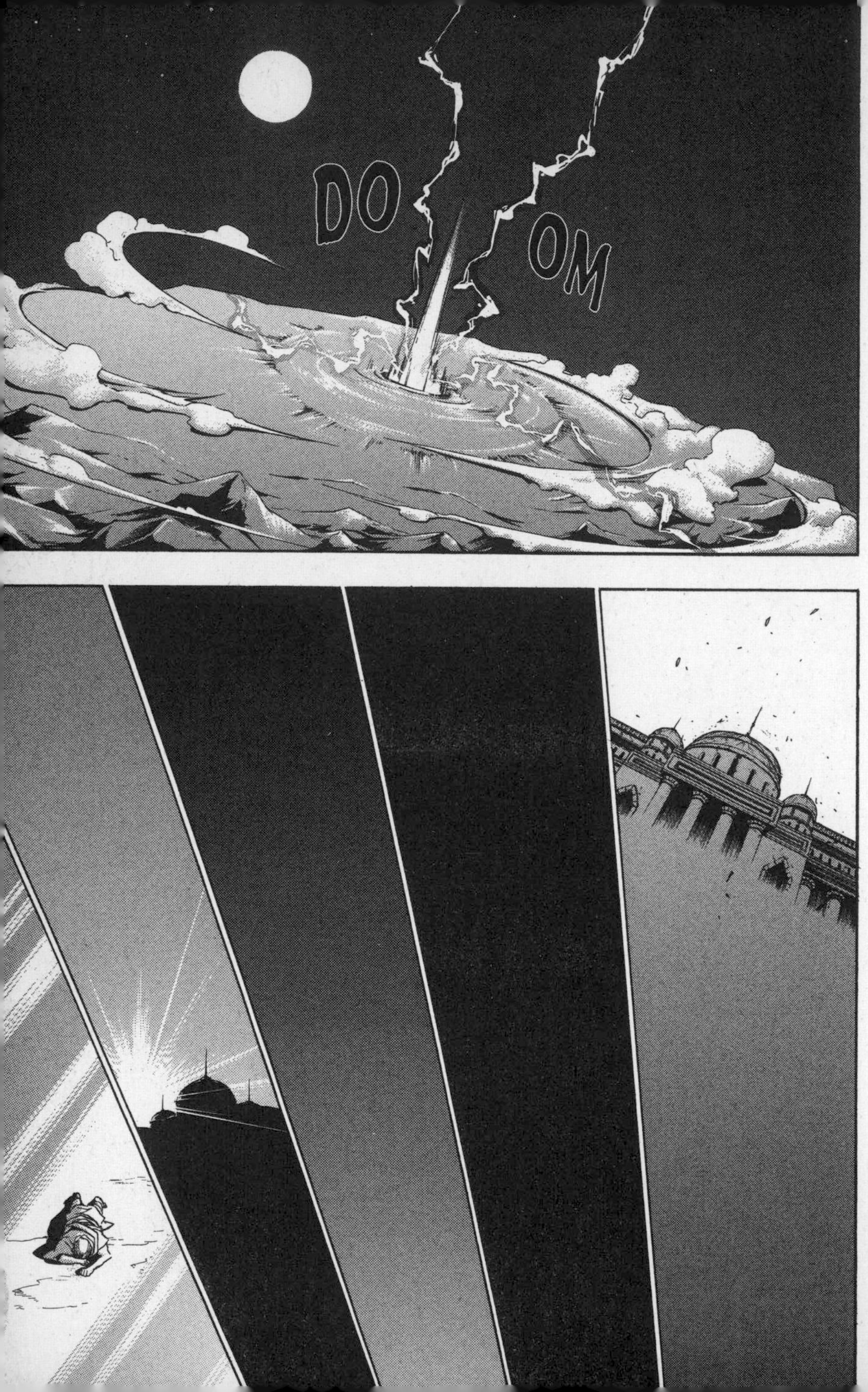
DO OM

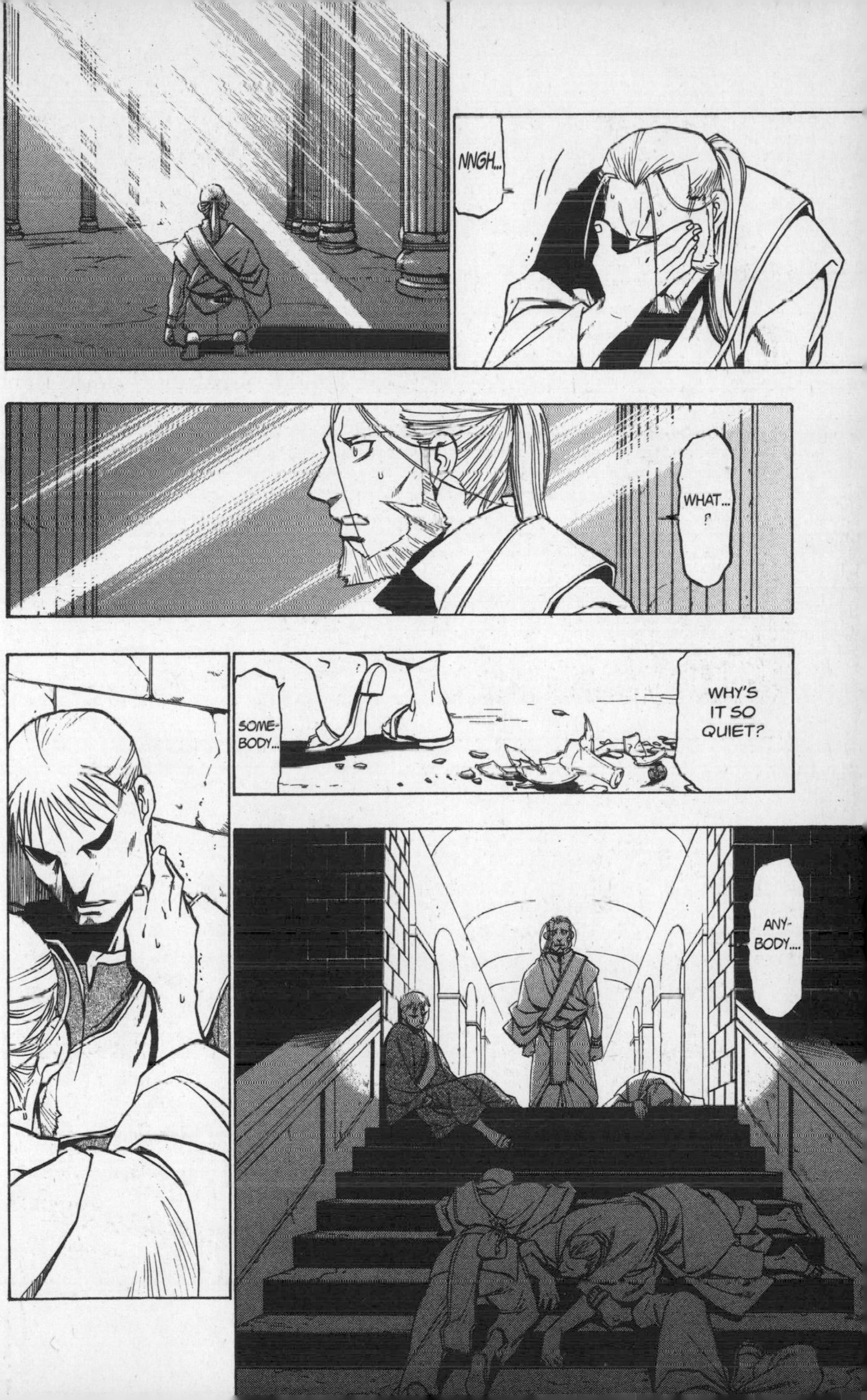
NNGH...
WHAT... ?
WHY'S IT SO QUIET?
SOME-BODY...
ANY-BODY....

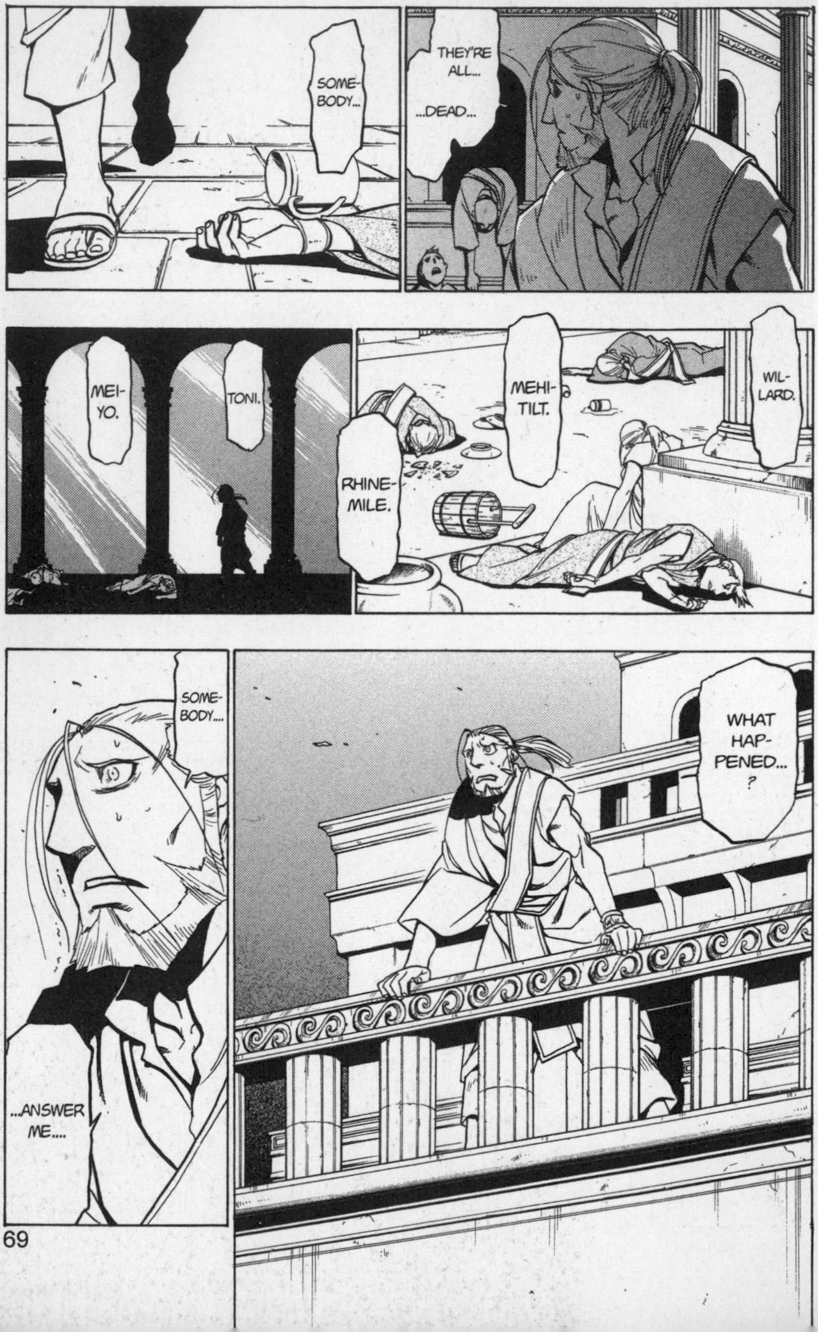
THEY'RE ALL...
...DEAD...
SOME-BODY...
WIL-LARD.
MEHI-TILT.
RHINE-MILE.
TONI.
MEI-YO.
WHAT HAP-PENED...?
SOME-BODY....
...ANSWER ME....

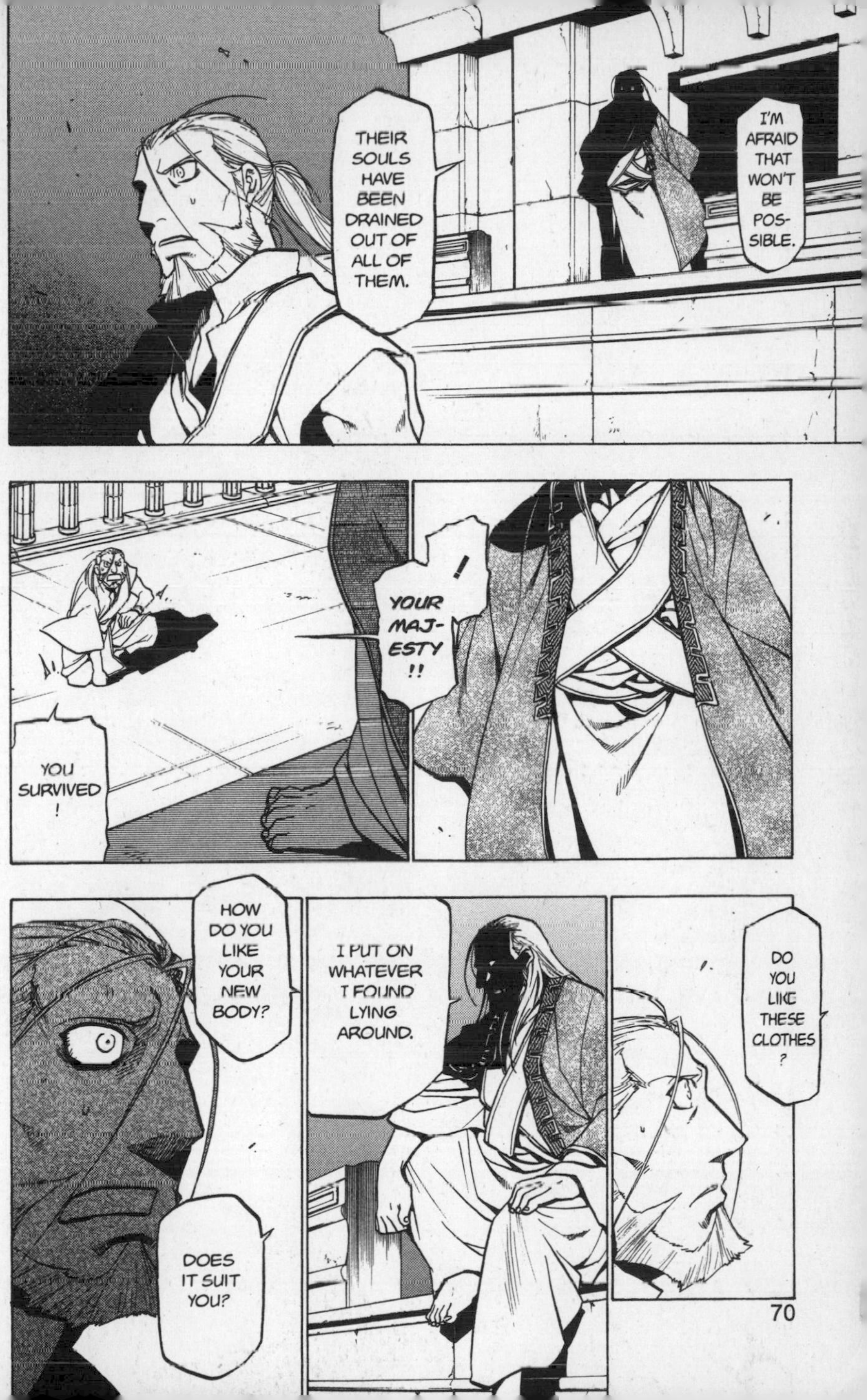
I'M AFRAID THAT WON'T BE POS-SIBLE.
THEIR SOULS HAVE BEEN DRAINED OUT OF ALL OF THEM.
!
YOUR MAJ-ESTY!!
YOU SURVIVED!
DO YOU LIKE THESE CLOTHES?
I PUT ON WHATEVER I FOUND LYING AROUND.
HOW DO YOU LIKE YOUR NEW BODY?
DOES IT SUIT YOU?

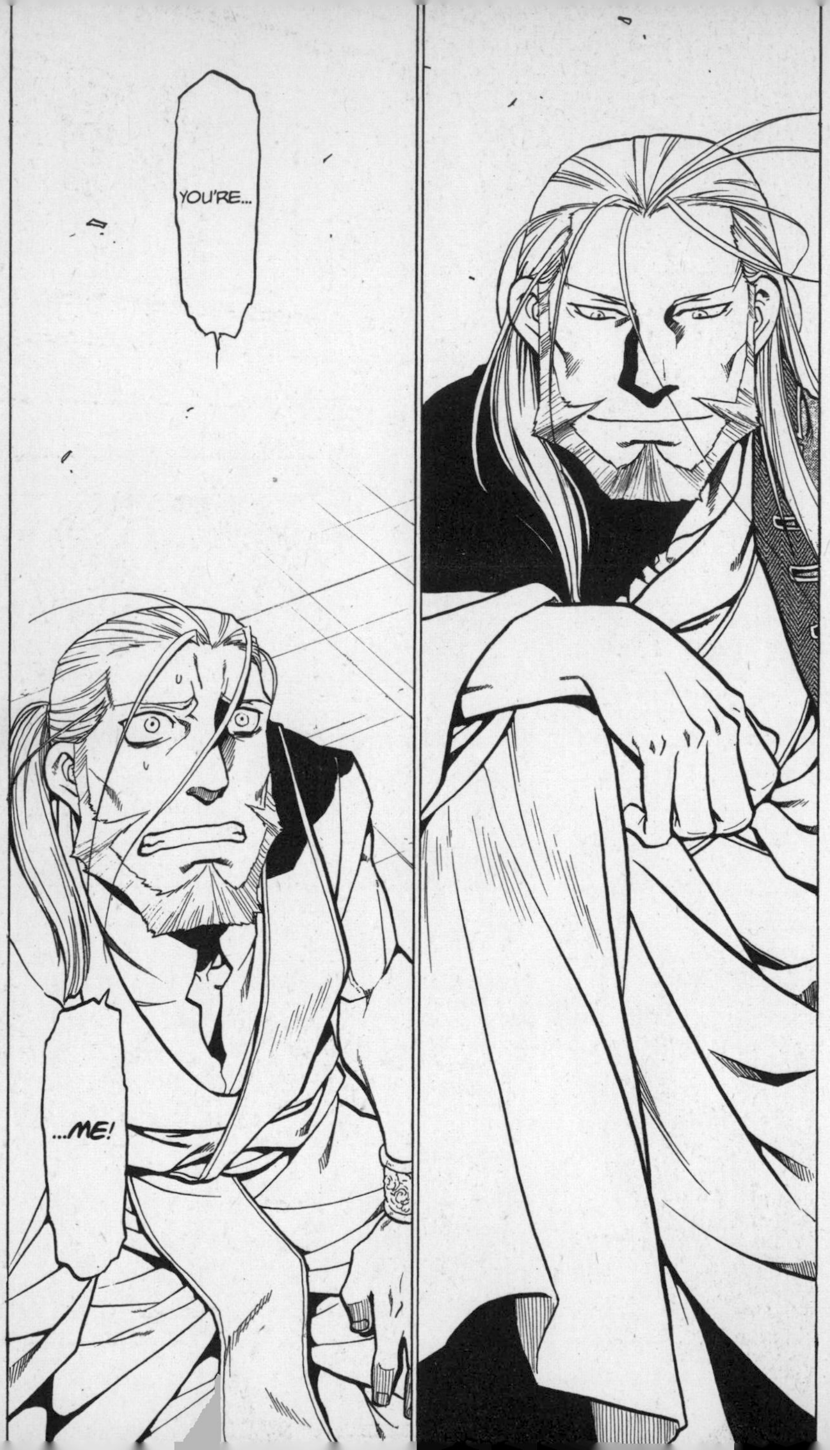
YOU'RE...
...ME!

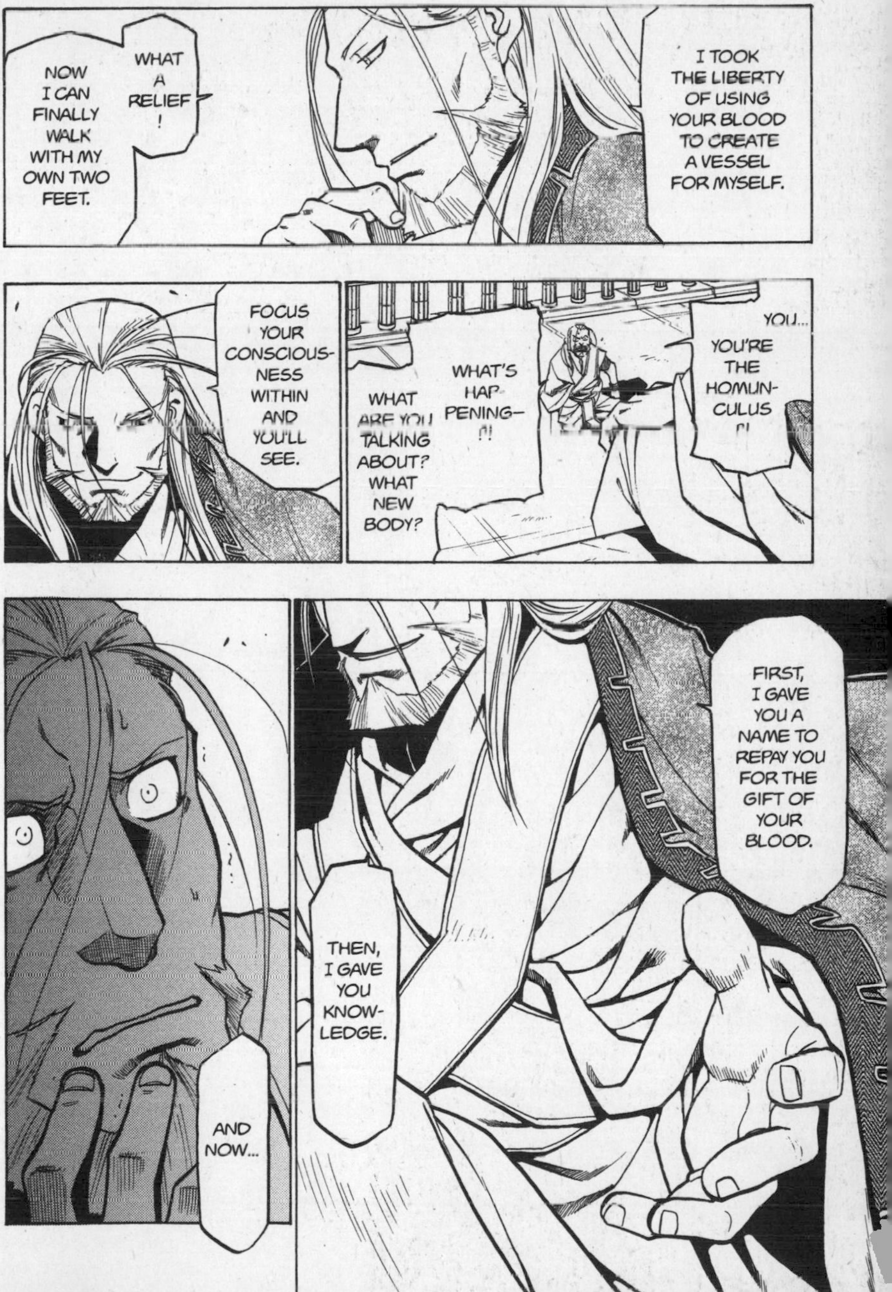
I TOOK THE LIBERTY OF USING YOUR BLOOD TO CREATE A VESSEL FOR MYSELF.
WHAT A RELIEF!
NOW I CAN FINALLY WALK WITH MY OWN TWO FEET.
YOU... YOU'RE THE HOMUNCULUS!!
WHAT'S HAPPENING—!!
WHAT ARE YOU TALKING ABOUT? WHAT NEW BODY?
FOCUS YOUR CONSCIOUSNESS WITHIN AND YOU'LL SEE.
FIRST, I GAVE YOU A NAME TO REPAY YOU FOR THE GIFT OF YOUR BLOOD.
THEN, I GAVE YOU KNOWLEDGE.
AND NOW...

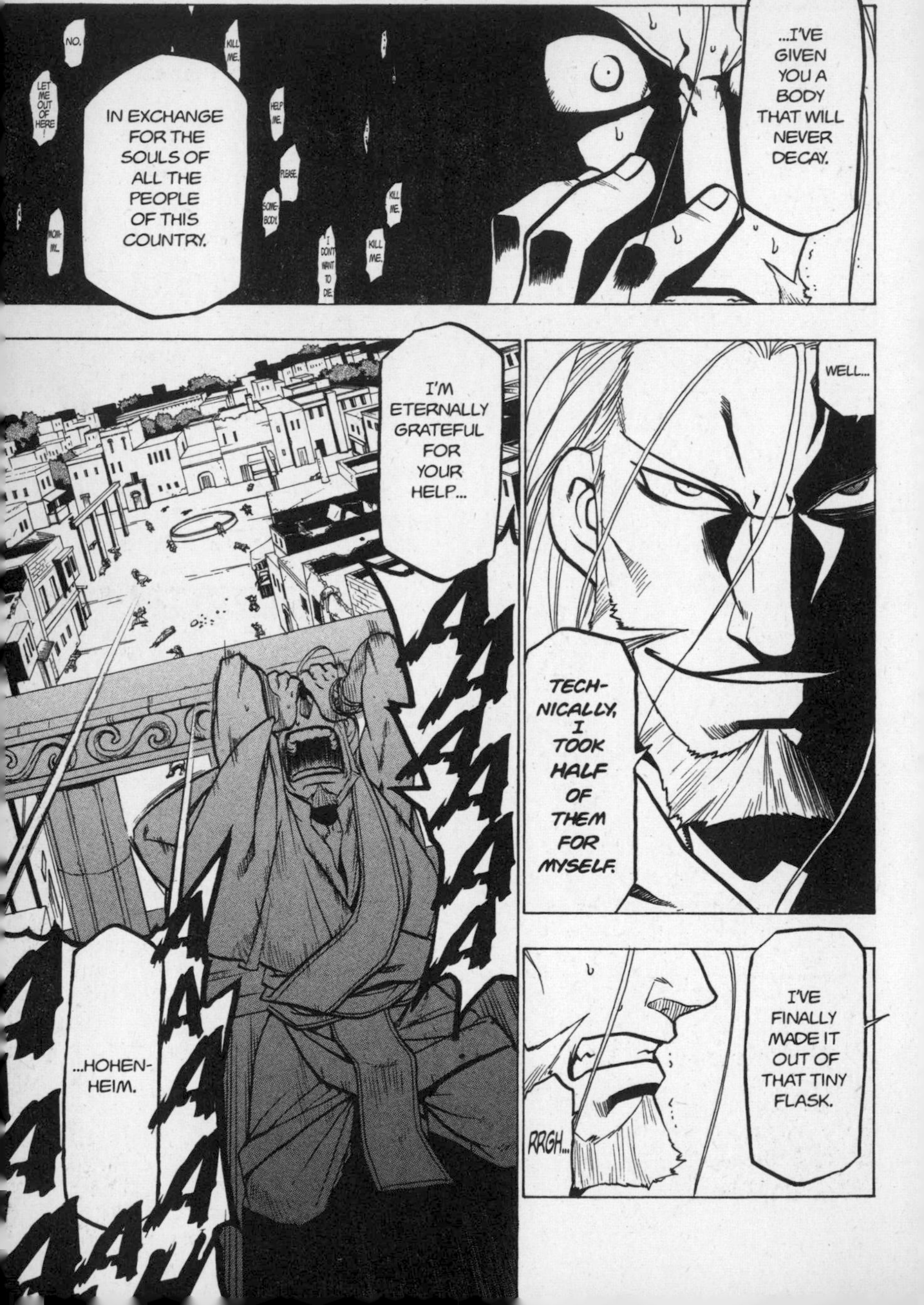
...I'VE GIVEN YOU A BODY THAT WILL NEVER DECAY.
KILL ME.
HELP ME.
PLEASE.
KILL ME.
SOME-BODY.
KILL ME.
I DON'T WANT TO DIE.
NO.
LET ME OUT OF HERE!
MOM-MY...
IN EXCHANGE FOR THE SOULS OF ALL THE PEOPLE OF THIS COUNTRY.
WELL...
TECH-NICALLY, I TOOK HALF OF THEM FOR MYSELF.
I'VE FINALLY MADE IT OUT OF THAT TINY FLASK.
RRGH...
I'M ETERNALLY GRATEFUL FOR YOUR HELP...
...HOHEN-HEIM.

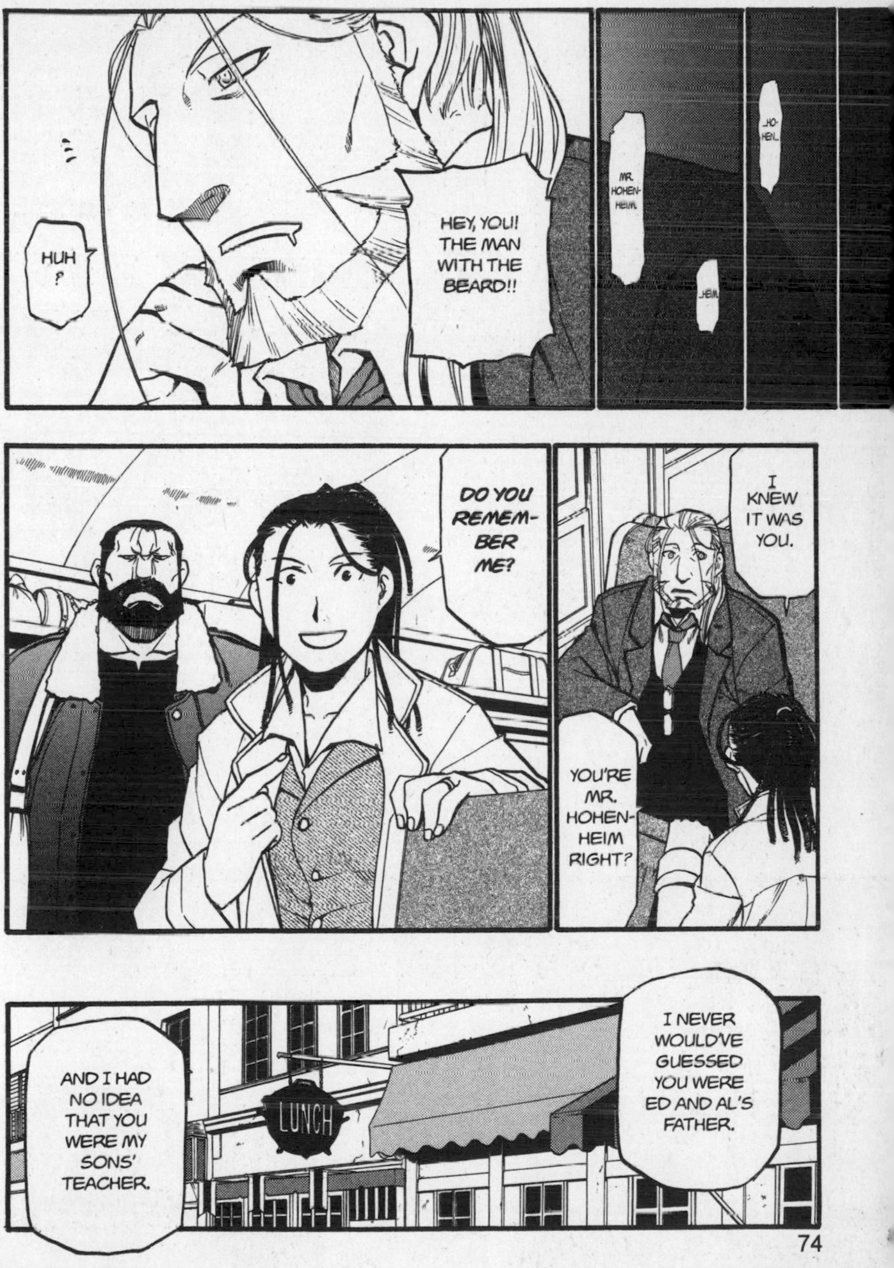

...HO-HEIM...
MR. HOHENHEIM
...HEIM...
HEY, YOU! THE MAN WITH THE BEARD!!
HUH?
I KNEW IT WAS YOU.
YOU'RE MR. HOHENHEIM RIGHT?
DO YOU REMEMBER ME?
I NEVER WOULD'VE GUESSED YOU WERE ED AND AL'S FATHER.
LUNCH
AND I HAD NO IDEA THAT YOU WERE MY SONS' TEACHER.

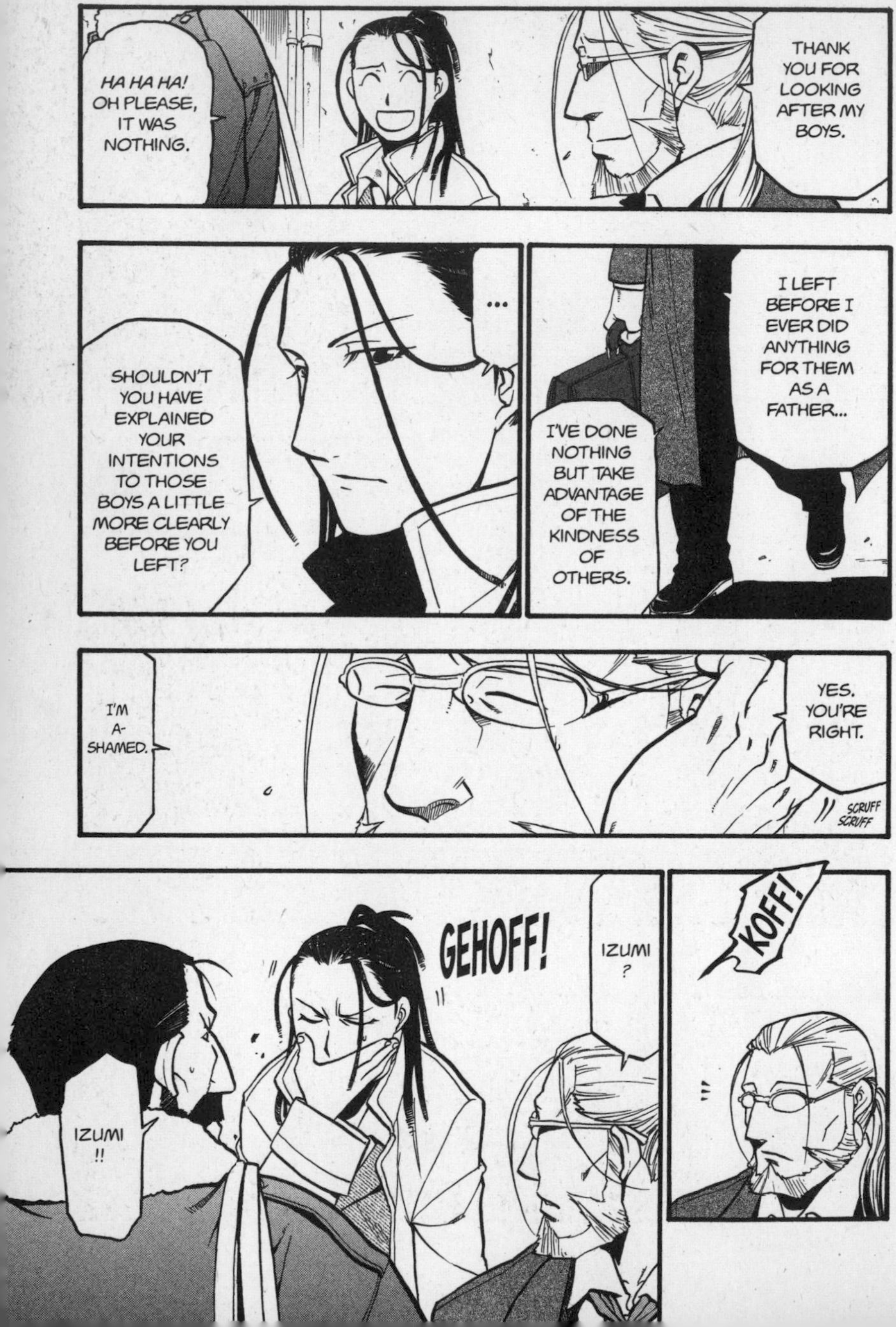
THANK YOU FOR LOOKING AFTER MY BOYS.
HA HA HA! OH PLEASE, IT WAS NOTHING.
I LEFT BEFORE I EVER DID ANYTHING FOR THEM AS A FATHER...
I'VE DONE NOTHING BUT TAKE ADVANTAGE OF THE KINDNESS OF OTHERS.
...
SHOULDN'T YOU HAVE EXPLAINED YOUR INTENTIONS TO THOSE BOYS A LITTLE MORE CLEARLY BEFORE YOU LEFT?
YES. YOU'RE RIGHT.
SCRUFF SCRUFF
I'M A-SHAMED.
KOFF!
IZUMI ?
GEHOFF!
IZUMI !!

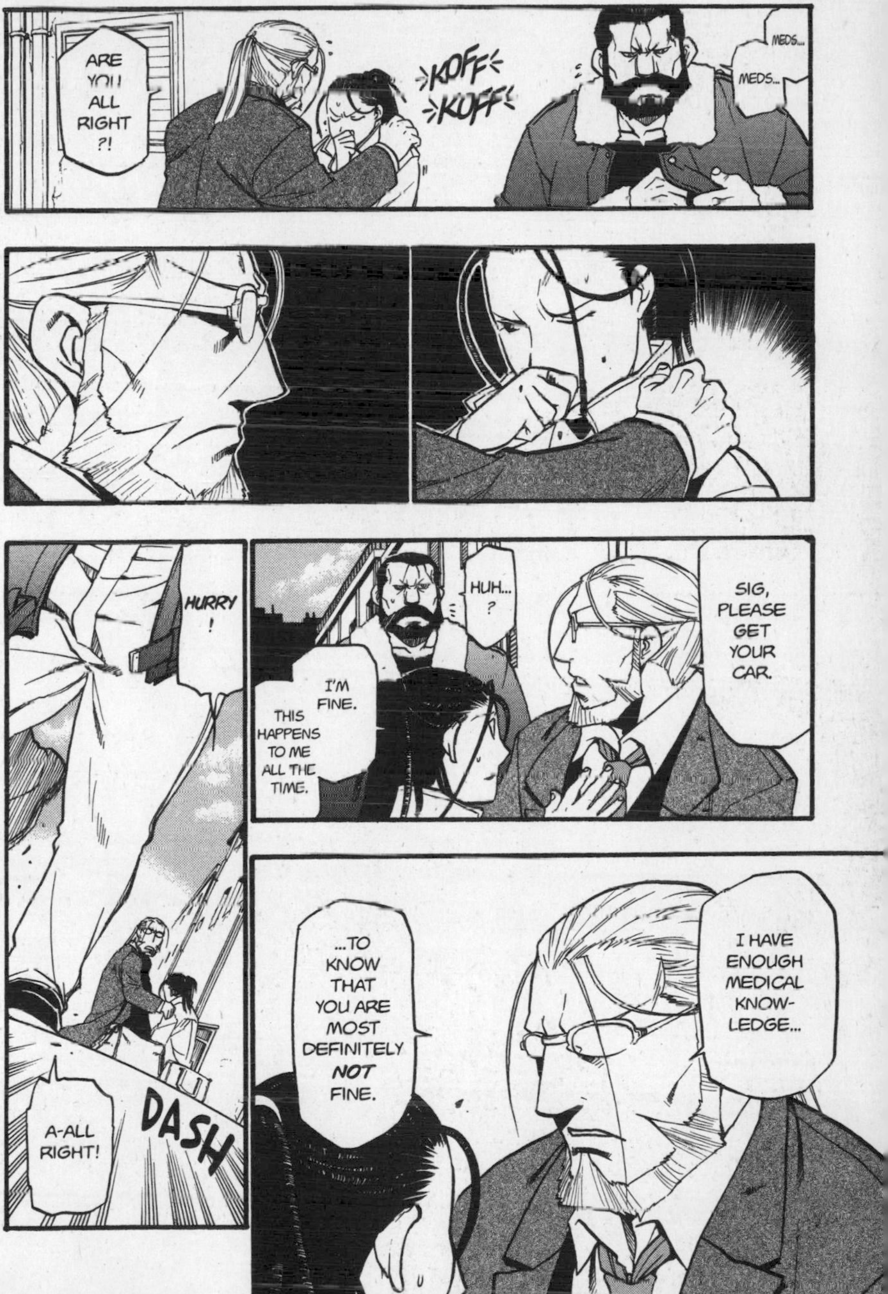
MEDS...
MEDS...
KOFF
KOFF
ARE YOU ALL RIGHT ?!
SIG, PLEASE GET YOUR CAR.
HUH... ?
I'M FINE. THIS HAPPENS TO ME ALL THE TIME.
I HAVE ENOUGH MEDICAL KNOW-LEDGE...
...TO KNOW THAT YOU ARE MOST DEFINITELY *NOT* FINE.
HURRY!
A-ALL RIGHT!
DASH

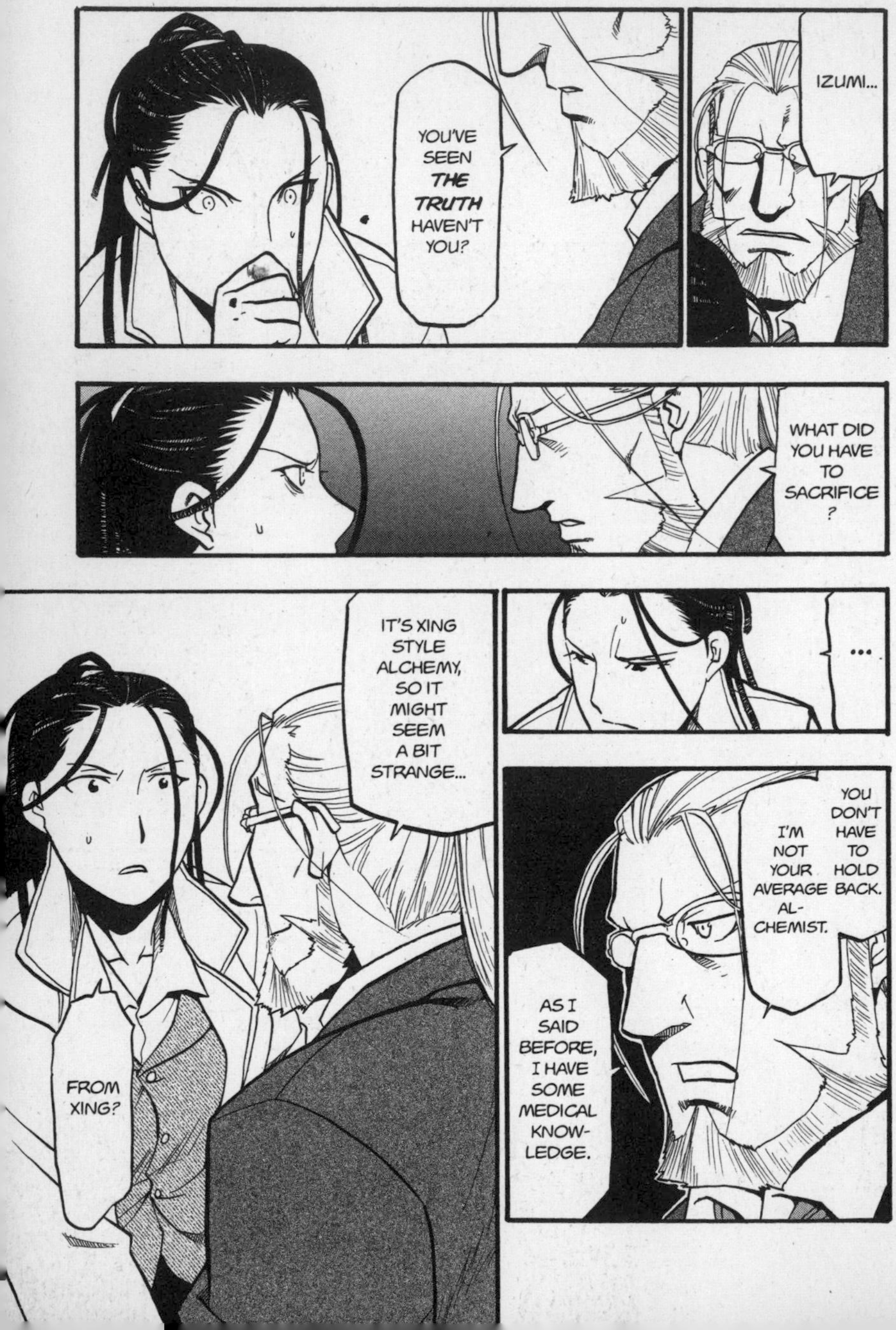
IZUMI...
YOU'VE SEEN THE TRUTH HAVEN'T YOU?
WHAT DID YOU HAVE TO SACRIFICE?
...
YOU DON'T HAVE TO HOLD BACK.
I'M NOT YOUR AVERAGE AL-CHEMIST.
AS I SAID BEFORE, I HAVE SOME MEDICAL KNOW-LEDGE.
IT'S XING STYLE ALCHEMY, SO IT MIGHT SEEM A BIT STRANGE...
FROM XING?

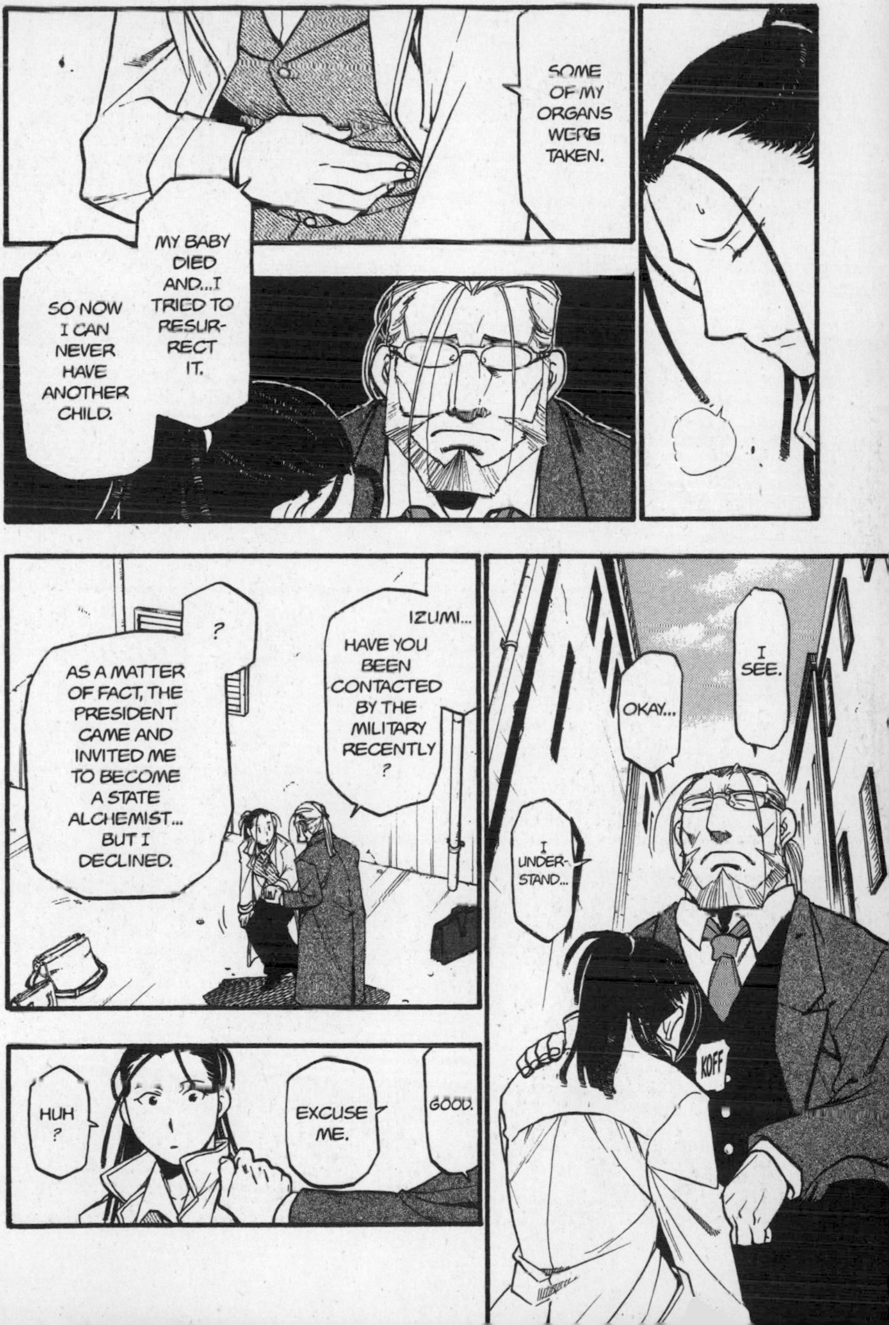
SOME OF MY ORGANS WERE TAKEN.
MY BABY DIED AND...I TRIED TO RESURRECT IT.
SO NOW I CAN NEVER HAVE ANOTHER CHILD.
I SEE.
OKAY...
I UNDERSTAND...
KOFF
IZUMI... HAVE YOU BEEN CONTACTED BY THE MILITARY RECENTLY?
?
AS A MATTER OF FACT, THE PRESIDENT CAME AND INVITED ME TO BECOME A STATE ALCHEMIST... BUT I DECLINED.
GOOD.
EXCUSE ME.
HUH?

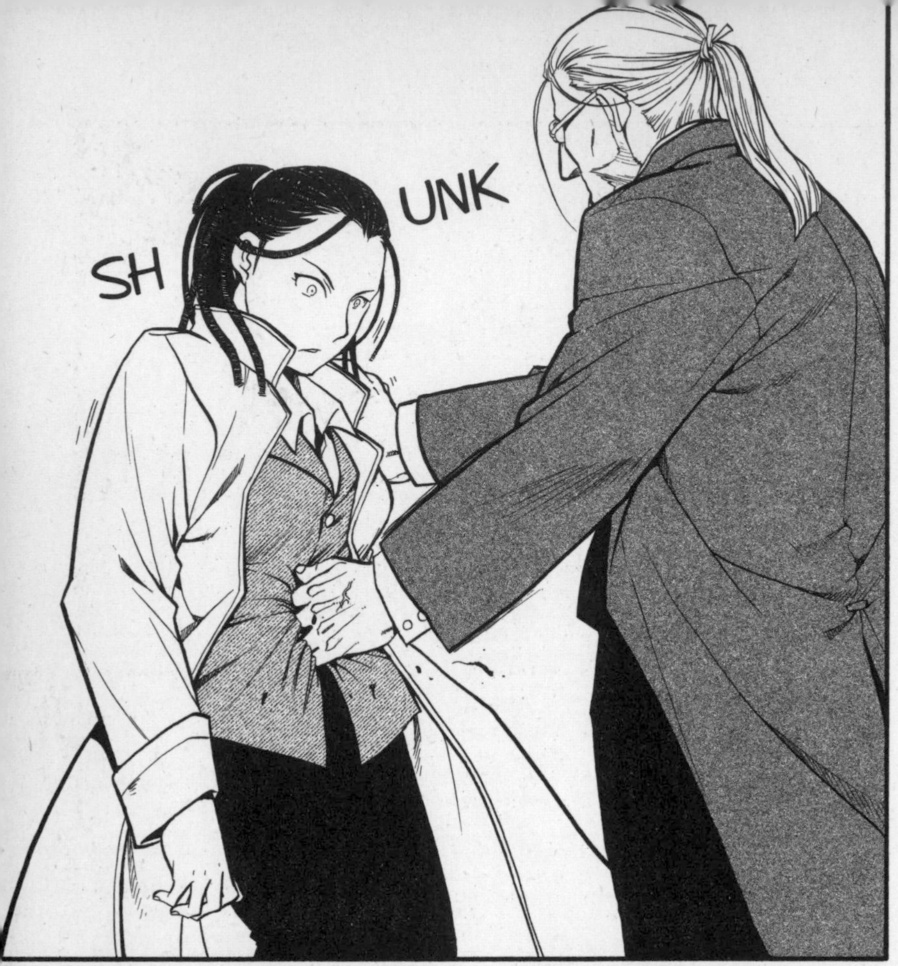
SH
UNK
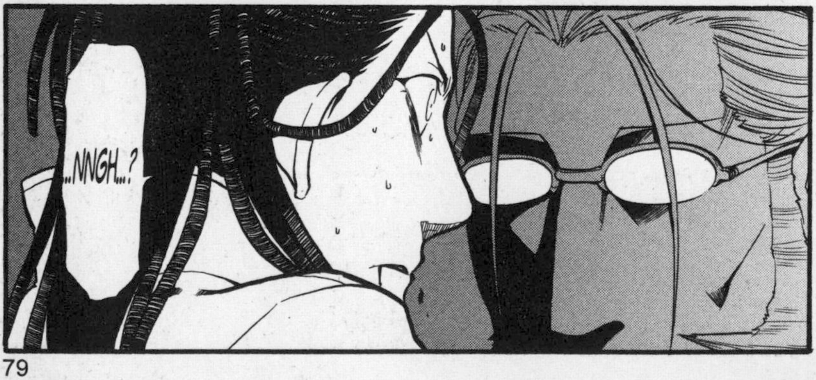
...NNGH...?

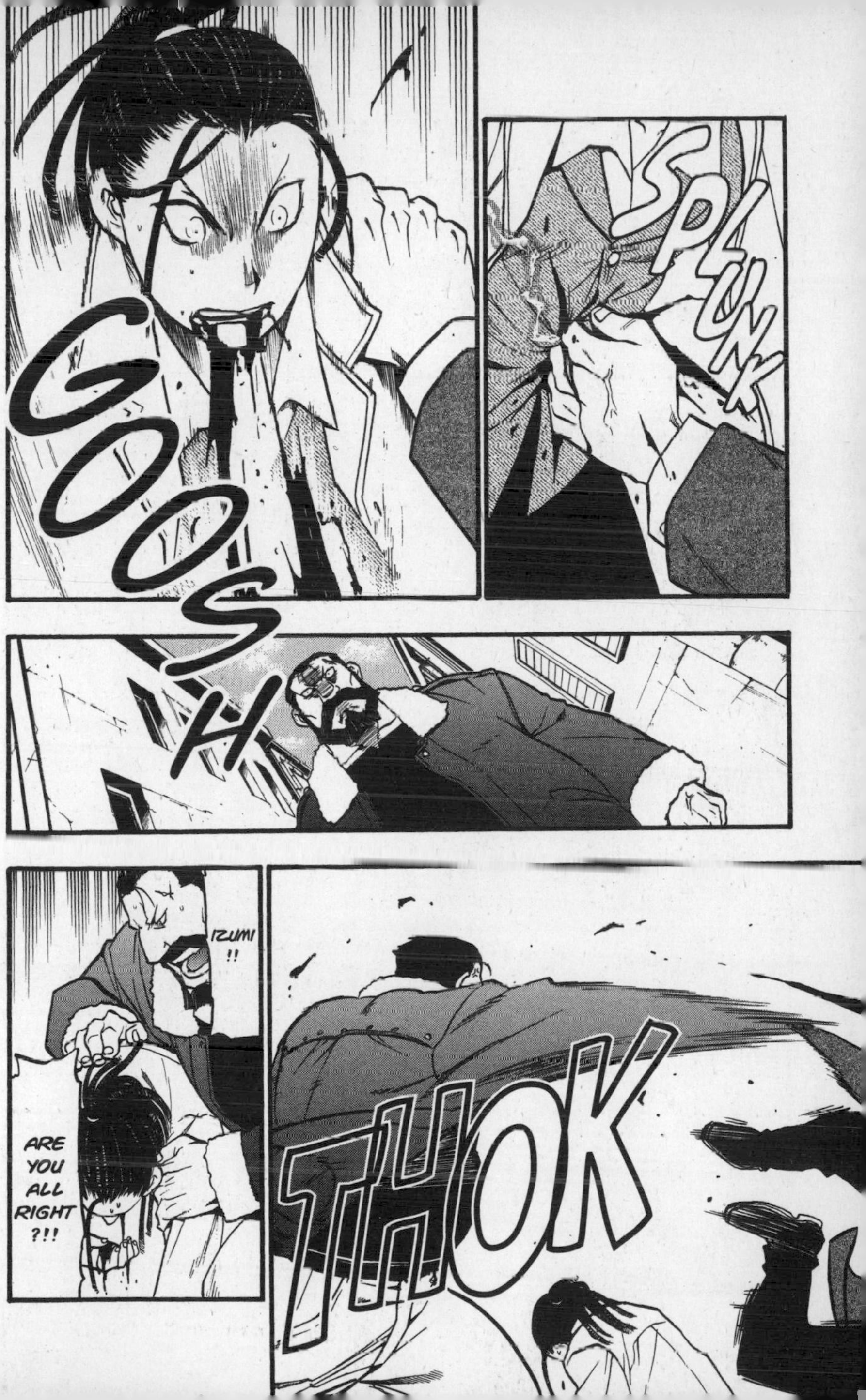
SPLUNK
GOOSH
THOK
IZUMI !!
ARE YOU ALL RIGHT ?!!

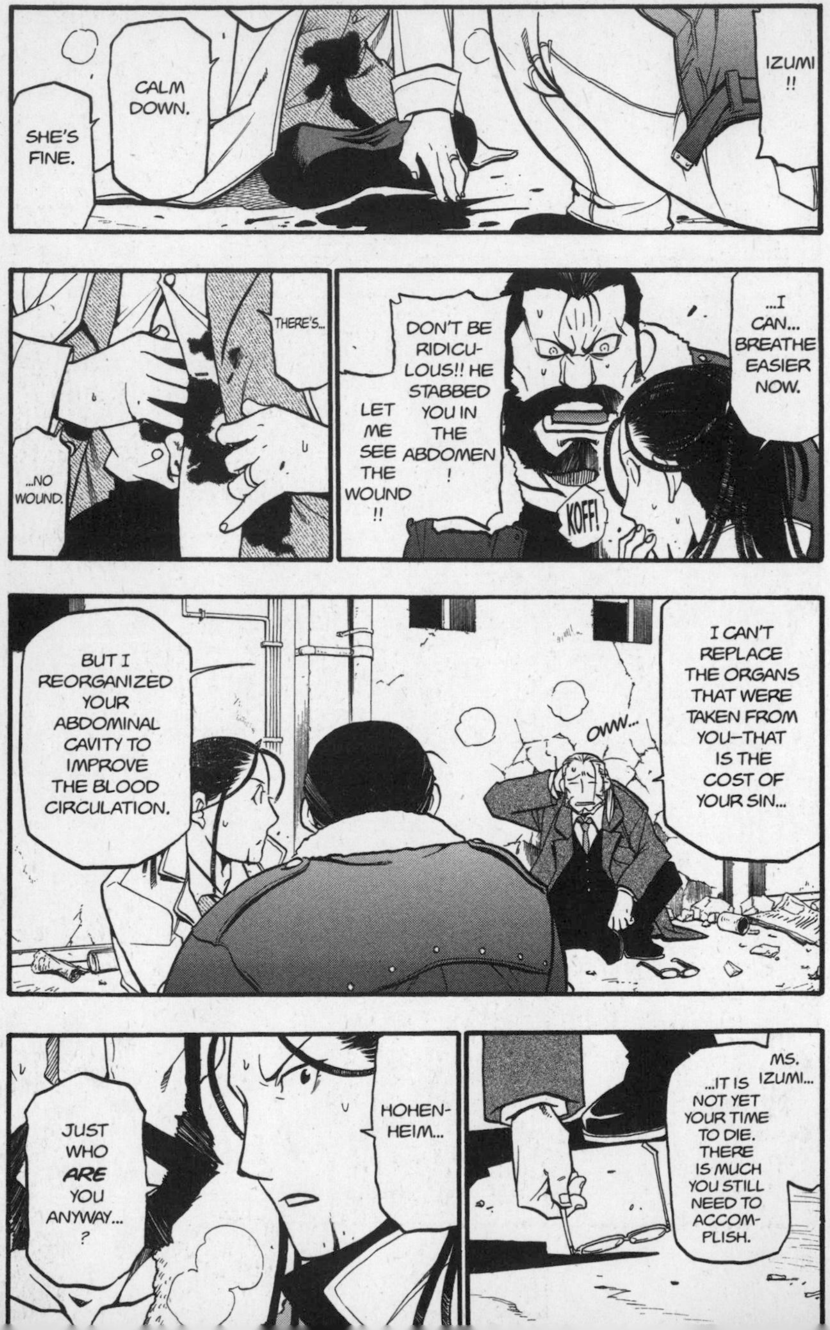

IZUMI!!
CALM DOWN.
SHE'S FINE.
...I CAN... BREATHE EASIER NOW.
DON'T BE RIDICULOUS!! HE STABBED YOU IN THE ABDOMEN!
KOFF!
LET ME SEE THE WOUND!!
THERE'S...
...NO WOUND.
I CAN'T REPLACE THE ORGANS THAT WERE TAKEN FROM YOU—THAT IS THE COST OF YOUR SIN...
OWW...
BUT I REORGANIZED YOUR ABDOMINAL CAVITY TO IMPROVE THE BLOOD CIRCULATION.
MS. IZUMI...
...IT IS NOT YET YOUR TIME TO DIE. THERE IS MUCH YOU STILL NEED TO ACCOMPLISH.
HOHENHEIM...
JUST WHO ARE YOU ANYWAY...?

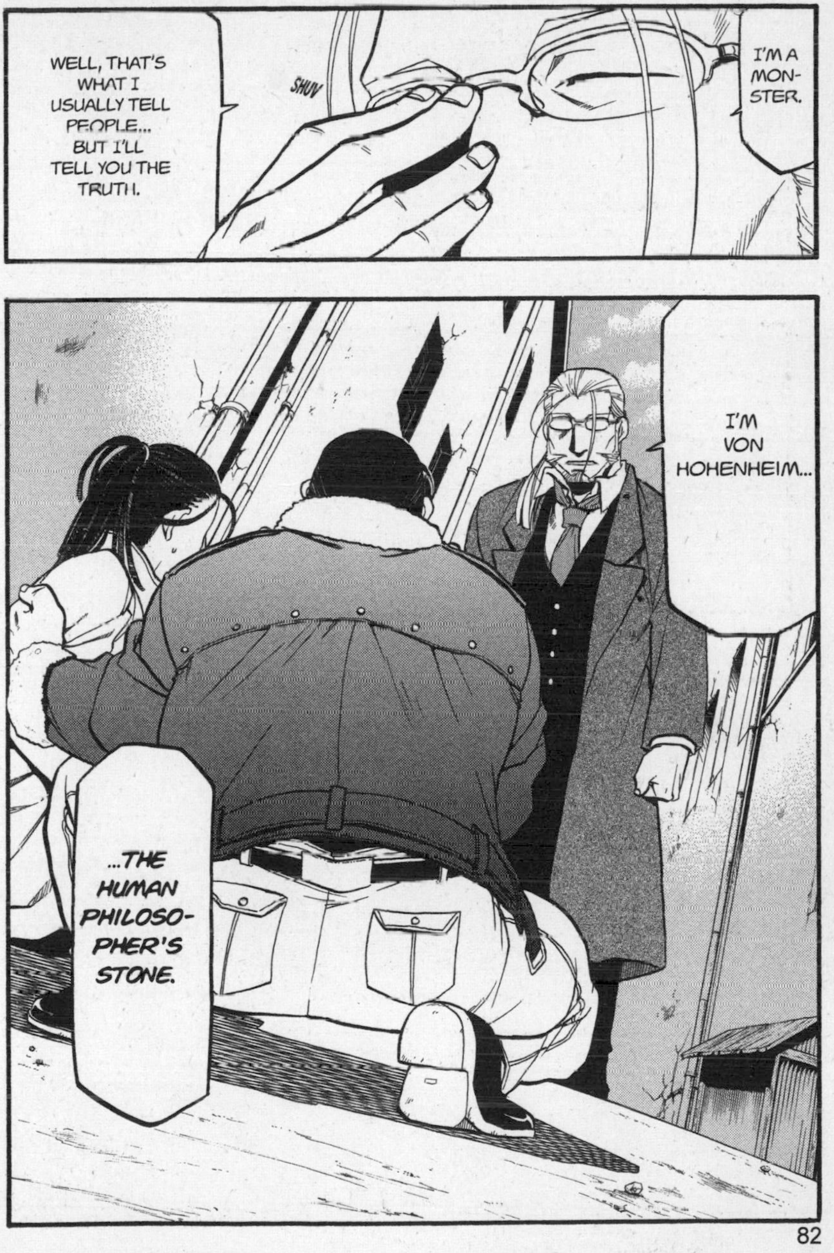
I'M A MONSTER.
SHUV
WELL, THAT'S WHAT I USUALLY TELL PEOPLE... BUT I'LL TELL YOU THE TRUTH.
I'M VON HOHENHEIM...
...THE HUMAN PHILOSOPHER'S STONE.

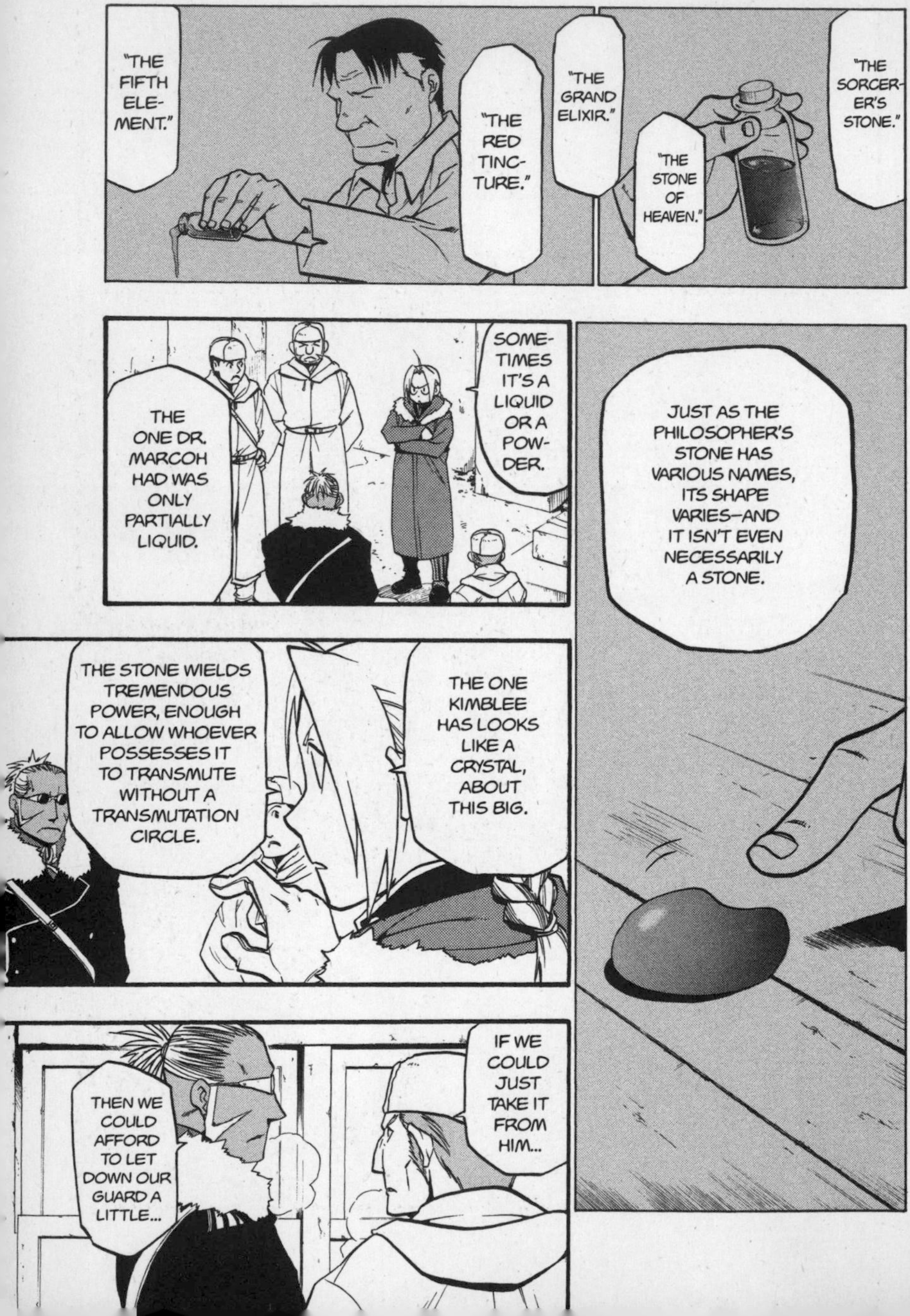
"THE SORCERER'S STONE."
"THE STONE OF HEAVEN."
"THE GRAND ELIXIR."
"THE RED TINCTURE."
"THE FIFTH ELEMENT."
JUST AS THE PHILOSOPHER'S STONE HAS VARIOUS NAMES, ITS SHAPE VARIES—AND IT ISN'T EVEN NECESSARILY A STONE.
SOMETIMES IT'S A LIQUID OR A POWDER.
THE ONE DR. MARCOH HAD WAS ONLY PARTIALLY LIQUID.
THE ONE KIMBLEE HAS LOOKS LIKE A CRYSTAL, ABOUT THIS BIG.
THE STONE WIELDS TREMENDOUS POWER, ENOUGH TO ALLOW WHOEVER POSSESSES IT TO TRANSMUTE WITHOUT A TRANSMUTATION CIRCLE.
IF WE COULD JUST TAKE IT FROM HIM...
THEN WE COULD AFFORD TO LET DOWN OUR GUARD A LITTLE...

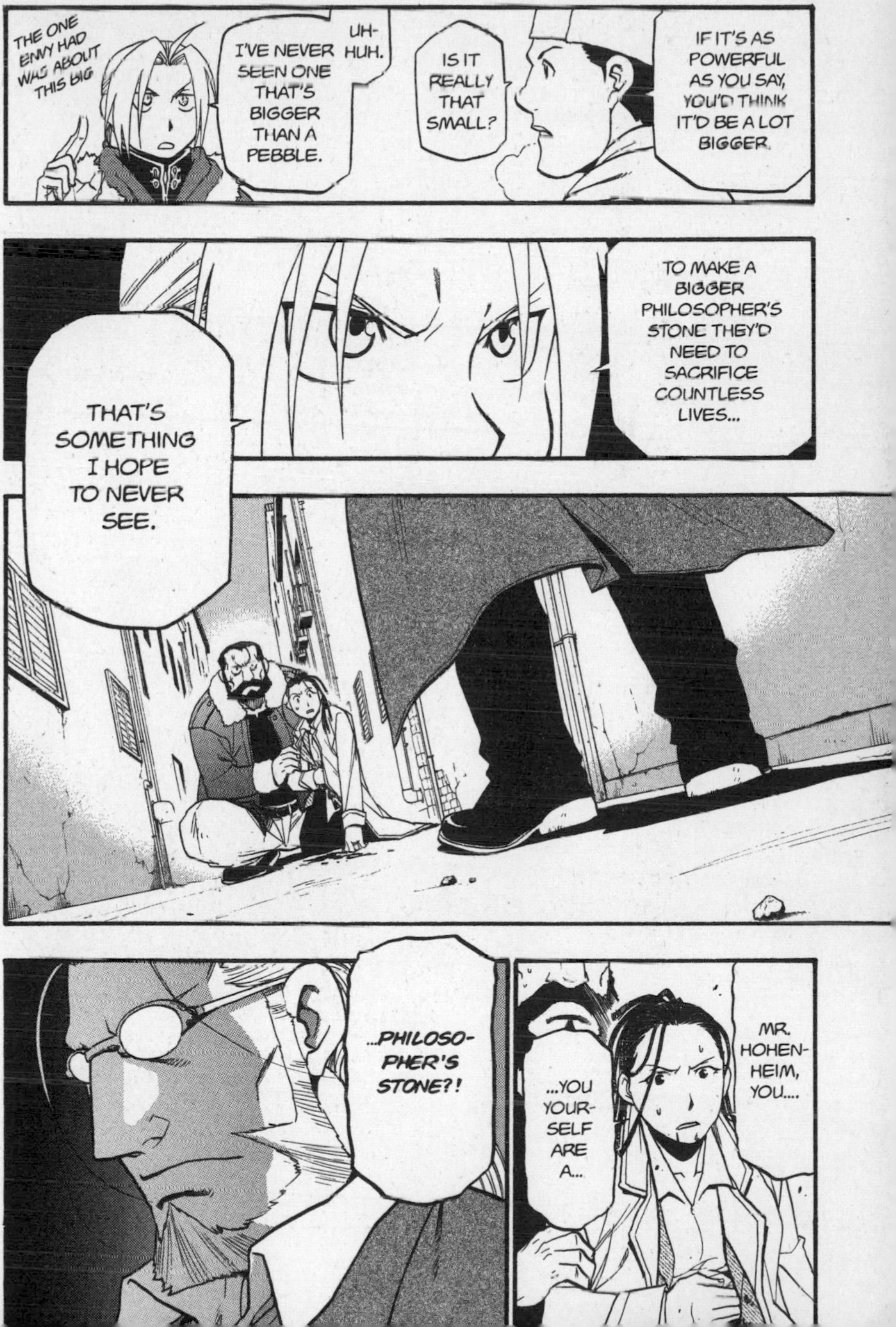
IF IT'S AS POWERFUL AS YOU SAY, YOU'D THINK IT'D BE A LOT BIGGER.
IS IT REALLY THAT SMALL?
UH-HUH.
I'VE NEVER SEEN ONE THAT'S BIGGER THAN A PEBBLE.
THE ONE ENVY HAD WAS ABOUT THIS BIG
TO MAKE A BIGGER PHILOSOPHER'S STONE THEY'D NEED TO SACRIFICE COUNTLESS LIVES...
THAT'S SOMETHING I HOPE TO NEVER SEE.
MR. HOHENHEIM, YOU....
...YOU YOURSELF ARE A...
...PHILOSOPHER'S STONE?!

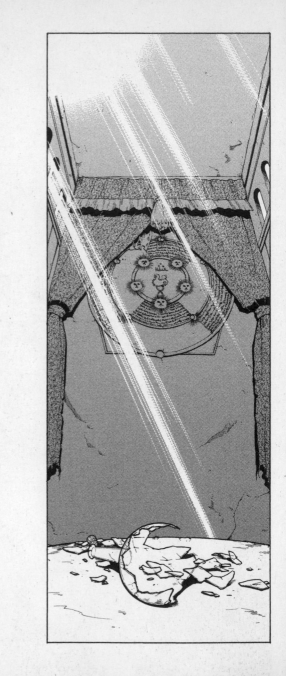

Chapter 76
Shape of a Person, Shape of a Stone

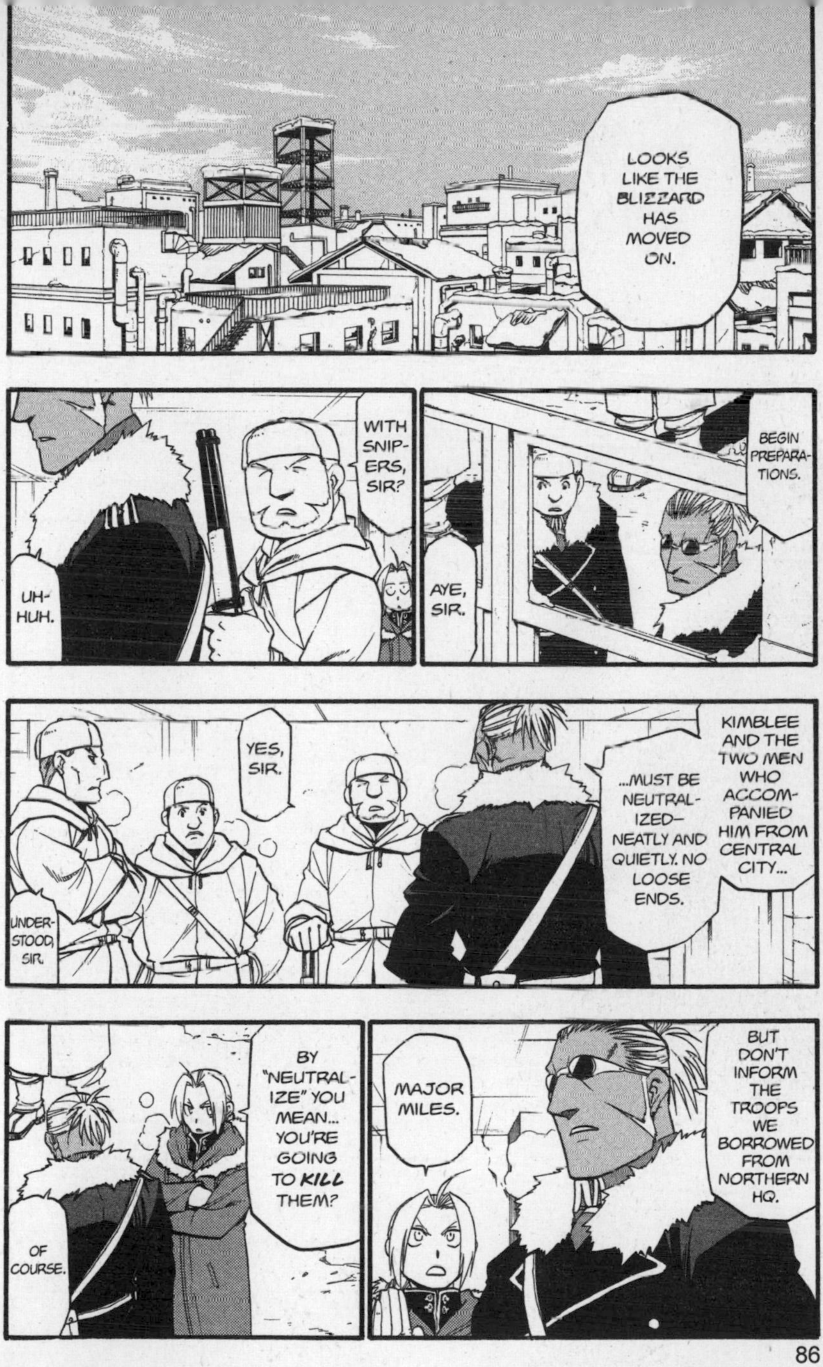
LOOKS LIKE THE BLIZZARD HAS MOVED ON.
BEGIN PREPARATIONS.
AYE, SIR.
WITH SNIPERS, SIR?
UH-HUH.
KIMBLEE AND THE TWO MEN WHO ACCOMPANIED HIM FROM CENTRAL CITY...
...MUST BE NEUTRALIZED— NEATLY AND QUIETLY. NO LOOSE ENDS.
YES, SIR.
UNDERSTOOD, SIR.
BUT DON'T INFORM THE TROOPS WE BORROWED FROM NORTHERN HQ.
MAJOR MILES.
BY "NEUTRALIZE" YOU MEAN... YOU'RE GOING TO **KILL** THEM?
OF COURSE.

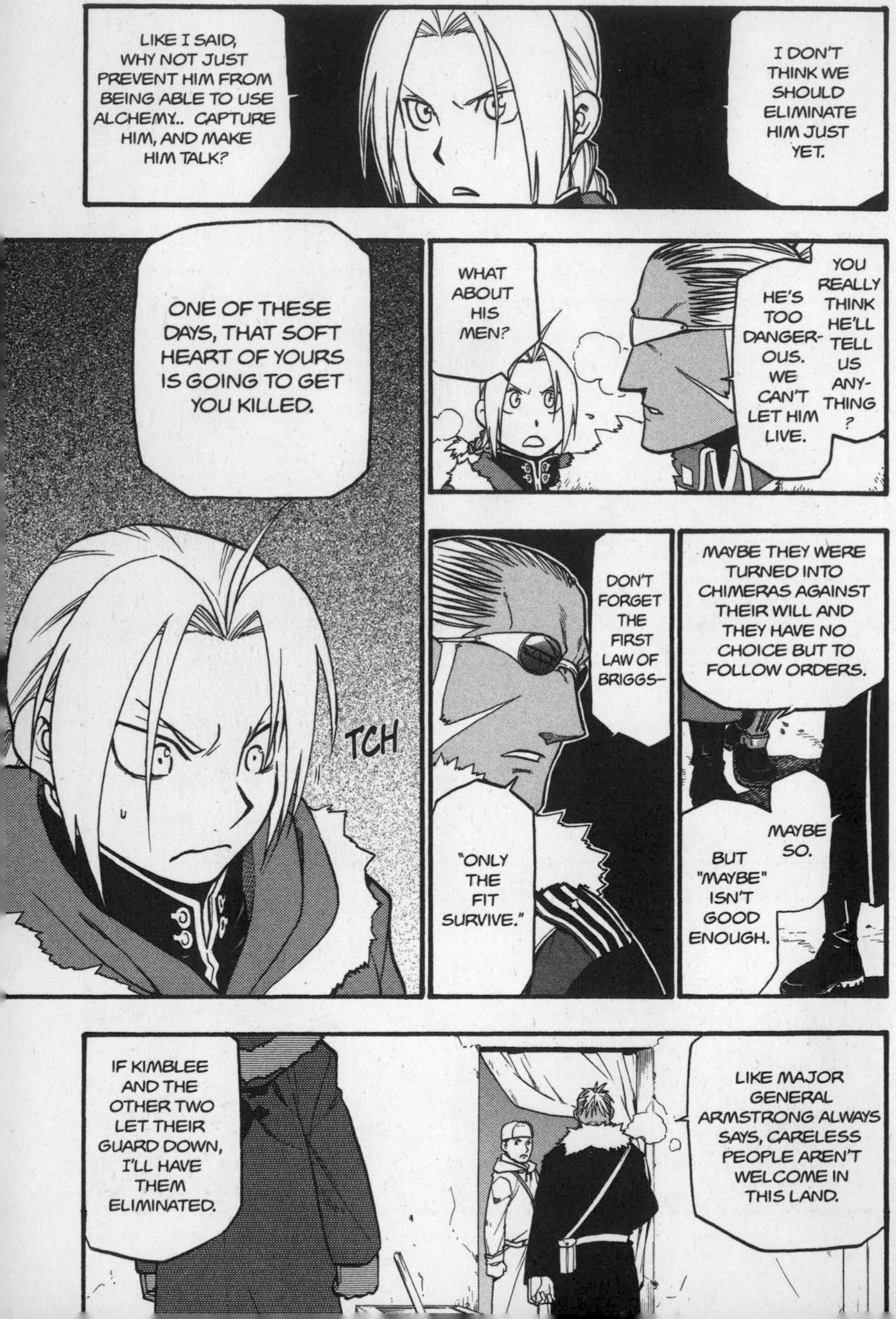
I DON'T THINK WE SHOULD ELIMINATE HIM JUST YET.
LIKE I SAID, WHY NOT JUST PREVENT HIM FROM BEING ABLE TO USE ALCHEMY.. CAPTURE HIM, AND MAKE HIM TALK?
YOU REALLY THINK HE'LL TELL US ANYTHING?
HE'S TOO DANGEROUS. WE CAN'T LET HIM LIVE.
WHAT ABOUT HIS MEN?
MAYBE THEY WERE TURNED INTO CHIMERAS AGAINST THEIR WILL AND THEY HAVE NO CHOICE BUT TO FOLLOW ORDERS.
MAYBE SO.
BUT "MAYBE" ISN'T GOOD ENOUGH.
DON'T FORGET THE FIRST LAW OF BRIGGS—
"ONLY THE FIT SURVIVE."
ONE OF THESE DAYS, THAT SOFT HEART OF YOURS IS GOING TO GET YOU KILLED.
TCH
LIKE MAJOR GENERAL ARMSTRONG ALWAYS SAYS, CARELESS PEOPLE AREN'T WELCOME IN THIS LAND.
IF KIMBLEE AND THE OTHER TWO LET THEIR GUARD DOWN, I'LL HAVE THEM ELIMINATED.

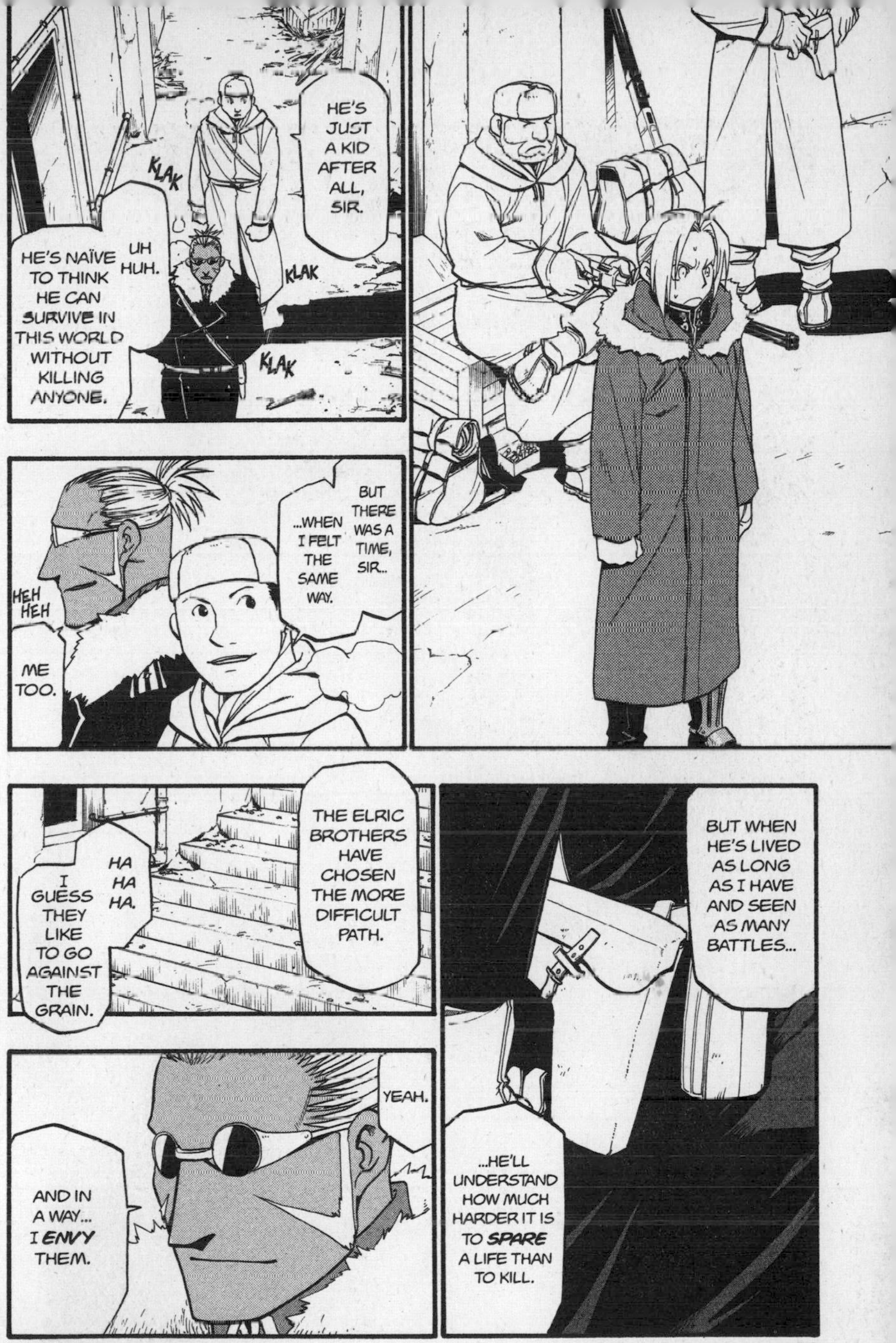
HE'S JUST A KID AFTER ALL, SIR.
KLAK
UH HUH.
KLAK
HE'S NAÏVE TO THINK HE CAN SURVIVE IN THIS WORLD WITHOUT KILLING ANYONE.
KLAK
BUT THERE WAS A TIME, SIR...
...WHEN I FELT THE SAME WAY.
HEH HEH
ME TOO.
BUT WHEN HE'S LIVED AS LONG AS I HAVE AND SEEN AS MANY BATTLES...
...HE'LL UNDERSTAND HOW MUCH HARDER IT IS TO *SPARE* A LIFE THAN TO KILL.
THE ELRIC BROTHERS HAVE CHOSEN THE MORE DIFFICULT PATH.
HA HA HA.
I GUESS THEY LIKE TO GO AGAINST THE GRAIN.
YEAH.
AND IN A WAY... I *ENVY* THEM.

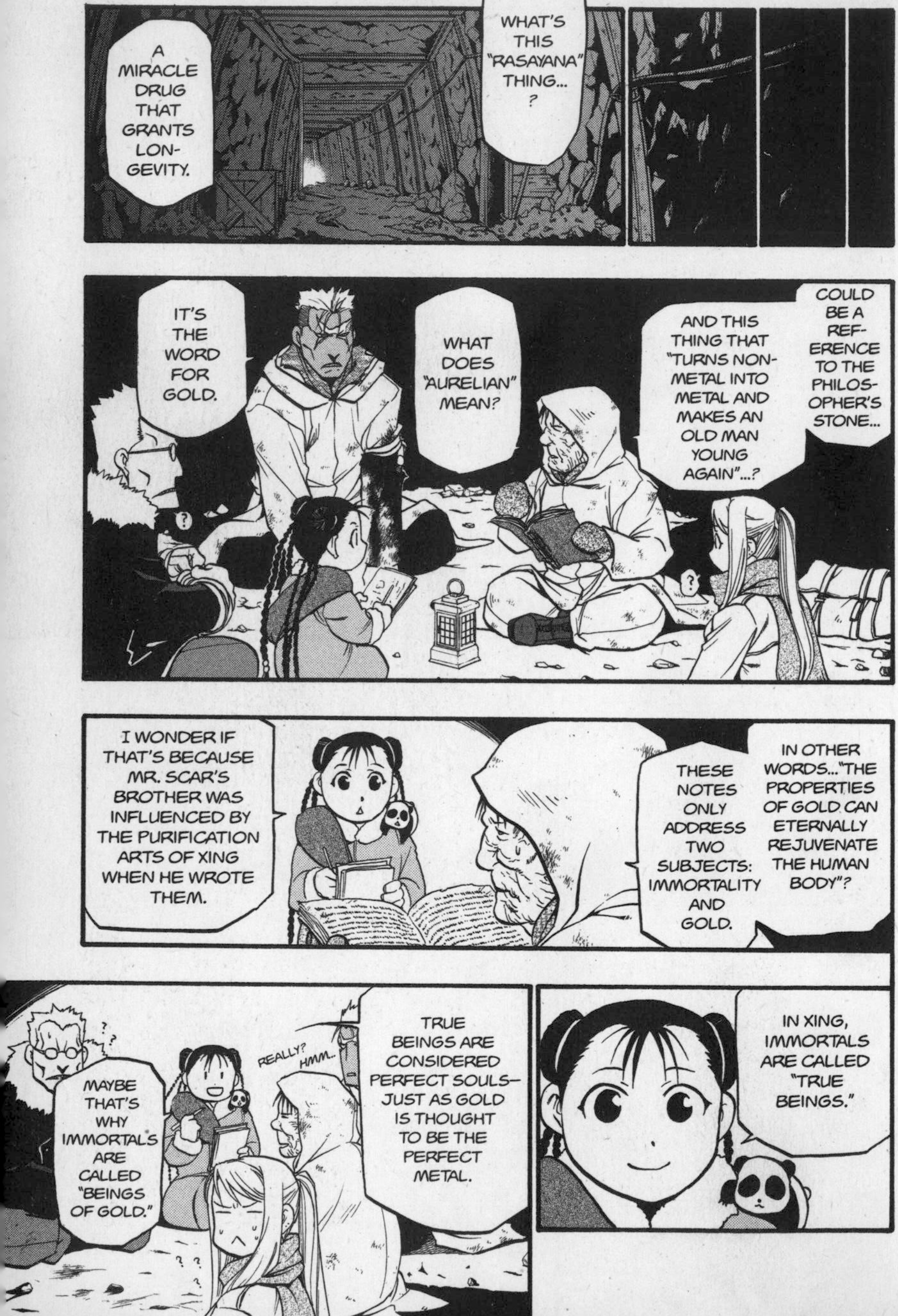
WHAT'S THIS "RASAYANA" THING...?
A MIRACLE DRUG THAT GRANTS LONGEVITY.
COULD BE A REFERENCE TO THE PHILOSOPHER'S STONE...
AND THIS THING THAT "TURNS NON-METAL INTO METAL AND MAKES AN OLD MAN YOUNG AGAIN"...?
WHAT DOES "AURELIAN" MEAN?
IT'S THE WORD FOR GOLD.
IN OTHER WORDS..."THE PROPERTIES OF GOLD CAN ETERNALLY REJUVENATE THE HUMAN BODY"?
THESE NOTES ONLY ADDRESS TWO SUBJECTS: IMMORTALITY AND GOLD.
I WONDER IF THAT'S BECAUSE MR. SCAR'S BROTHER WAS INFLUENCED BY THE PURIFICATION ARTS OF XING WHEN HE WROTE THEM.
IN XING, IMMORTALS ARE CALLED "TRUE BEINGS."
TRUE BEINGS ARE CONSIDERED PERFECT SOULS–JUST AS GOLD IS THOUGHT TO BE THE PERFECT METAL.
REALLY? HMM...
MAYBE THAT'S WHY IMMORTALS ARE CALLED "BEINGS OF GOLD."

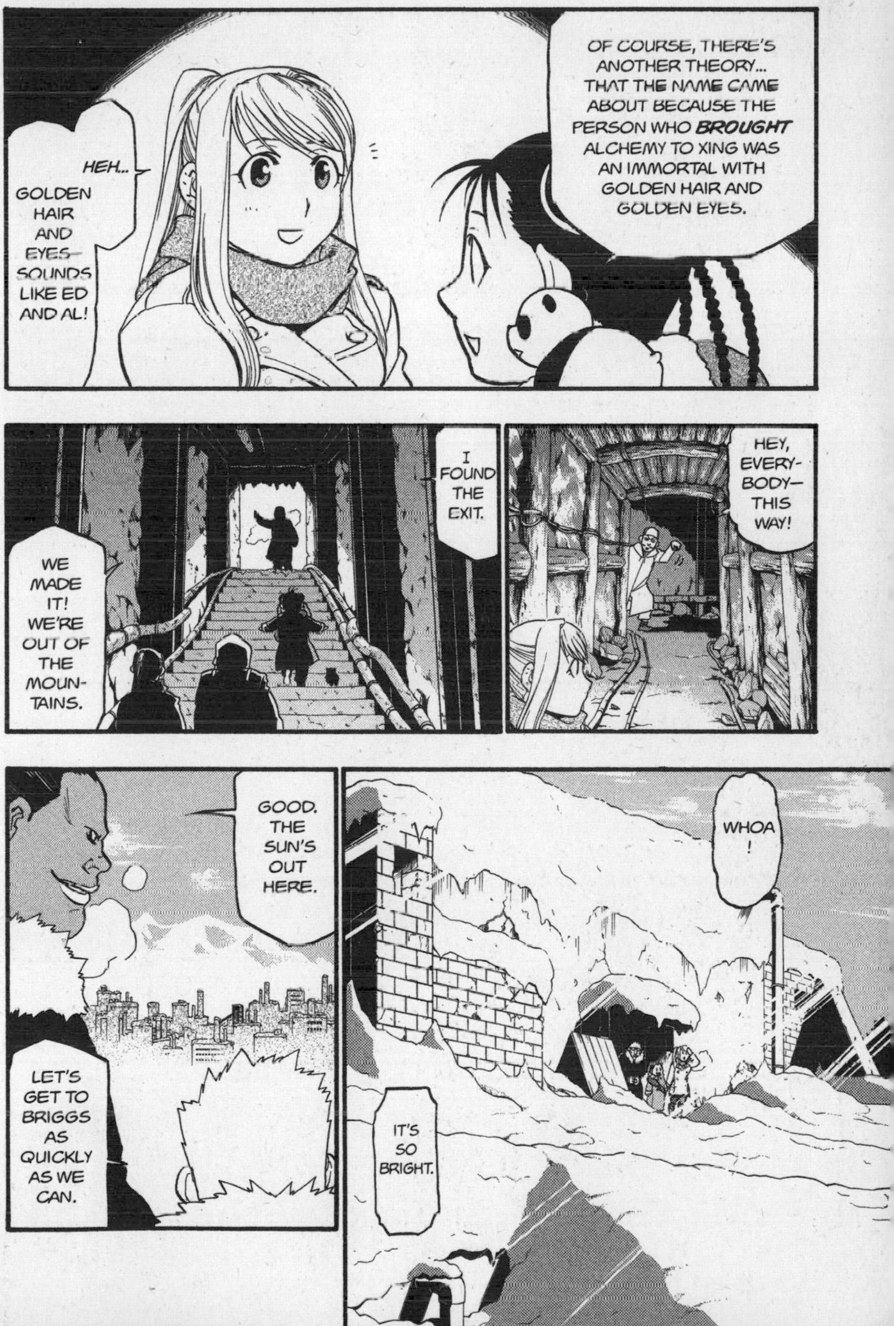
OF COURSE, THERE'S ANOTHER THEORY... THAT THE NAME CAME ABOUT BECAUSE THE PERSON WHO **BROUGHT** ALCHEMY TO XING WAS AN IMMORTAL WITH GOLDEN HAIR AND GOLDEN EYES.
HEH... GOLDEN HAIR AND EYES—SOUNDS LIKE ED AND AL!
HEY, EVERYBODY—THIS WAY!
I FOUND THE EXIT.
WE MADE IT! WE'RE OUT OF THE MOUNTAINS.
WHOA!
IT'S SO BRIGHT.
GOOD. THE SUN'S OUT HERE.
LET'S GET TO BRIGGS AS QUICKLY AS WE CAN.

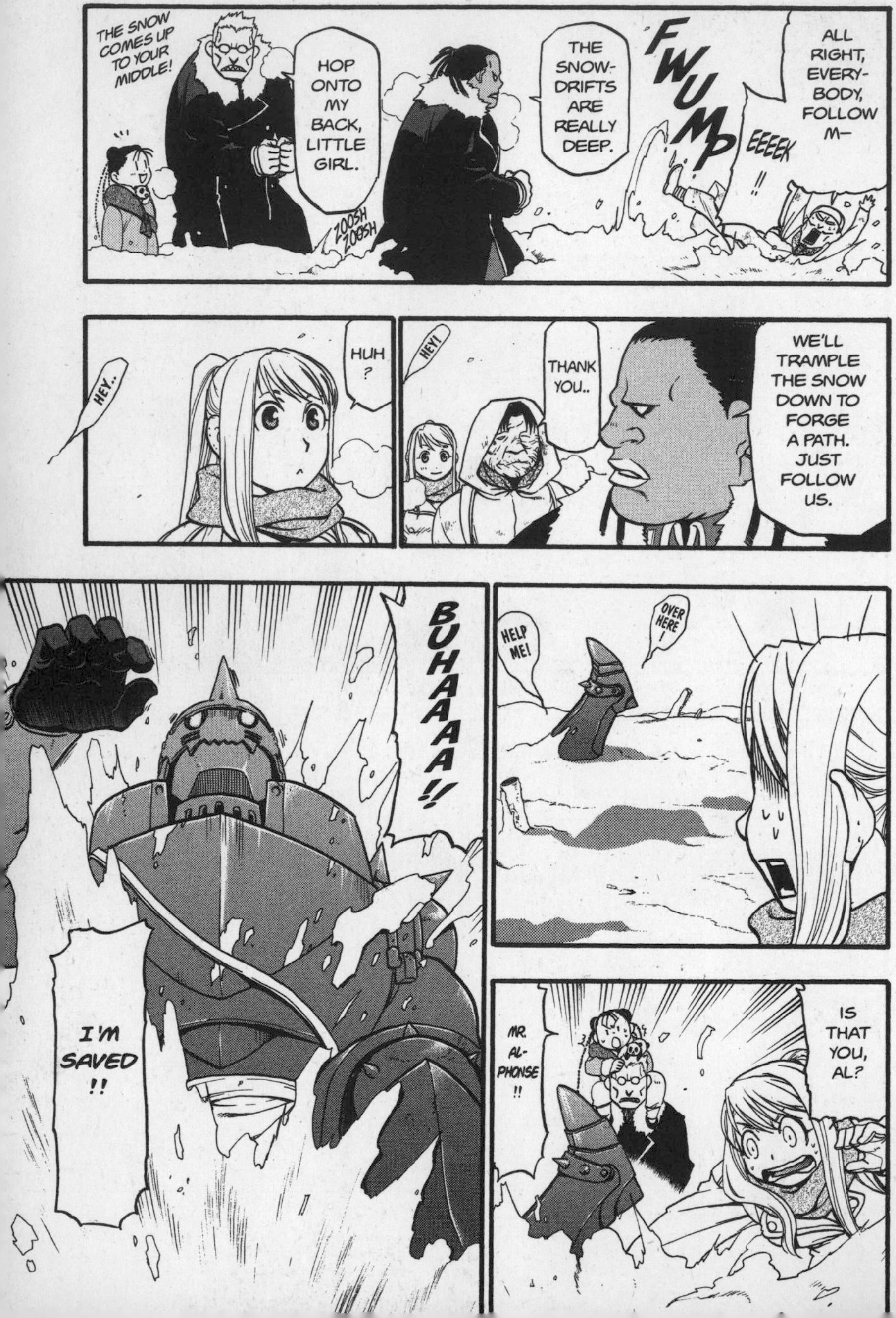
ALL RIGHT, EVERYBODY, FOLLOW M—
EEEEK!!
FWUMP
THE SNOW-DRIFTS ARE REALLY DEEP.
ZOOSH ZOOSH
HOP ONTO MY BACK, LITTLE GIRL.
THE SNOW COMES UP TO YOUR MIDDLE!
WE'LL TRAMPLE THE SNOW DOWN TO FORGE A PATH. JUST FOLLOW US.
THANK YOU..
HEY!
HUH?
HEY..
OVER HERE!
HELP ME!
IS THAT YOU, AL?
MR. AL-PHONSE!!
BUHAAAAA!!
I'M SAVED!!

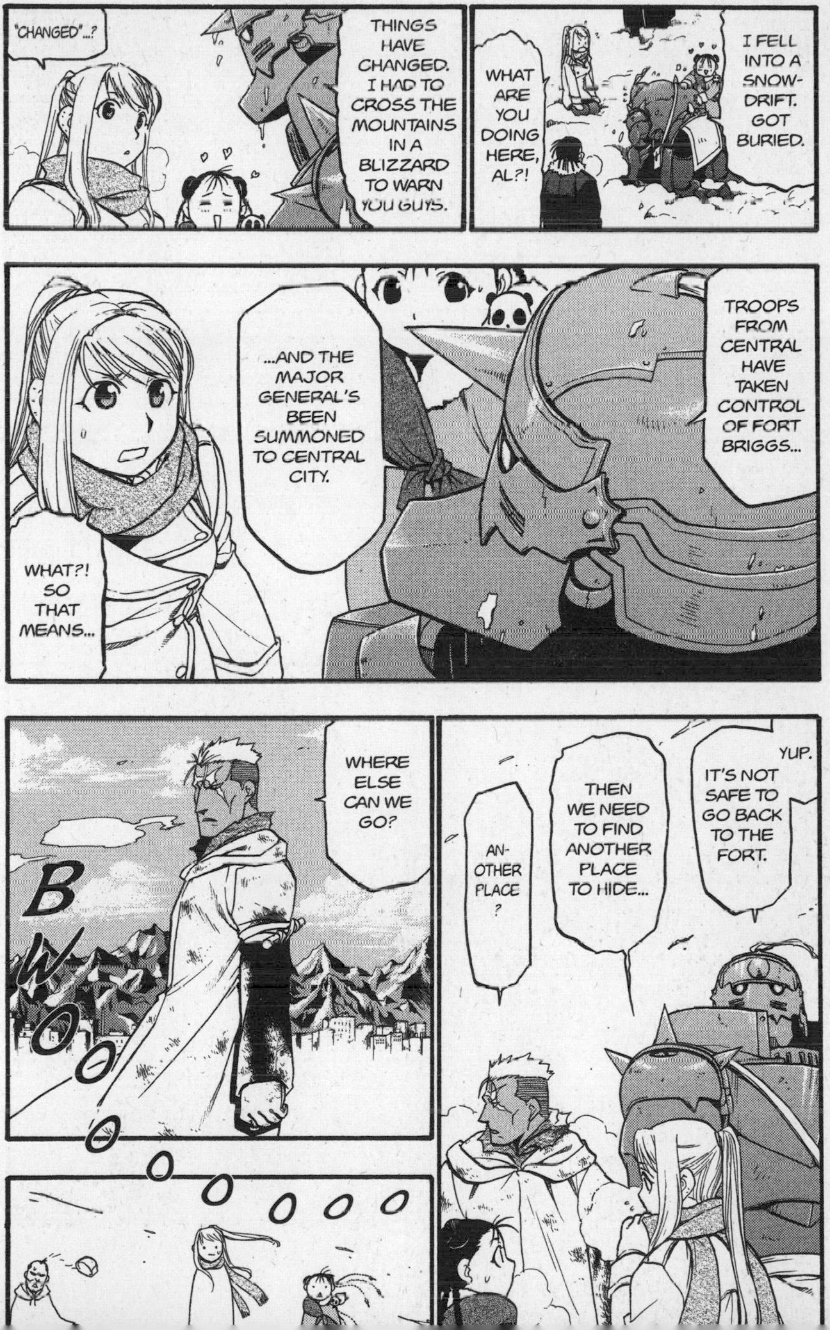
I FELL INTO A SNOW-DRIFT. GOT BURIED.
WHAT ARE YOU DOING HERE, AL?!
THINGS HAVE CHANGED. I HAD TO CROSS THE MOUNTAINS IN A BLIZZARD TO WARN YOU GUYS.
"CHANGED"...?
TROOPS FROM CENTRAL HAVE TAKEN CONTROL OF FORT BRIGGS...
...AND THE MAJOR GENERAL'S BEEN SUMMONED TO CENTRAL CITY.
WHAT?! SO THAT MEANS...
YUP.
IT'S NOT SAFE TO GO BACK TO THE FORT.
THEN WE NEED TO FIND ANOTHER PLACE TO HIDE...
AN-OTHER PLACE?
WHERE ELSE CAN WE GO?
BWOOOOOOOOOO

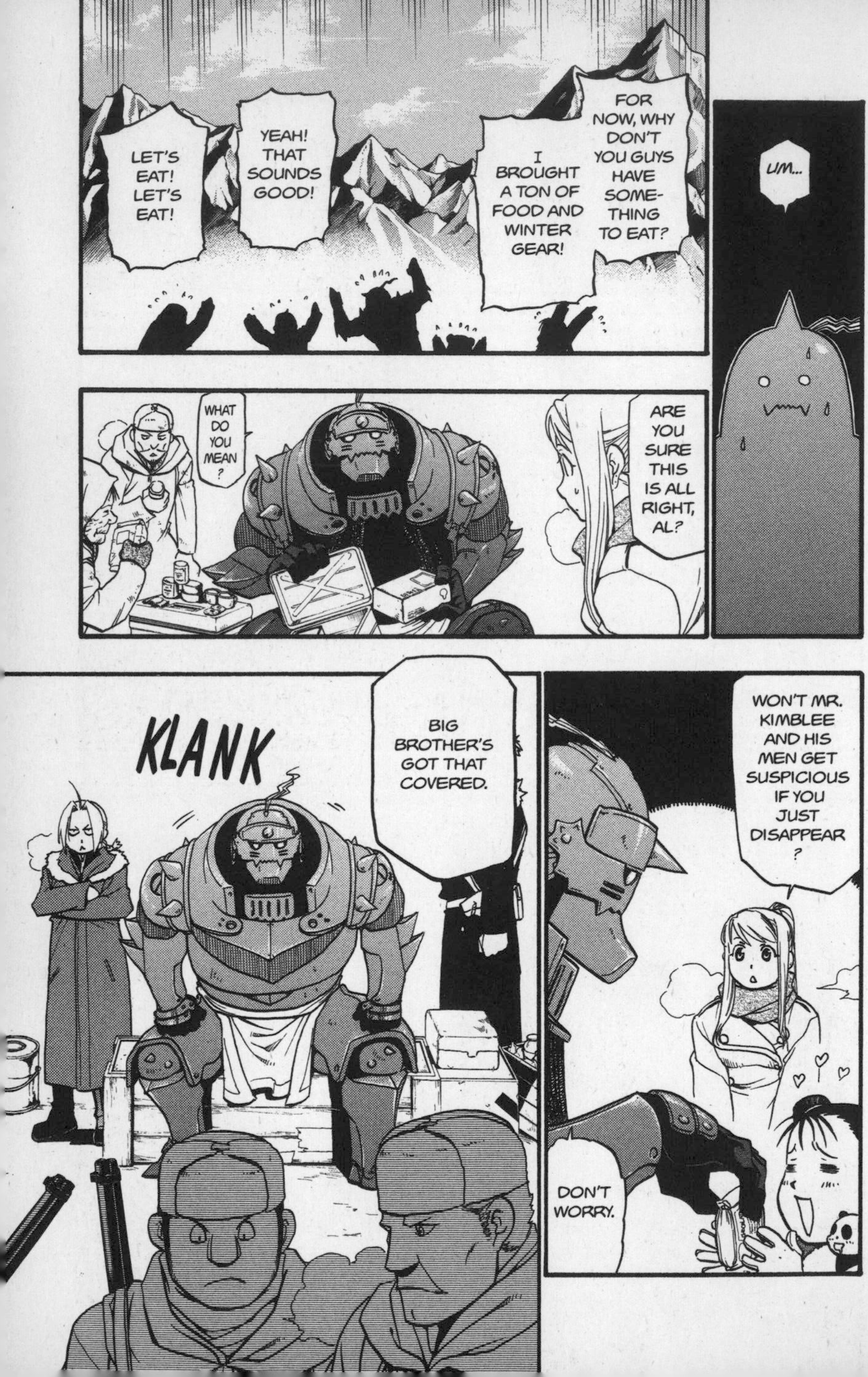
UM...
FOR NOW, WHY DON'T YOU GUYS HAVE SOME-THING TO EAT?
I BROUGHT A TON OF FOOD AND WINTER GEAR!
YEAH! THAT SOUNDS GOOD!
LET'S EAT! LET'S EAT!
ARE YOU SURE THIS IS ALL RIGHT, AL?
WHAT DO YOU MEAN?
WON'T MR. KIMBLEE AND HIS MEN GET SUSPICIOUS IF YOU JUST DISAPPEAR?
DON'T WORRY.
BIG BROTHER'S GOT THAT COVERED.
KLANK

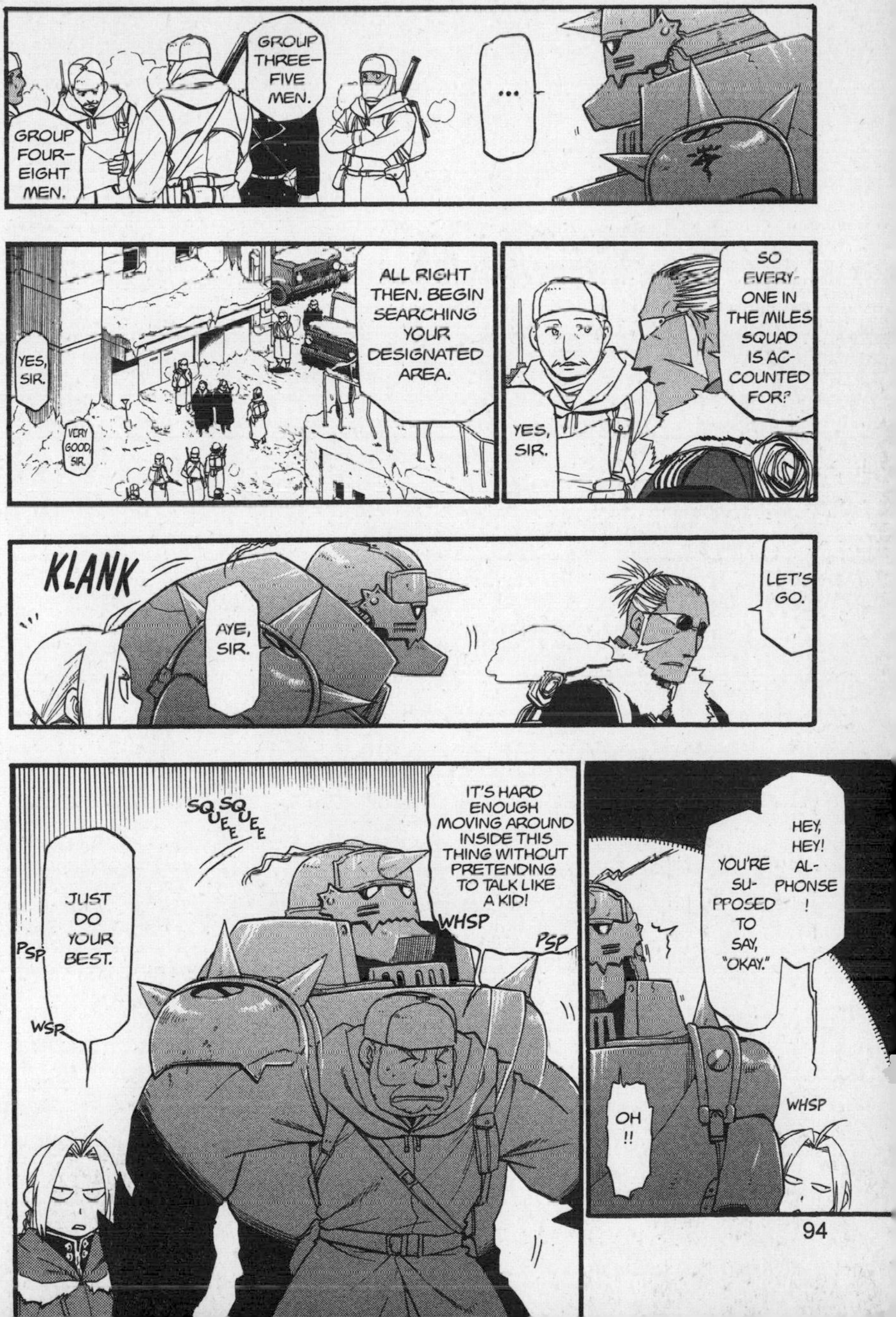
...
GROUP THREE—FIVE MEN.
GROUP FOUR—EIGHT MEN.
SO EVERYONE IN THE MILES SQUAD IS ACCOUNTED FOR?
YES, SIR.
ALL RIGHT THEN. BEGIN SEARCHING YOUR DESIGNATED AREA.
YES, SIR.
VERY GOOD, SIR.
LET'S GO.
AYE, SIR.
KLANK
HEY, HEY! ALPHONSE!
YOU'RE SUPPOSED TO SAY, "OKAY."
OH!!
WHSP
IT'S HARD ENOUGH MOVING AROUND INSIDE THIS THING WITHOUT PRETENDING TO TALK LIKE A KID!
WHSP
PSP
SQUEE SQUEE
JUST DO YOUR BEST.
PSP
WSP

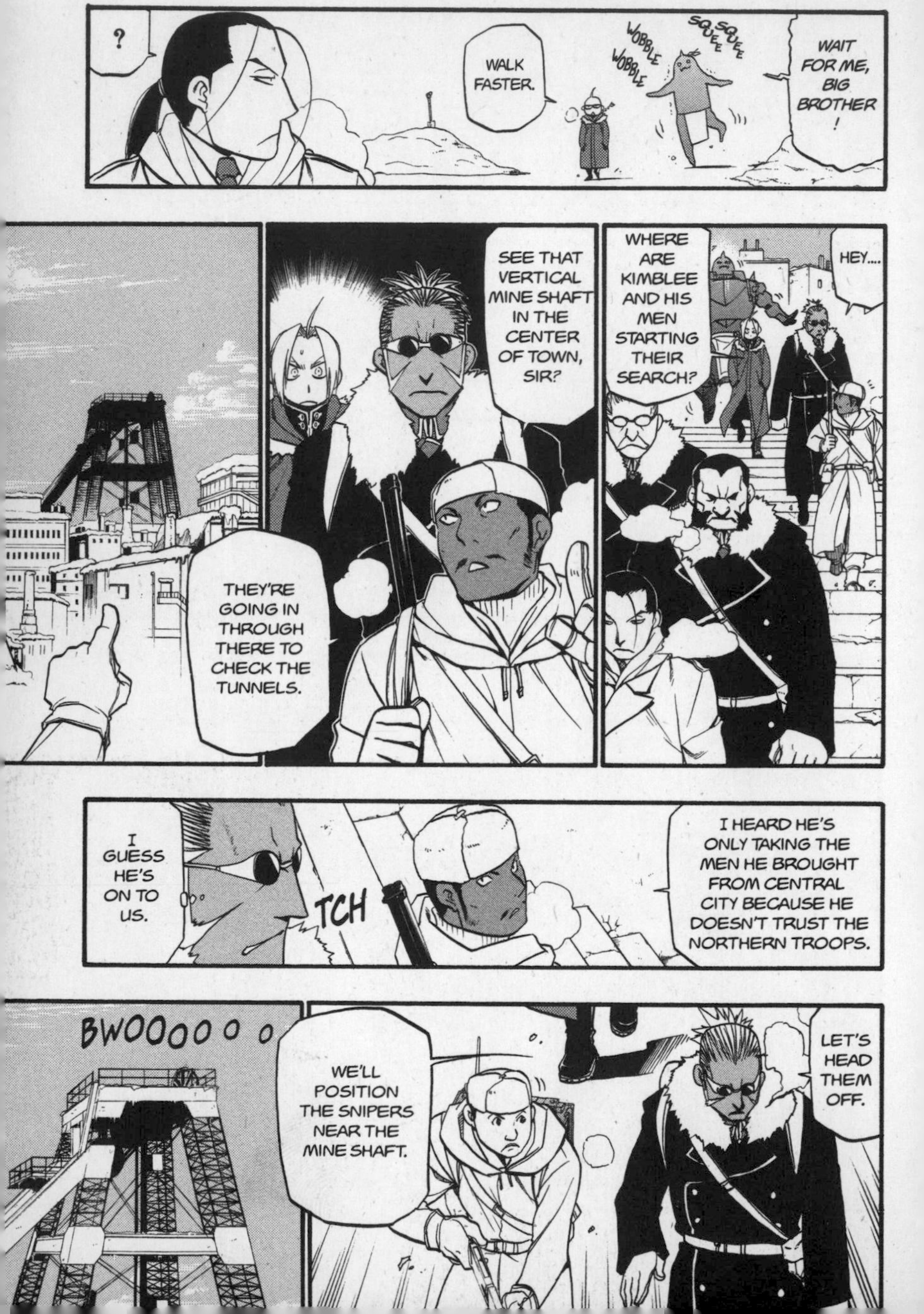
WAIT FOR ME, BIG BROTHER!
SQUEE SQUEE
WOBBLE WOBBLE
WALK FASTER.
?
HEY....
WHERE ARE KIMBLEE AND HIS MEN STARTING THEIR SEARCH?
SEE THAT VERTICAL MINE SHAFT IN THE CENTER OF TOWN, SIR?
THEY'RE GOING IN THROUGH THERE TO CHECK THE TUNNELS.
I HEARD HE'S ONLY TAKING THE MEN HE BROUGHT FROM CENTRAL CITY BECAUSE HE DOESN'T TRUST THE NORTHERN TROOPS.
TCH
I GUESS HE'S ON TO US.
LET'S HEAD THEM OFF.
WE'LL POSITION THE SNIPERS NEAR THE MINE SHAFT.
BWOOOOO O O

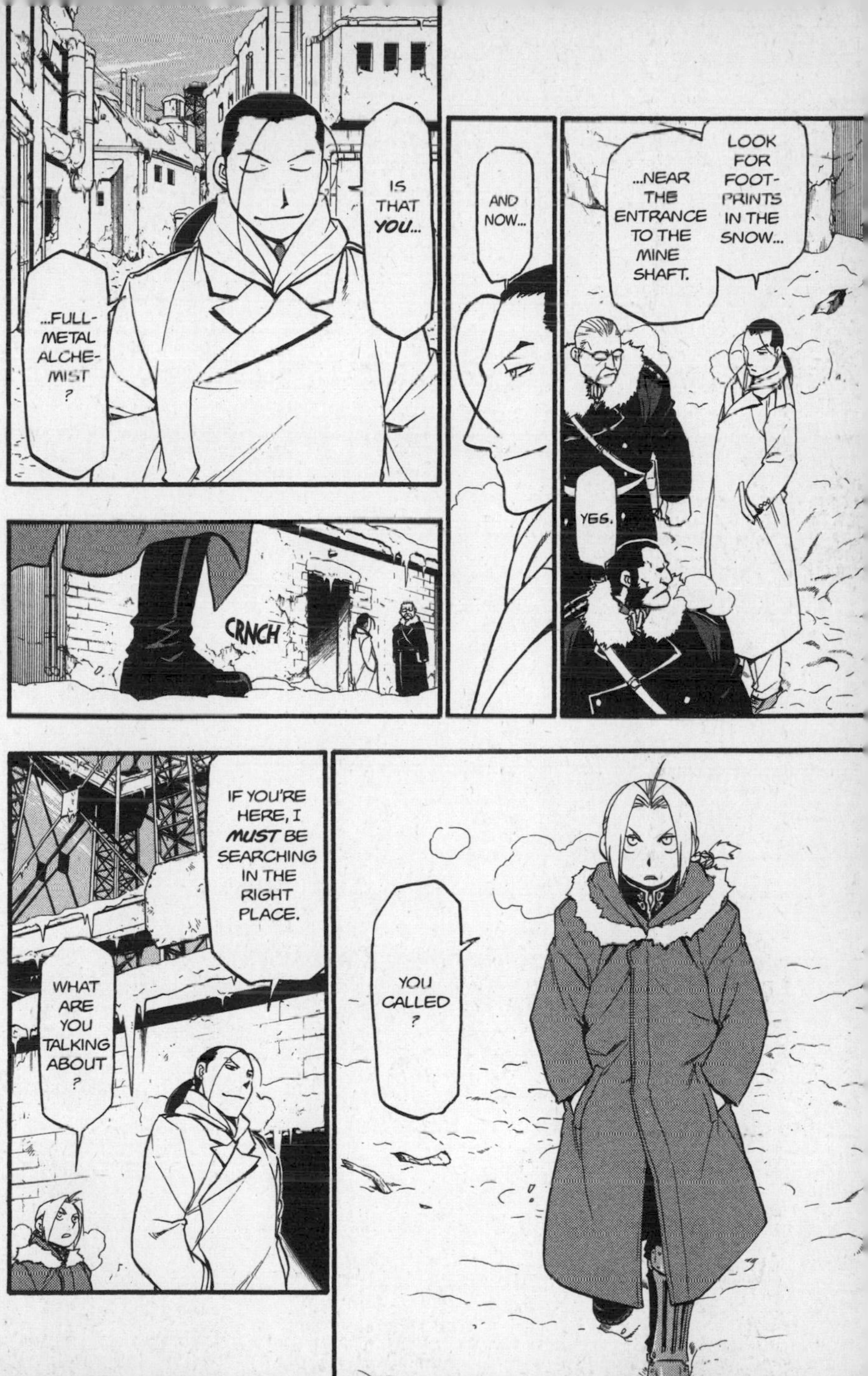
LOOK FOR FOOT-PRINTS IN THE SNOW...
...NEAR THE ENTRANCE TO THE MINE SHAFT.
YES.
AND NOW...
IS THAT *YOU*...
...FULL-METAL ALCHE-MIST?
CRNCH
YOU CALLED?
IF YOU'RE HERE, I *MUST* BE SEARCHING IN THE RIGHT PLACE.
WHAT ARE YOU TALKING ABOUT?

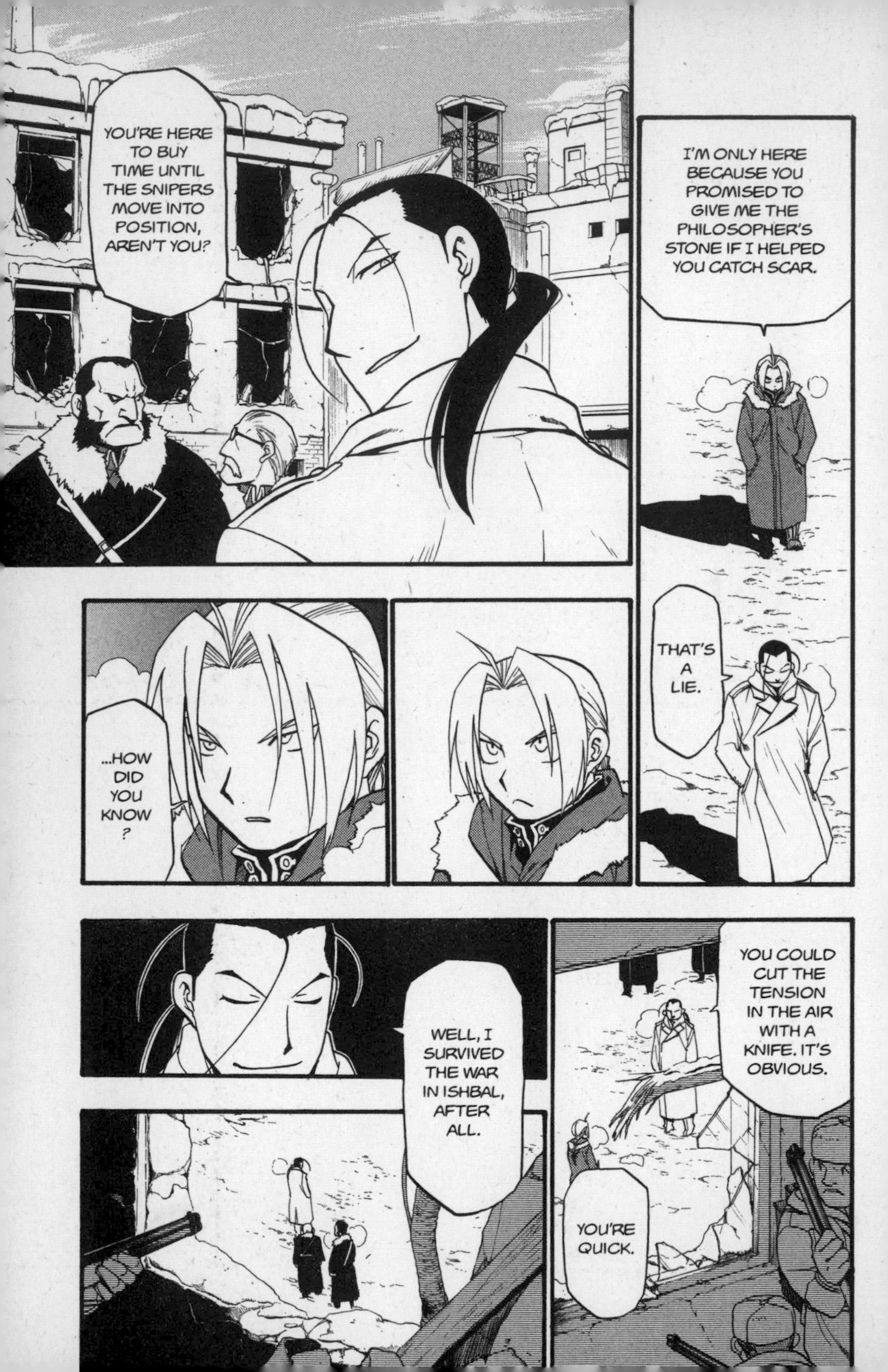
I'M ONLY HERE BECAUSE YOU PROMISED TO GIVE ME THE PHILOSOPHER'S STONE IF I HELPED YOU CATCH SCAR.
THAT'S A LIE.
YOU'RE HERE TO BUY TIME UNTIL THE SNIPERS MOVE INTO POSITION, AREN'T YOU?
...HOW DID YOU KNOW?
YOU COULD CUT THE TENSION IN THE AIR WITH A KNIFE. IT'S OBVIOUS.
YOU'RE QUICK.
WELL, I SURVIVED THE WAR IN ISHBAL, AFTER ALL.

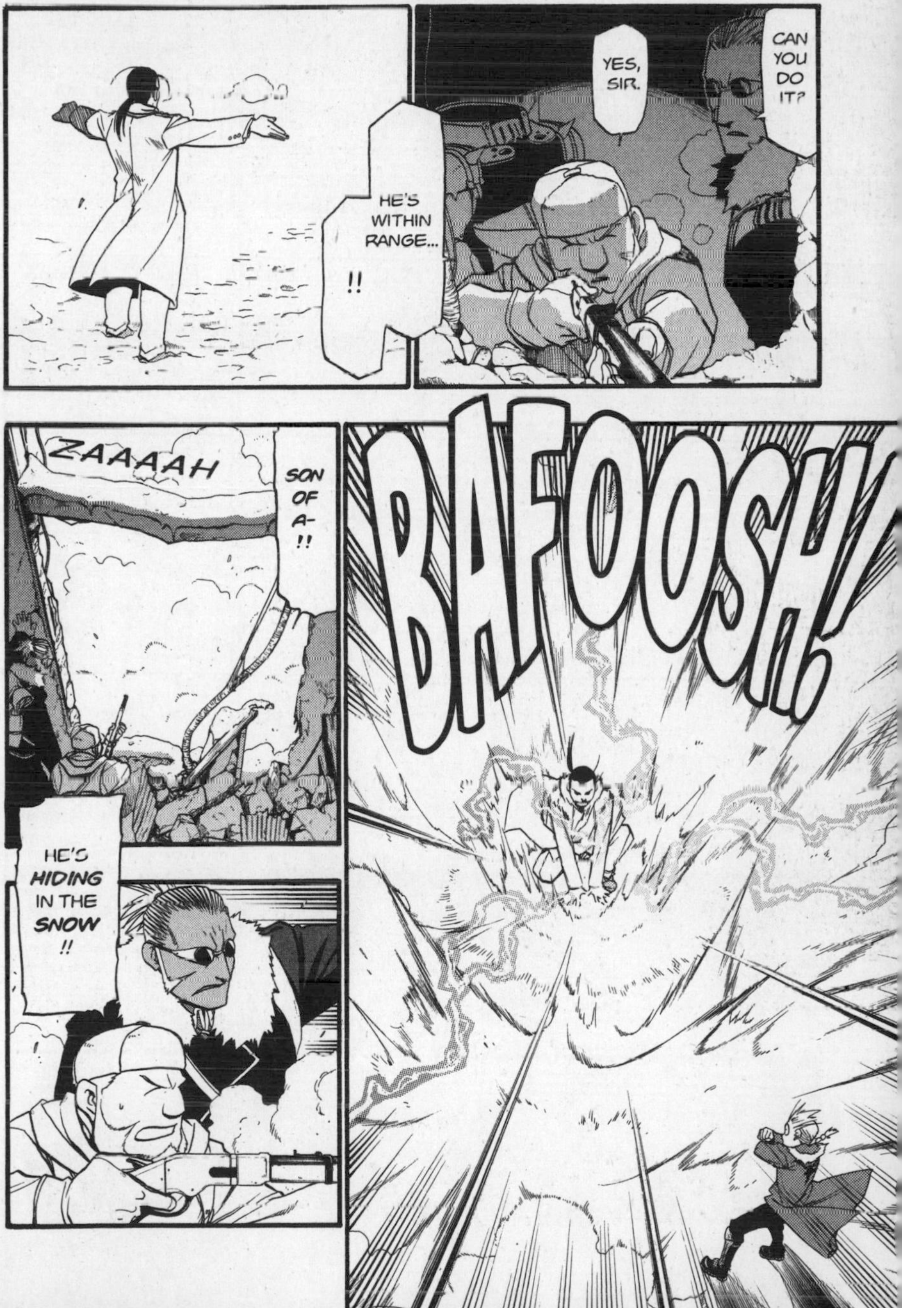
CAN YOU DO IT?
YES, SIR.
HE'S WITHIN RANGE...
!!
BAFOOSH!
SON OF A-!!
ZAAAAH
HE'S HIDING IN THE SNOW!!

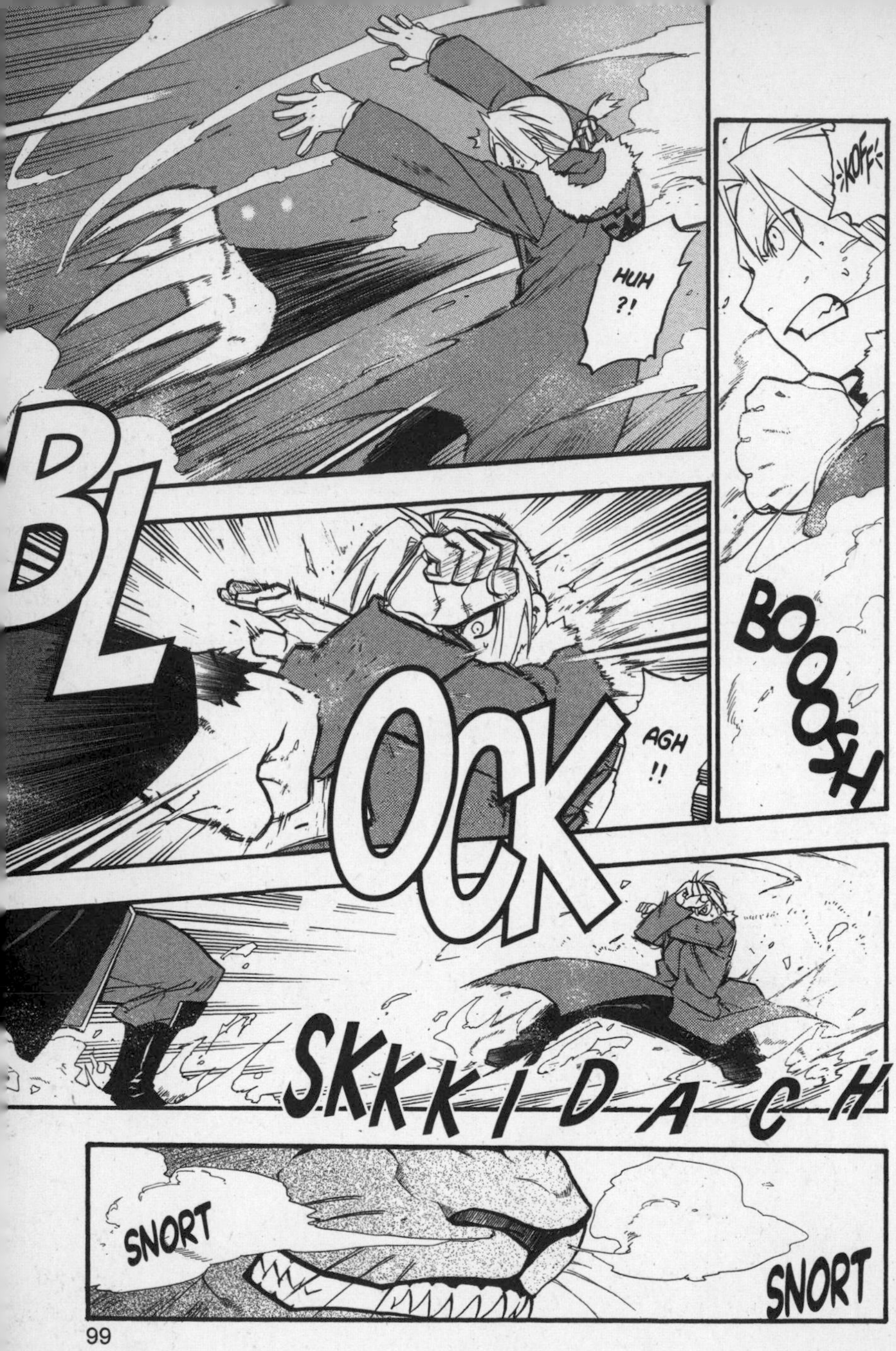
KOFF
BOOOSH
HUH ?!
BLOCK
AGH !!
SKKIDACH
SNORT
SNORT

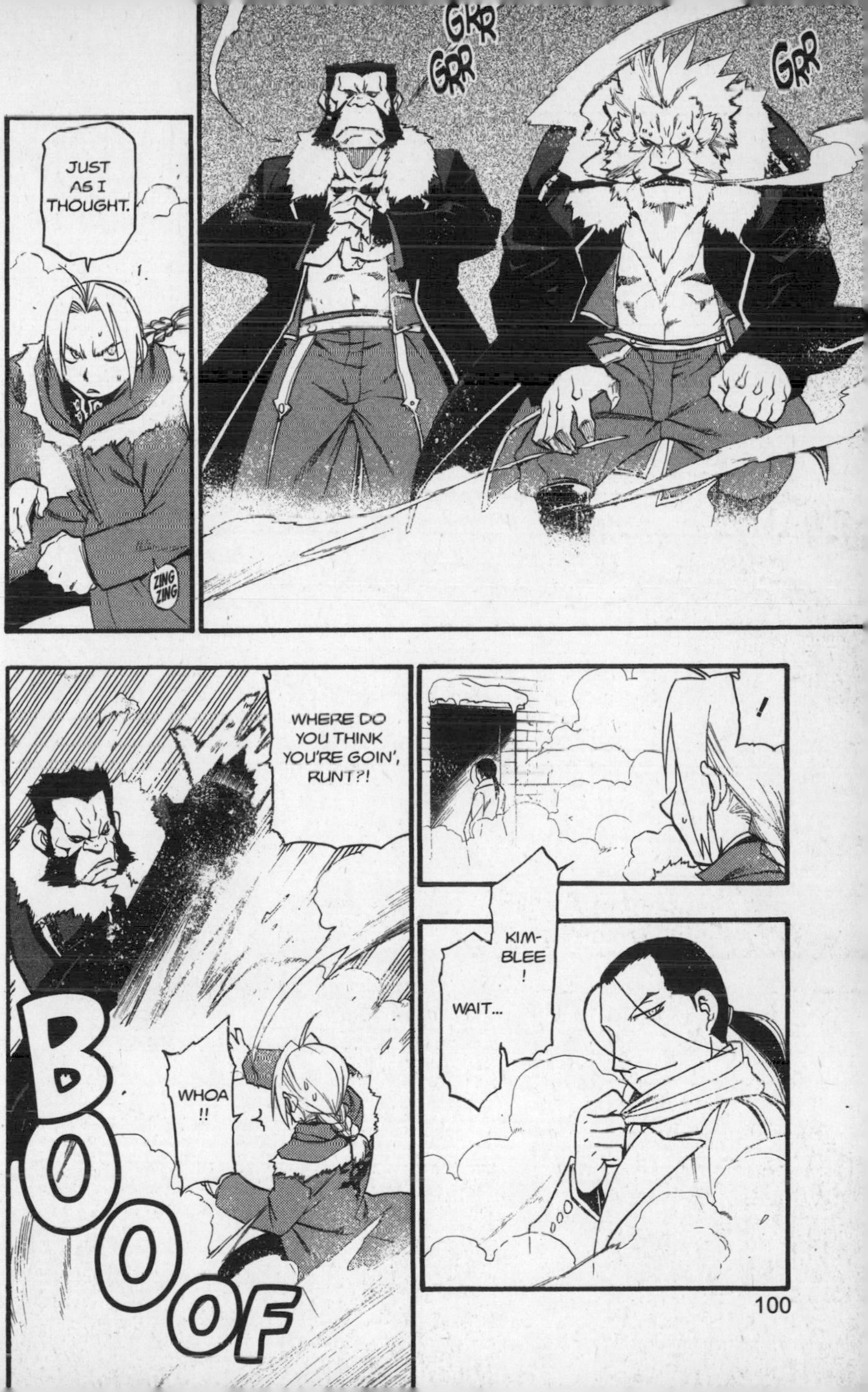
GRR
GRR
GRR
JUST AS I THOUGHT.
ZING ZING
!
KIM-BLEE!
WAIT...
WHERE DO YOU THINK YOU'RE GOIN', RUNT?!
WHOA!!
BOOOOF

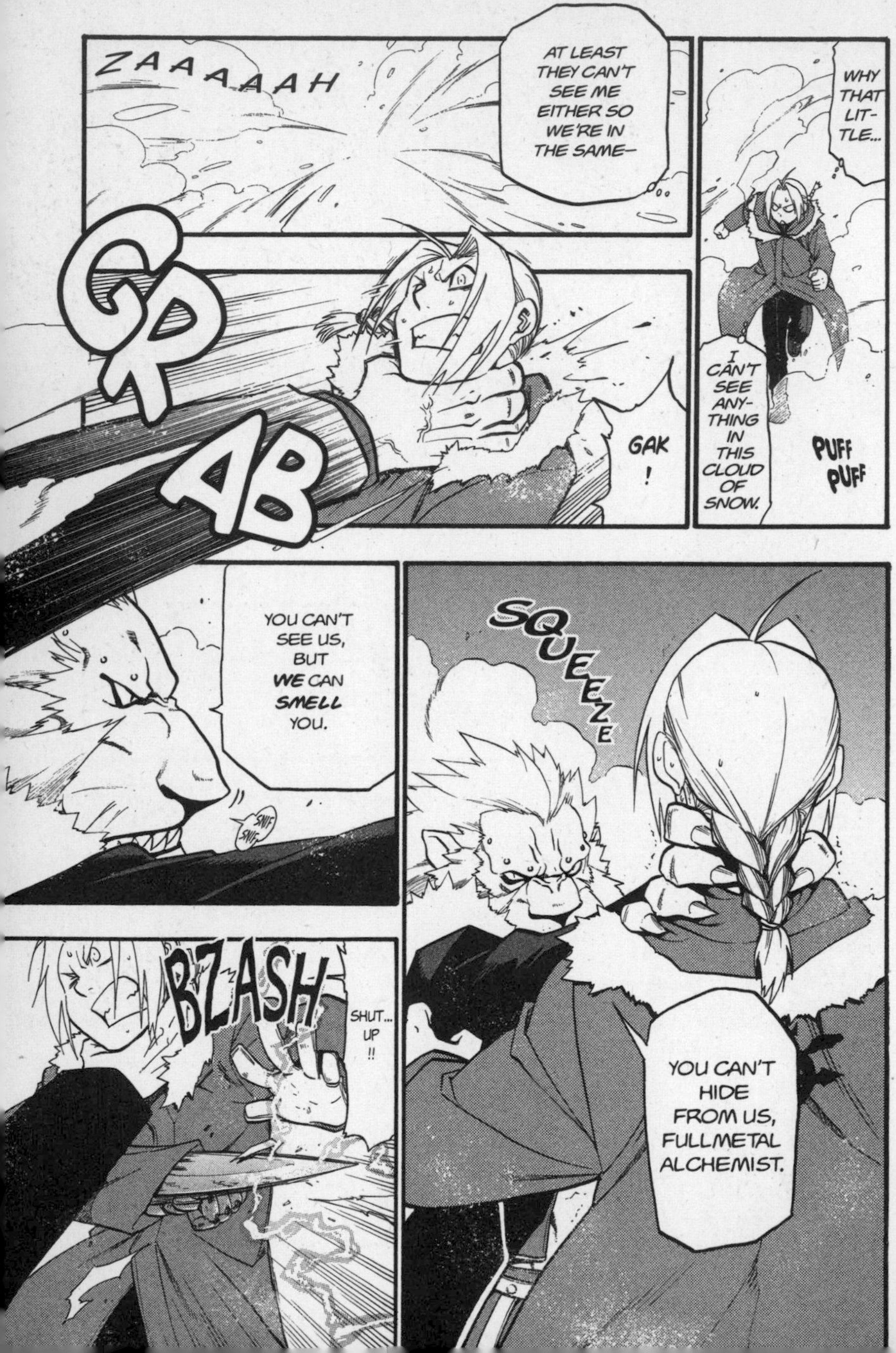
WHY THAT LIT-TLE...
I CAN'T SEE ANY-THING IN THIS CLOUD OF SNOW.
PUFF PUFF
ZAAAAAAH
AT LEAST THEY CAN'T SEE ME EITHER SO WE'RE IN THE SAME—
GRAB
GAK!
SQUEEZE
YOU CAN'T HIDE FROM US, FULLMETAL ALCHEMIST.
YOU CAN'T SEE US, BUT **WE** CAN **SMELL** YOU.
SNIF SNIF
BZASH
SHUT... UP!!

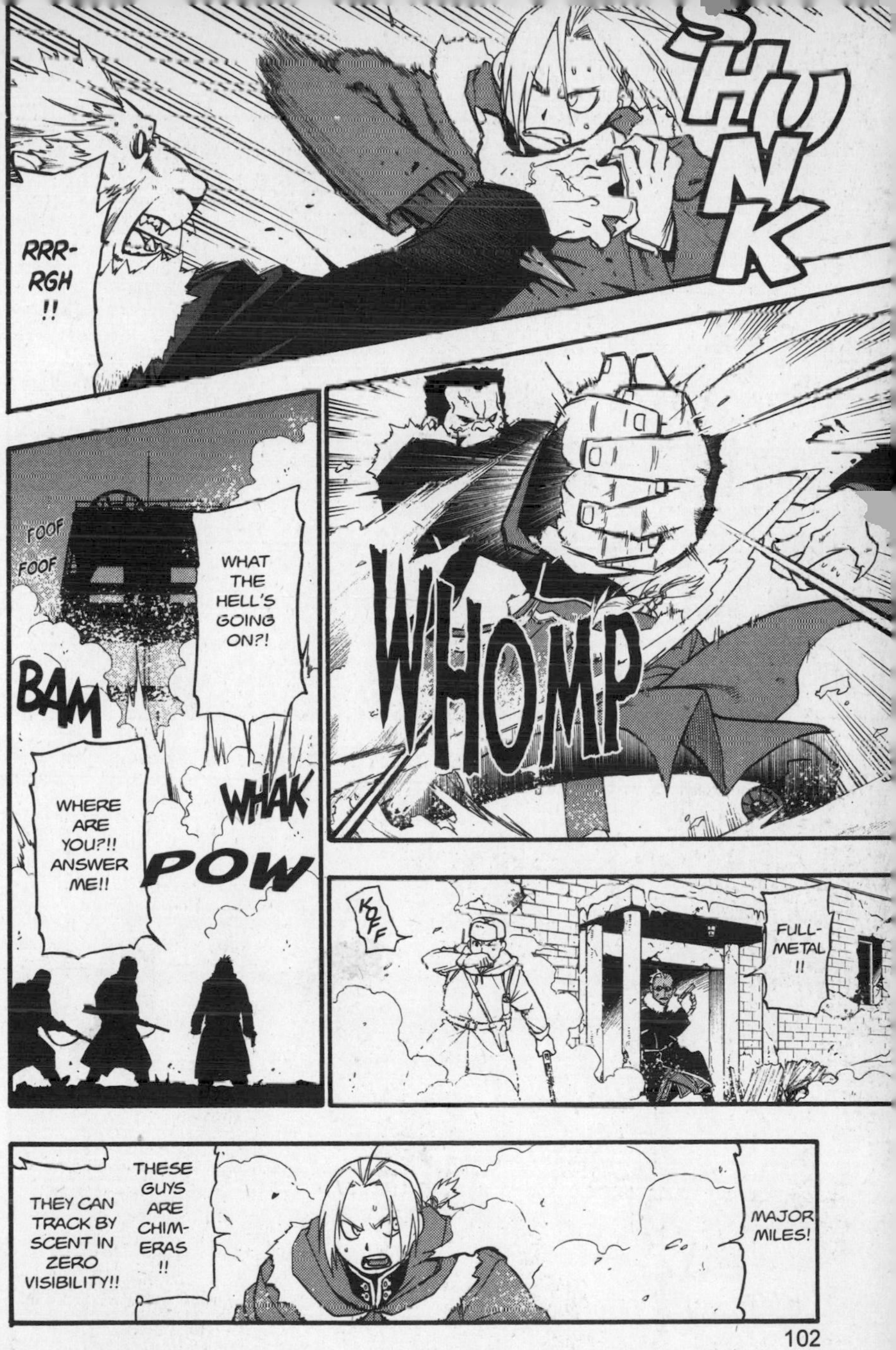
SHUNK
RRR-RGH!!
WHOMP
FULL-METAL!!
KOFF
WHAT THE HELL'S GOING ON?!
FOOF FOOF
BAM
WHAK
WHERE ARE YOU?!! ANSWER ME!!
POW
MAJOR MILES!
THESE GUYS ARE CHIMERAS!!
THEY CAN TRACK BY SCENT IN ZERO VISIBILITY!!

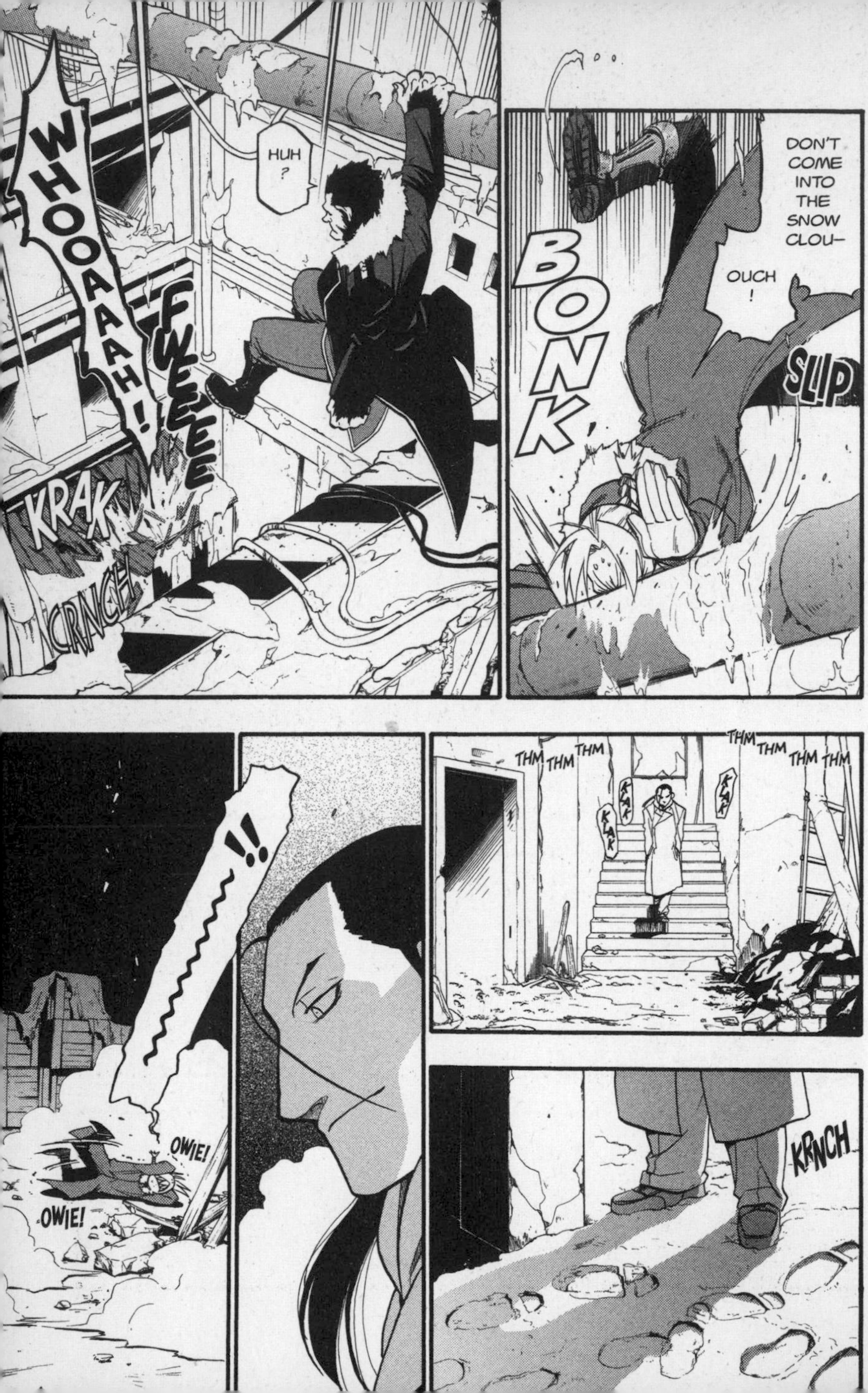

DON'T COME INTO THE SNOW CLOU—
OUCH!
SLIP
BONK
HUH?
WHOOAAAAH!
FWEEEE
KRAK
CRNCH
THM THM THM
THM THM THM THM
KLAK
KLAK
KLAK
KRNCH
~~~!!
OWIE!
OWIE!
~~~

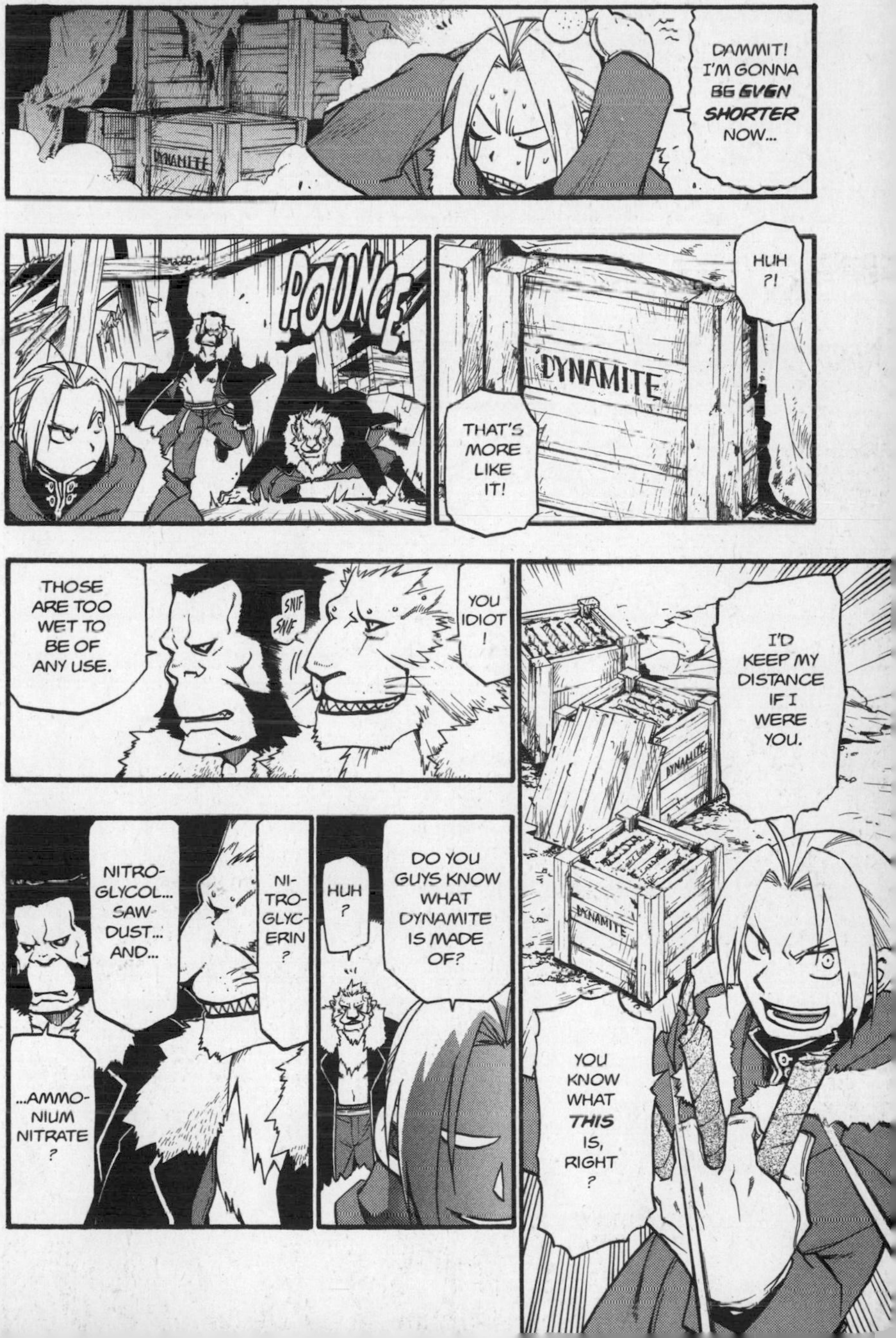
DAMMIT! I'M GONNA BE *EVEN SHORTER* NOW...
DYNAMITE
HUH ?!
DYNAMITE
THAT'S MORE LIKE IT!
POUNCE
I'D KEEP MY DISTANCE IF I WERE YOU.
DYNAMITE
DYNAMITE
YOU KNOW WHAT *THIS* IS, RIGHT ?
YOU IDIOT !
SNIF SNIF
THOSE ARE TOO WET TO BE OF ANY USE.
DO YOU GUYS KNOW WHAT DYNAMITE IS MADE OF?
HUH ?
NI-TRO-GLYC-ERIN ?
NITRO-GLYCOL... SAW-DUST... AND...
...AMMO-NIUM NITRATE ?

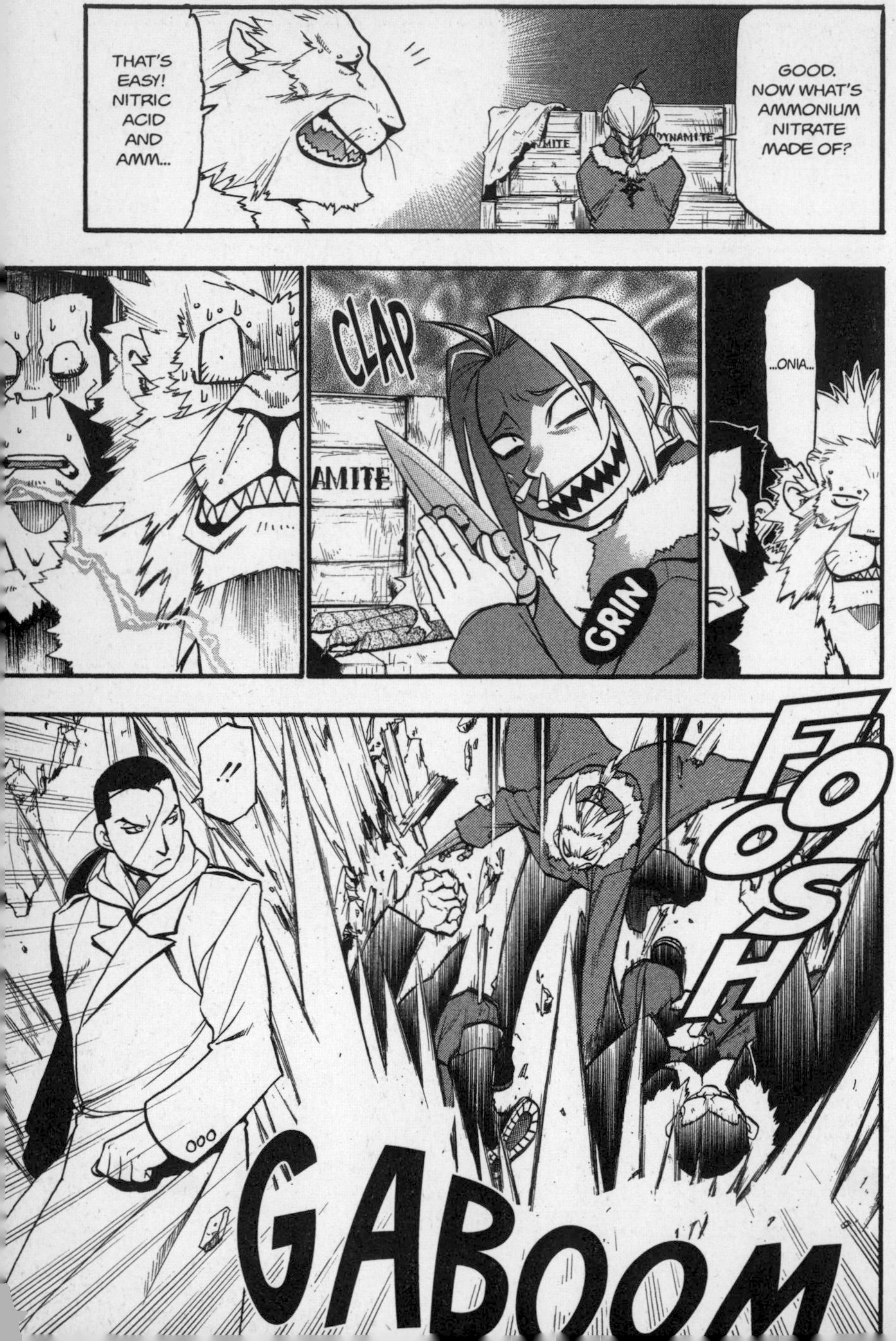
GOOD. NOW WHAT'S AMMONIUM NITRATE MADE OF?
THAT'S EASY! NITRIC ACID AND AMM...
...ONIA...
CLAP
GRIN
FOOSH
!!
GABOOM

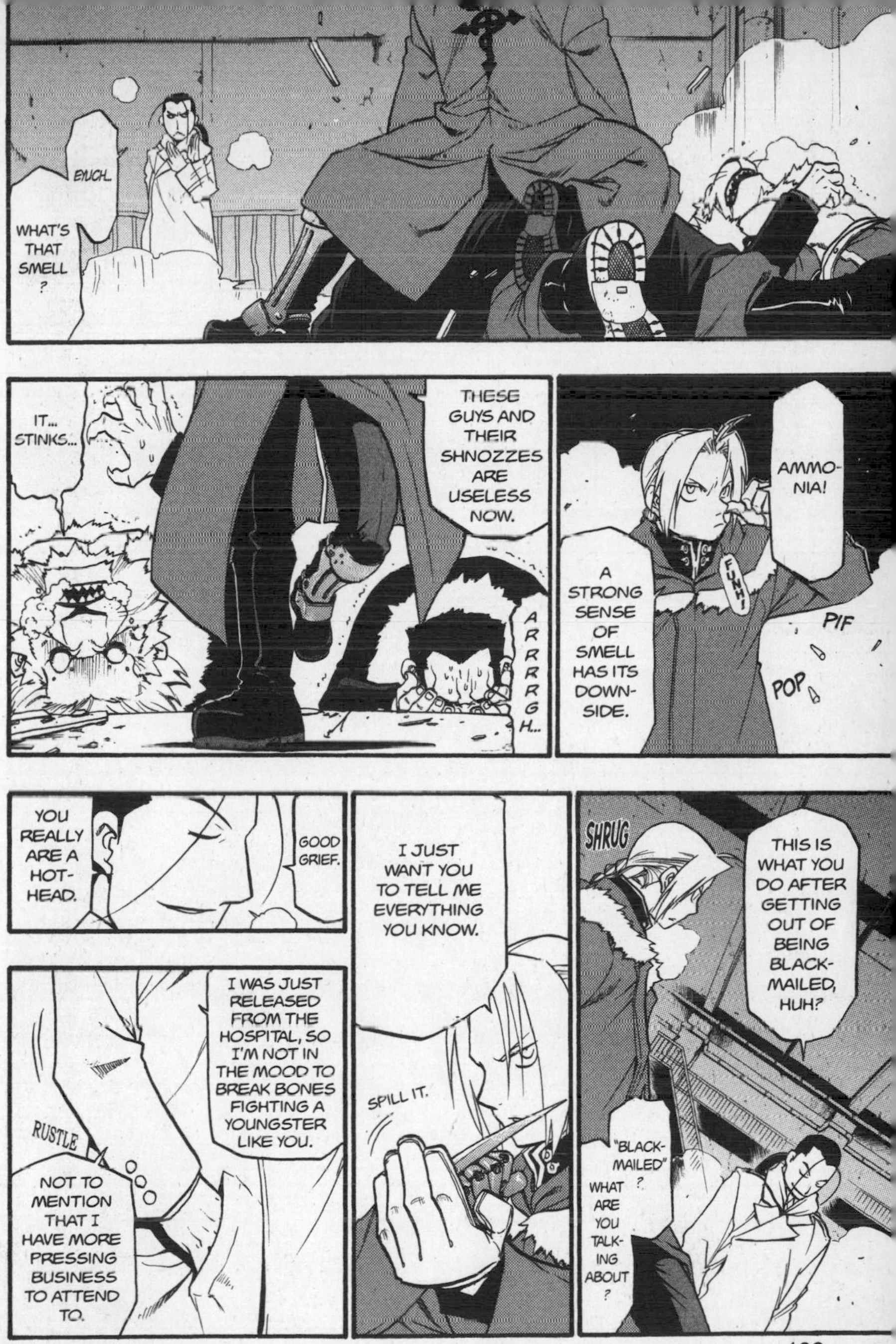
EYUCH.
WHAT'S THAT SMELL?
AMMONIA!
FUNH!
PIF
POP
A STRONG SENSE OF SMELL HAS ITS DOWNSIDE.
THESE GUYS AND THEIR SHNOZZES ARE USELESS NOW.
ARRRRGH...
IT... STINKS...
SHRUG
THIS IS WHAT YOU DO AFTER GETTING OUT OF BEING BLACKMAILED, HUH?
"BLACKMAILED"?
WHAT ARE YOU TALKING ABOUT?
I JUST WANT YOU TO TELL ME EVERYTHING YOU KNOW.
SPILL IT.
GOOD GRIEF.
YOU REALLY ARE A HOT-HEAD.
I WAS JUST RELEASED FROM THE HOSPITAL, SO I'M NOT IN THE MOOD TO BREAK BONES FIGHTING A YOUNGSTER LIKE YOU.
RUSTLE
NOT TO MENTION THAT I HAVE MORE PRESSING BUSINESS TO ATTEND TO.

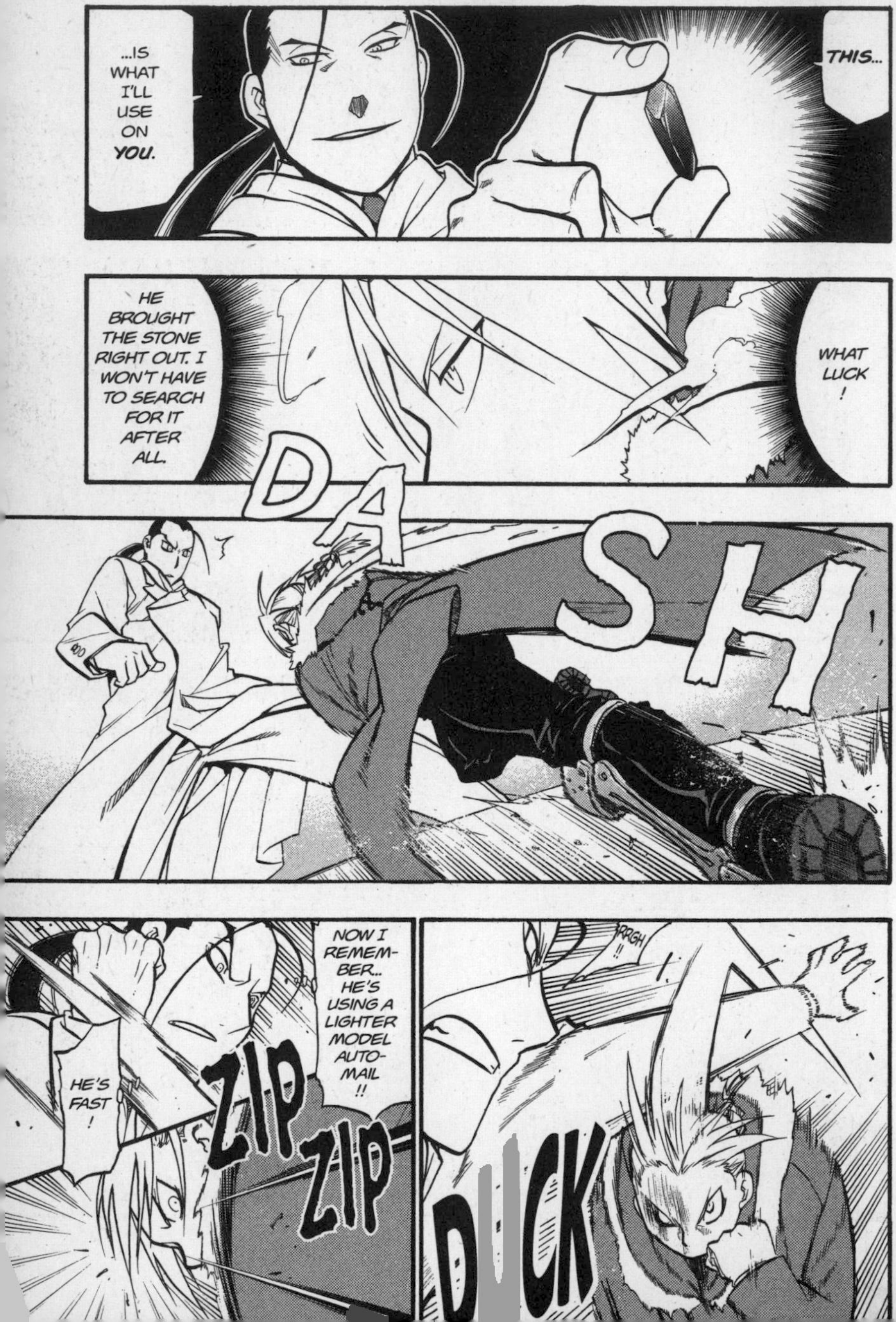
THIS...
...IS WHAT I'LL USE ON YOU.
WHAT LUCK!
HE BROUGHT THE STONE RIGHT OUT. I WON'T HAVE TO SEARCH FOR IT AFTER ALL.
DASH
RRRGH!!
DUCK
NOW I REMEMBER... HE'S USING A LIGHTER MODEL AUTO-MAIL!!
ZIP ZIP
HE'S FAST!

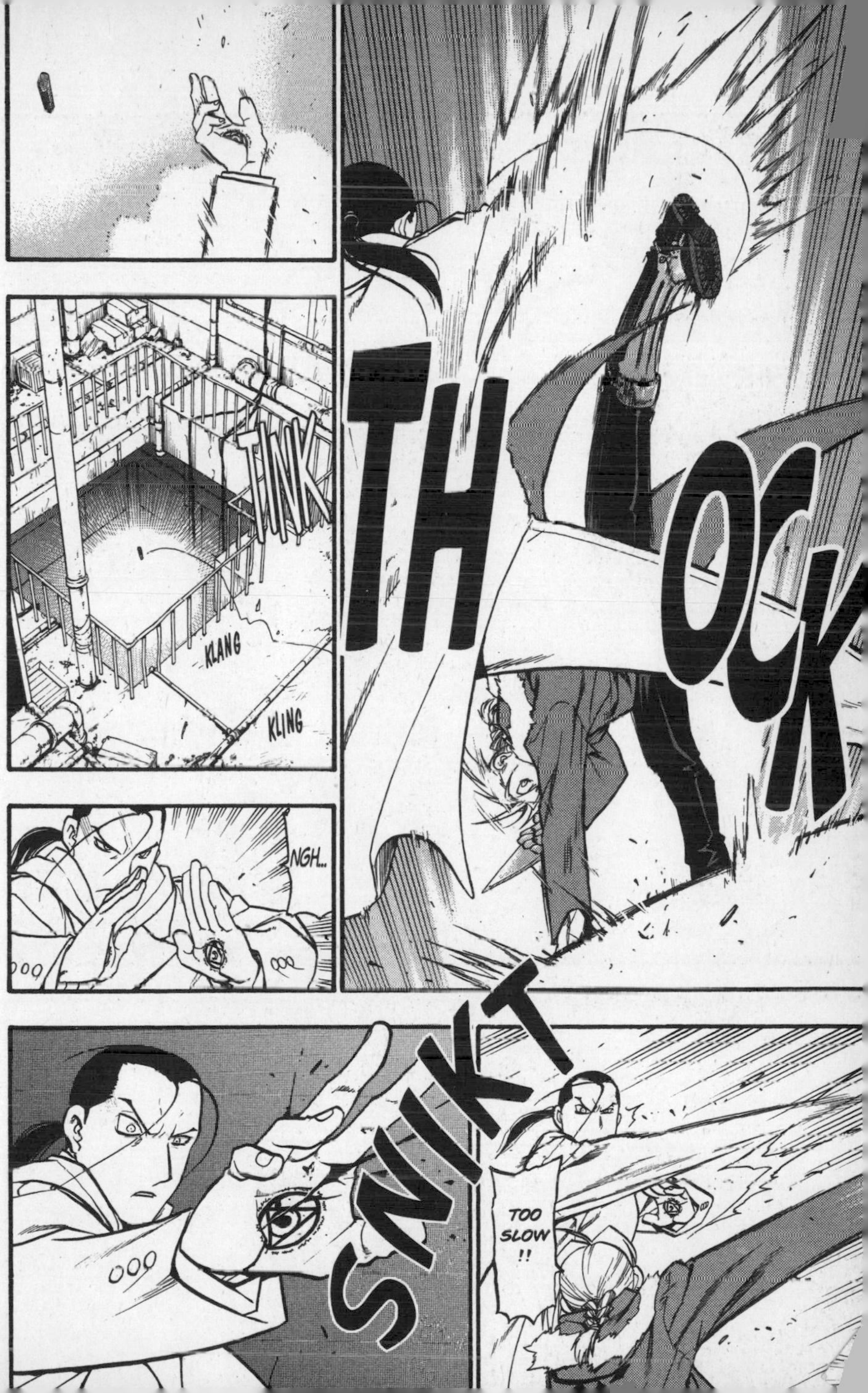
THOCK
TINK
KLANG
KLING
NGH...
TOO SLOW!!
SNIKT

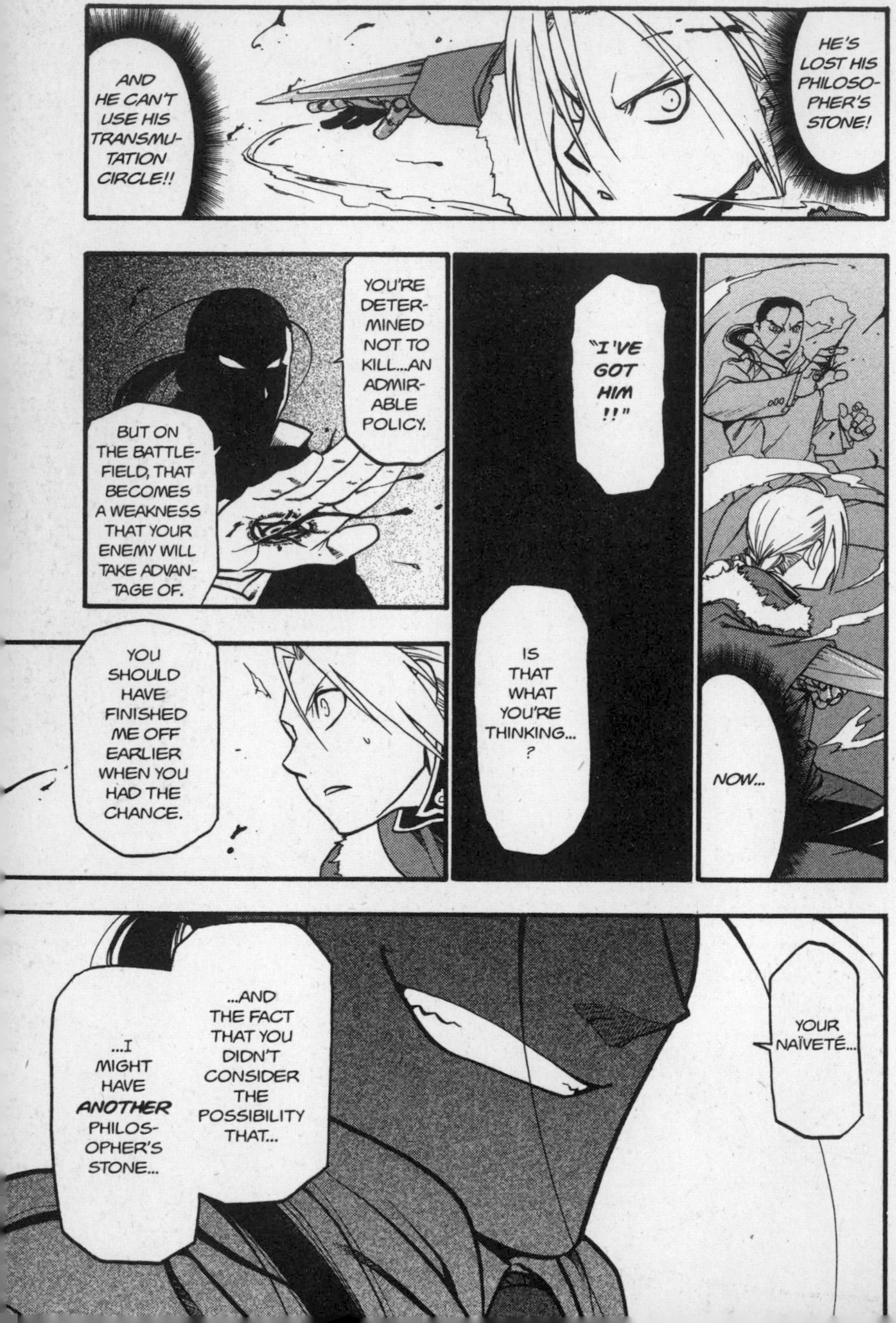
HE'S LOST HIS PHILOSOPHER'S STONE!
AND HE CAN'T USE HIS TRANSMUTATION CIRCLE!!
NOW...
"I'VE GOT HIM!!"
IS THAT WHAT YOU'RE THINKING...?
YOU'RE DETERMINED NOT TO KILL...AN ADMIRABLE POLICY.
BUT ON THE BATTLEFIELD, THAT BECOMES A WEAKNESS THAT YOUR ENEMY WILL TAKE ADVANTAGE OF.
YOU SHOULD HAVE FINISHED ME OFF EARLIER WHEN YOU HAD THE CHANCE.
YOUR NAÏVETÉ...
...AND THE FACT THAT YOU DIDN'T CONSIDER THE POSSIBILITY THAT...
...I MIGHT HAVE ANOTHER PHILOSOPHER'S STONE...

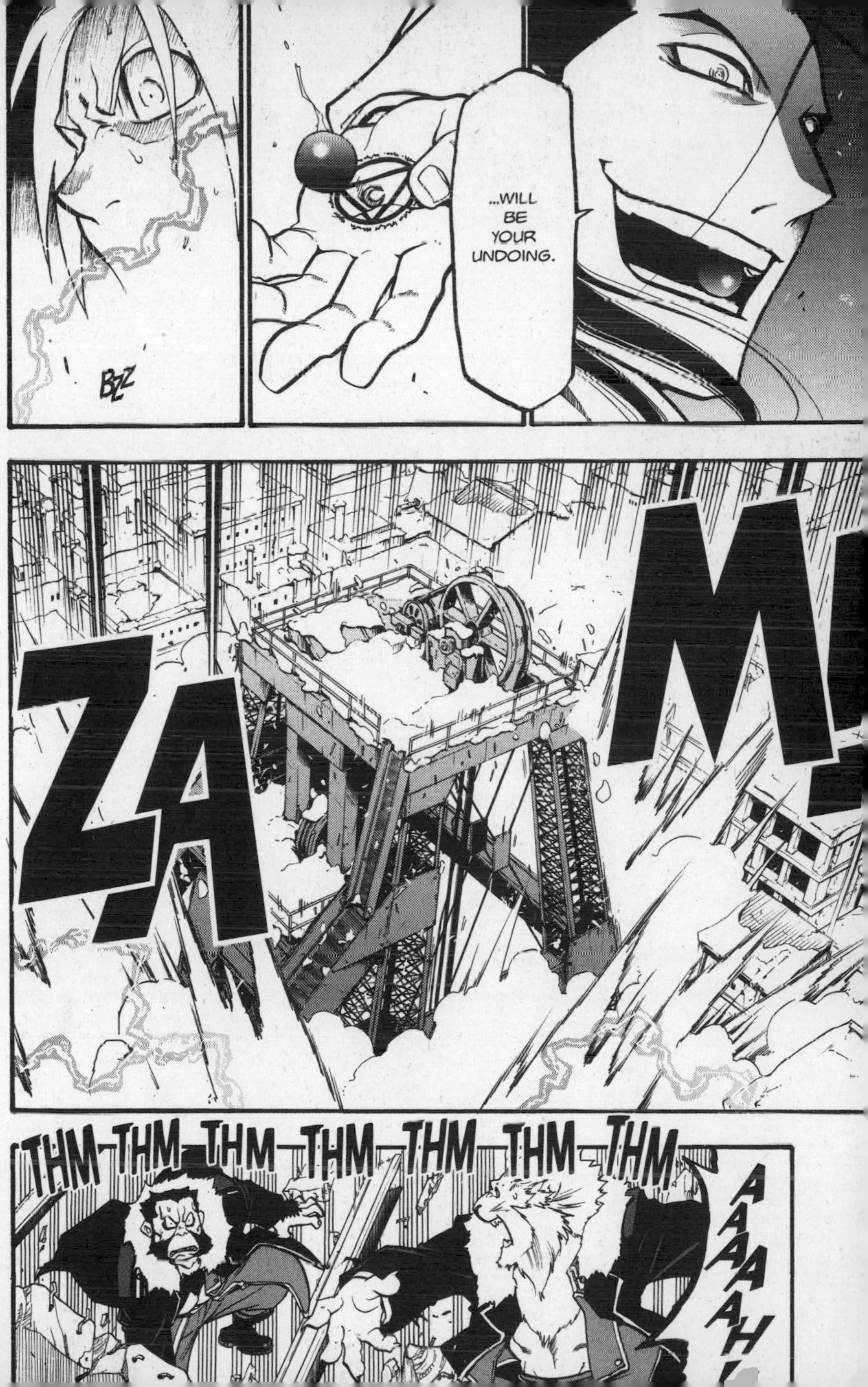
...WILL BE YOUR UNDOING.
BZZ
ZAM!
THM THM THM THM THM THM THM
AAAAAH!

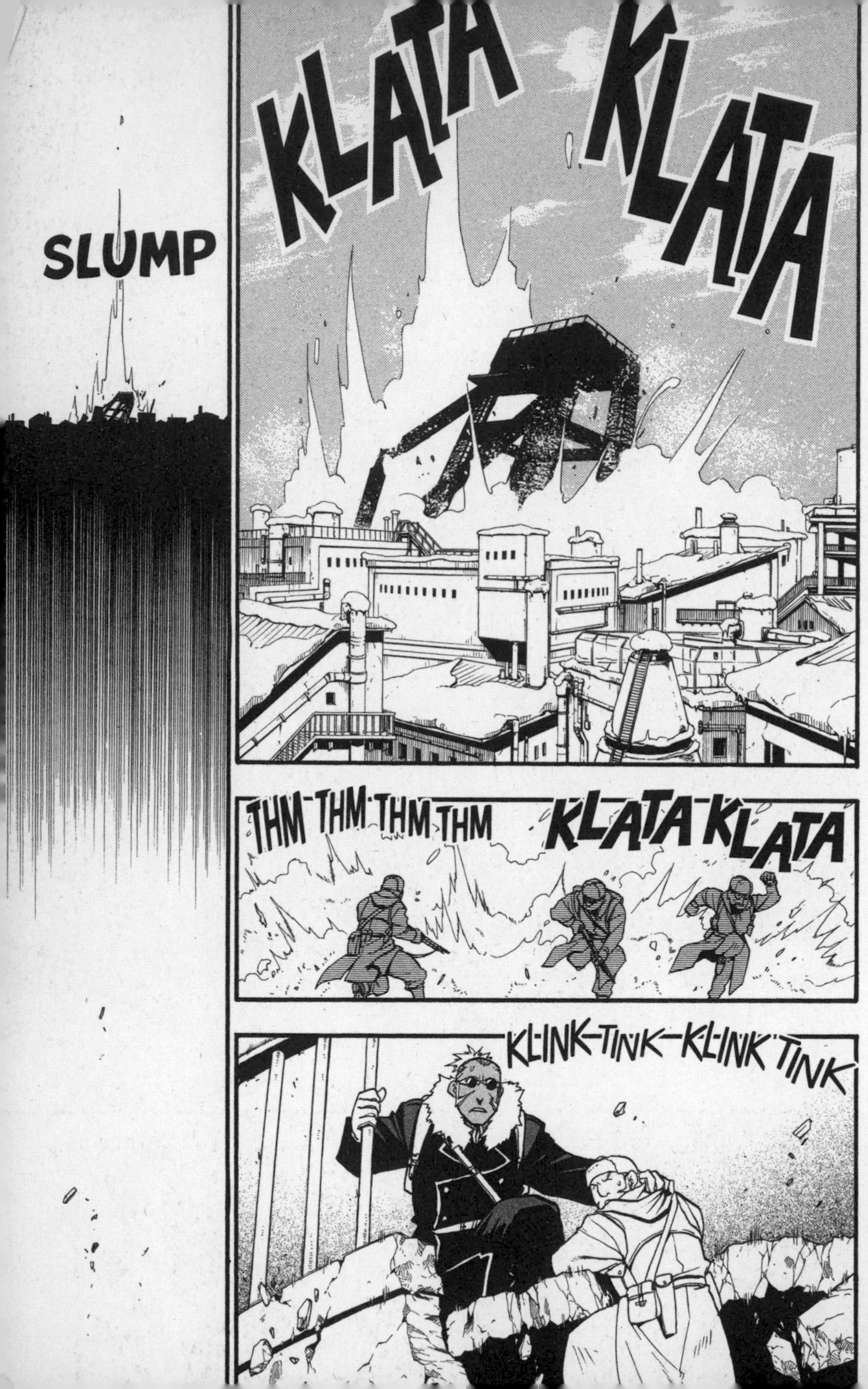
KLATA KLATA
KLATA KLATA
THM THM THM THM
KLINK TINK KLINK TINK
SLUMP

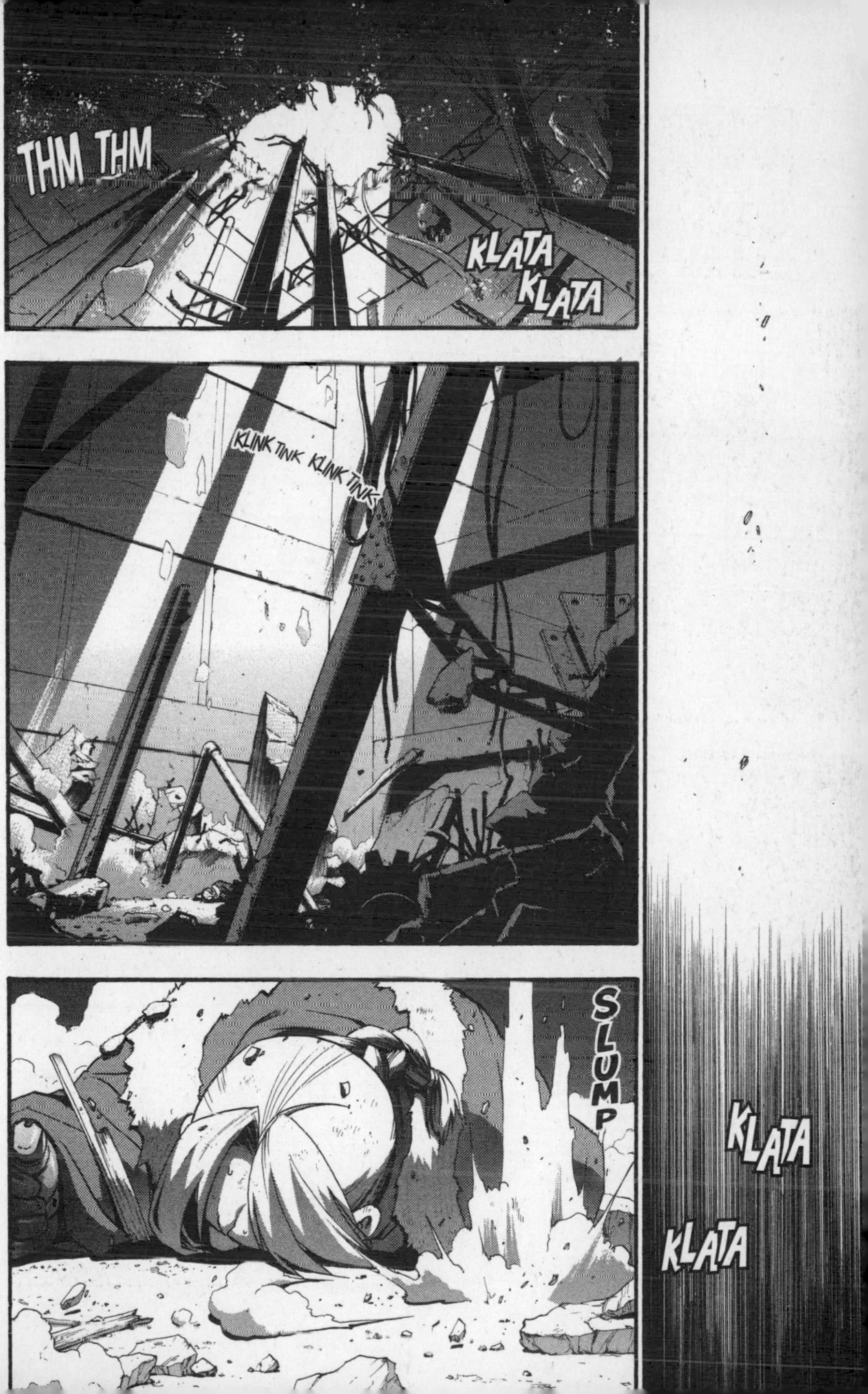
THM THM
KLATA KLATA
KLINK TINK KLINK TINK
KLATA
KLATA
SLUMP

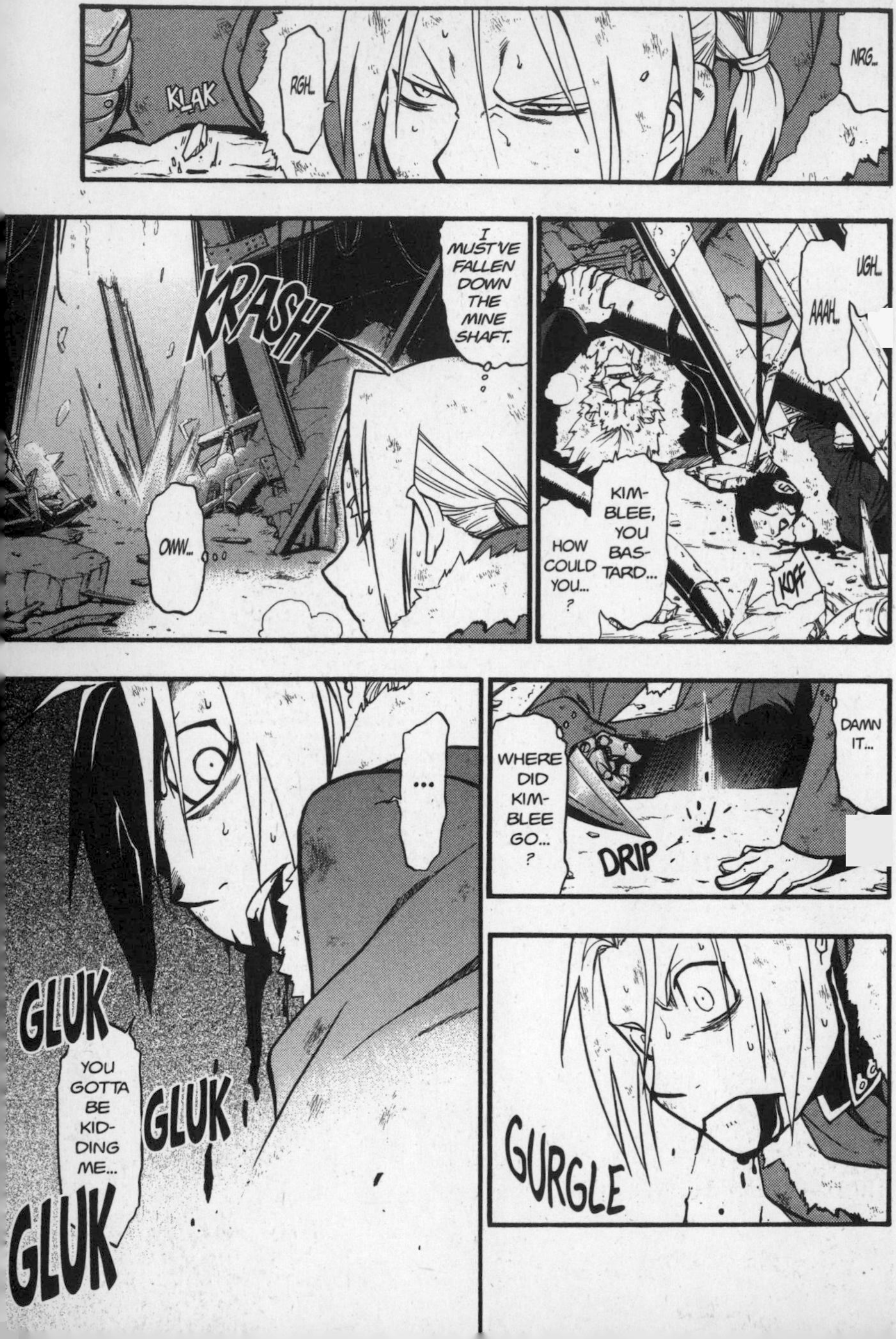
NRG...
RGH...
KLAK
UGH...
AAAH...
KIMBLEE, YOU BASTARD...
HOW COULD YOU...?
KOFF
I MUST'VE FALLEN DOWN THE MINE SHAFT.
KRASH
OWW...
DAMN IT...
WHERE DID KIMBLEE GO...?
DRIP
GURGLE
...
GLUK
YOU GOTTA BE KIDDING ME...
GLUK
GLUK

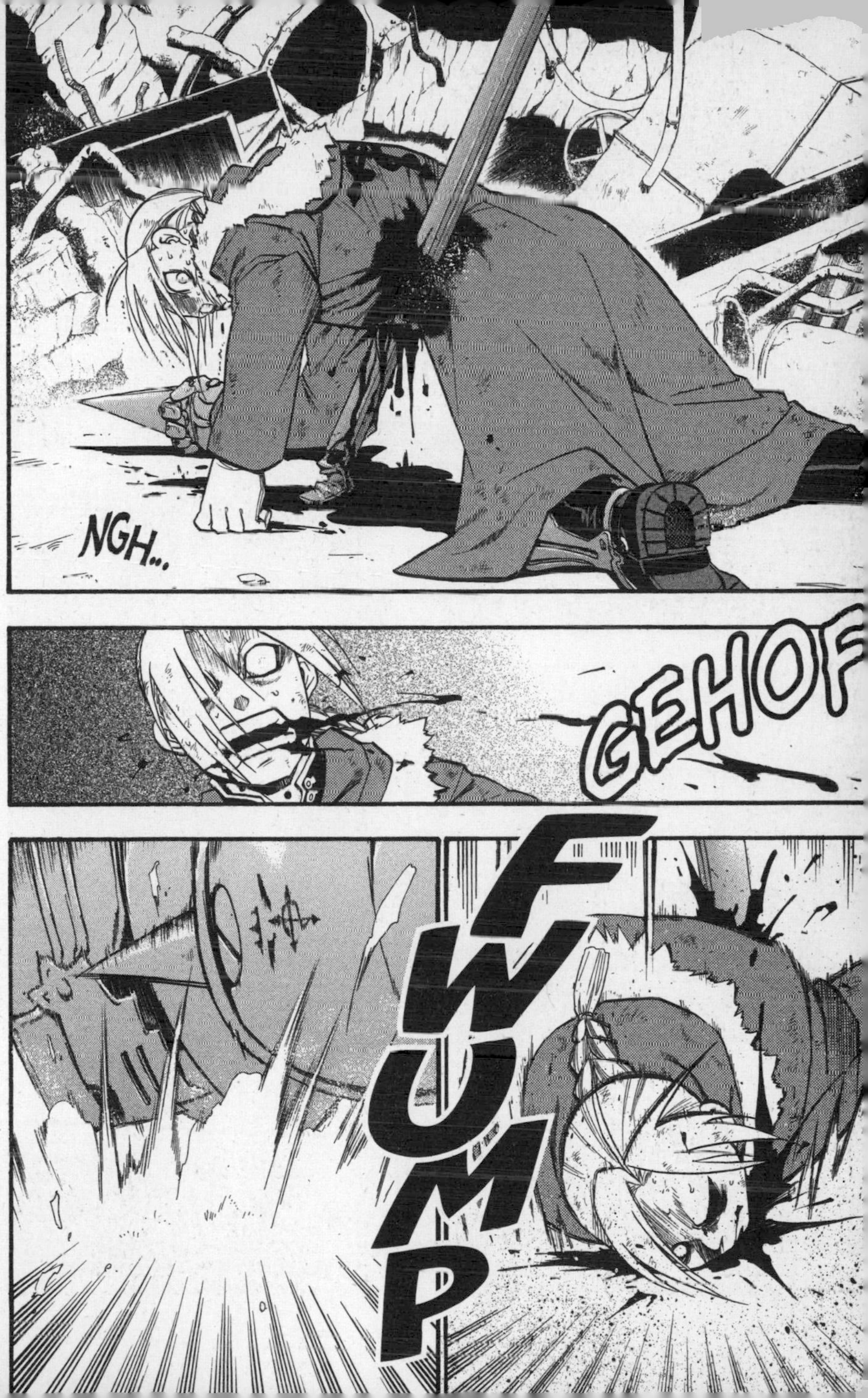
NGH...
GEHOF
FWUMP

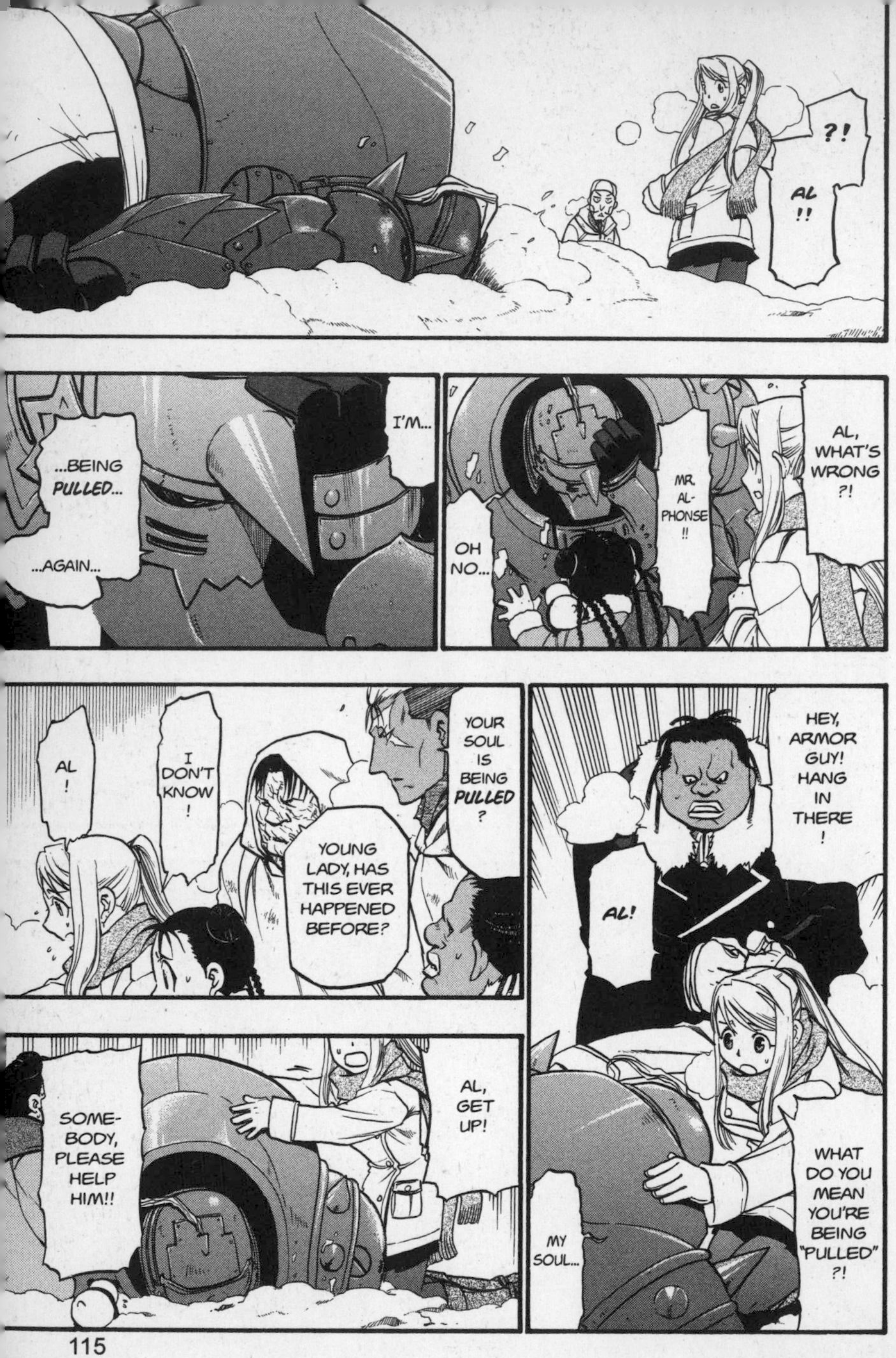
?!
AL !!
AL, WHAT'S WRONG ?!
MR. AL-PHONSE !!
OH NO...
I'M...
...BEING PULLED...
...AGAIN...
HEY, ARMOR GUY! HANG IN THERE !
AL!
WHAT DO YOU MEAN YOU'RE BEING "PULLED" ?!
MY SOUL...
YOUR SOUL IS BEING PULLED ?
YOUNG LADY, HAS THIS EVER HAPPENED BEFORE?
I DON'T KNOW !
AL !
AL, GET UP!
SOME-BODY, PLEASE HELP HIM!!

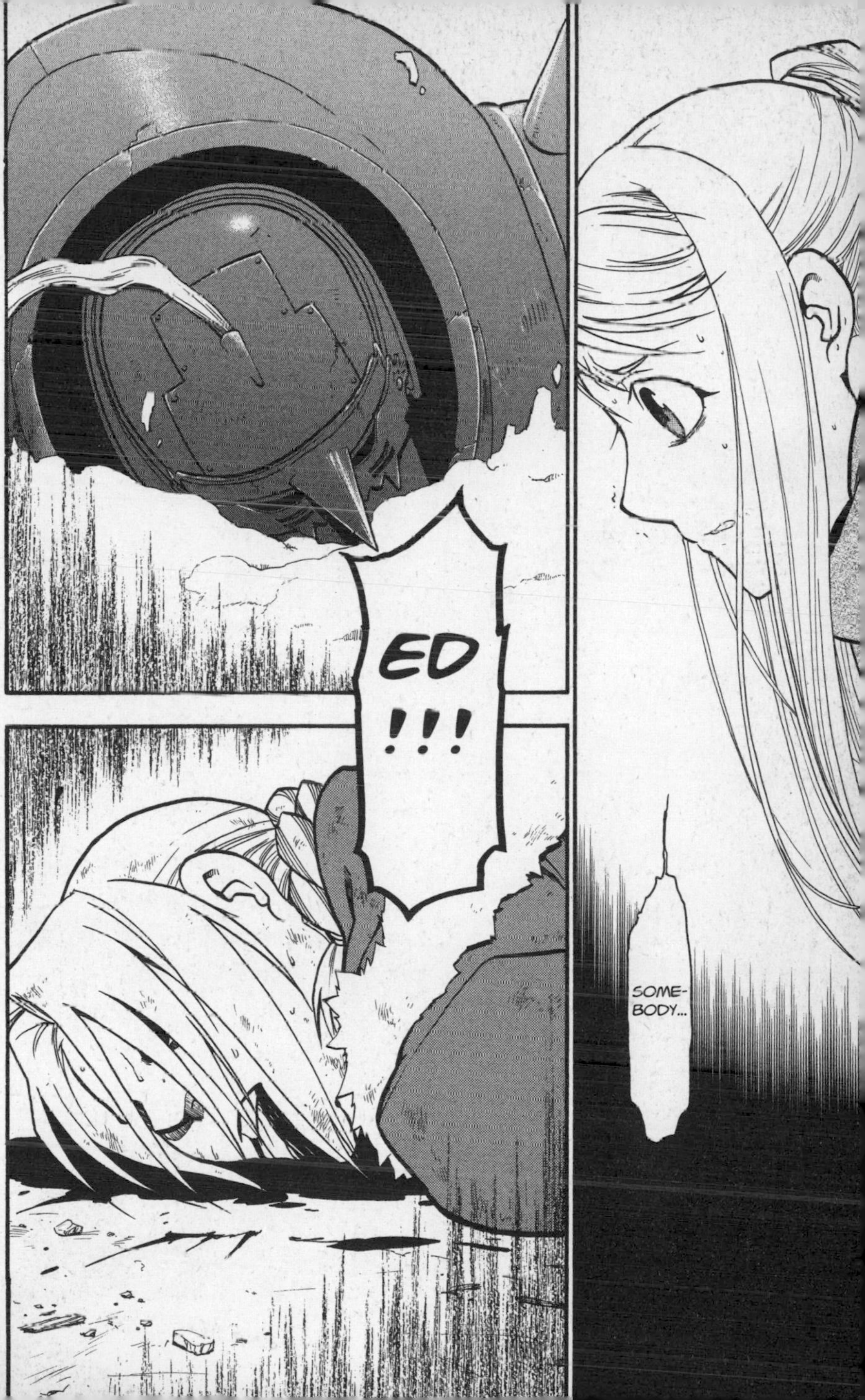
SOME-BODY...
ED!!!

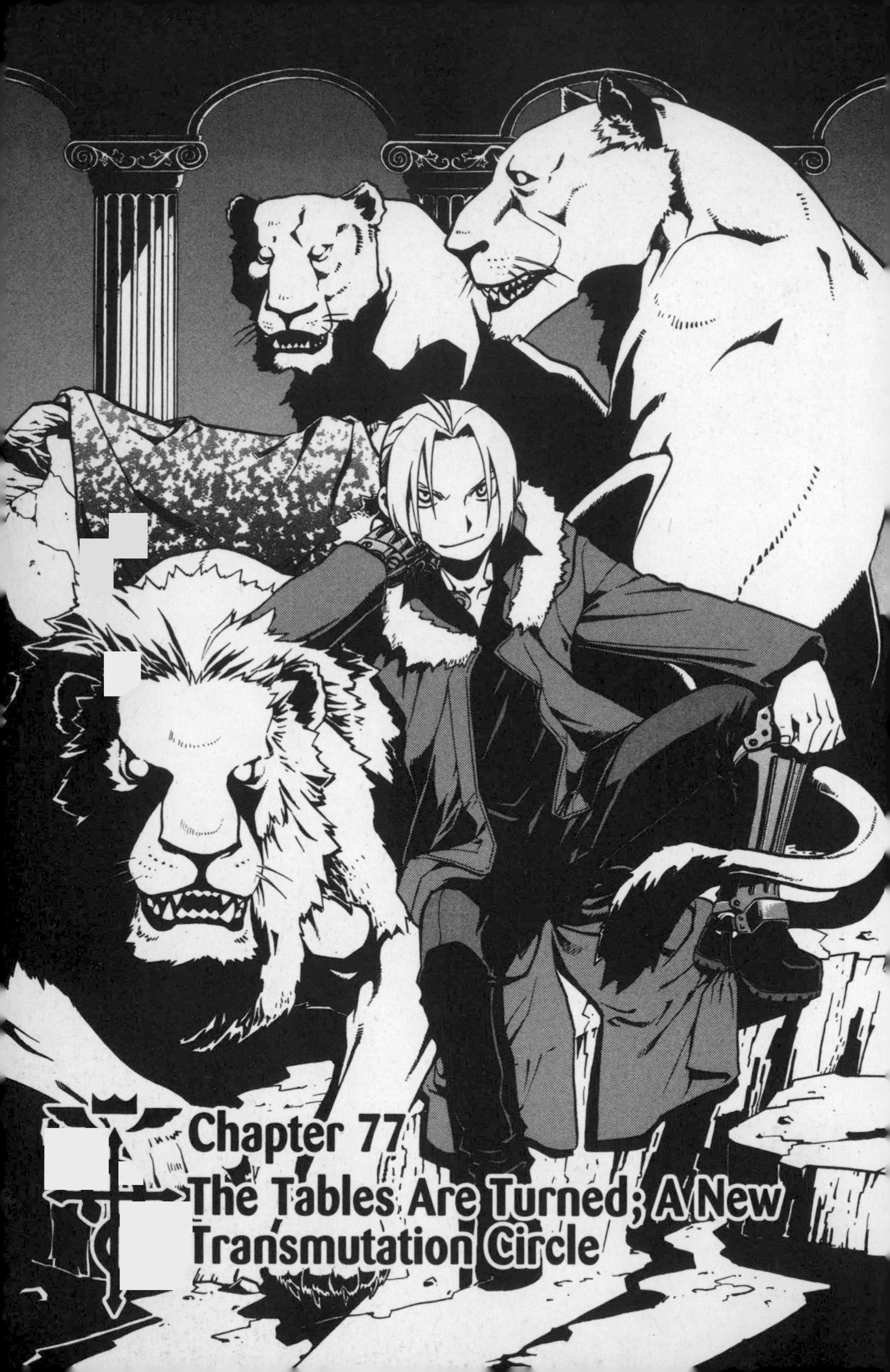

Chapter 77
The Tables Are Turned; A New Transmutation Circle

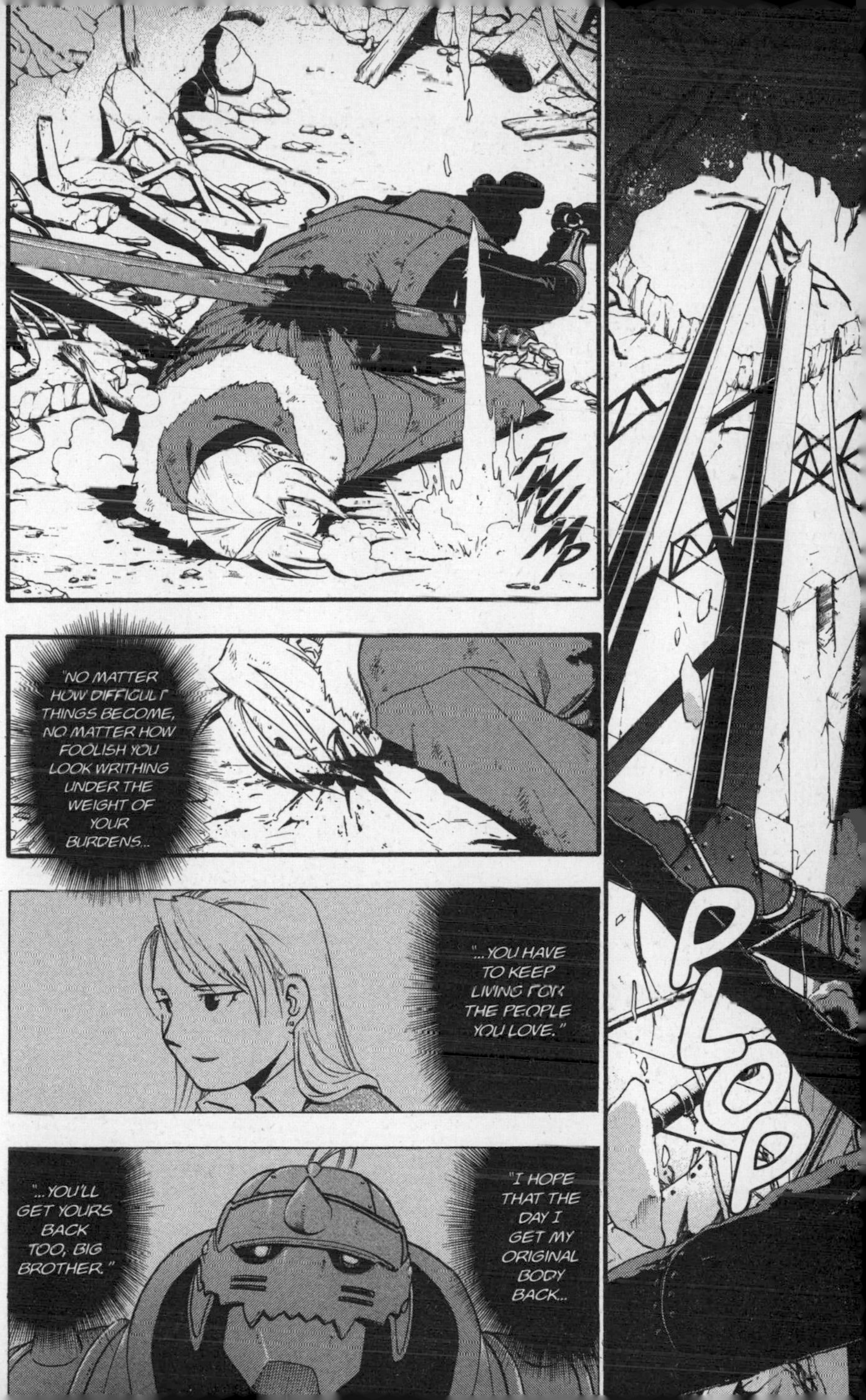
PLOP
FWUMP
"NO MATTER HOW DIFFICULT THINGS BECOME, NO MATTER HOW FOOLISH YOU LOOK WRITHING UNDER THE WEIGHT OF YOUR BURDENS...
"...YOU HAVE TO KEEP LIVING FOR THE PEOPLE YOU LOVE."
"I HOPE THAT THE DAY I GET MY ORIGINAL BODY BACK...
"...YOU'LL GET YOURS BACK TOO, BIG BROTHER."

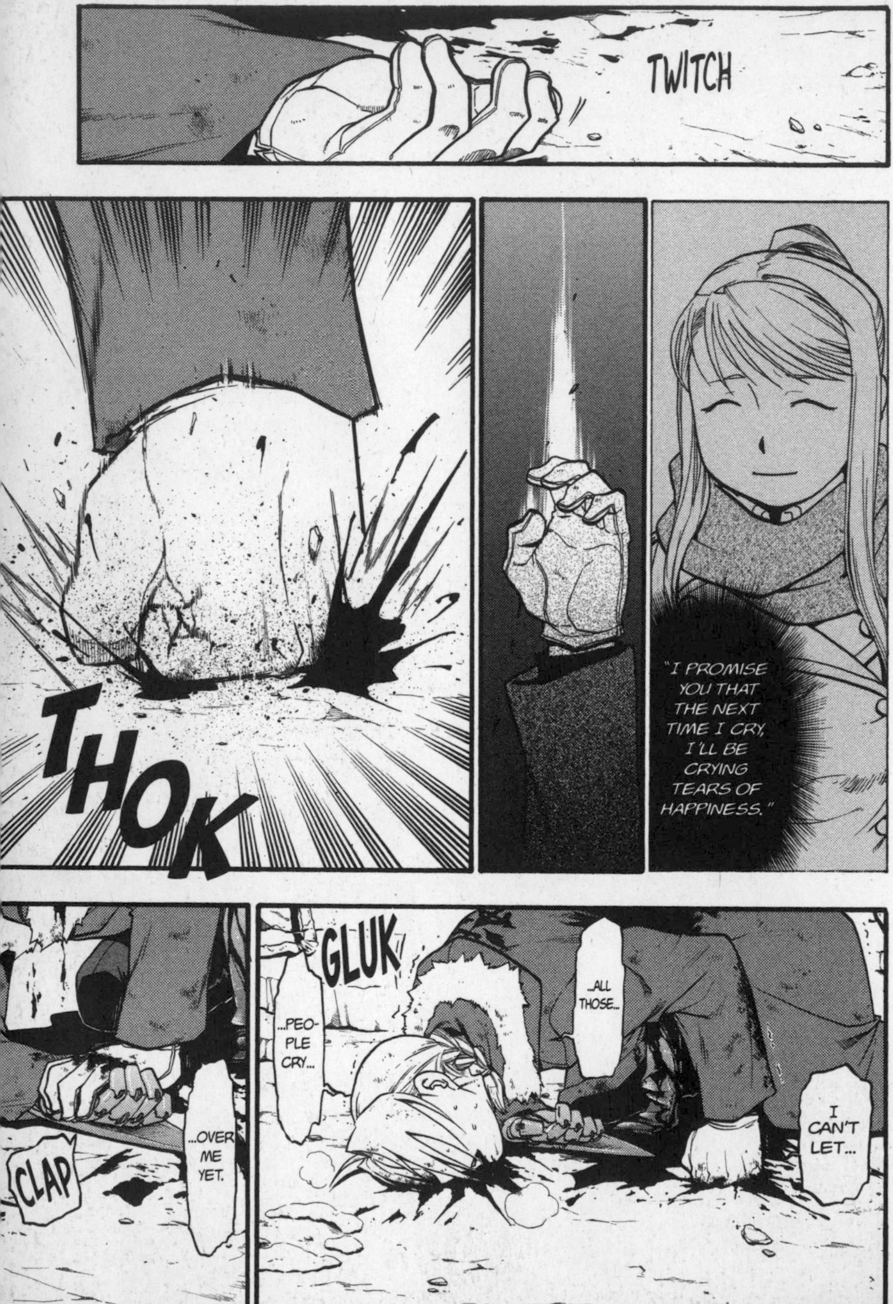
TWITCH
"I PROMISE YOU THAT THE NEXT TIME I CRY, I'LL BE CRYING TEARS OF HAPPINESS."
THOK
GLUK
I CAN'T LET...
...ALL THOSE...
...PEO-PLE CRY...
...OVER ME YET.
CLAP

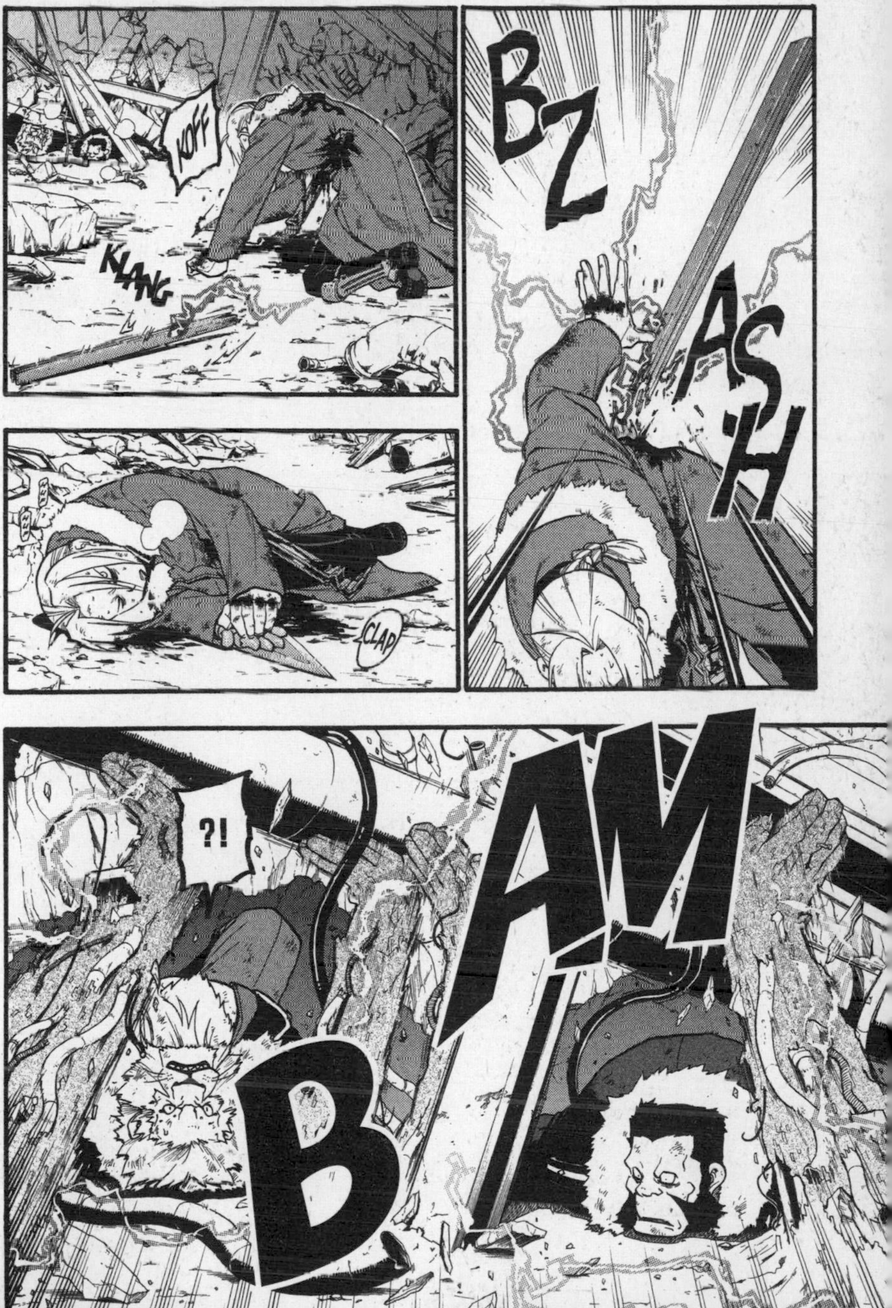
BZ
ASH
KOFF
KLANG
CLAP
BAM
?!

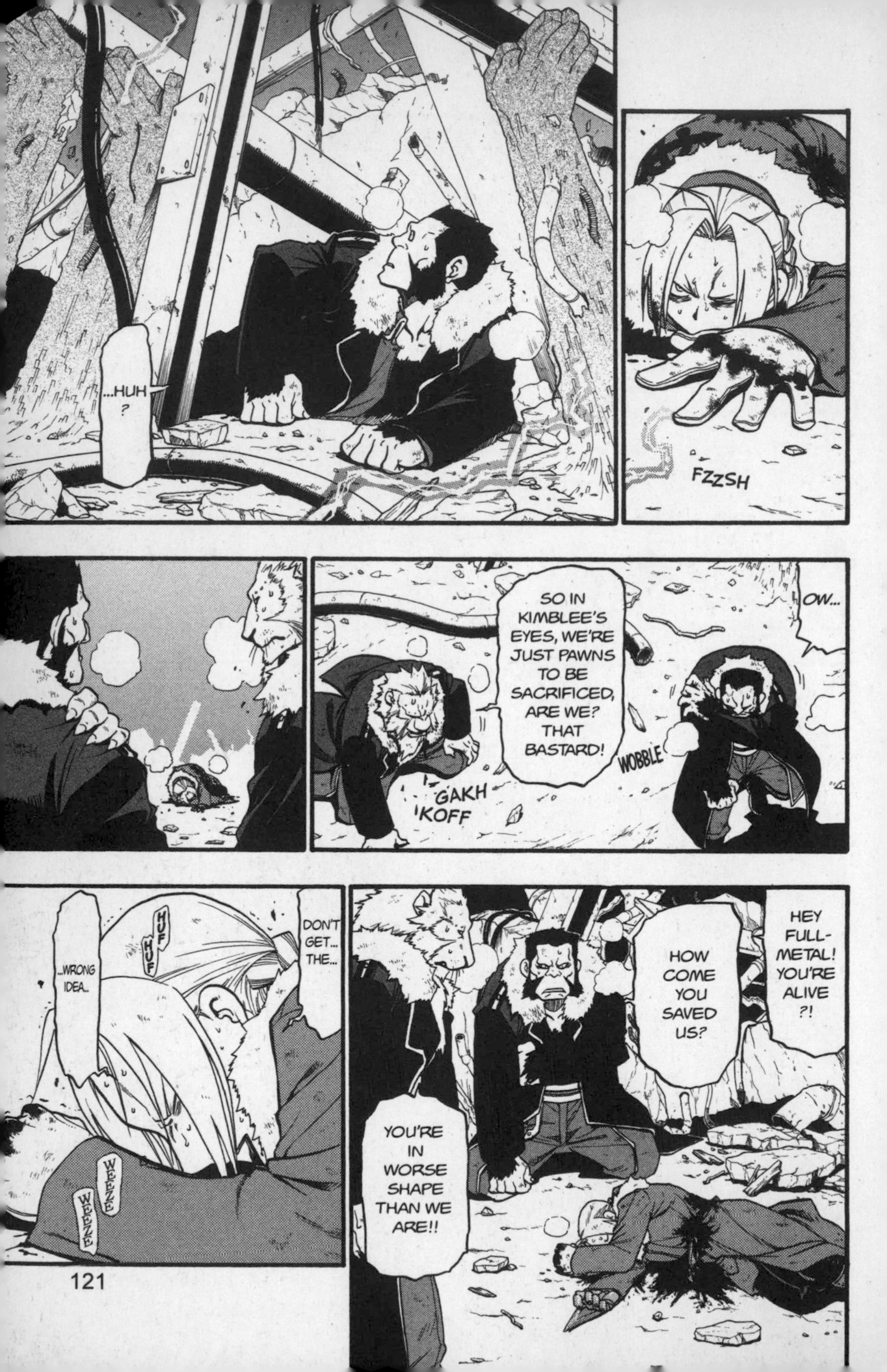
FZZSH
...HUH ?
OW...
SO IN KIMBLEE'S EYES, WE'RE JUST PAWNS TO BE SACRIFICED, ARE WE? THAT BASTARD!
WOBBLE
GAKH KOFF
HEY FULL-METAL! YOU'RE ALIVE ?!
HOW COME YOU SAVED US?
YOU'RE IN WORSE SHAPE THAN WE ARE!!
DON'T GET... THE...
HUF HUF
...WRONG IDEA...
WEEZE WEEZE

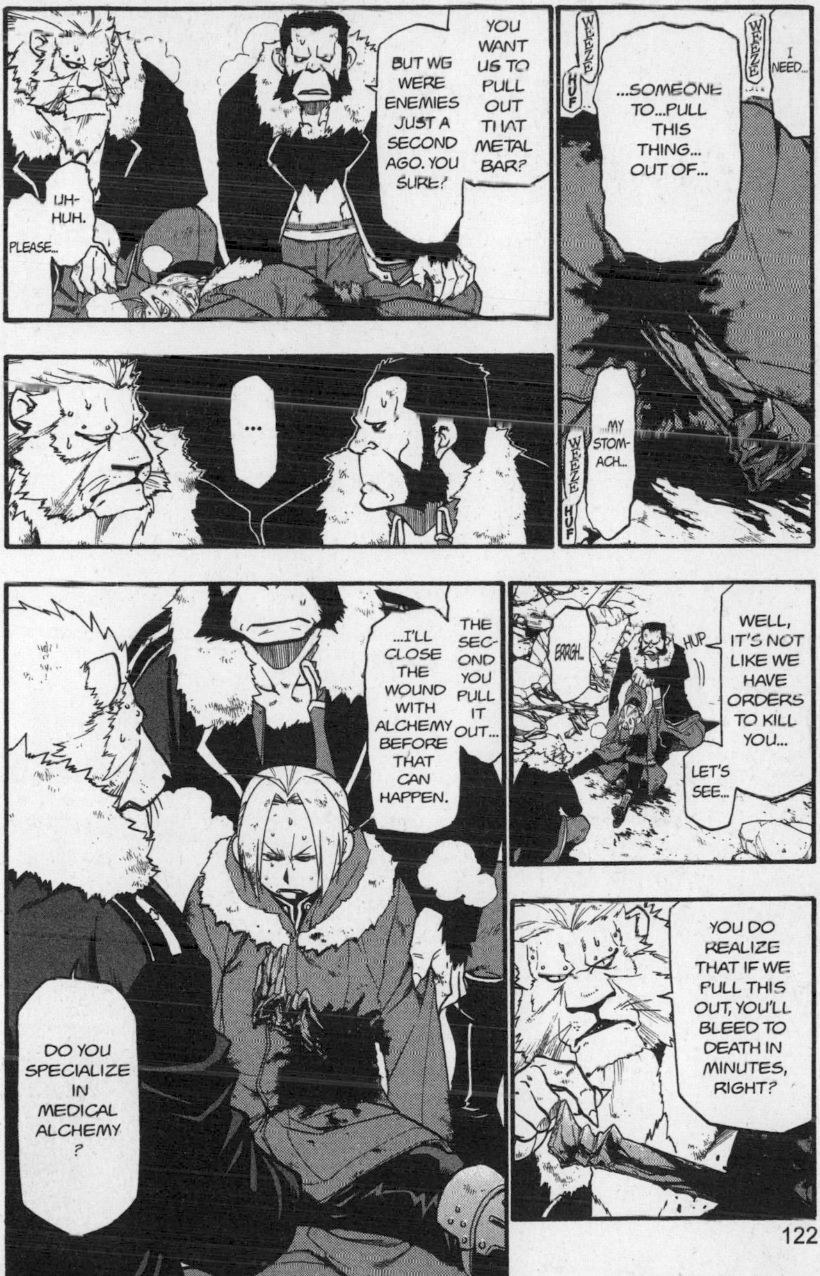

WEEZE
I NEED...
...SOMEONE TO...PULL THIS THING... OUT OF...
WEEZE HUF
...MY STOMACH...
WEEZE HUF
YOU WANT US TO PULL OUT THAT METAL BAR?
BUT WE WERE ENEMIES JUST A SECOND AGO. YOU SURE?
UH-HUH.
PLEASE...
...
WELL, IT'S NOT LIKE WE HAVE ORDERS TO KILL YOU...
HUP
ERRGH.
LET'S SEE...
YOU DO REALIZE THAT IF WE PULL THIS OUT, YOU'LL BLEED TO DEATH IN MINUTES, RIGHT?
THE SECOND YOU PULL IT OUT...
...I'LL CLOSE THE WOUND WITH ALCHEMY BEFORE THAT CAN HAPPEN.
DO YOU SPECIALIZE IN MEDICAL ALCHEMY?

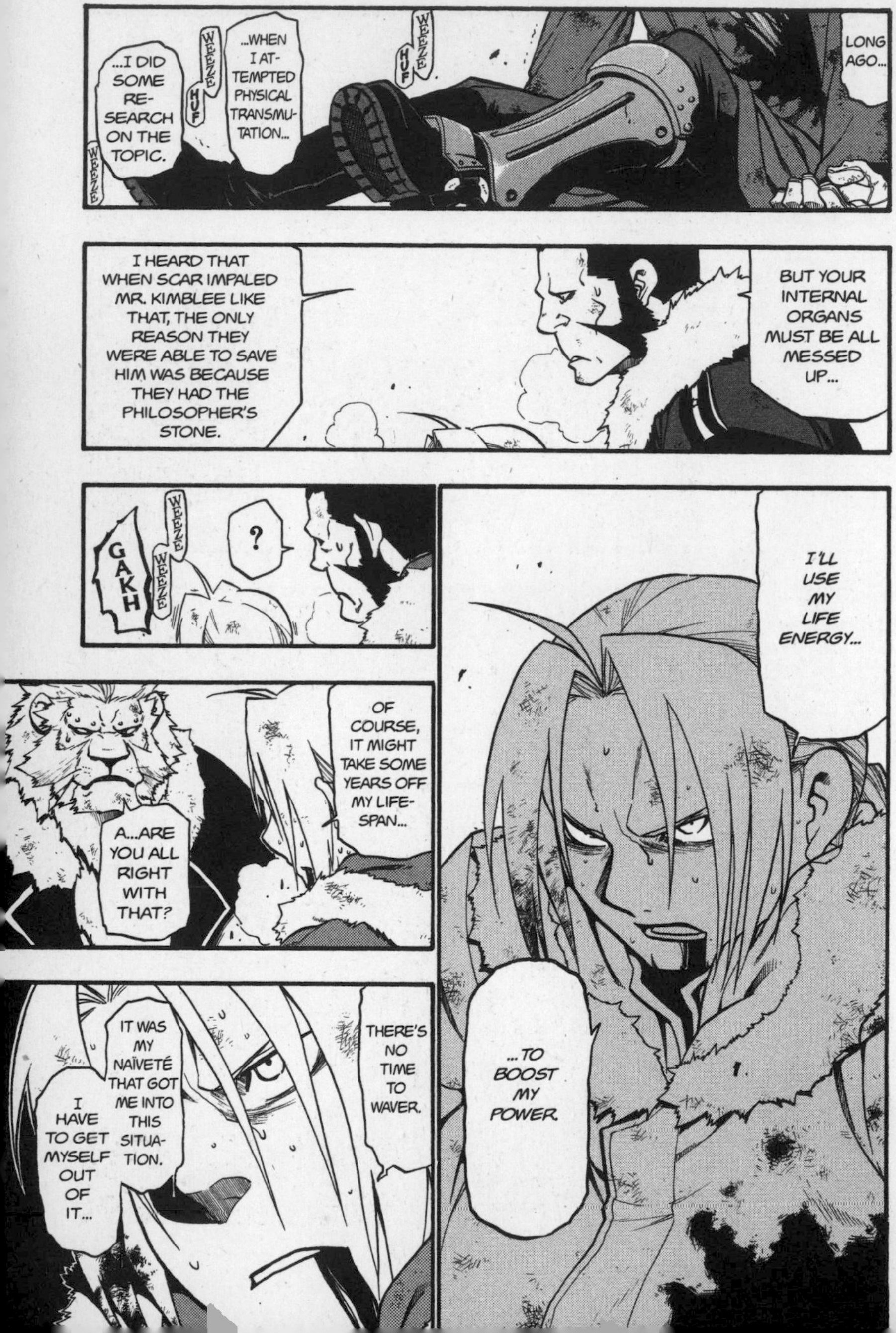
LONG AGO...
WEEZE HUF
...WHEN I ATTEMPTED PHYSICAL TRANSMUTATION...
WEEZE HUF
...I DID SOME RESEARCH ON THE TOPIC.
WEEZE
BUT YOUR INTERNAL ORGANS MUST BE ALL MESSED UP...
I HEARD THAT WHEN SCAR IMPALED MR. KIMBLEE LIKE THAT, THE ONLY REASON THEY WERE ABLE TO SAVE HIM WAS BECAUSE THEY HAD THE PHILOSOPHER'S STONE.
I'LL USE MY LIFE ENERGY...
...TO BOOST MY POWER.
?
WEEZE
WEEZE
GAKH
OF COURSE, IT MIGHT TAKE SOME YEARS OFF MY LIFESPAN...
A...ARE YOU ALL RIGHT WITH THAT?
THERE'S NO TIME TO WAVER.
IT WAS MY NAÏVETÉ THAT GOT ME INTO THIS SITUATION.
I HAVE TO GET MYSELF OUT OF IT...

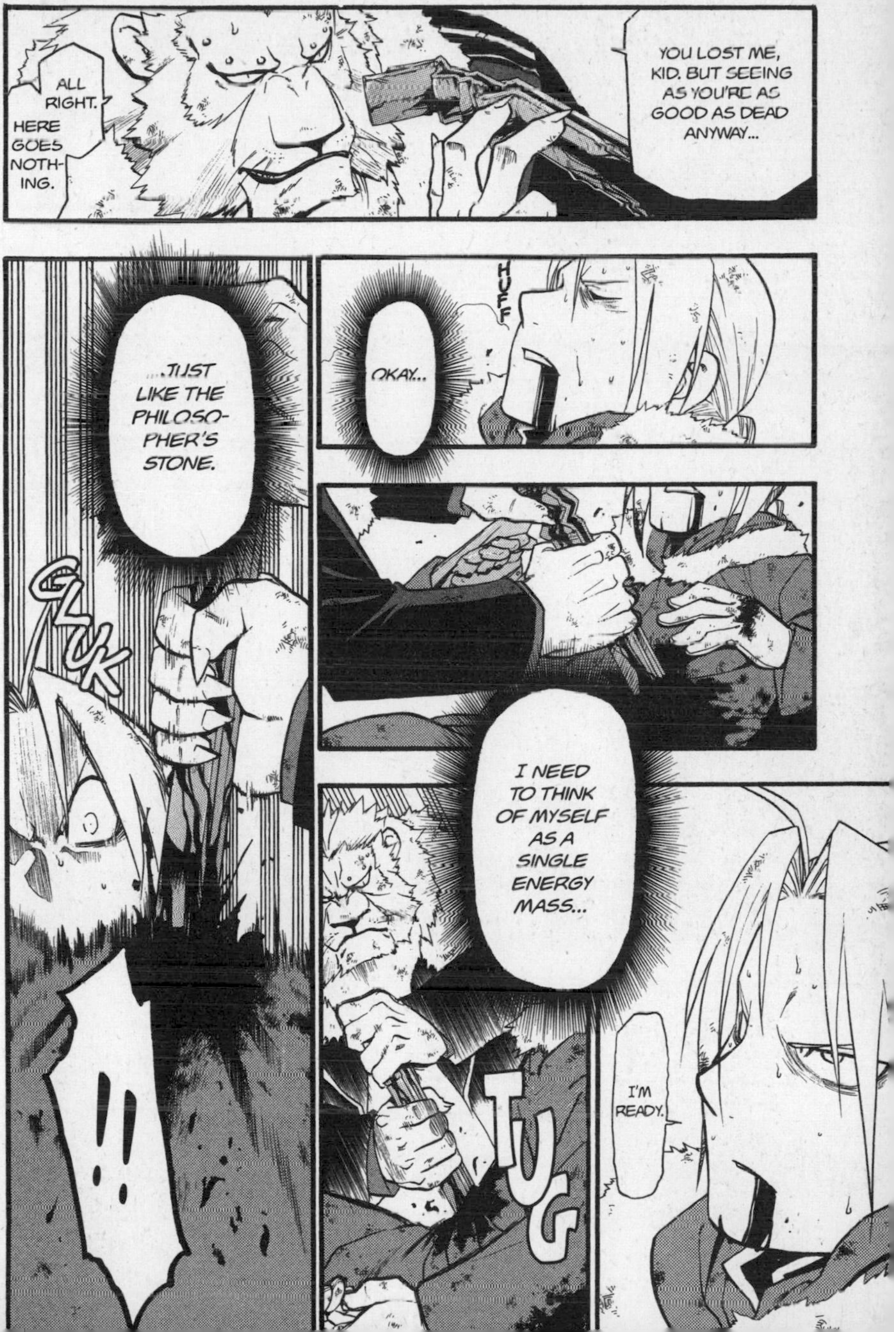
YOU LOST ME, KID. BUT SEEING AS YOU'RE AS GOOD AS DEAD ANYWAY...
ALL RIGHT. HERE GOES NOTHING.
HUFF
OKAY...
I NEED TO THINK OF MYSELF AS A SINGLE ENERGY MASS...
I'M READY.
TUG
...JUST LIKE THE PHILOSOPHER'S STONE.
GLUK
!!

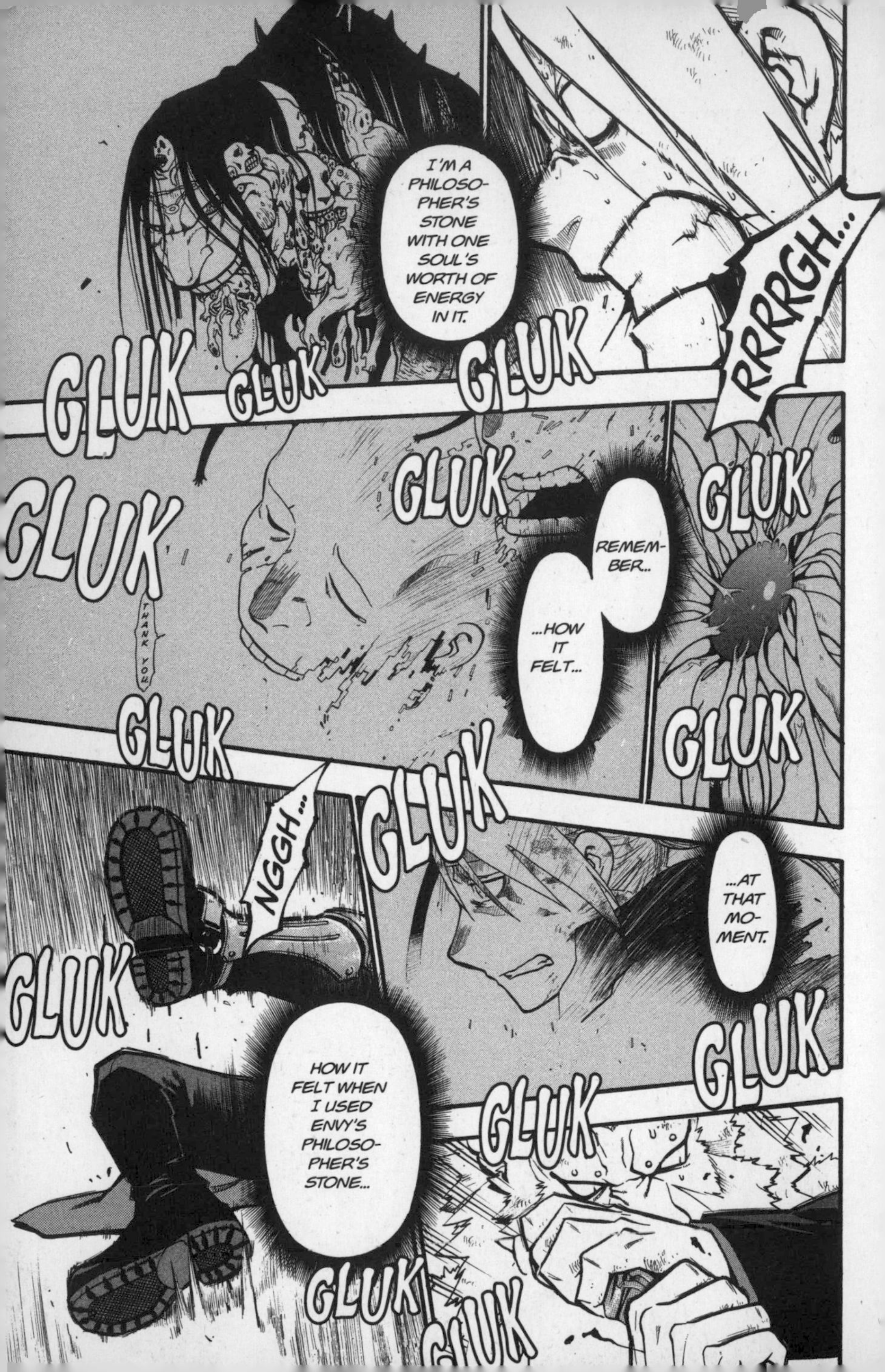
RRRRGH...
I'M A PHILOSOPHER'S STONE WITH ONE SOUL'S WORTH OF ENERGY IN IT.
GLUK
GLUK
GLUK
GLUK
GLUK
GLUK
REMEMBER...
...HOW IT FELT...
GLUK
THANK YOU
GLUK
...AT THAT MOMENT.
GLUK
GLUK
NGGH...
GLUK
HOW IT FELT WHEN I USED ENVY'S PHILOSOPHER'S STONE...
GLUK
GLUK
GLUK

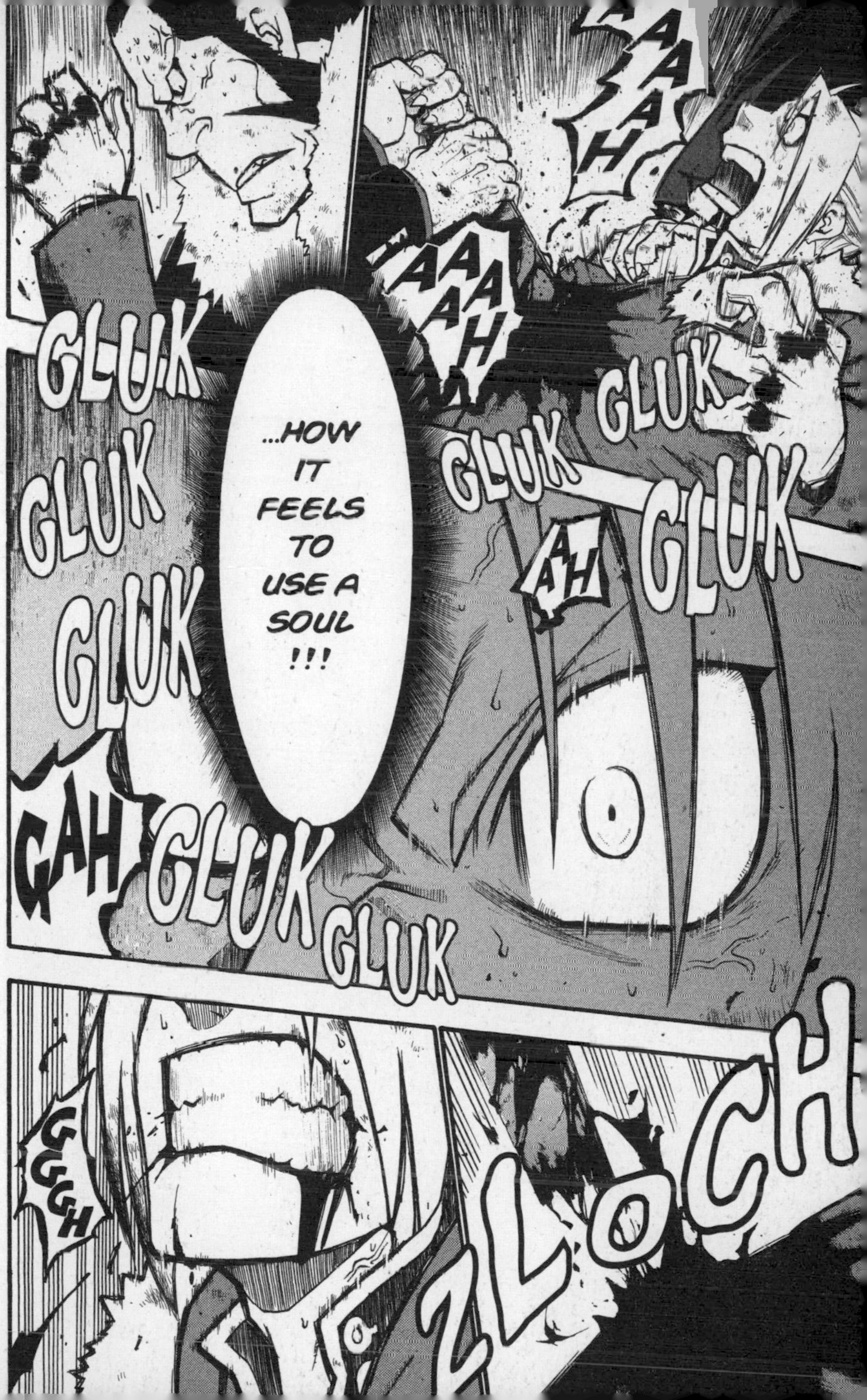
AAAAH
AAAAH
GLUK GLUK
GLUK GLUK
GLUK GLUK
...HOW IT FEELS TO USE A SOUL!!!
GLUK GLUK
AH
GAH GLUK GLUK
ZLOOCH
GGGH

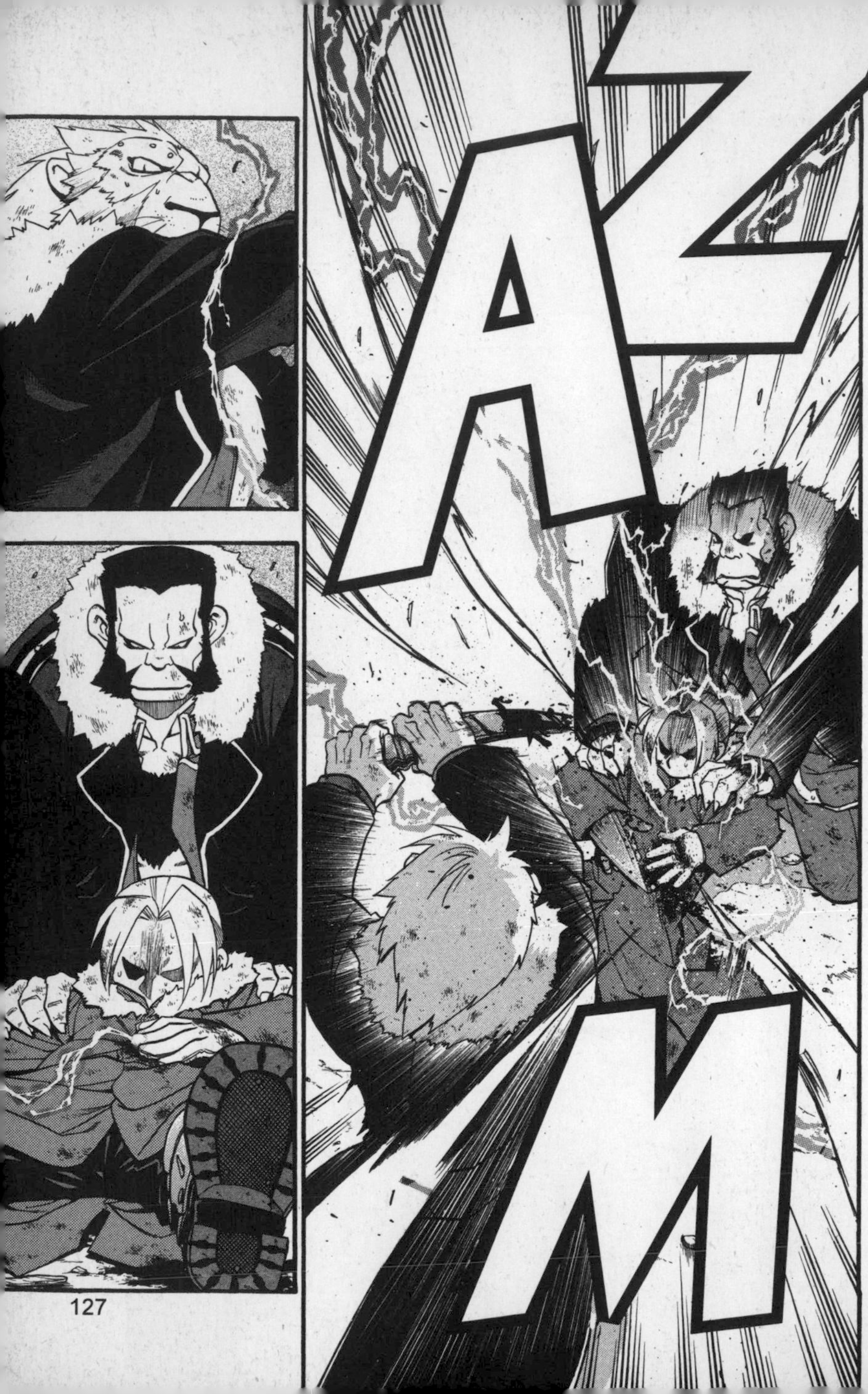
ZAM

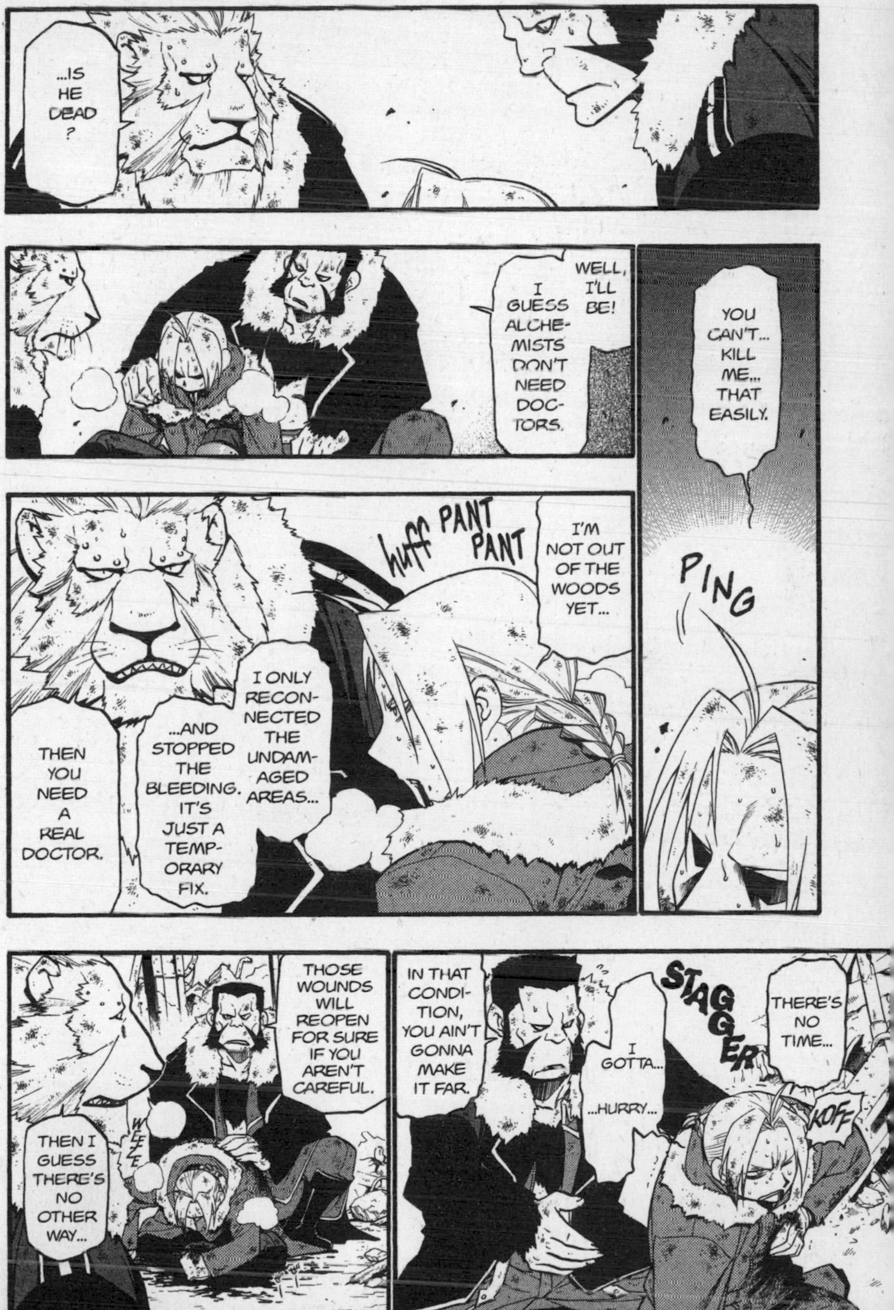
...IS HE DEAD ?
YOU CAN'T... KILL ME... THAT EASILY.
PING
WELL, I'LL BE!
I GUESS ALCHEMISTS DON'T NEED DOCTORS.
I'M NOT OUT OF THE WOODS YET...
huff PANT PANT
I ONLY RECONNECTED THE UNDAMAGED AREAS...
...AND STOPPED THE BLEEDING. IT'S JUST A TEMPORARY FIX.
THEN YOU NEED A REAL DOCTOR.
THERE'S NO TIME...
STAGGER
I GOTTA...
...HURRY...
KOFF
IN THAT CONDITION, YOU AIN'T GONNA MAKE IT FAR.
THOSE WOUNDS WILL REOPEN FOR SURE IF YOU AREN'T CAREFUL.
WHEEZE
THEN I GUESS THERE'S NO OTHER WAY...

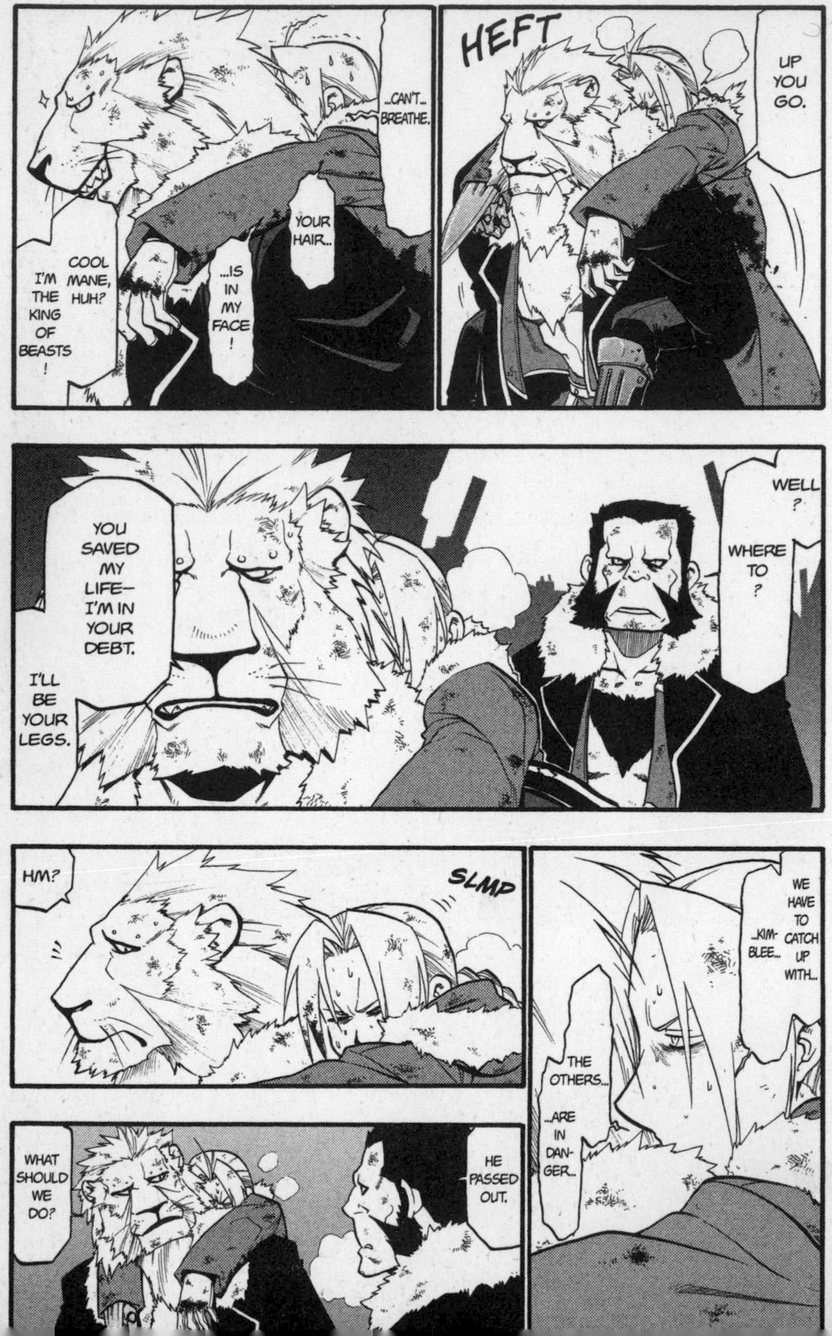
HEFT
UP YOU GO.
...CAN'T... BREATHE.
YOUR HAIR...
...IS IN MY FACE!
COOL MANE, HUH?
I'M THE KING OF BEASTS!
WELL?
WHERE TO?
YOU SAVED MY LIFE— I'M IN YOUR DEBT.
I'LL BE YOUR LEGS.
WE HAVE TO CATCH UP WITH...
...KIM-BLEE...
THE OTHERS...
...ARE IN DAN-GER...
HM?
SLMP
HE PASSED OUT.
WHAT SHOULD WE DO?

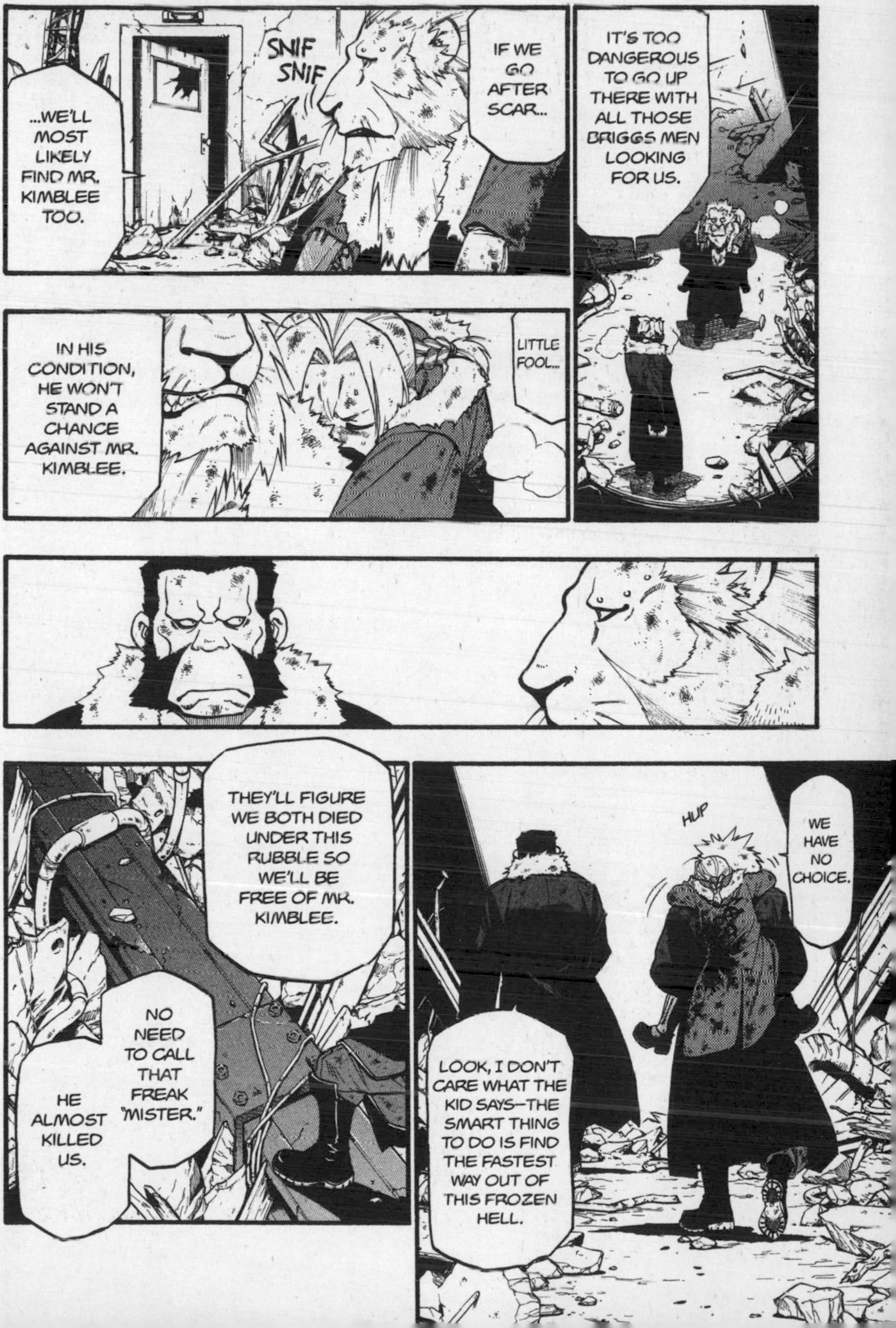
IT'S TOO DANGEROUS TO GO UP THERE WITH ALL THOSE BRIGGS MEN LOOKING FOR US.
IF WE GO AFTER SCAR...
SNIF SNIF
...WE'LL MOST LIKELY FIND MR. KIMBLEE TOO.
LITTLE FOOL...
IN HIS CONDITION, HE WON'T STAND A CHANCE AGAINST MR. KIMBLEE.
WE HAVE NO CHOICE.
HUP
LOOK, I DON'T CARE WHAT THE KID SAYS—THE SMART THING TO DO IS FIND THE FASTEST WAY OUT OF THIS FROZEN HELL.
THEY'LL FIGURE WE BOTH DIED UNDER THIS RUBBLE SO WE'LL BE FREE OF MR. KIMBLEE.
NO NEED TO CALL THAT FREAK "MISTER."
HE ALMOST KILLED US.

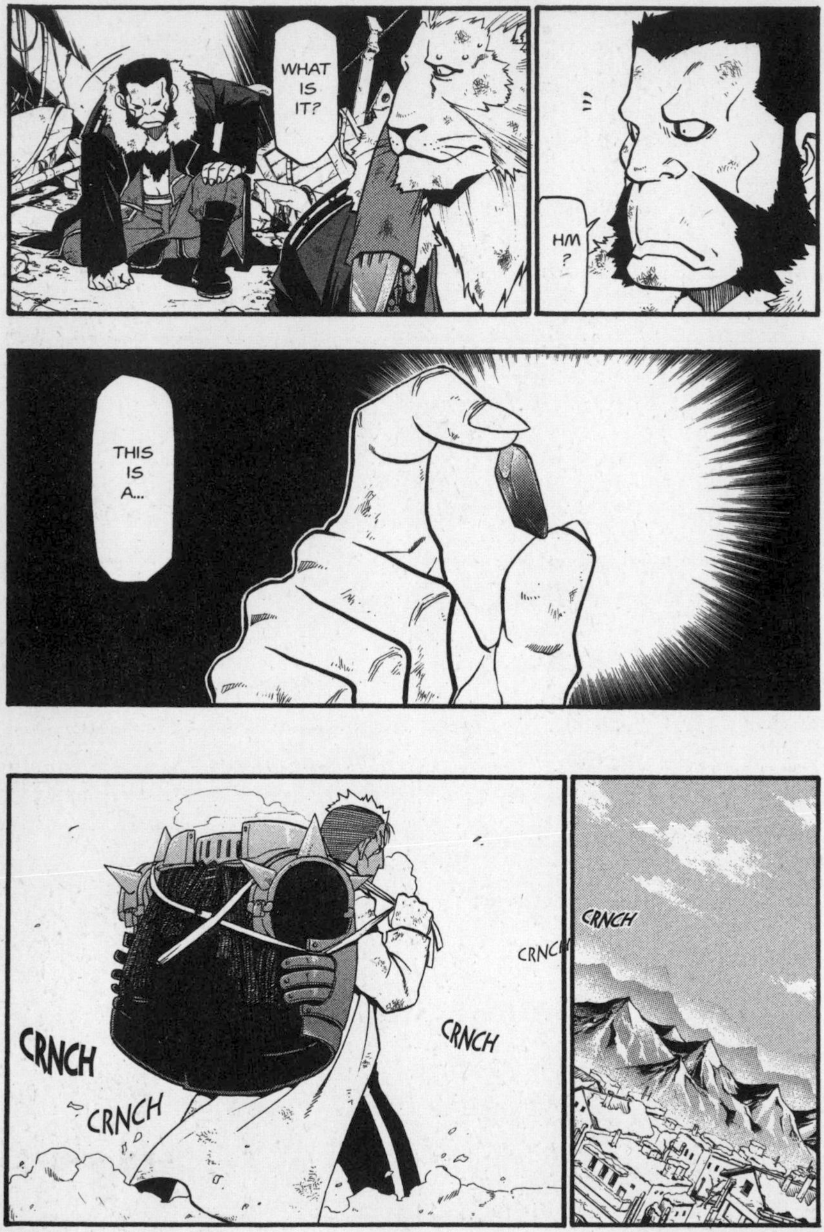
HM ?
WHAT IS IT?
THIS IS A...
CRNCH
CRNCH
CRNCH
CRNCH
CRNCH

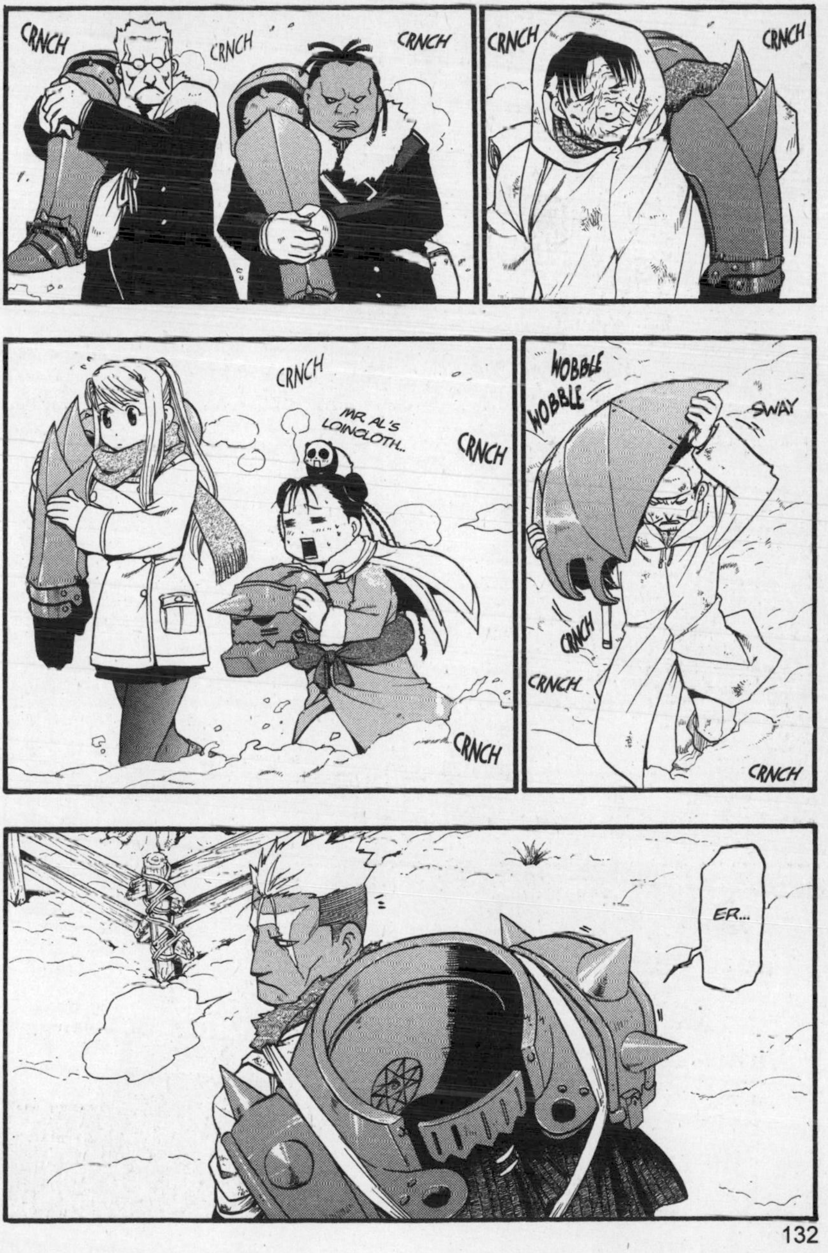
CRNCH
CRNCH
CRNCH
CRNCH
CRNCH
WOBBLE
WOBBLE
SWAY
CRNCH
CRNCH
CRNCH
CRNCH
MR. AL'S LOINCLOTH..
CRNCH
CRNCH
ER...

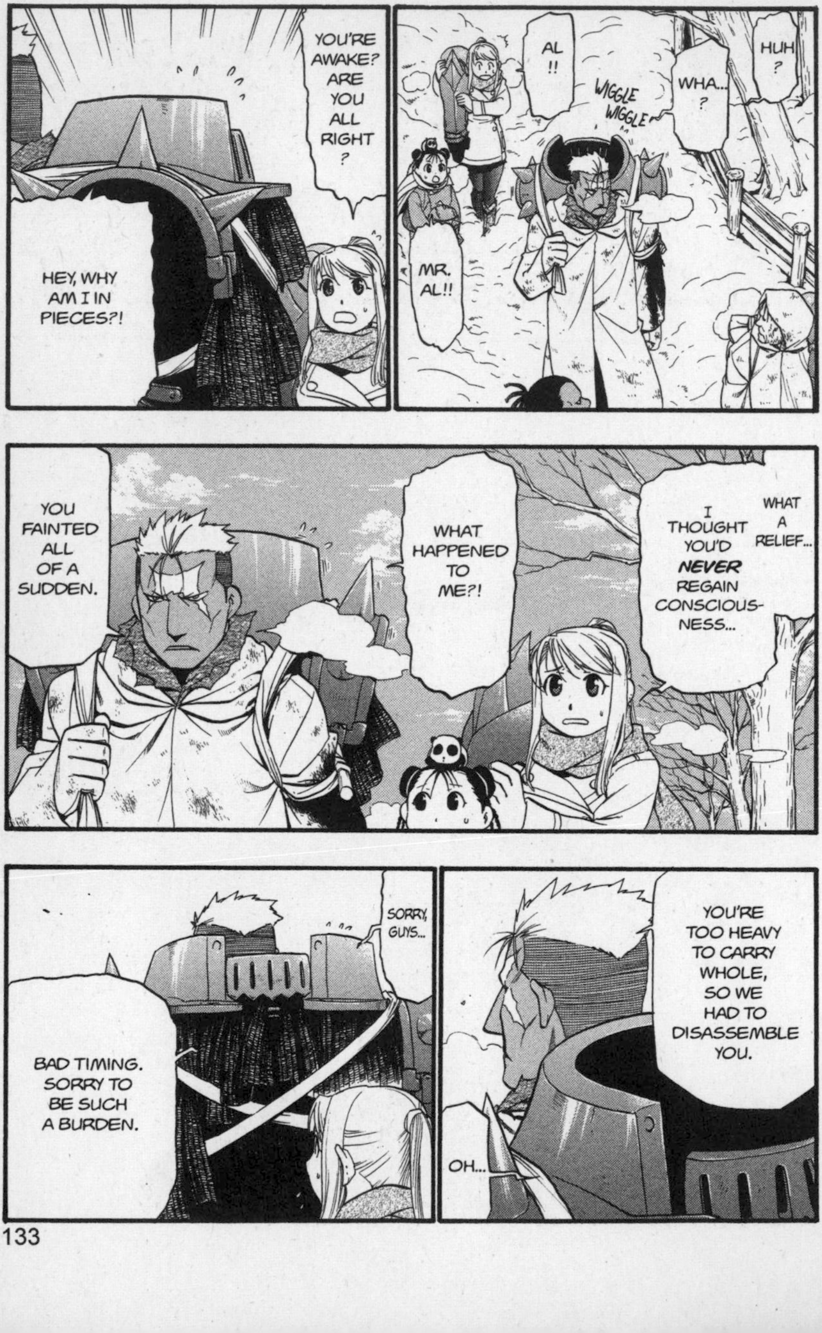
HUH?
WHA...?
WIGGLE WIGGLE
AL!!
MR. AL!!
YOU'RE AWAKE? ARE YOU ALL RIGHT?
HEY, WHY AM I IN PIECES?!
WHAT A RELIEF...
I THOUGHT YOU'D ***NEVER*** REGAIN CONSCIOUSNESS...
WHAT HAPPENED TO ME?!
YOU FAINTED ALL OF A SUDDEN.
YOU'RE TOO HEAVY TO CARRY WHOLE, SO WE HAD TO DISASSEMBLE YOU.
OH...
SORRY, GUYS...
BAD TIMING. SORRY TO BE SUCH A BURDEN.

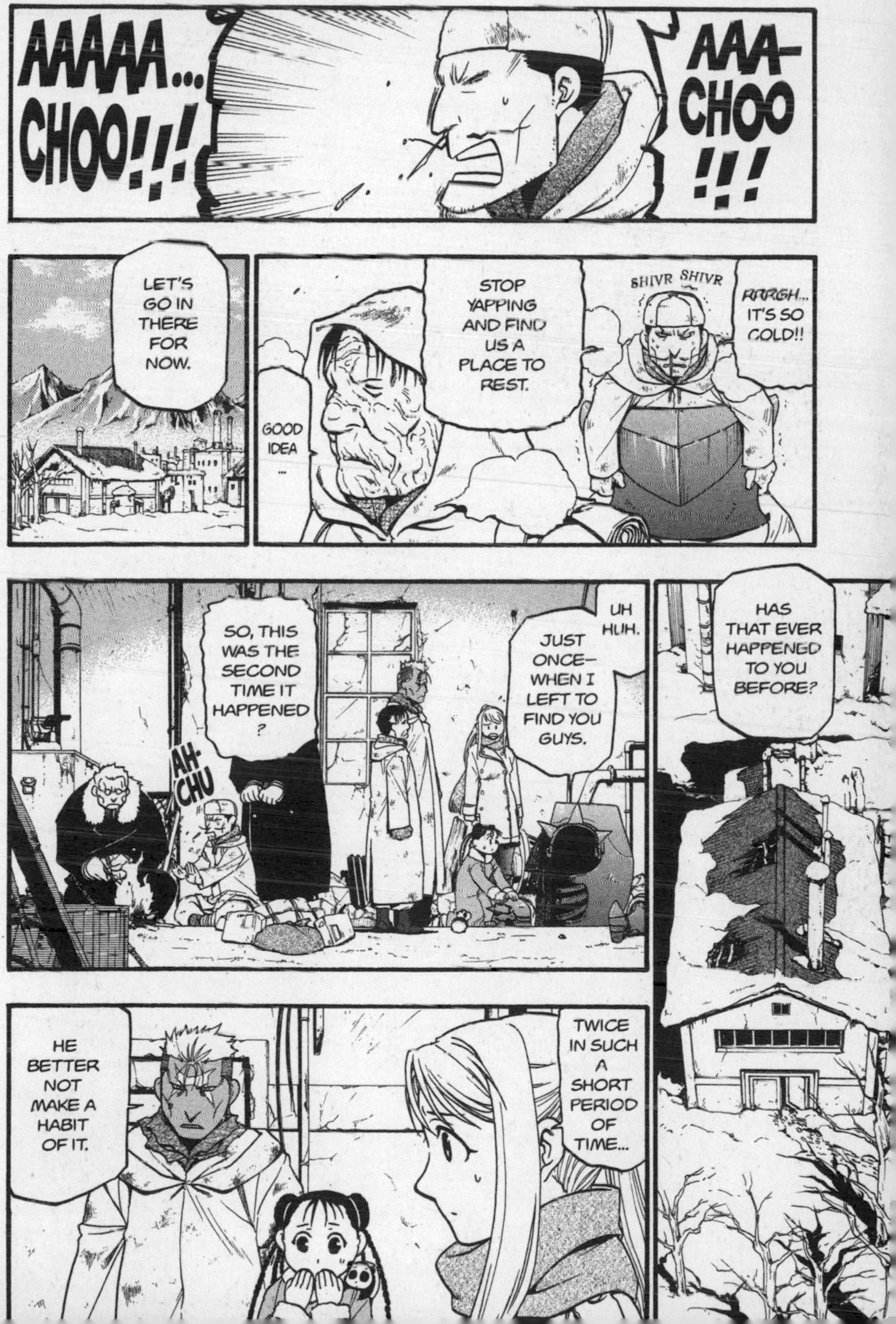
AAA-CHOO!!!
AAAAA... CHOO!!!
RRRGH... IT'S SO COLD!!
SHIVR SHIVR
STOP YAPPING AND FIND US A PLACE TO REST.
GOOD IDEA...
LET'S GO IN THERE FOR NOW.
HAS THAT EVER HAPPENED TO YOU BEFORE?
UH HUH.
JUST ONCE— WHEN I LEFT TO FIND YOU GUYS.
SO, THIS WAS THE SECOND TIME IT HAPPENED?
AH-CHU
TWICE IN SUCH A SHORT PERIOD OF TIME...
HE BETTER NOT MAKE A HABIT OF IT.

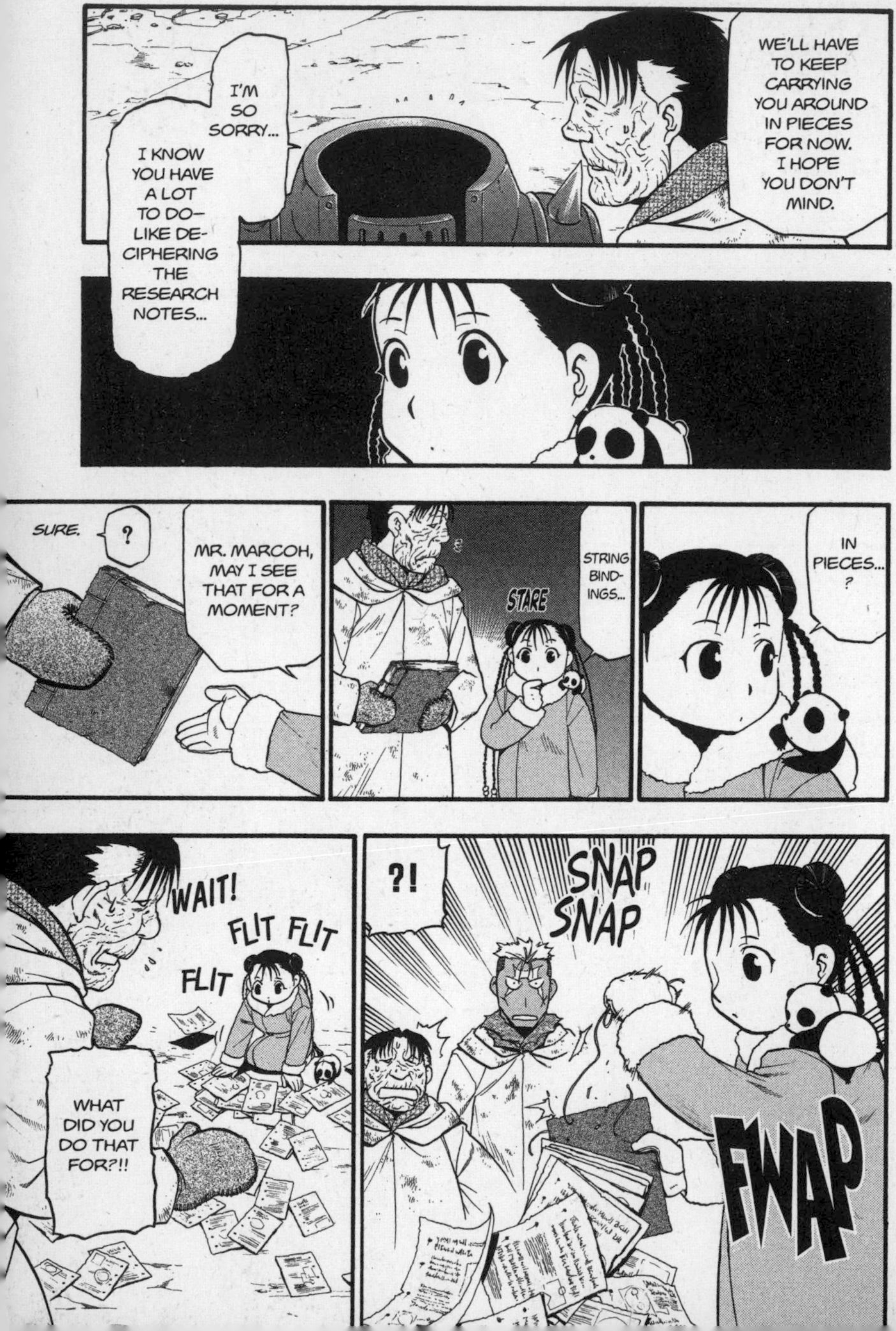
WE'LL HAVE TO KEEP CARRYING YOU AROUND IN PIECES FOR NOW. I HOPE YOU DON'T MIND.
I'M SO SORRY...
I KNOW YOU HAVE A LOT TO DO—LIKE DE-CIPHERING THE RESEARCH NOTES...
IN PIECES...?
STRING BIND-INGS...
STARE
MR. MARCOH, MAY I SEE THAT FOR A MOMENT?
?
SURE.
?!
SNAP SNAP
FWAP
WAIT!
FLIT FLIT
FLIT
WHAT DID YOU DO THAT FOR?!!

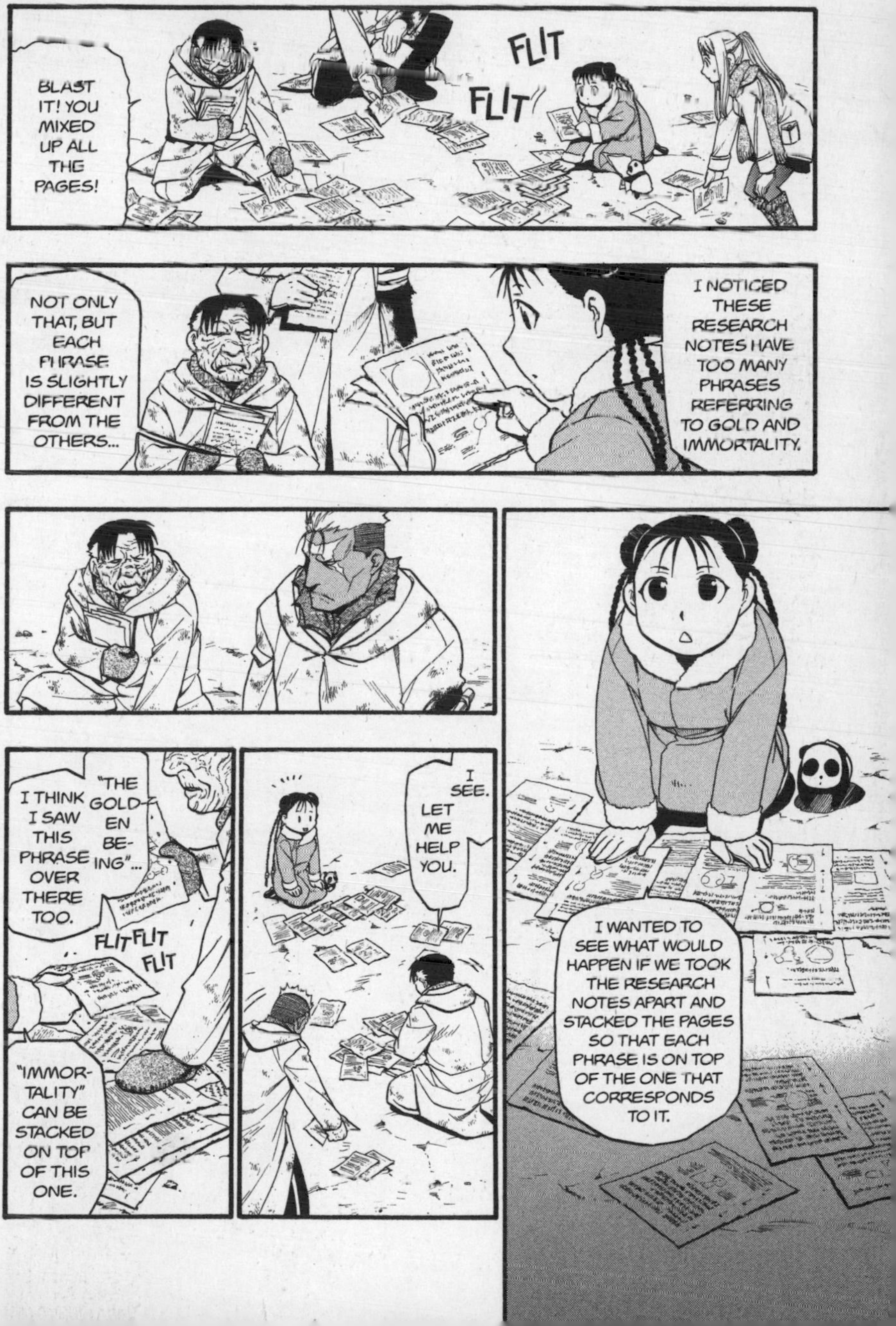
FLIT
FLIT
BLAST IT! YOU MIXED UP ALL THE PAGES!
I NOTICED THESE RESEARCH NOTES HAVE TOO MANY PHRASES REFERRING TO GOLD AND IMMORTALITY.
NOT ONLY THAT, BUT EACH PHRASE IS SLIGHTLY DIFFERENT FROM THE OTHERS...
I WANTED TO SEE WHAT WOULD HAPPEN IF WE TOOK THE RESEARCH NOTES APART AND STACKED THE PAGES SO THAT EACH PHRASE IS ON TOP OF THE ONE THAT CORRESPONDS TO IT.
I SEE. LET ME HELP YOU.
"THE GOLDEN BEING"... I THINK I SAW THIS PHRASE OVER THERE TOO.
FLIT FLIT FLIT
"IMMORTALITY" CAN BE STACKED ON TOP OF THIS ONE.

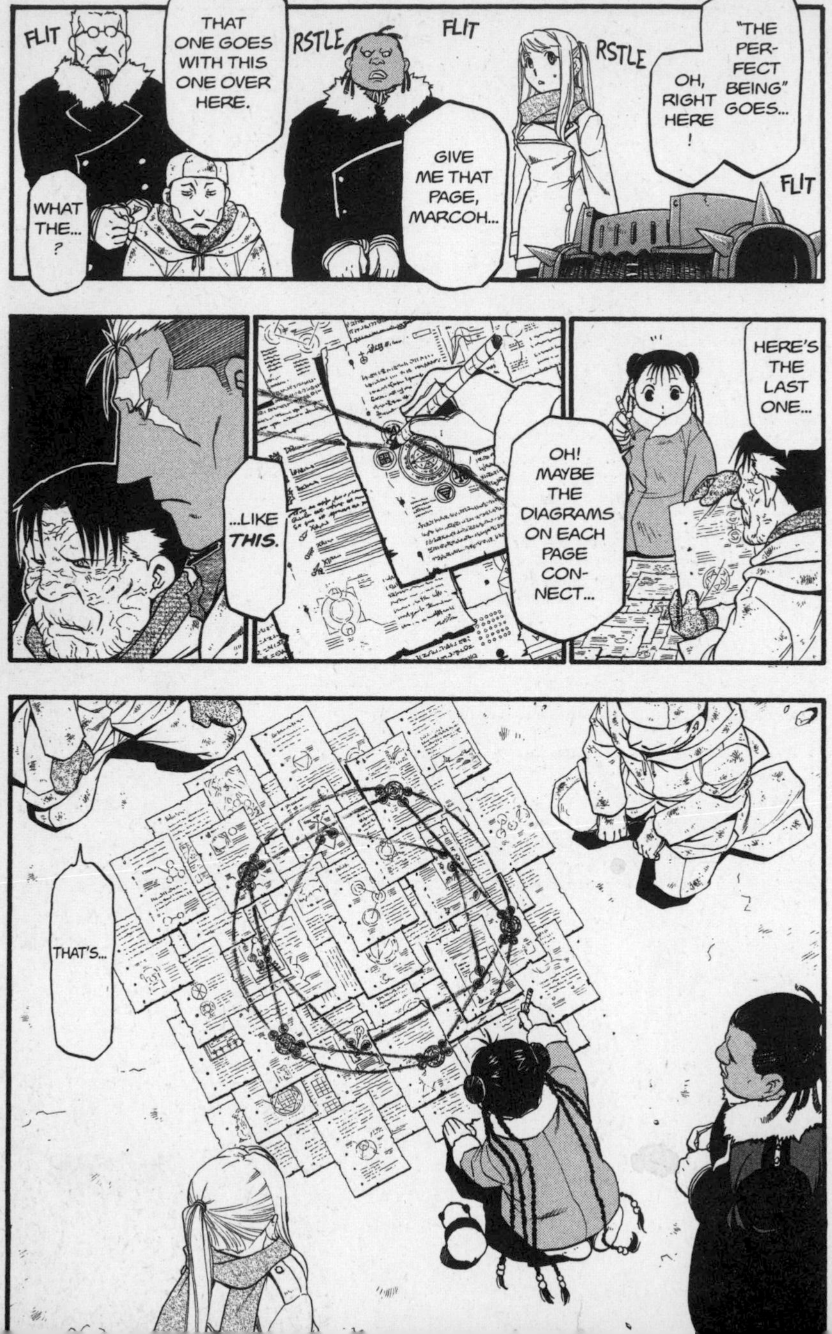
"THE PERFECT BEING" GOES...
FLIT
OH, RIGHT HERE!
RSTLE
FLIT
GIVE ME THAT PAGE, MARCOH...
RSTLE
THAT ONE GOES WITH THIS ONE OVER HERE.
FLIT
WHAT THE...?
HERE'S THE LAST ONE...
OH! MAYBE THE DIAGRAMS ON EACH PAGE CONNECT...
...LIKE THIS.
THAT'S...

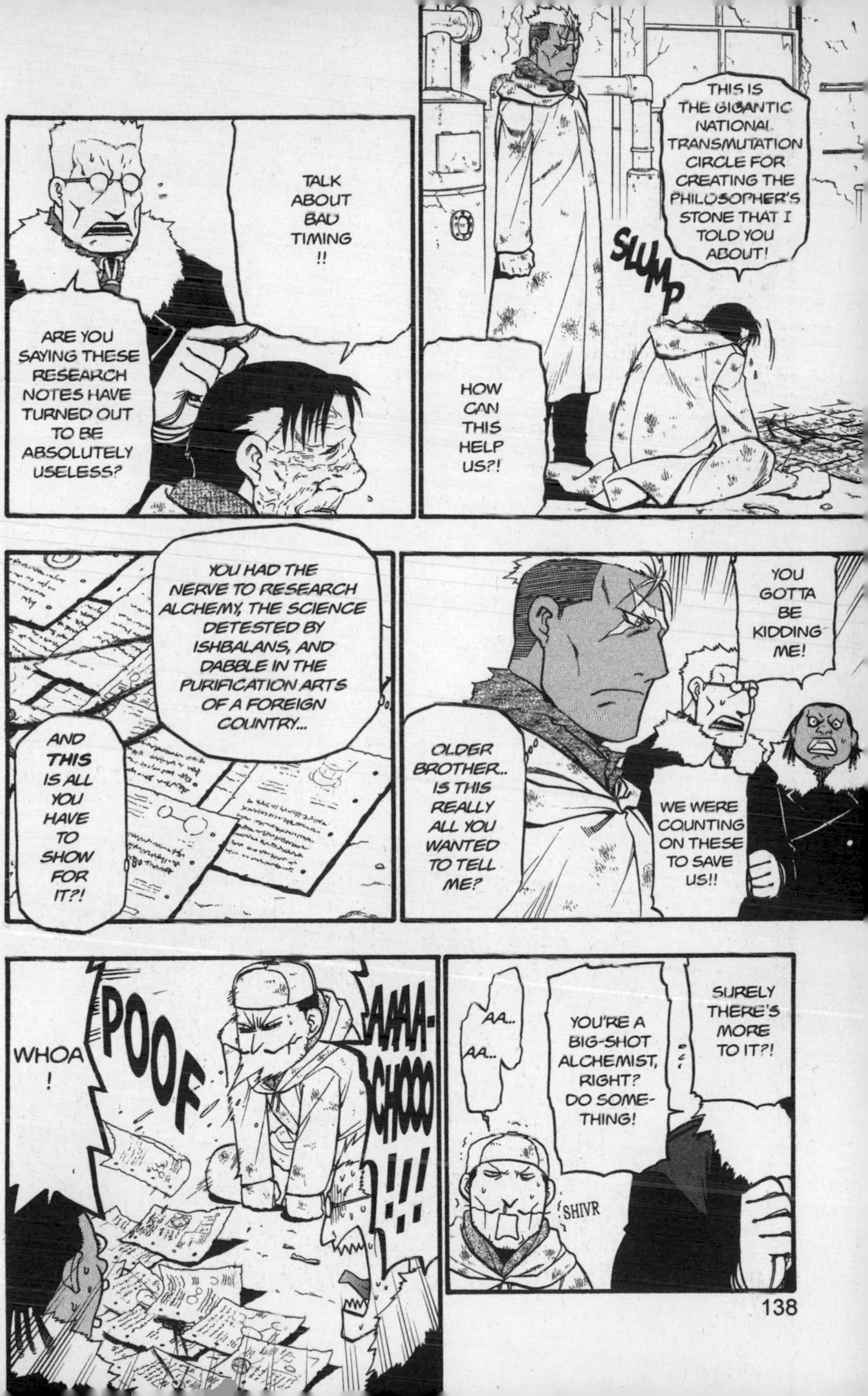
THIS IS THE GIGANTIC NATIONAL TRANSMUTATION CIRCLE FOR CREATING THE PHILOSOPHER'S STONE THAT I TOLD YOU ABOUT!
SLUMP
HOW CAN THIS HELP US?!
TALK ABOUT BAD TIMING!!
ARE YOU SAYING THESE RESEARCH NOTES HAVE TURNED OUT TO BE ABSOLUTELY USELESS?
YOU GOTTA BE KIDDING ME!
WE WERE COUNTING ON THESE TO SAVE US!!
OLDER BROTHER... IS THIS REALLY ALL YOU WANTED TO TELL ME?
YOU HAD THE NERVE TO RESEARCH ALCHEMY, THE SCIENCE DETESTED BY ISHBALANS, AND DABBLE IN THE PURIFICATION ARTS OF A FOREIGN COUNTRY...
AND THIS IS ALL YOU HAVE TO SHOW FOR IT?!
SURELY THERE'S MORE TO IT?!
YOU'RE A BIG-SHOT ALCHEMIST, RIGHT? DO SOMETHING!
AA... AA...
SHIVR
AAAA-CHOOO!!!
POOF
WHOA!

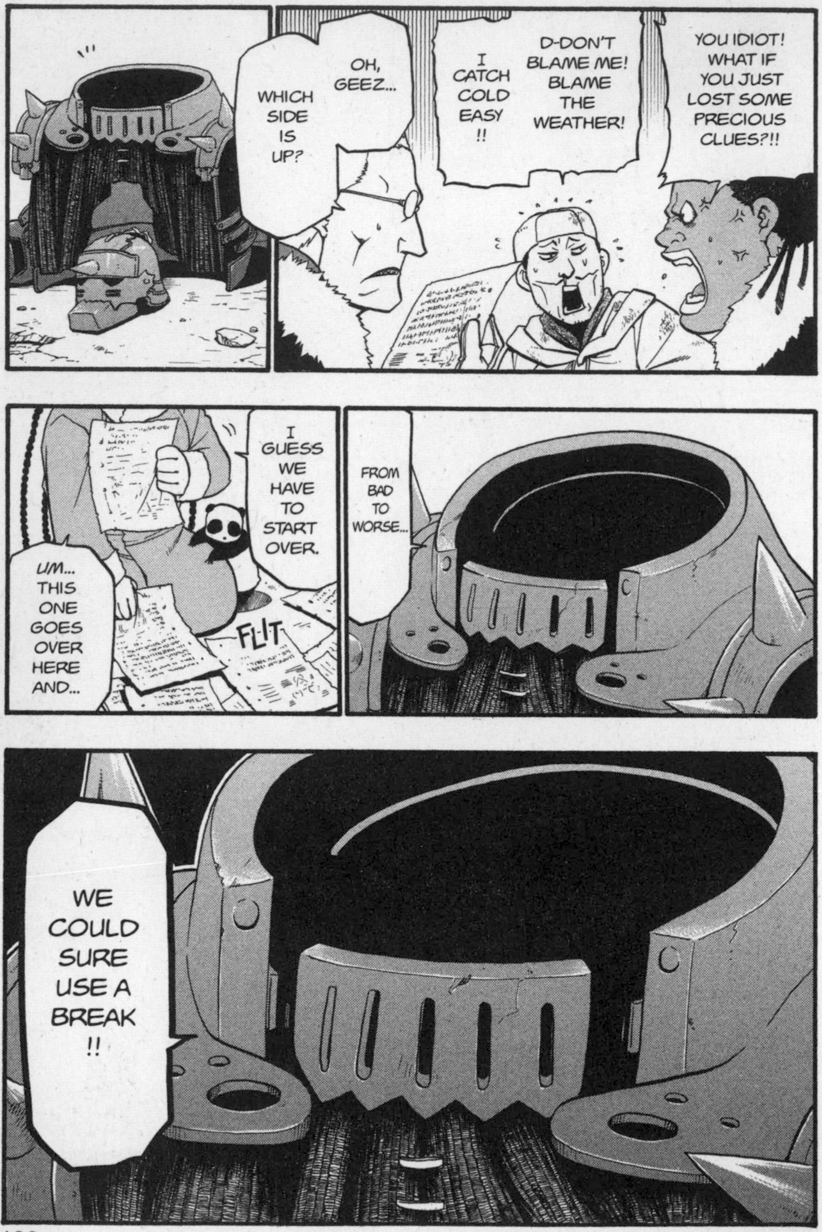
YOU IDIOT! WHAT IF YOU JUST LOST SOME PRECIOUS CLUES?!!
D-DON'T BLAME ME! BLAME THE WEATHER!
I CATCH COLD EASY !!
OH, GEEZ...
WHICH SIDE IS UP?
FROM BAD TO WORSE...
I GUESS WE HAVE TO START OVER.
FLIT
UM... THIS ONE GOES OVER HERE AND...
WE COULD SURE USE A BREAK !!

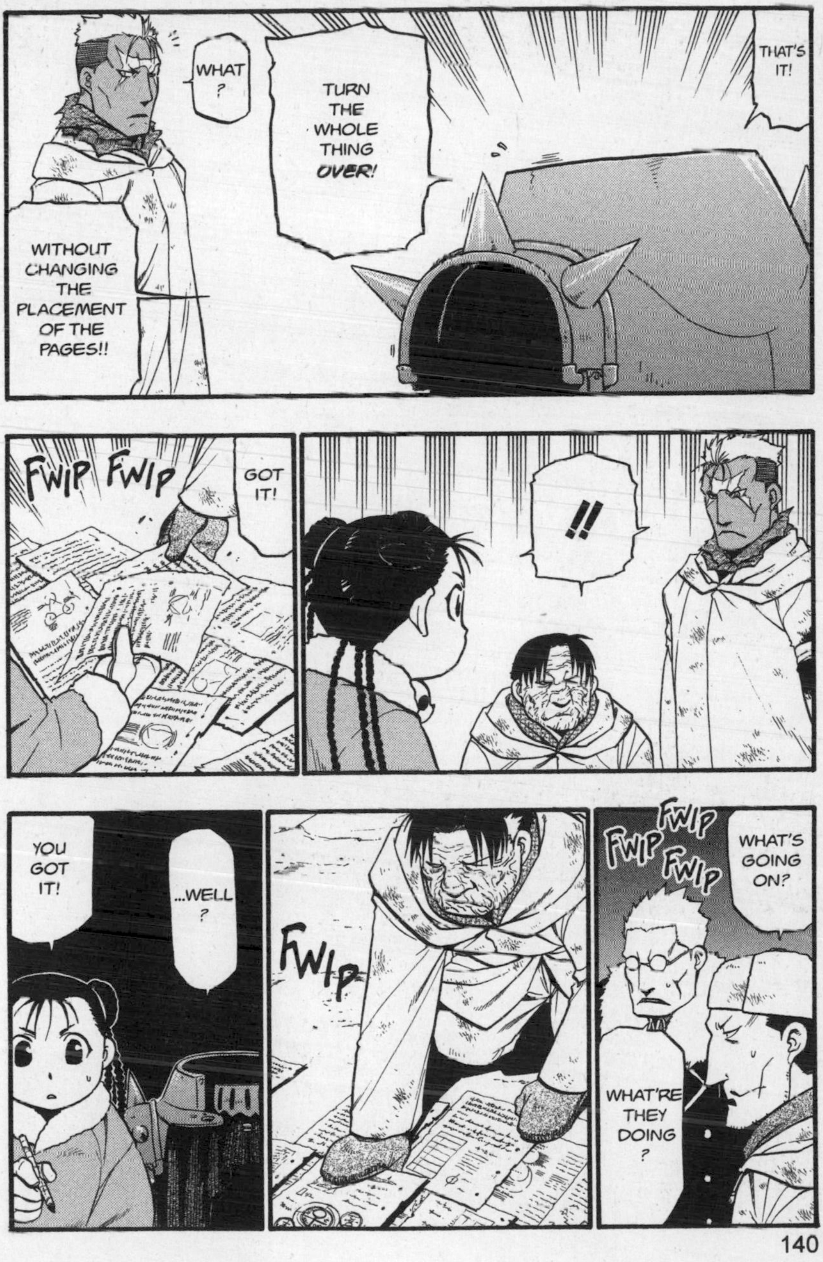
THAT'S IT!
TURN THE WHOLE THING OVER!
WHAT?
WITHOUT CHANGING THE PLACEMENT OF THE PAGES!!
!!
GOT IT!
FWIP FWIP
WHAT'S GOING ON?
FWIP FWIP FWIP
WHAT'RE THEY DOING?
FWIP
...WELL?
YOU GOT IT!

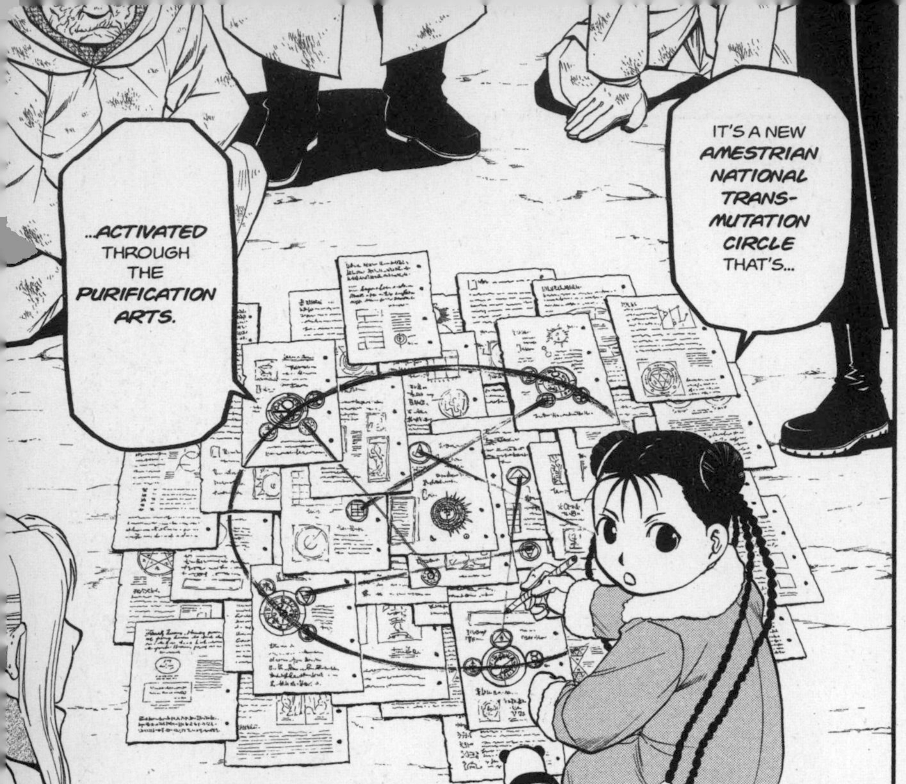
IT'S A NEW AMESTRIAN NATIONAL TRANS-MUTATION CIRCLE THAT'S...
...ACTIVATED THROUGH THE PURIFICATION ARTS.

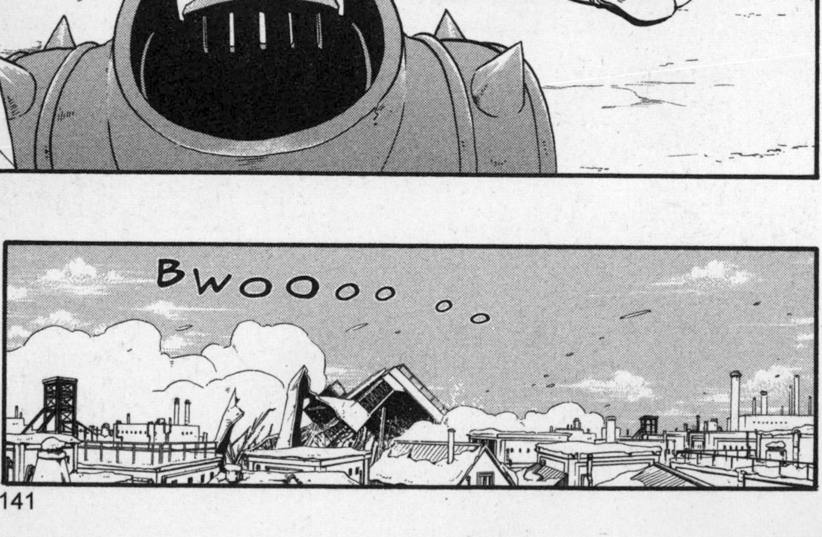
BWOOooo o o

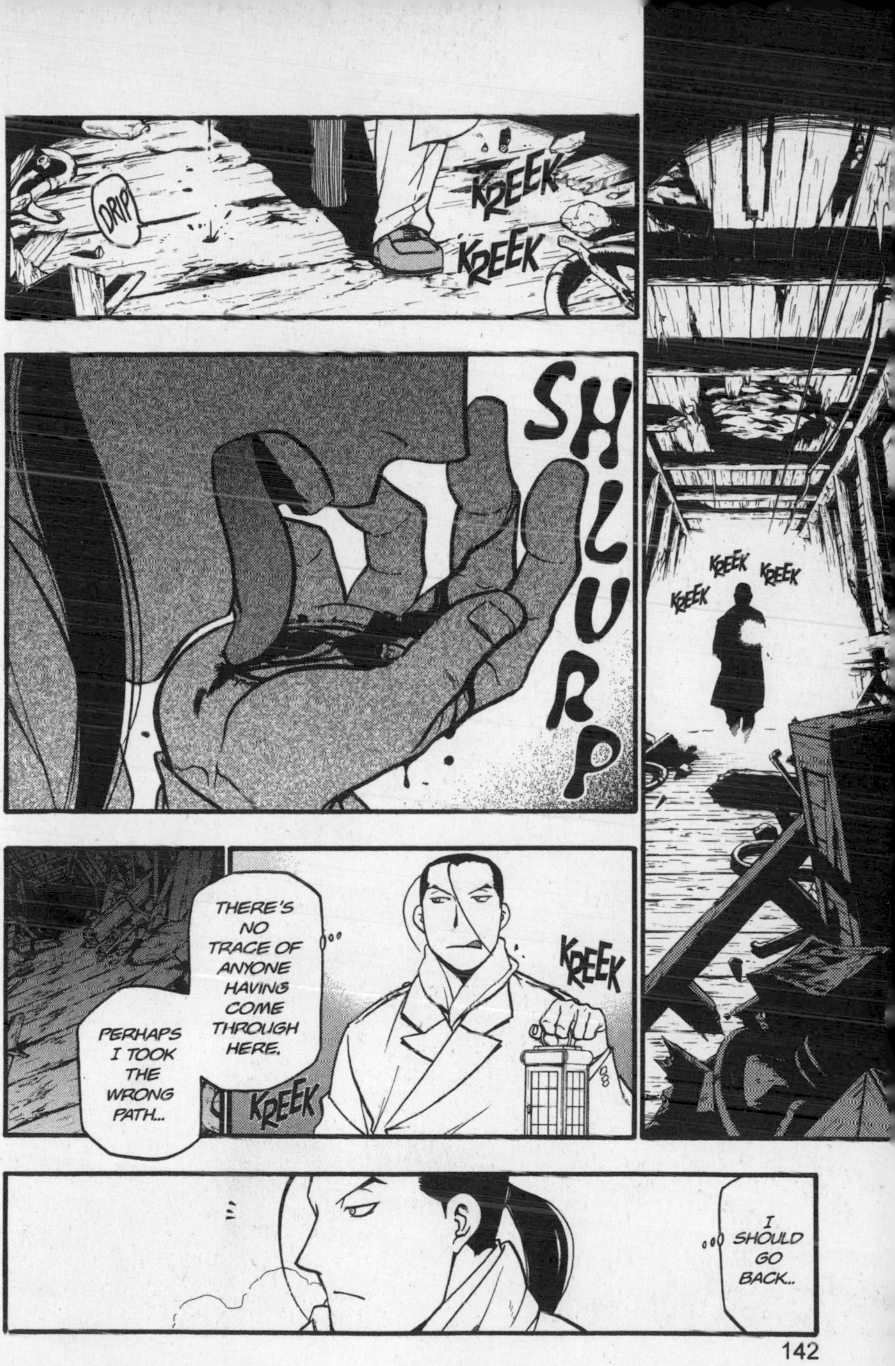
KREEK
KREEK
KREEK
KREEK
KREEK
DRIP
SHLURP
KREEK
THERE'S NO TRACE OF ANYONE HAVING COME THROUGH HERE.
PERHAPS I TOOK THE WRONG PATH...
KREEK
...
...I SHOULD GO BACK...

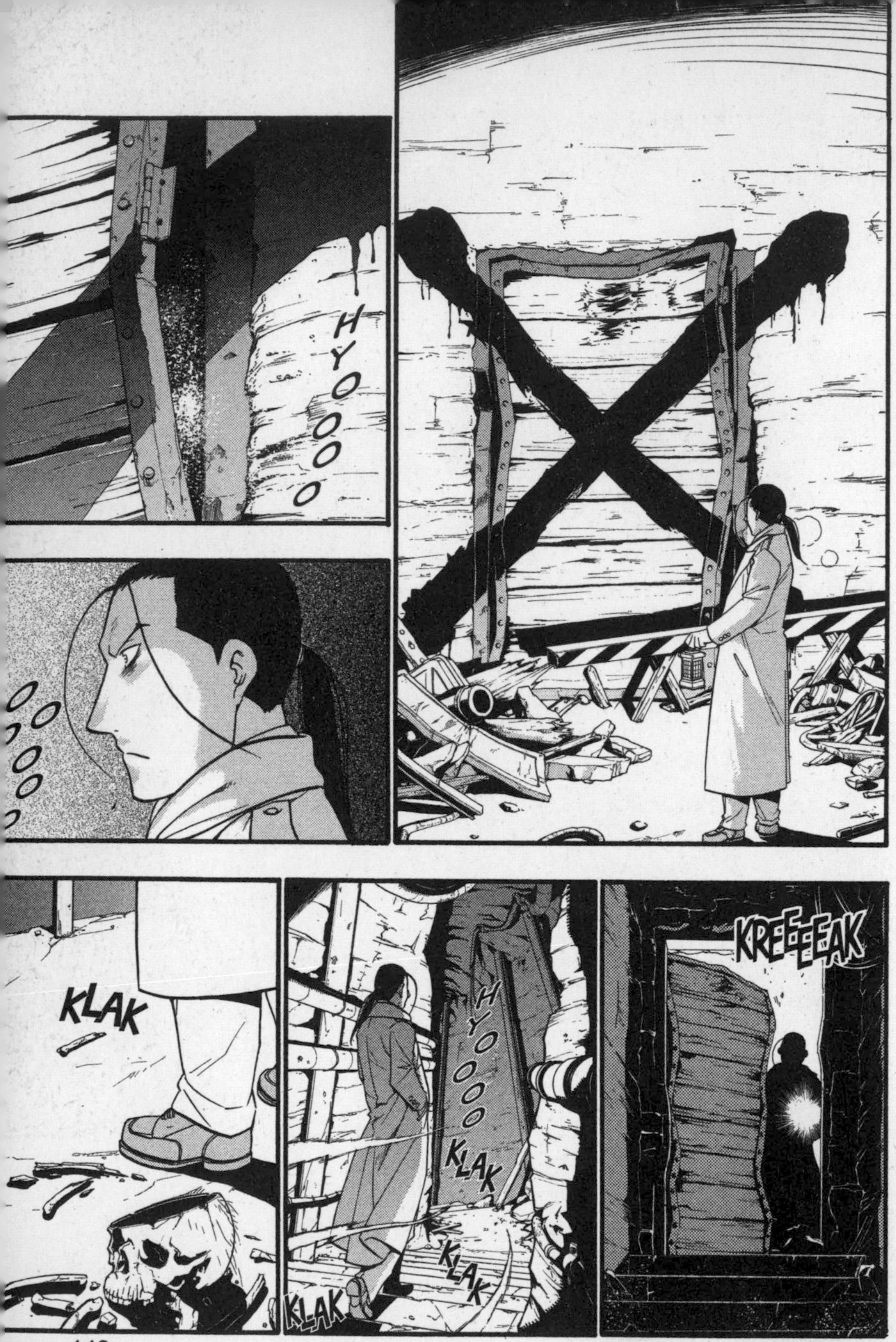

HYOOOOO
OOOOOO
KREEEEAK
HYOOOOO
KLAK
KLAK
KLAK
KLAK
KLAK

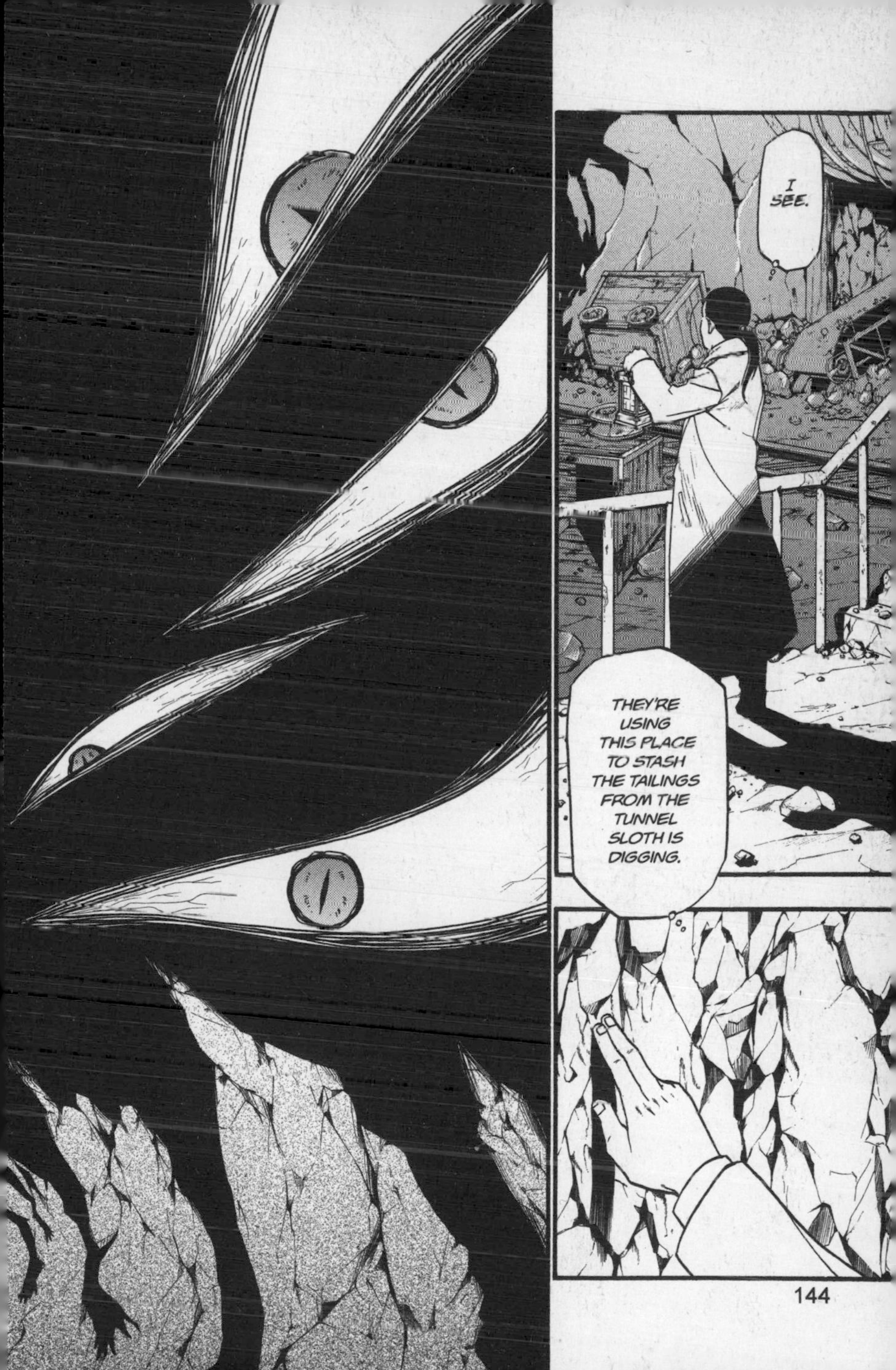
I SEE.
THEY'RE USING THIS PLACE TO STASH THE TAILINGS FROM THE TUNNEL SLOTH IS DIGGING.

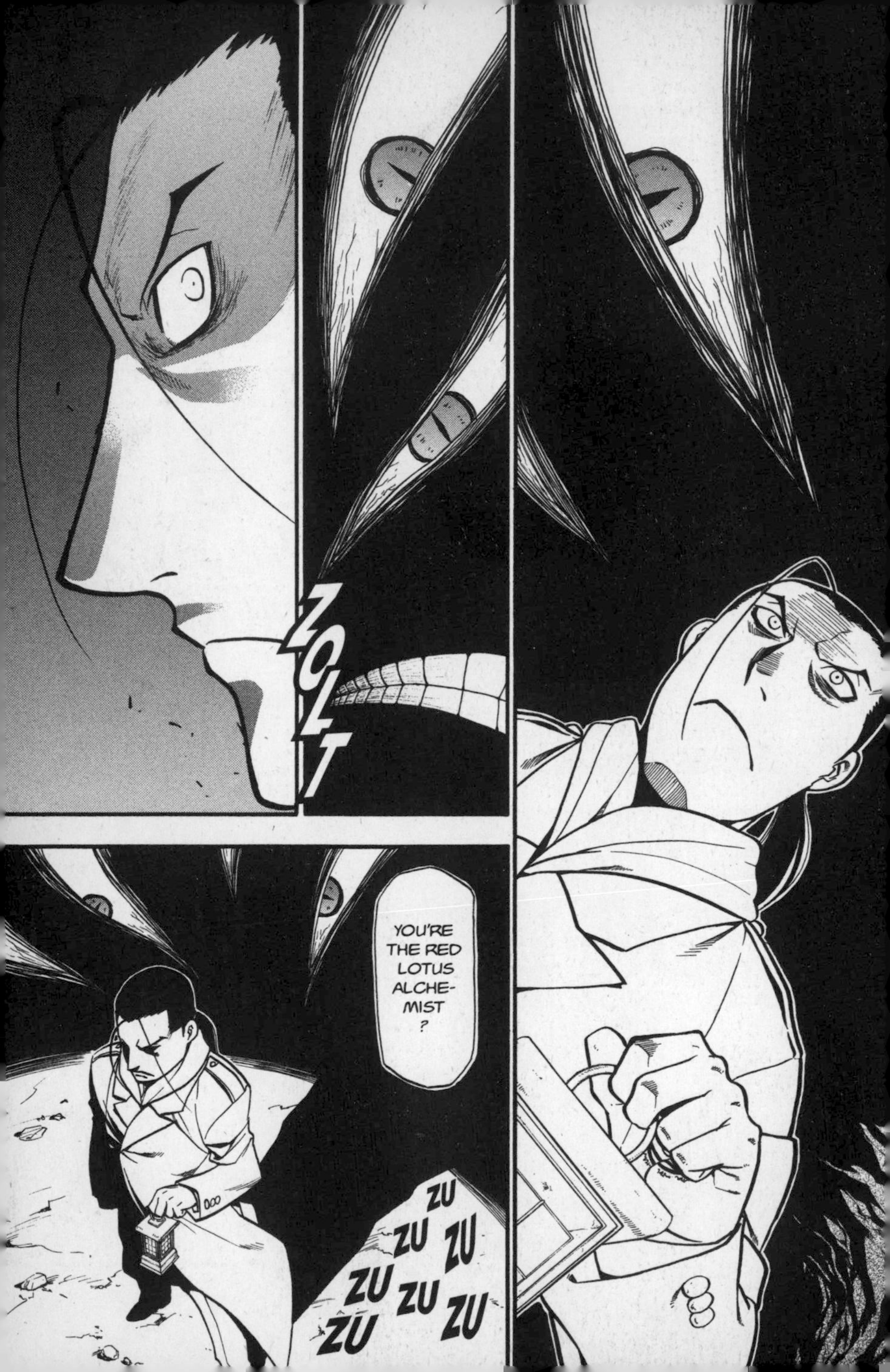
ZOLT
YOU'RE THE RED LOTUS ALCHEMIST?
ZU ZU ZU ZU ZU ZU ZU ZU

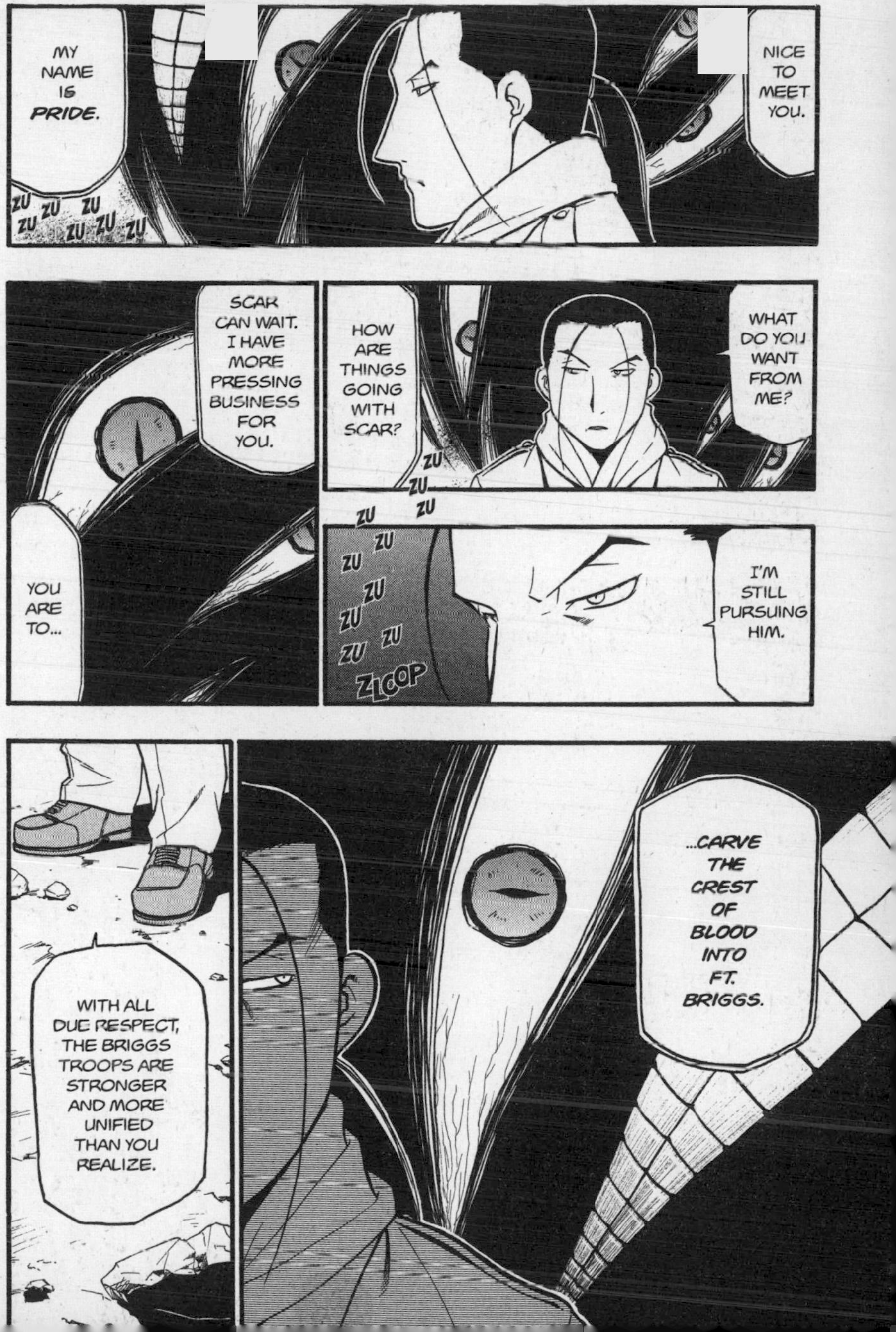
NICE TO MEET YOU.
MY NAME IS PRIDE.
ZU ZU ZU ZU ZU ZU ZU ZU
WHAT DO YOU WANT FROM ME?
HOW ARE THINGS GOING WITH SCAR?
ZU ZU ZU
I'M STILL PURSUING HIM.
ZU ZU ZU ZU ZU ZU ZU
ZLOOP
SCAR CAN WAIT. I HAVE MORE PRESSING BUSINESS FOR YOU.
YOU ARE TO...
...CARVE THE CREST OF BLOOD INTO FT. BRIGGS.
WITH ALL DUE RESPECT, THE BRIGGS TROOPS ARE STRONGER AND MORE UNIFIED THAN YOU REALIZE.

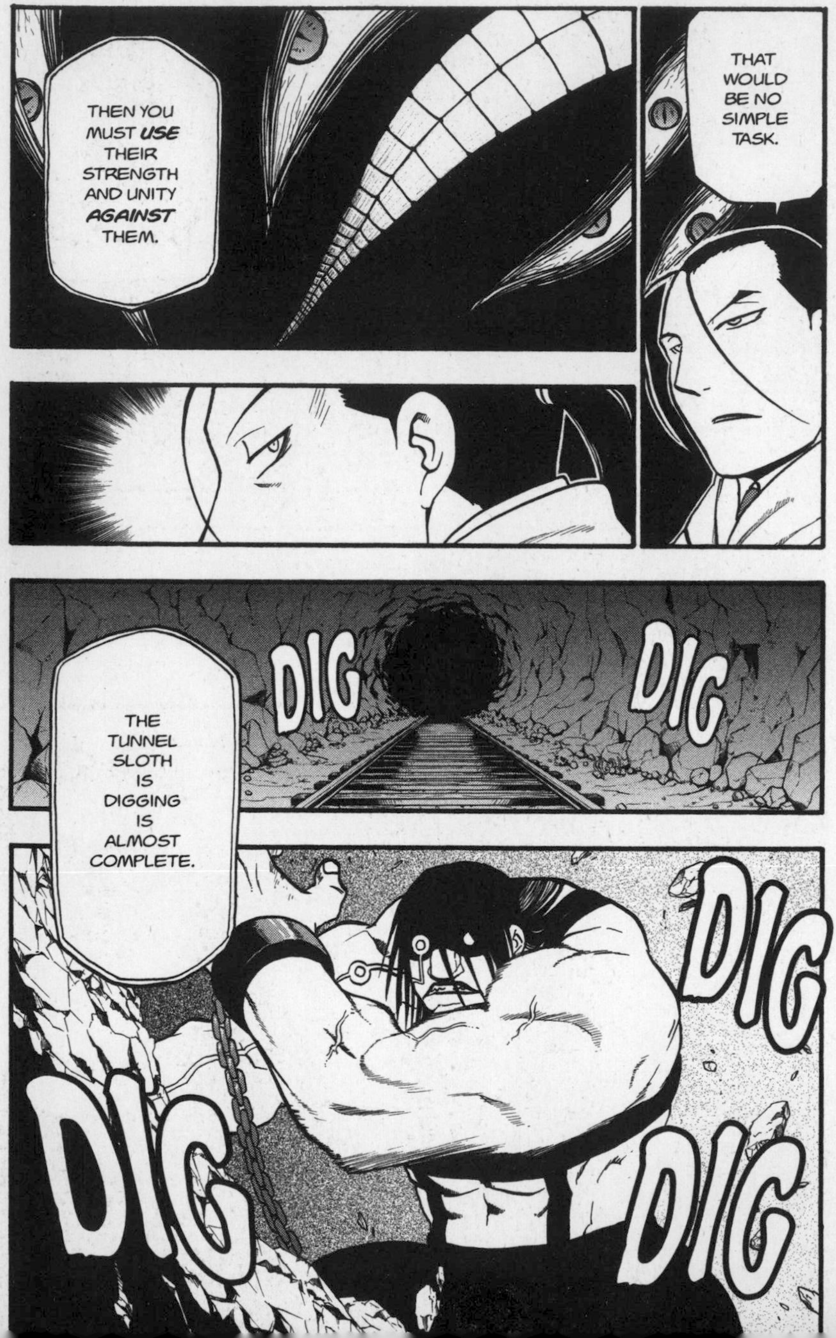
THEN YOU MUST *USE* THEIR STRENGTH AND UNITY *AGAINST* THEM.
THAT WOULD BE NO SIMPLE TASK.
DIG DIG
THE TUNNEL SLOTH IS DIGGING IS ALMOST COMPLETE.
DIG DIG DIG DIG

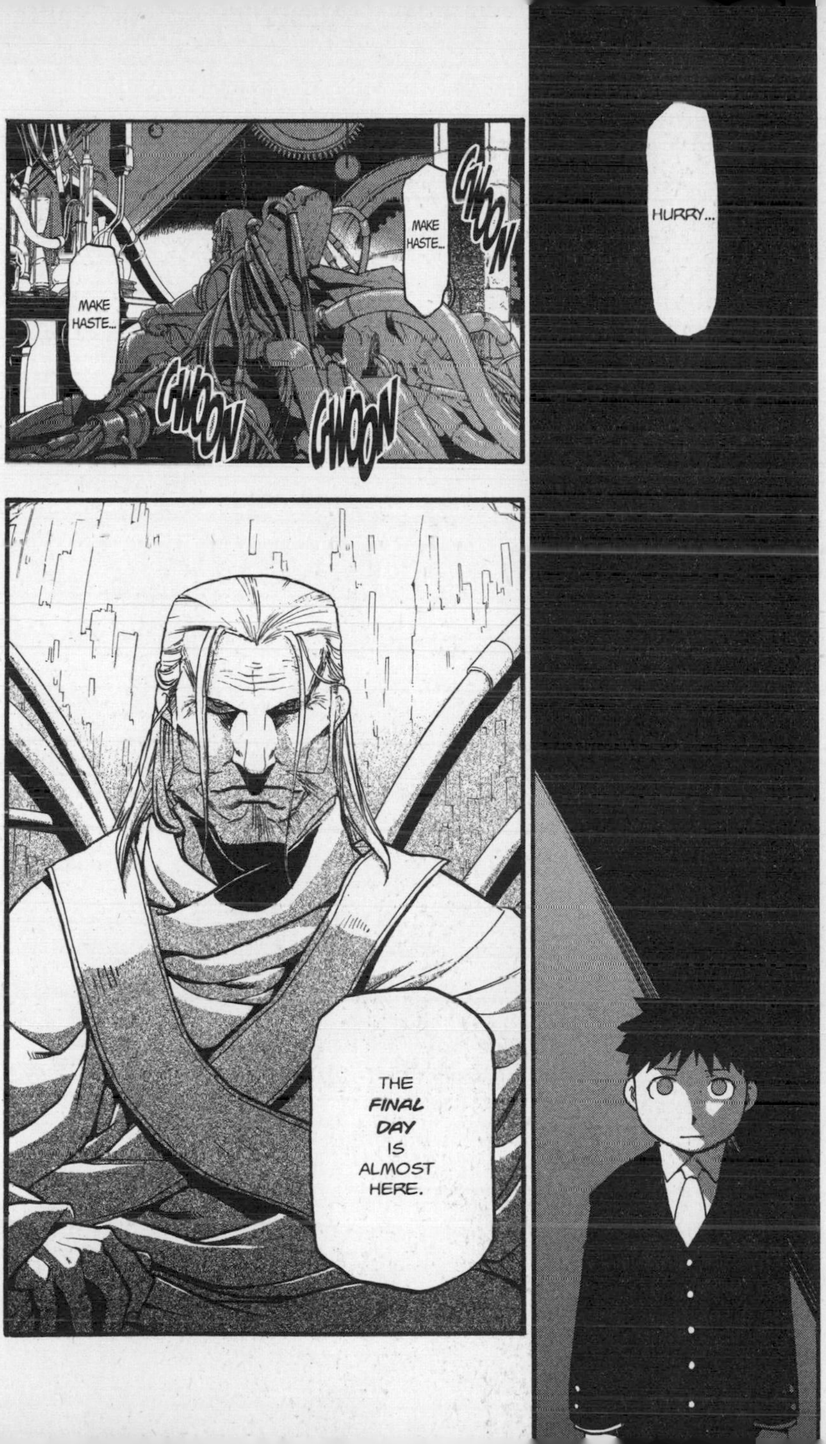
HURRY...
MAKE HASTE...
GWOON
MAKE HASTE...
GWOON
GWOON
THE *FINAL DAY* IS ALMOST HERE.

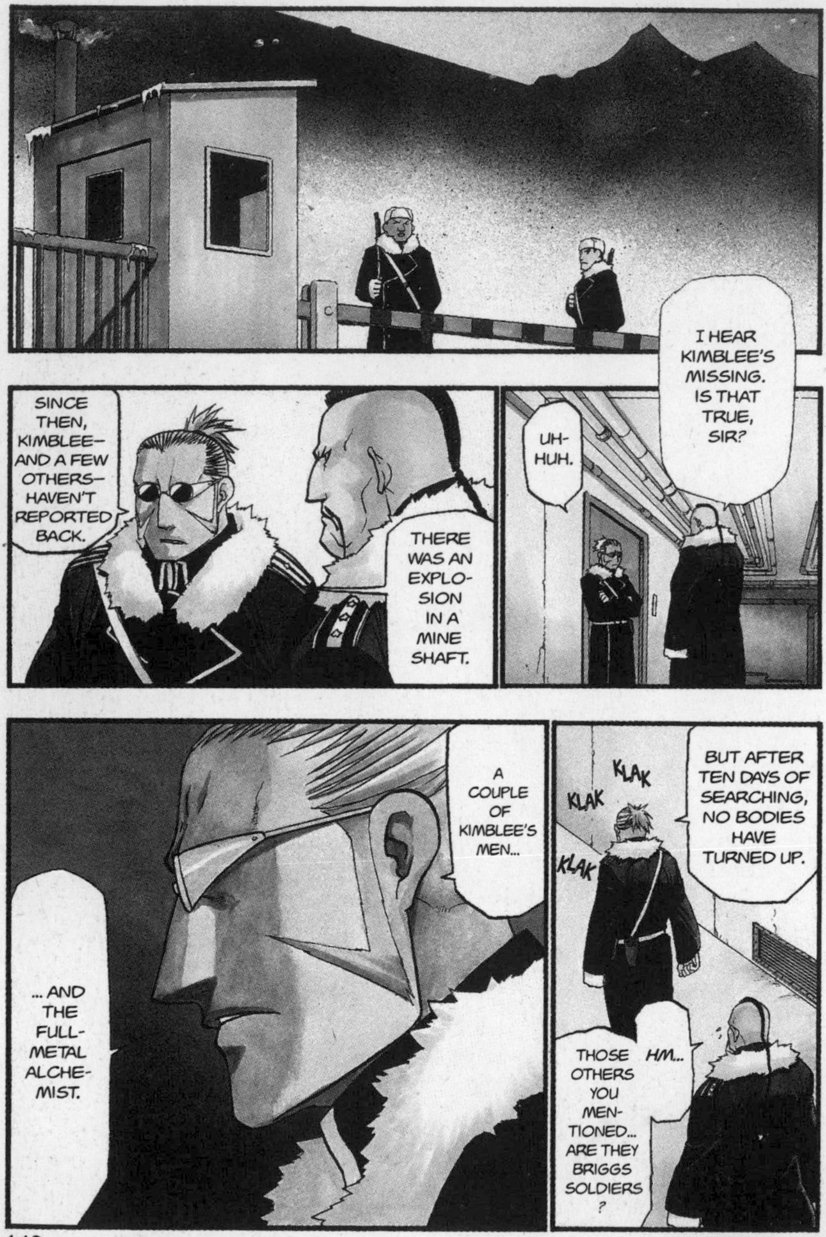
I HEAR KIMBLEE'S MISSING. IS THAT TRUE, SIR?
UH-HUH.
THERE WAS AN EXPLOSION IN A MINE SHAFT.
SINCE THEN, KIMBLEE—AND A FEW OTHERS—HAVEN'T REPORTED BACK.
BUT AFTER TEN DAYS OF SEARCHING, NO BODIES HAVE TURNED UP.
KLAK
KLAK
KLAK
HM...
THOSE OTHERS YOU MENTIONED... ARE THEY BRIGGS SOLDIERS?
A COUPLE OF KIMBLEE'S MEN...
...AND THE FULLMETAL ALCHEMIST.

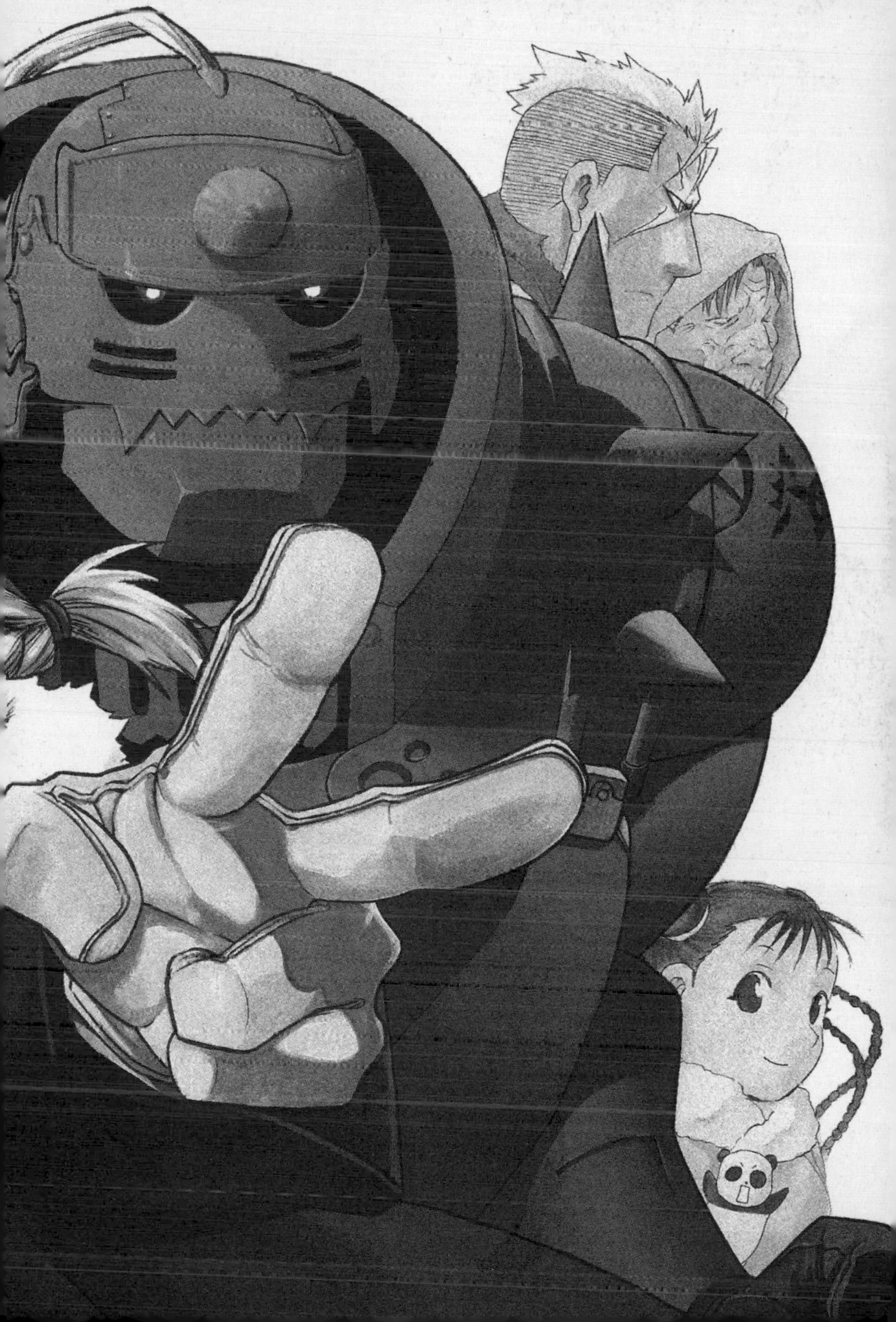

Chapter 78
The Seven Deadly Sins

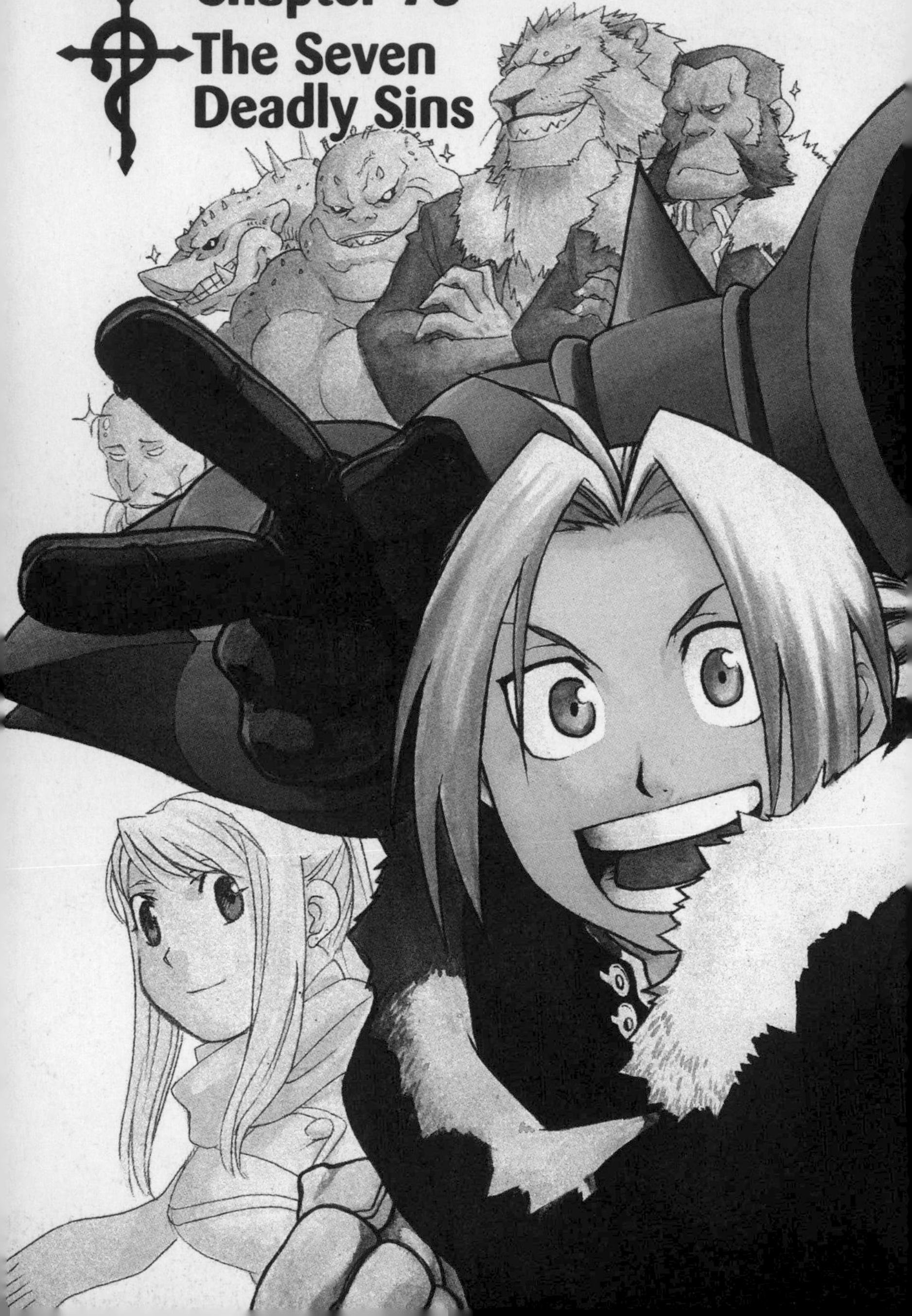

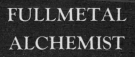

FULLMETAL
ALCHEMIST

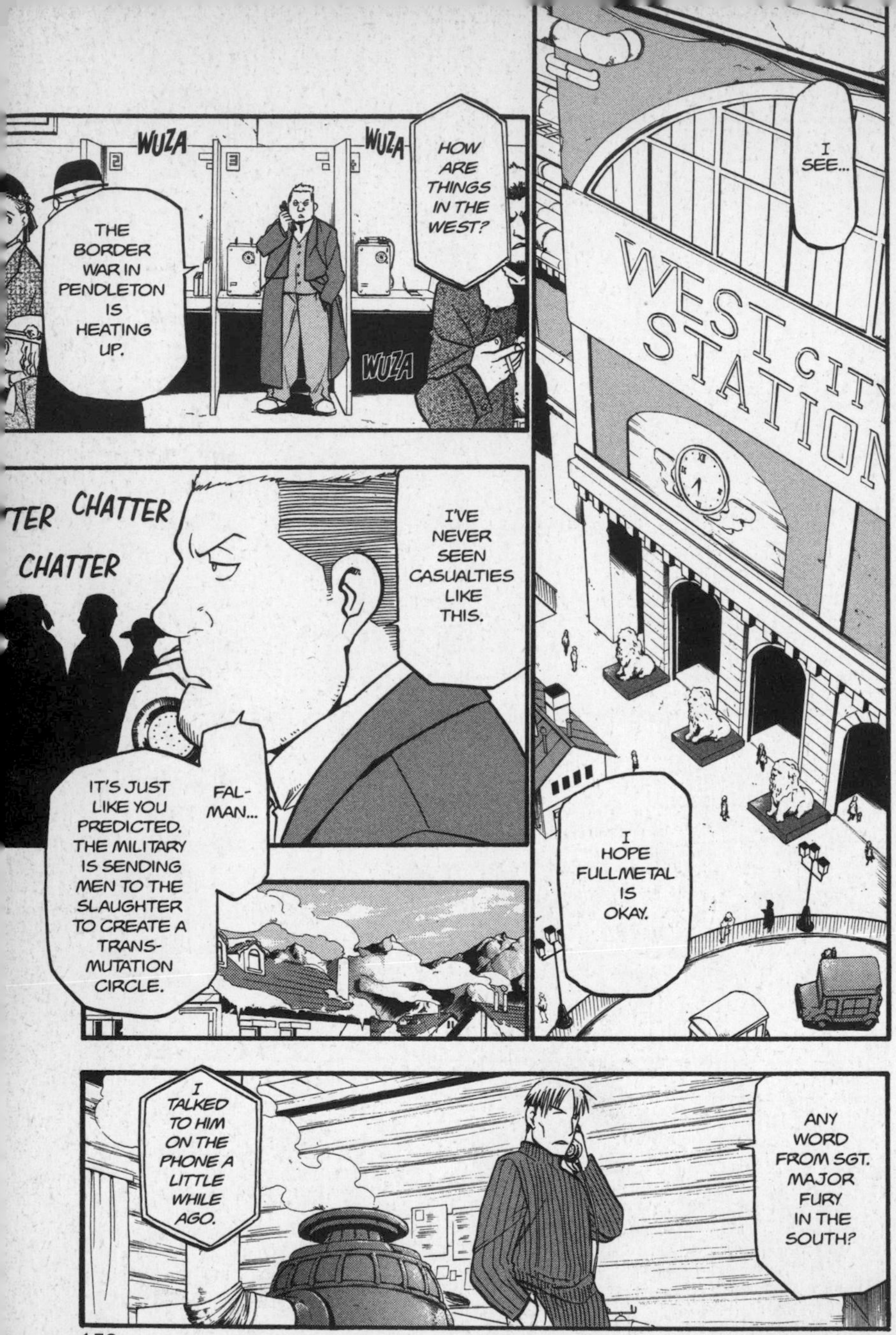
I SEE...
WEST CITY STATION
I HOPE FULLMETAL IS OKAY.
HOW ARE THINGS IN THE WEST?
WUZA
WUZA
THE BORDER WAR IN PENDLETON IS HEATING UP.
WUZA
I'VE NEVER SEEN CASUALTIES LIKE THIS.
CHATTER
TER
CHATTER
FAL-MAN...
IT'S JUST LIKE YOU PREDICTED. THE MILITARY IS SENDING MEN TO THE SLAUGHTER TO CREATE A TRANS-MUTATION CIRCLE.
ANY WORD FROM SGT. MAJOR FURY IN THE SOUTH?
I TALKED TO HIM ON THE PHONE A LITTLE WHILE AGO.

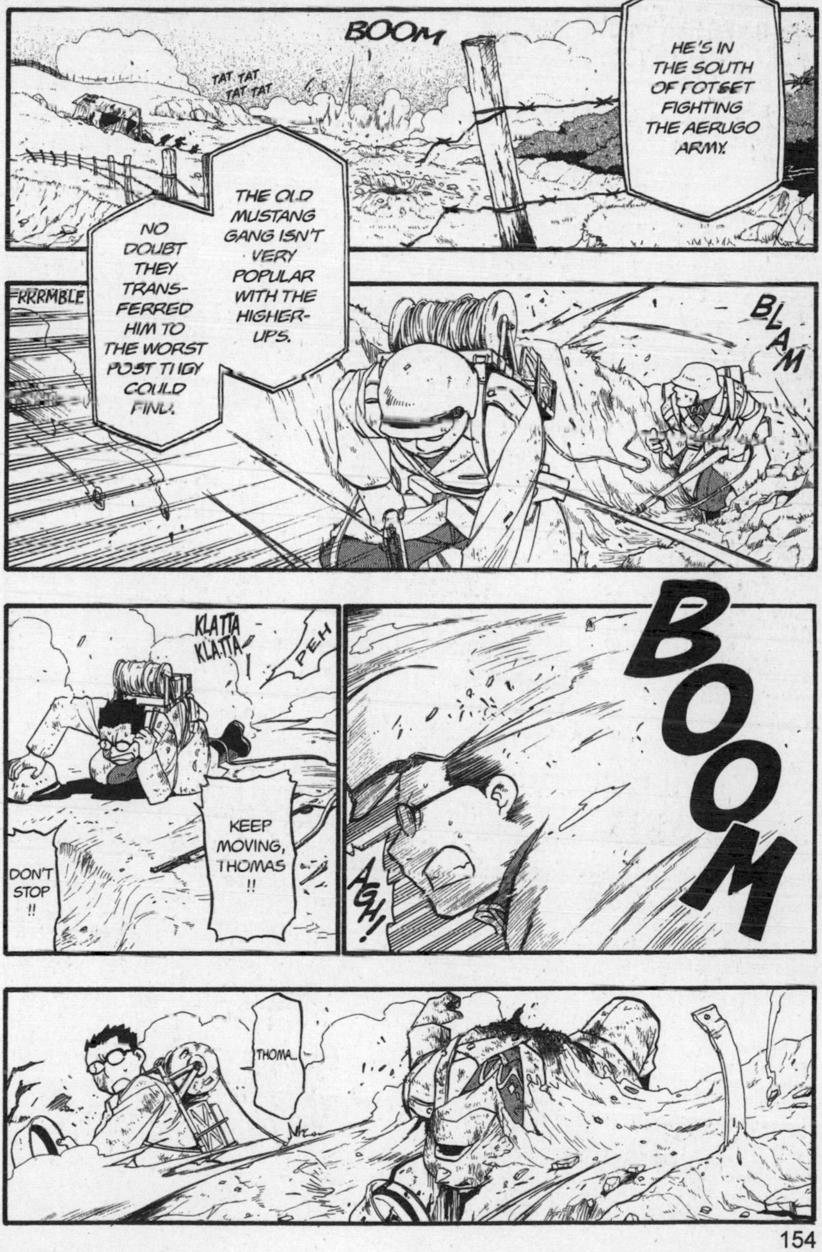
BOOM
TAT TAT TAT TAT
HE'S IN THE SOUTH OF FOTSET FIGHTING THE AERUGO ARMY.
THE OLD MUSTANG GANG ISN'T VERY POPULAR WITH THE HIGHER-UPS.
NO DOUBT THEY TRANSFERRED HIM TO THE WORST POST THEY COULD FIND.
BLAM
KKRMBLE
BOOM
AGH!
PEH
KLATTA KLATTA
KEEP MOVING, THOMAS!!
DON'T STOP!!
THOMA...

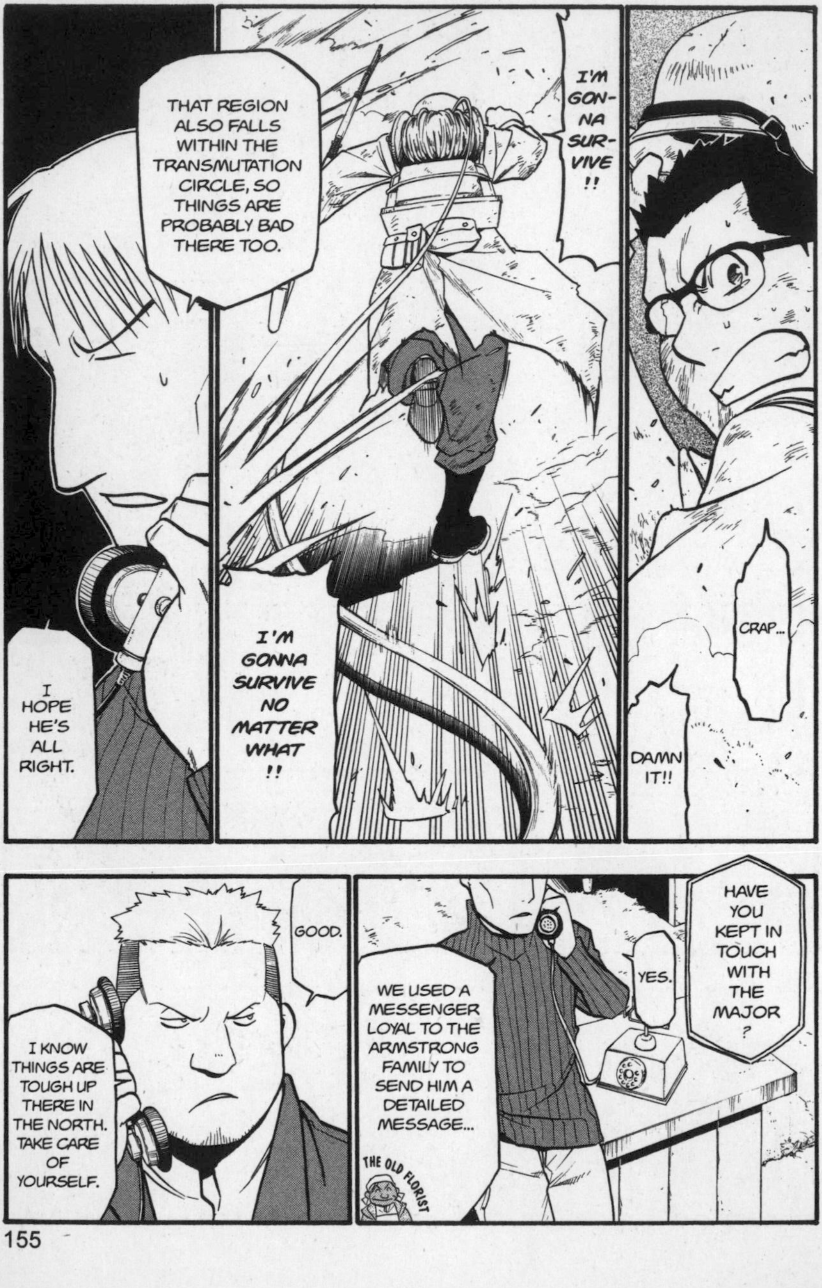
CRAP...
DAMN IT!!
I'M GONNA SURVIVE!!
I'M GONNA SURVIVE NO MATTER WHAT!!
THAT REGION ALSO FALLS WITHIN THE TRANSMUTATION CIRCLE, SO THINGS ARE PROBABLY BAD THERE TOO.
I HOPE HE'S ALL RIGHT.
HAVE YOU KEPT IN TOUCH WITH THE MAJOR?
YES.
WE USED A MESSENGER LOYAL TO THE ARMSTRONG FAMILY TO SEND HIM A DETAILED MESSAGE...
THE OLD FLORIST
GOOD.
I KNOW THINGS ARE TOUGH UP THERE IN THE NORTH. TAKE CARE OF YOURSELF.

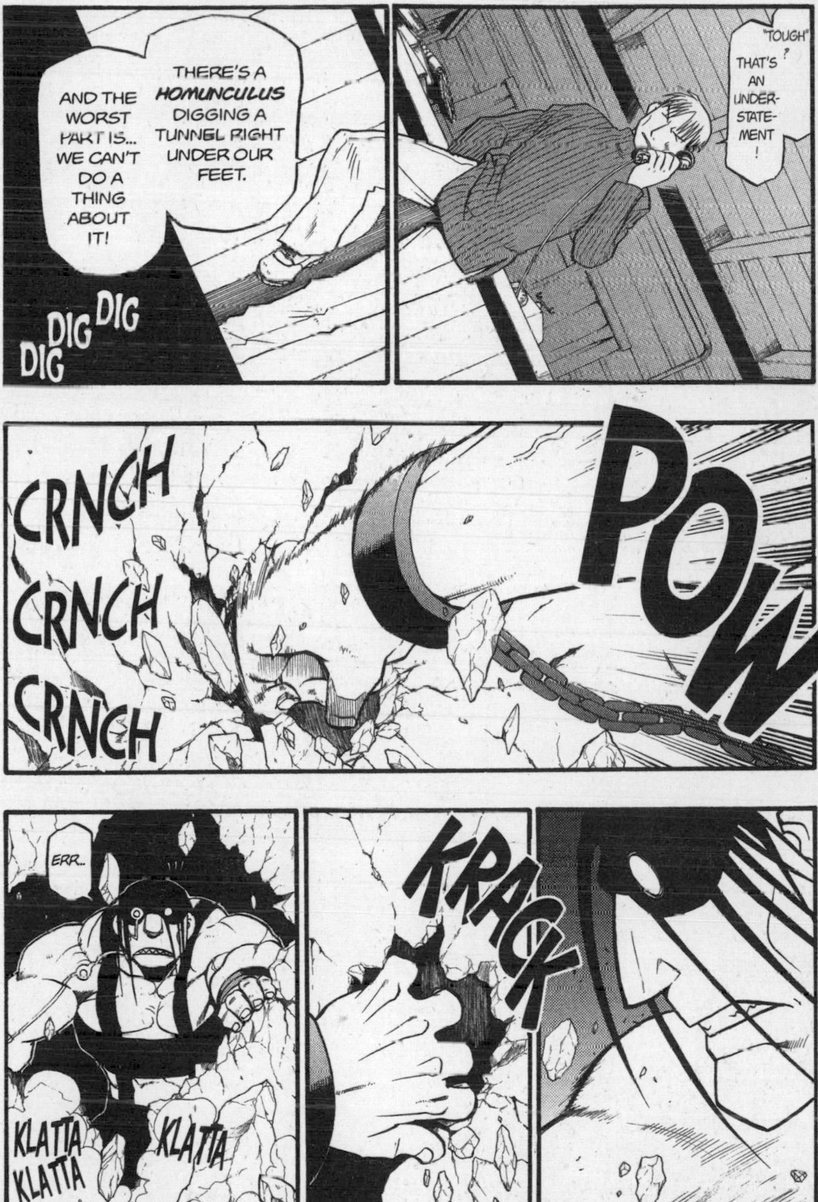
"TOUGH"? THAT'S AN UNDER-STATE-MENT!
THERE'S A *HOMUNCULUS* DIGGING A TUNNEL RIGHT UNDER OUR FEET.
AND THE WORST PART IS... WE CAN'T DO A THING ABOUT IT!
DIG DIG DIG
POW
CRNCH CRNCH CRNCH
KRACK
ERR..
KLATTA
KLATTA KLATTA

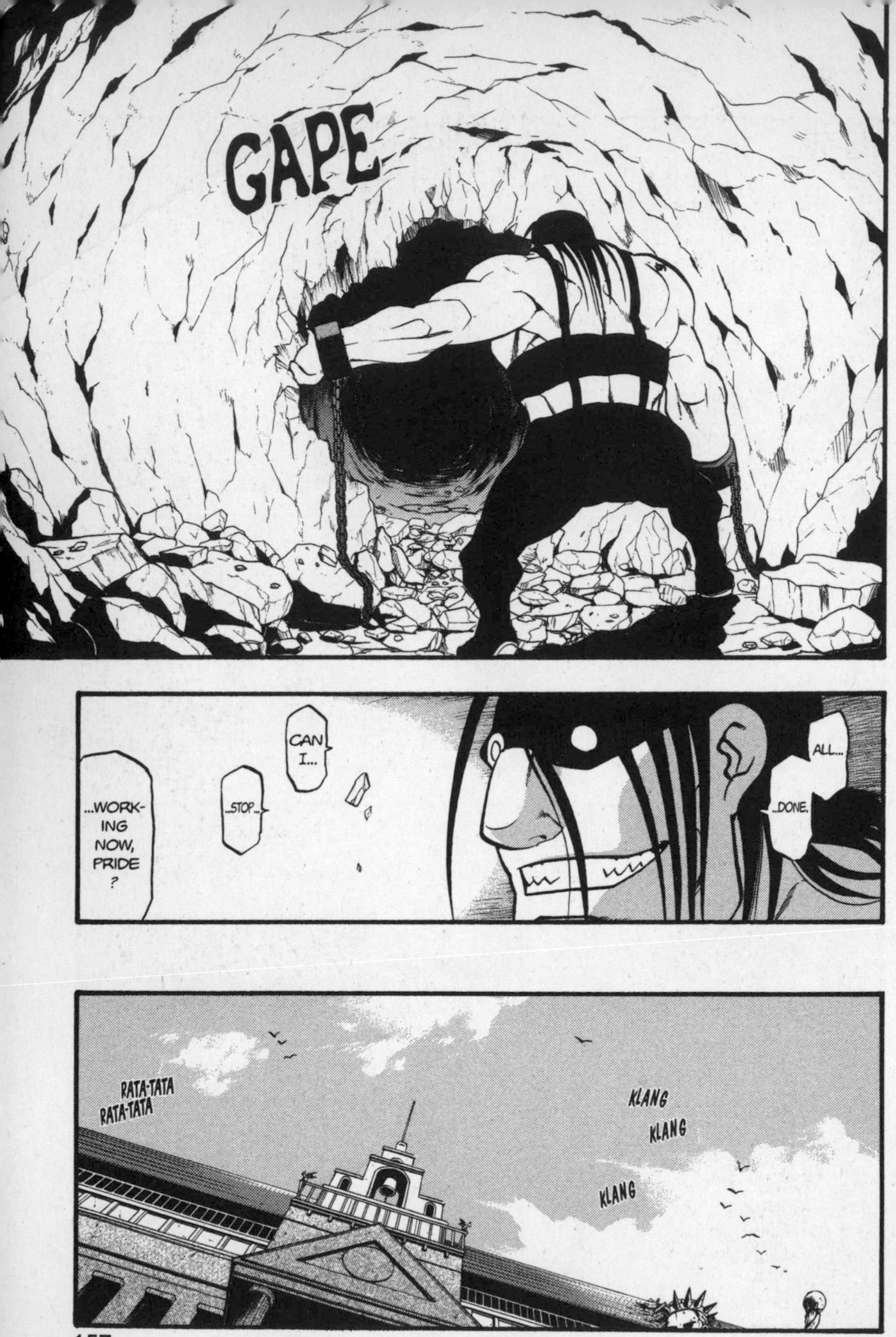
GAPE
ALL...
...DONE.
CAN I...
...STOP...
...WORKING-ING NOW, PRIDE?
KLANG
KLANG
KLANG
RATA-TATA
RATA-TATA

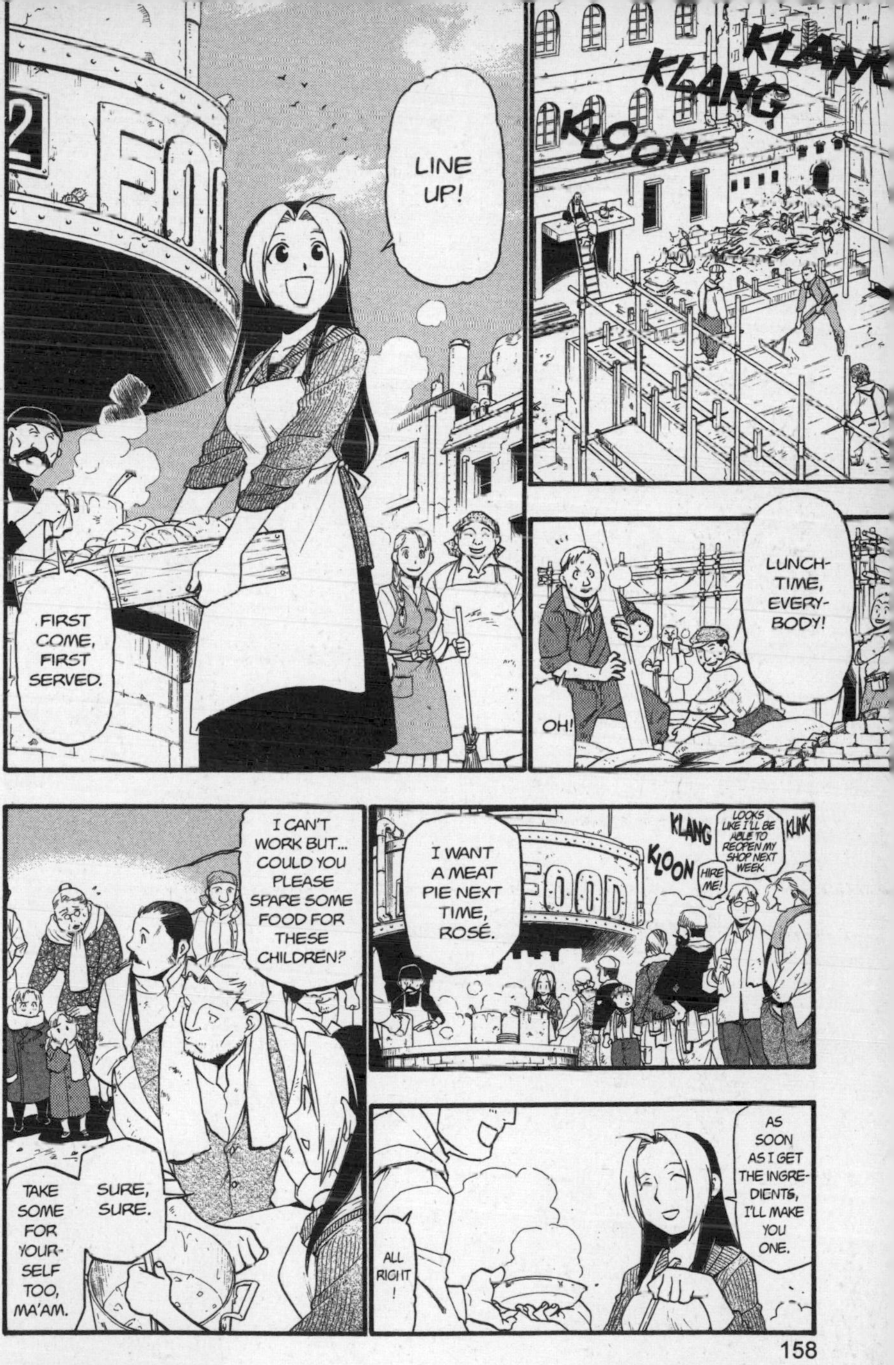
KLAN
KLANG
KLOON
LUNCH-TIME, EVERY-BODY!
OH!
LINE UP!
FIRST COME, FIRST SERVED.
KLANG
KLINK
LOOKS LIKE I'LL BE ABLE TO REOPEN MY SHOP NEXT WEEK
KLOON
HIRE ME!
I WANT A MEAT PIE NEXT TIME, ROSÉ.
AS SOON AS I GET THE INGRE-DIENTS, I'LL MAKE YOU ONE.
ALL RIGHT!
I CAN'T WORK BUT... COULD YOU PLEASE SPARE SOME FOOD FOR THESE CHILDREN?
SURE, SURE.
TAKE SOME FOR YOUR-SELF TOO, MA'AM.

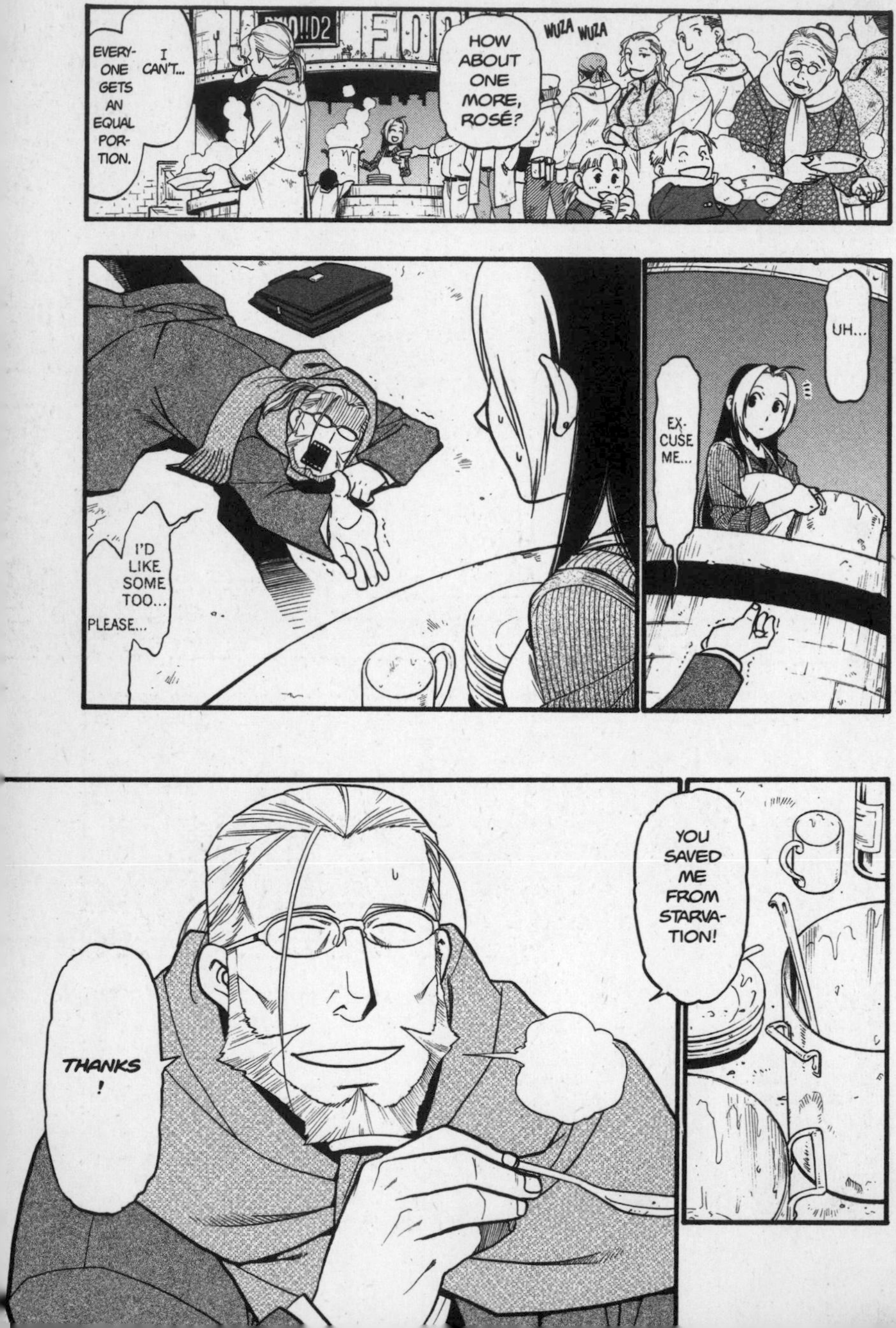
WUZA WUZA
HOW ABOUT ONE MORE, ROSÉ?
I CAN'T...
EVERYONE GETS AN EQUAL PORTION.
UH...
EXCUSE ME...
I'D LIKE SOME TOO... PLEASE...
YOU SAVED ME FROM STARVATION!
THANKS!

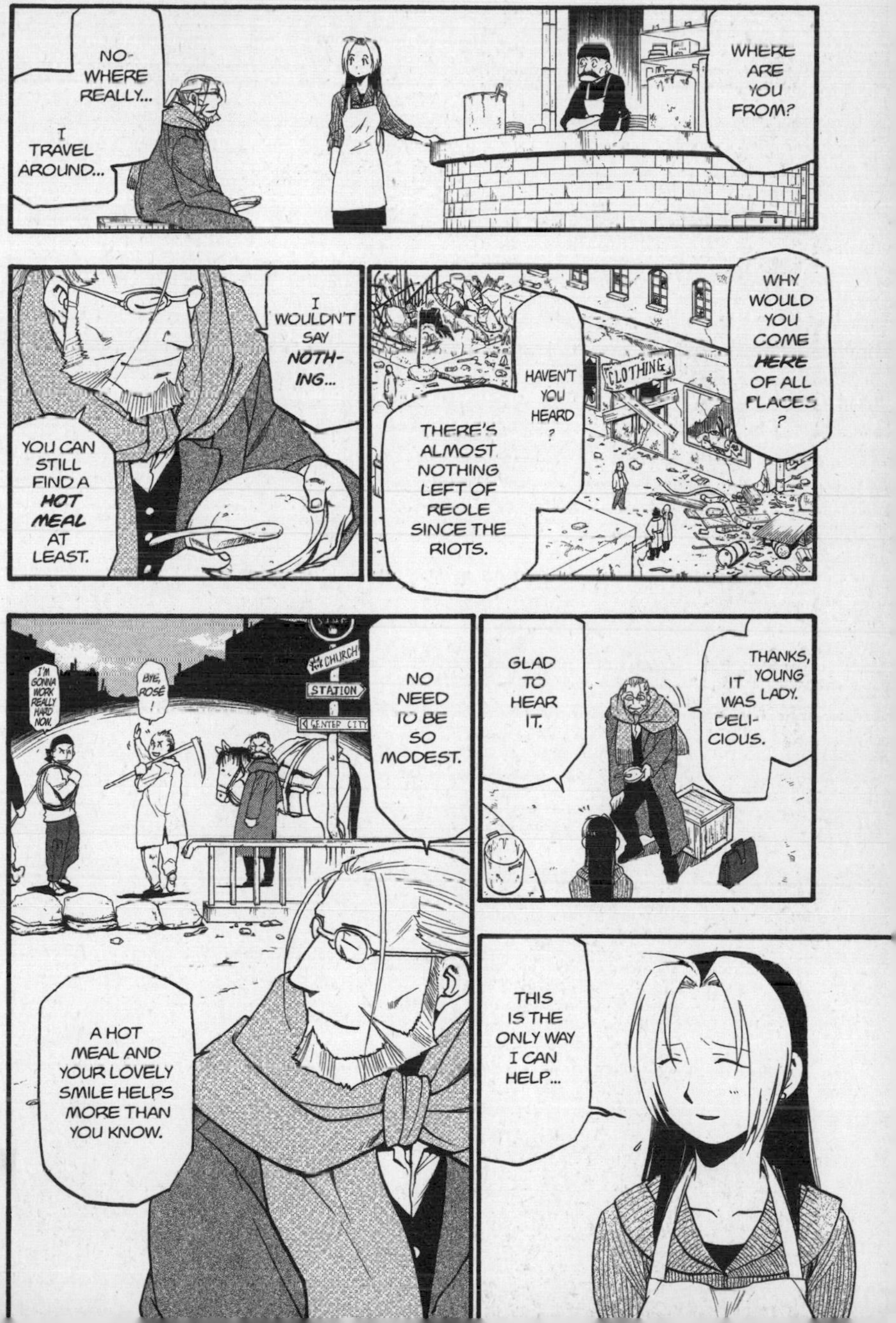
WHERE ARE YOU FROM?
NO-WHERE REALLY...
I TRAVEL AROUND...
WHY WOULD YOU COME HERE OF ALL PLACES?
HAVEN'T YOU HEARD?
THERE'S ALMOST NOTHING LEFT OF REOLE SINCE THE RIOTS.
I WOULDN'T SAY NOTHING...
YOU CAN STILL FIND A HOT MEAL AT LEAST.
THANKS, YOUNG LADY.
IT WAS DELICIOUS.
GLAD TO HEAR IT.
THIS IS THE ONLY WAY I CAN HELP...
NO NEED TO BE SO MODEST.
CHURCH
STATION
CENTER CITY
BYE, ROSÉ!
I'M GONNA WORK REALLY HARD NOW.
A HOT MEAL AND YOUR LOVELY SMILE HELPS MORE THAN YOU KNOW.

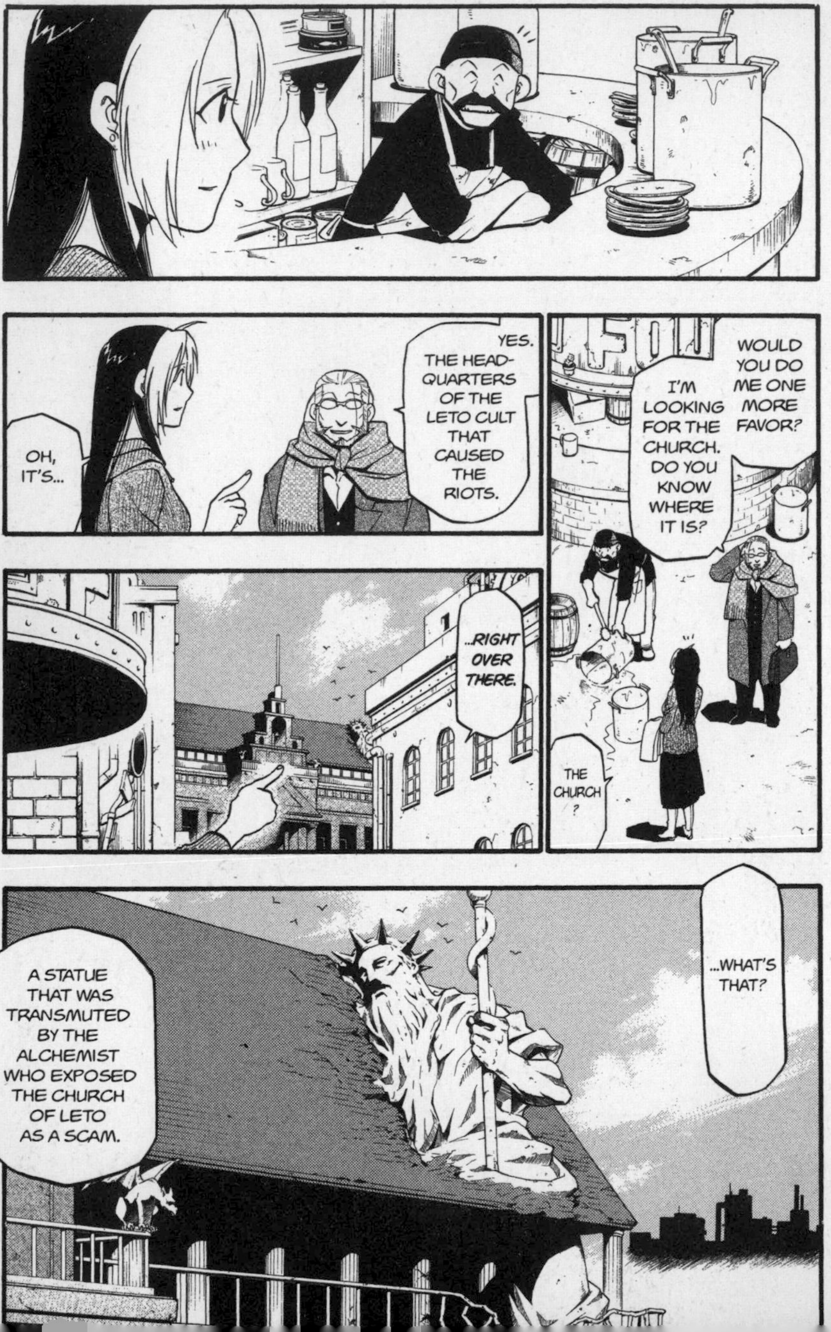
WOULD YOU DO ME ONE MORE FAVOR?
I'M LOOKING FOR THE CHURCH. DO YOU KNOW WHERE IT IS?
THE CHURCH?
YES. THE HEAD-QUARTERS OF THE LETO CULT THAT CAUSED THE RIOTS.
OH, IT'S...
...RIGHT OVER THERE.
...WHAT'S THAT?
A STATUE THAT WAS TRANSMUTED BY THE ALCHEMIST WHO EXPOSED THE CHURCH OF LETO AS A SCAM.

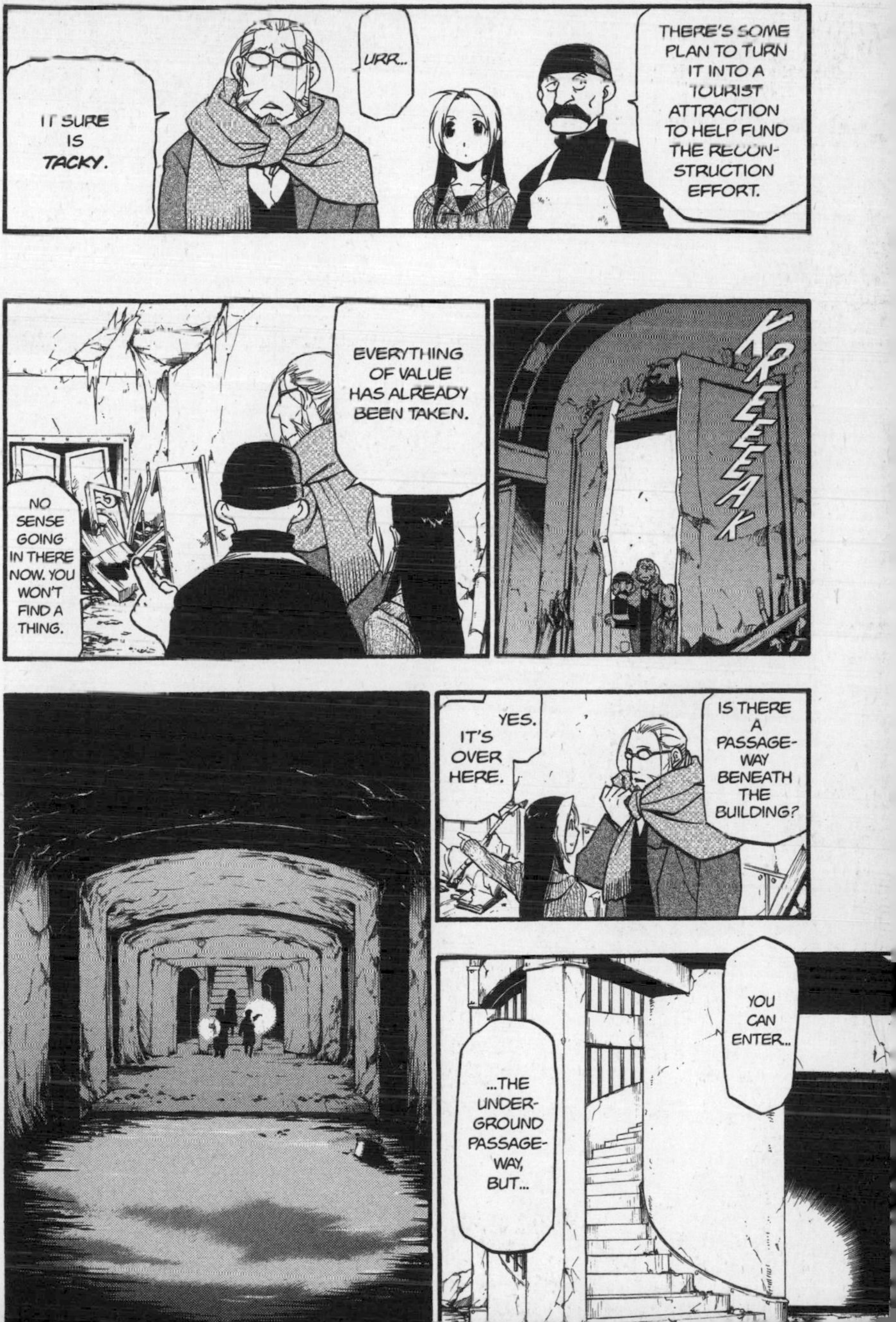
THERE'S SOME PLAN TO TURN IT INTO A TOURIST ATTRACTION TO HELP FUND THE RECONSTRUCTION EFFORT.
URR...
IT SURE IS TACKY.
KREEEAK
EVERYTHING OF VALUE HAS ALREADY BEEN TAKEN.
NO SENSE GOING IN THERE NOW. YOU WON'T FIND A THING.
IS THERE A PASSAGEWAY BENEATH THE BUILDING?
YES. IT'S OVER HERE.
YOU CAN ENTER...
...THE UNDERGROUND PASSAGEWAY, BUT...

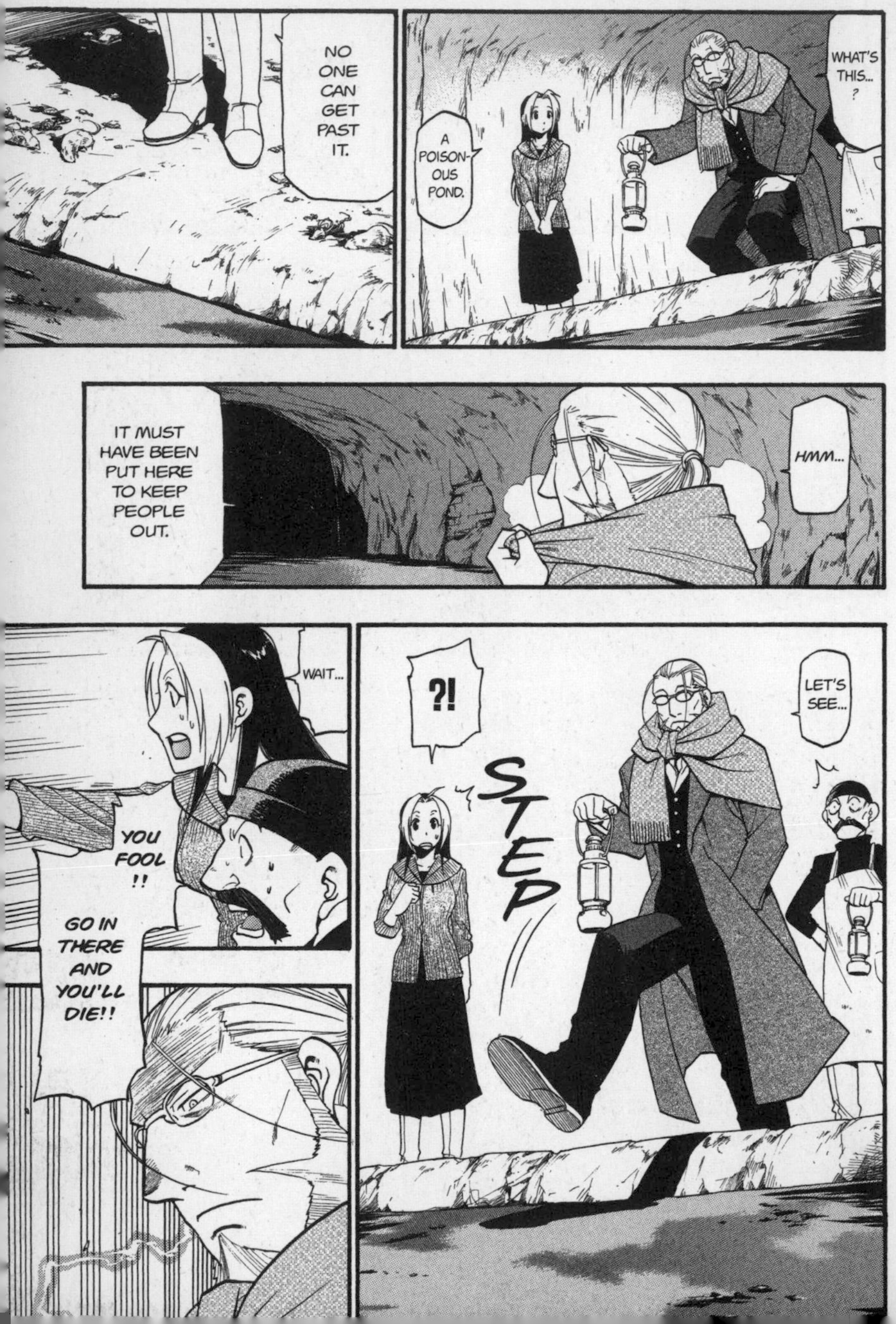
WHAT'S THIS...?
A POISONOUS POND.
NO ONE CAN GET PAST IT.
HMM...
IT MUST HAVE BEEN PUT HERE TO KEEP PEOPLE OUT.
LET'S SEE...
?!
STEP
WAIT...
YOU FOOL!!
GO IN THERE AND YOU'LL DIE!!

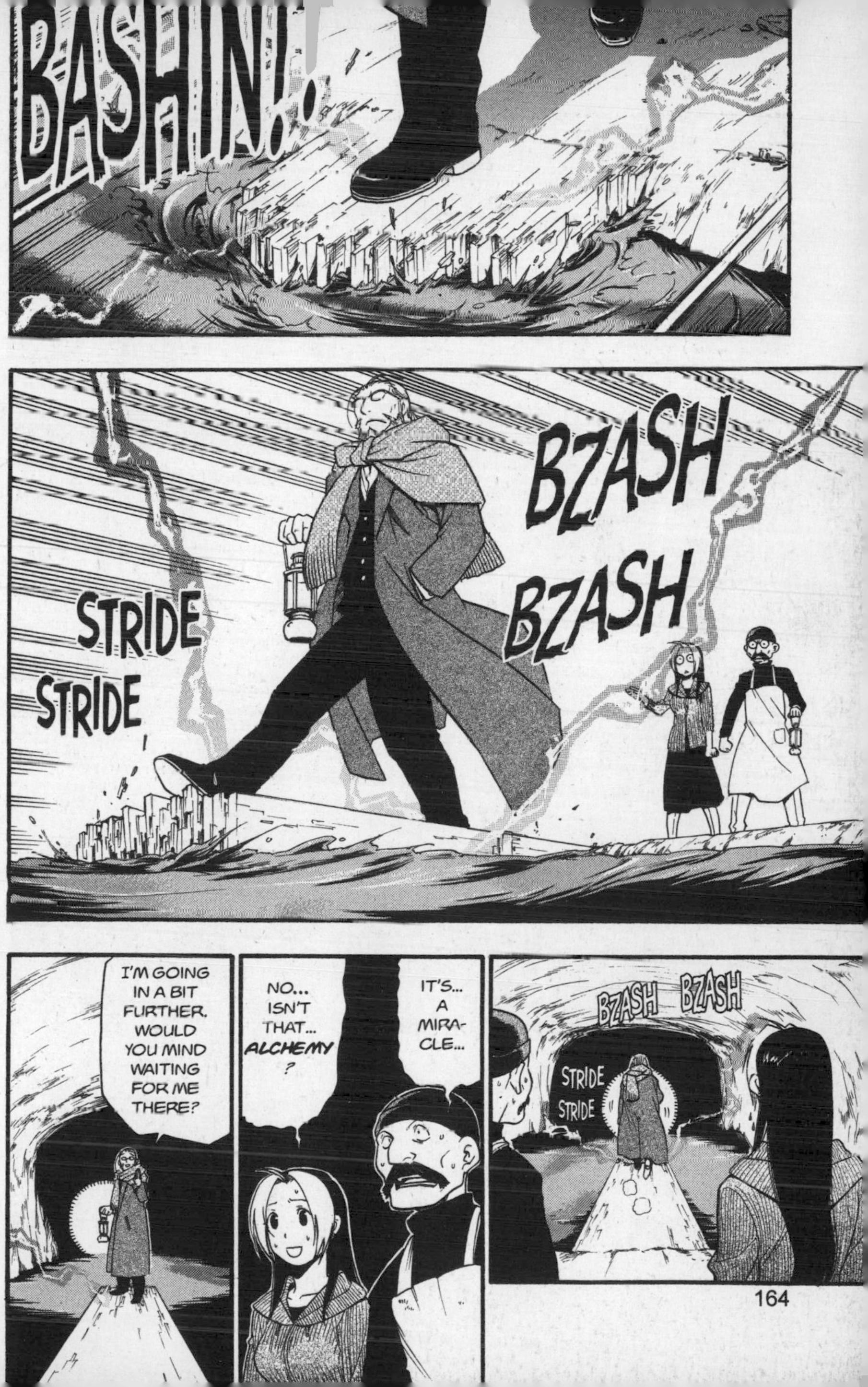
BASHIN
BZASH BZASH
STRIDE STRIDE
BZASH BZASH
STRIDE STRIDE
IT'S... A MIRA-CLE...
NO... ISN'T THAT... ALCHEMY?
I'M GOING IN A BIT FURTHER. WOULD YOU MIND WAITING FOR ME THERE?

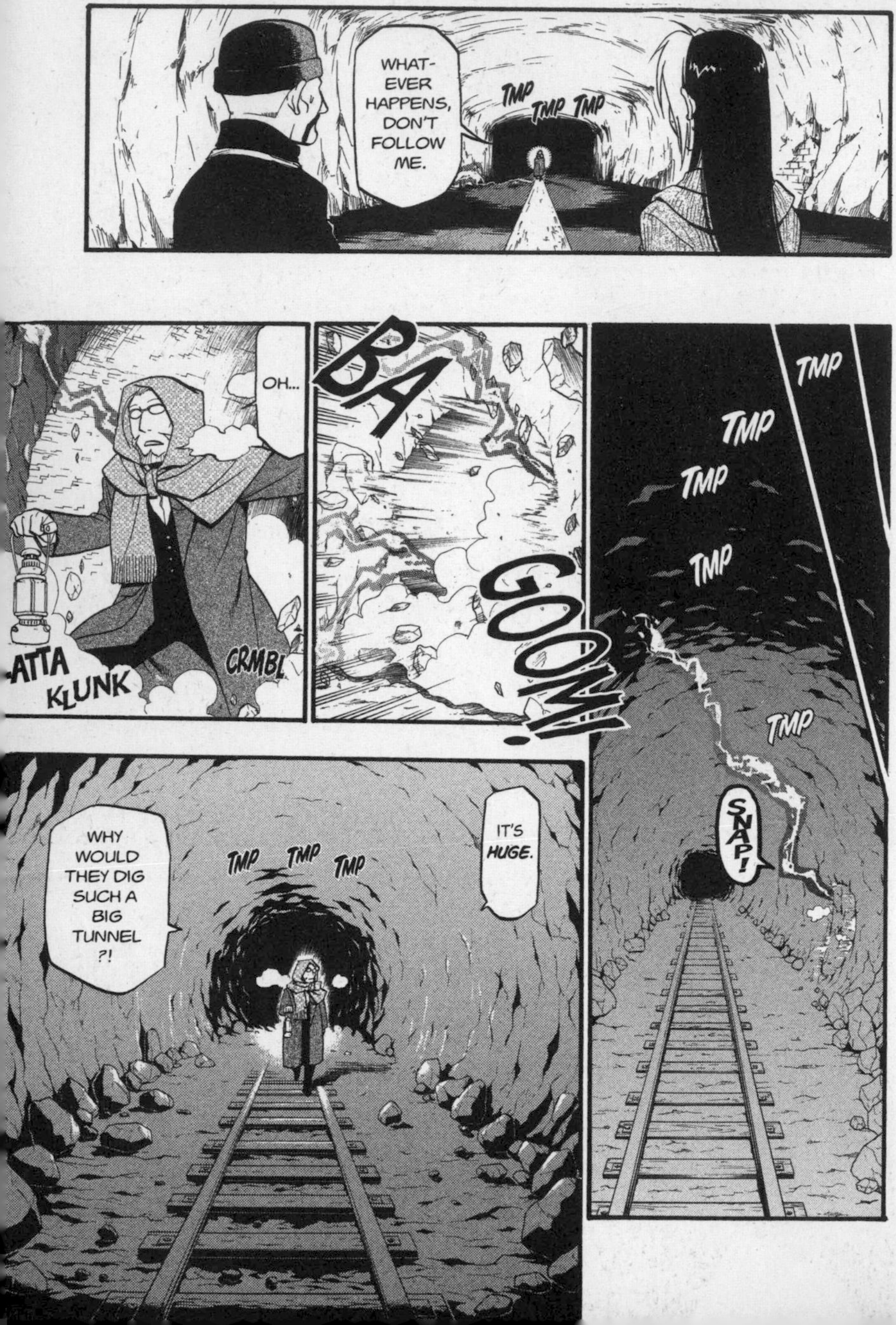
TMP
TMP TMP
WHATEVER HAPPENS, DON'T FOLLOW ME.
TMP
TMP
TMP
TMP
TMP
SNAP!
BA
GOOM!
OH...
CRMBL
ATTA
KLUNK
IT'S HUGE.
WHY WOULD THEY DIG SUCH A BIG TUNNEL ?!
TMP TMP TMP

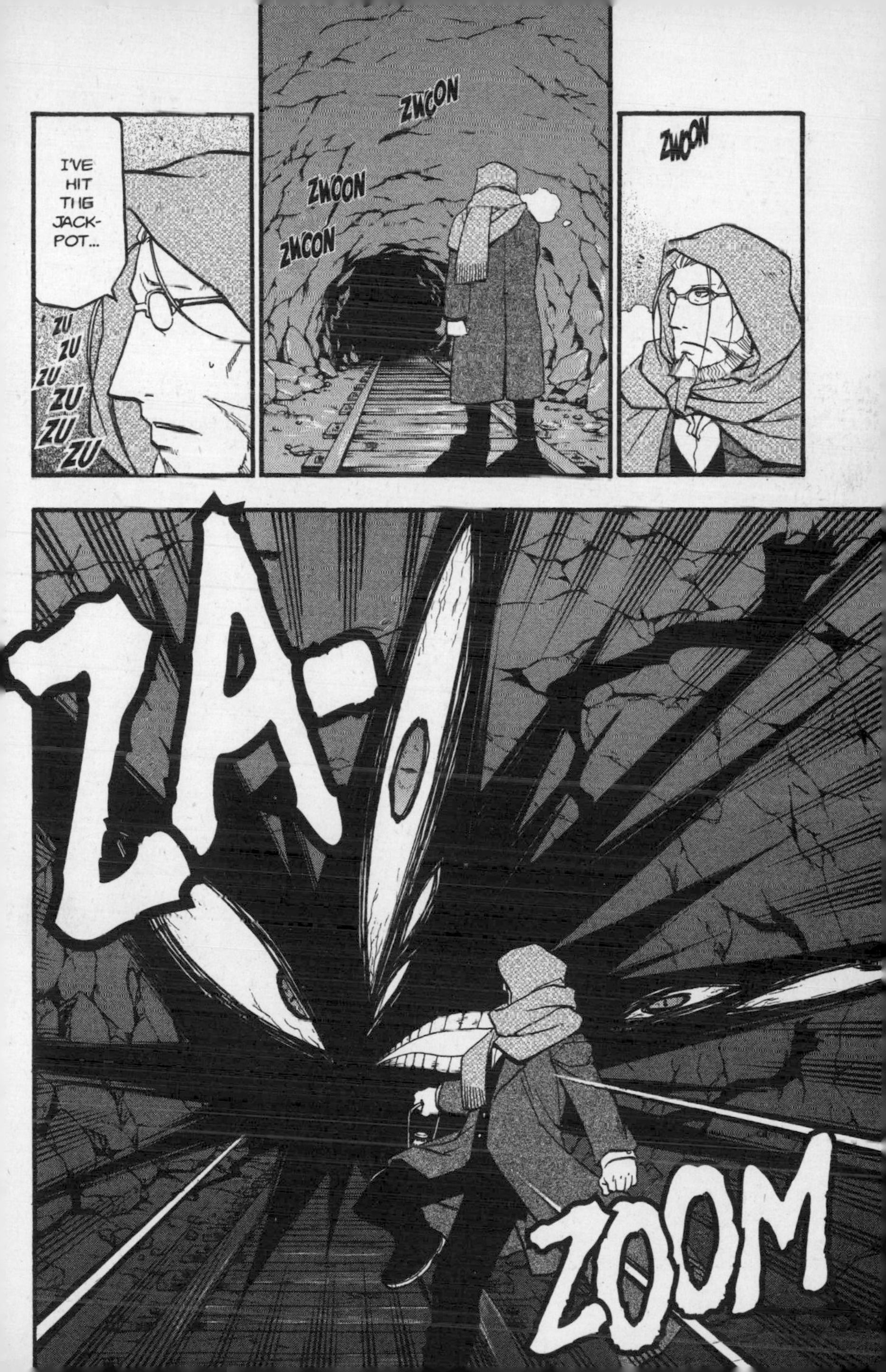
ZWOON
ZWOON
ZWOON
ZWOON
I'VE HIT THE JACKPOT...
ZU ZU ZU ZU ZU ZU
ZA
ZOOM

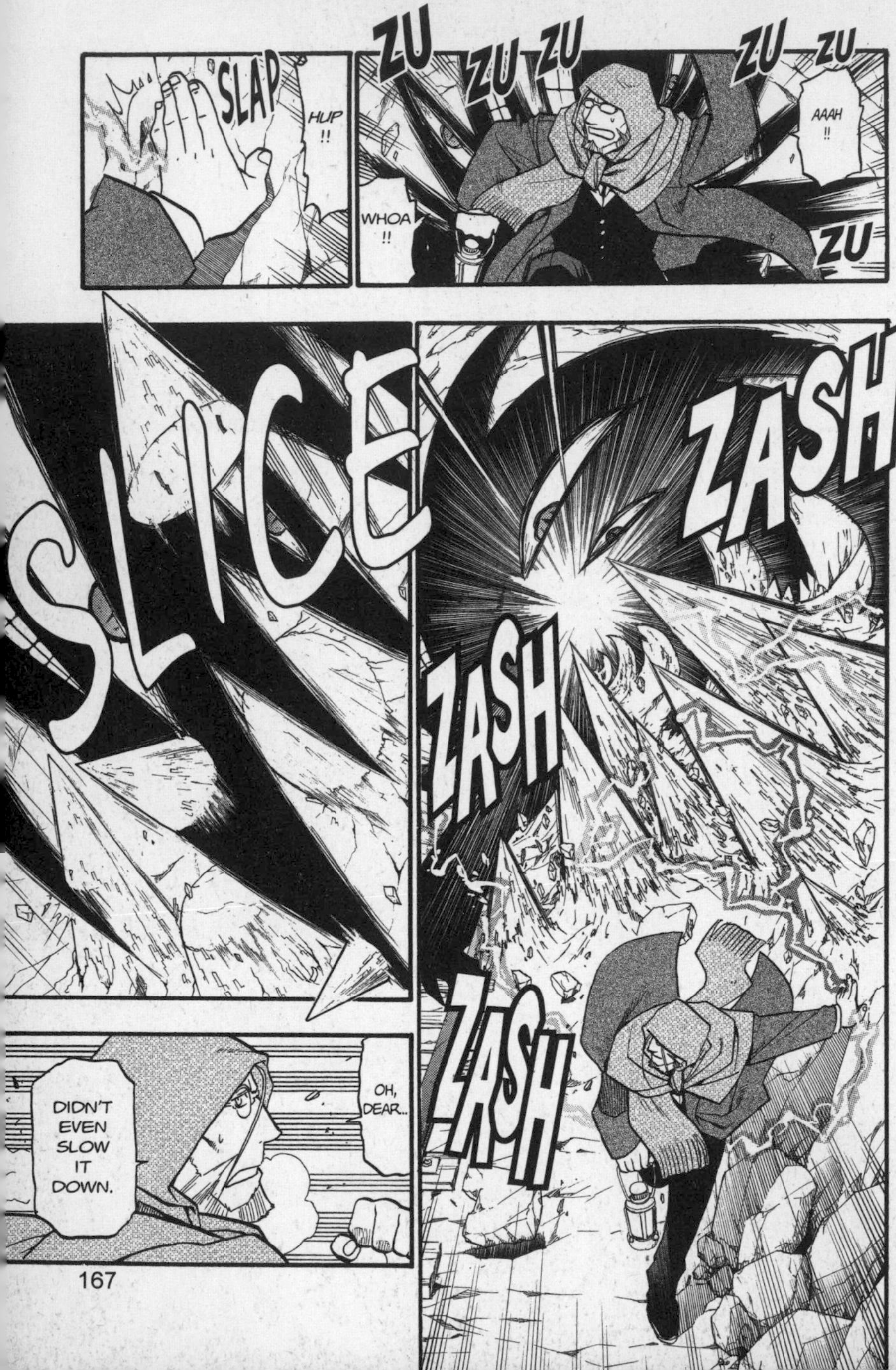
ZU
ZU
ZU
ZU
ZU
AAAH!!
WHOA!!
ZU
SLAP
HUP!!
ZASH
ZASH
ZASH
ZASH
SLICE
OH, DEAR...
DIDN'T EVEN SLOW IT DOWN.

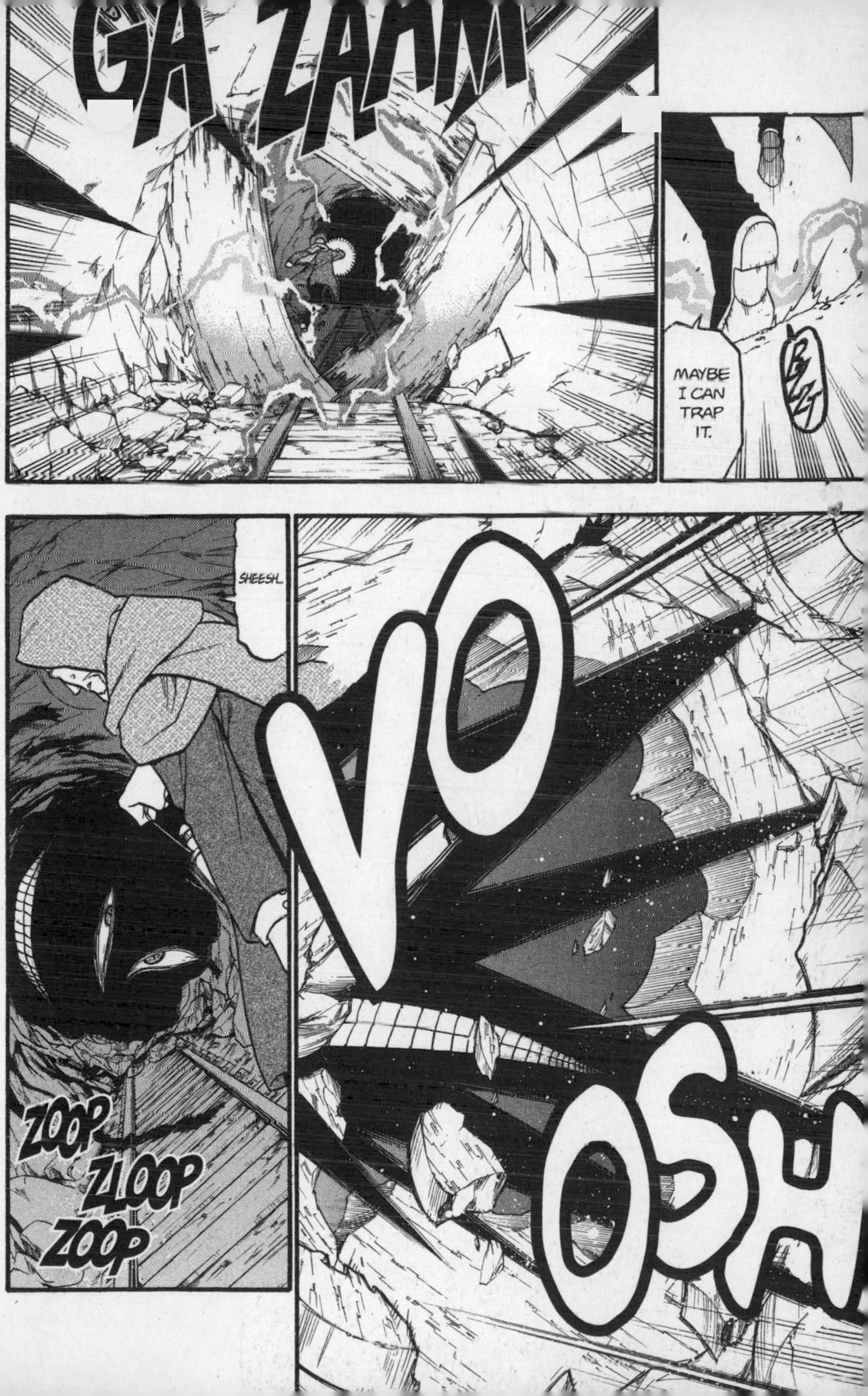
MAYBE I CAN TRAP IT.
GA ZAM
VOOSH
SHEESH.
ZOOP
ZLOOP
ZOOP

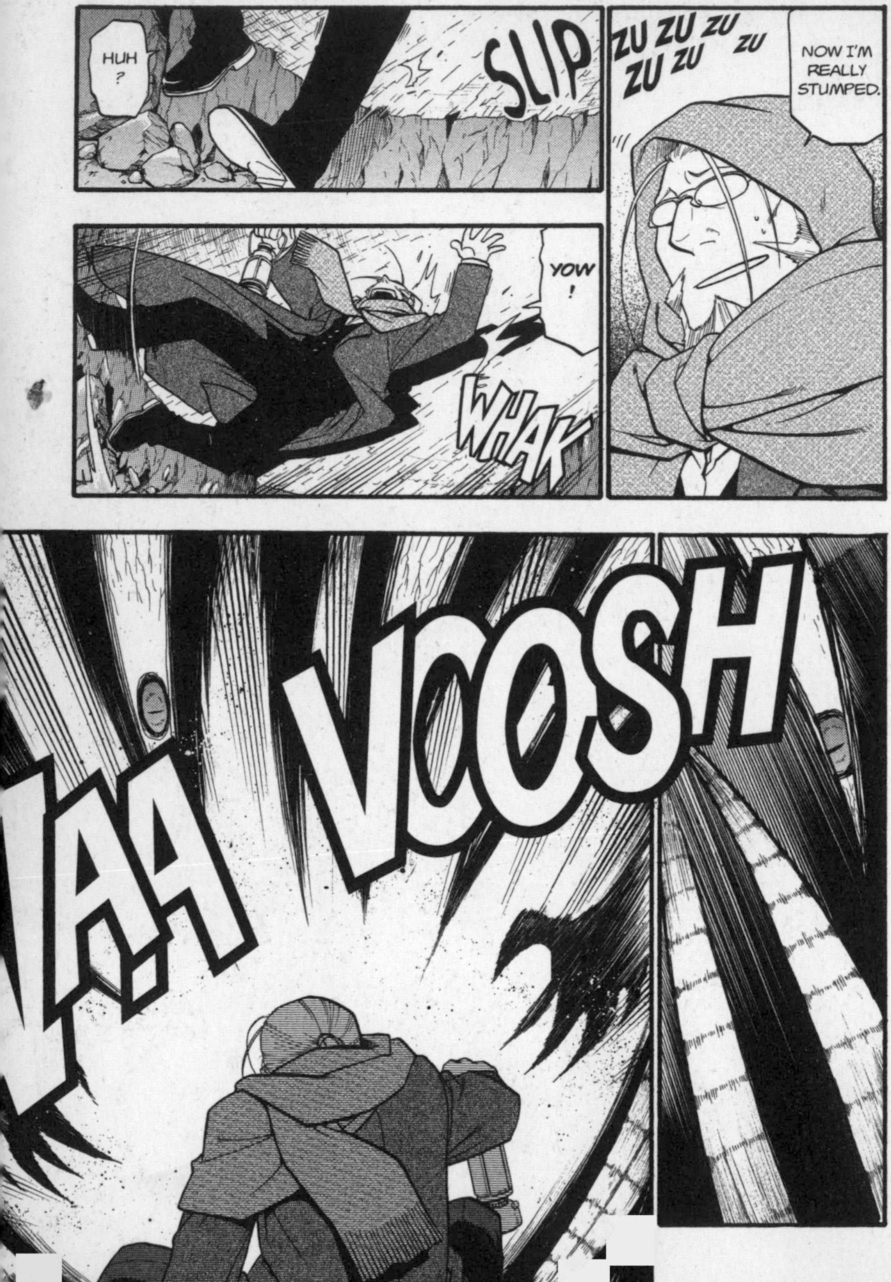
ZU ZU ZU
ZU ZU
ZU
NOW I'M REALLY STUMPED.
SLIP
HUH?
YOW!
WHAK
VOOSH
AA

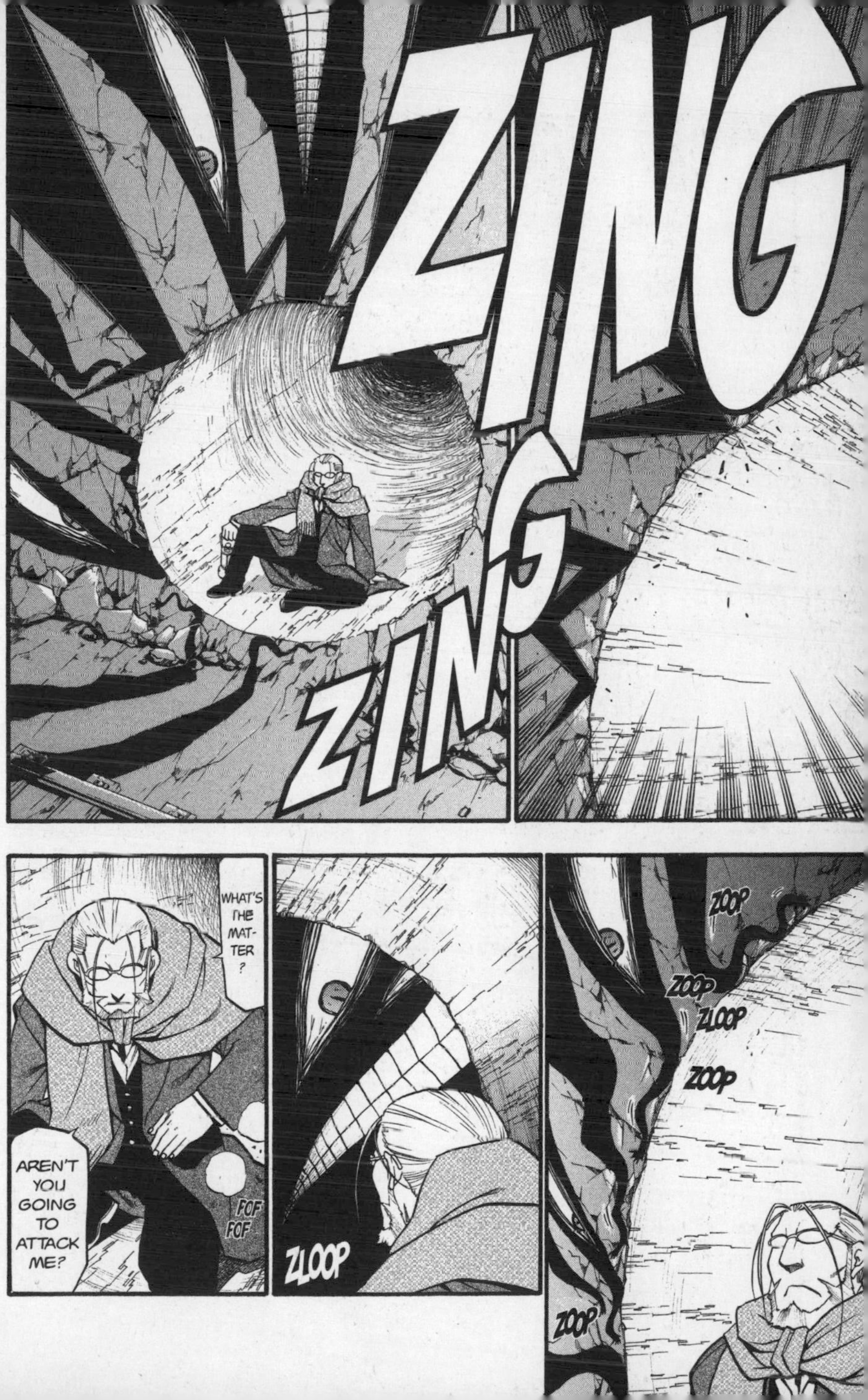
ZING
ZING
ZOOP
ZOOP
ZLOOP
ZOOP
ZOOP
ZLOOP
WHAT'S THE MATTER?
AREN'T YOU GOING TO ATTACK ME?
FOF FOF

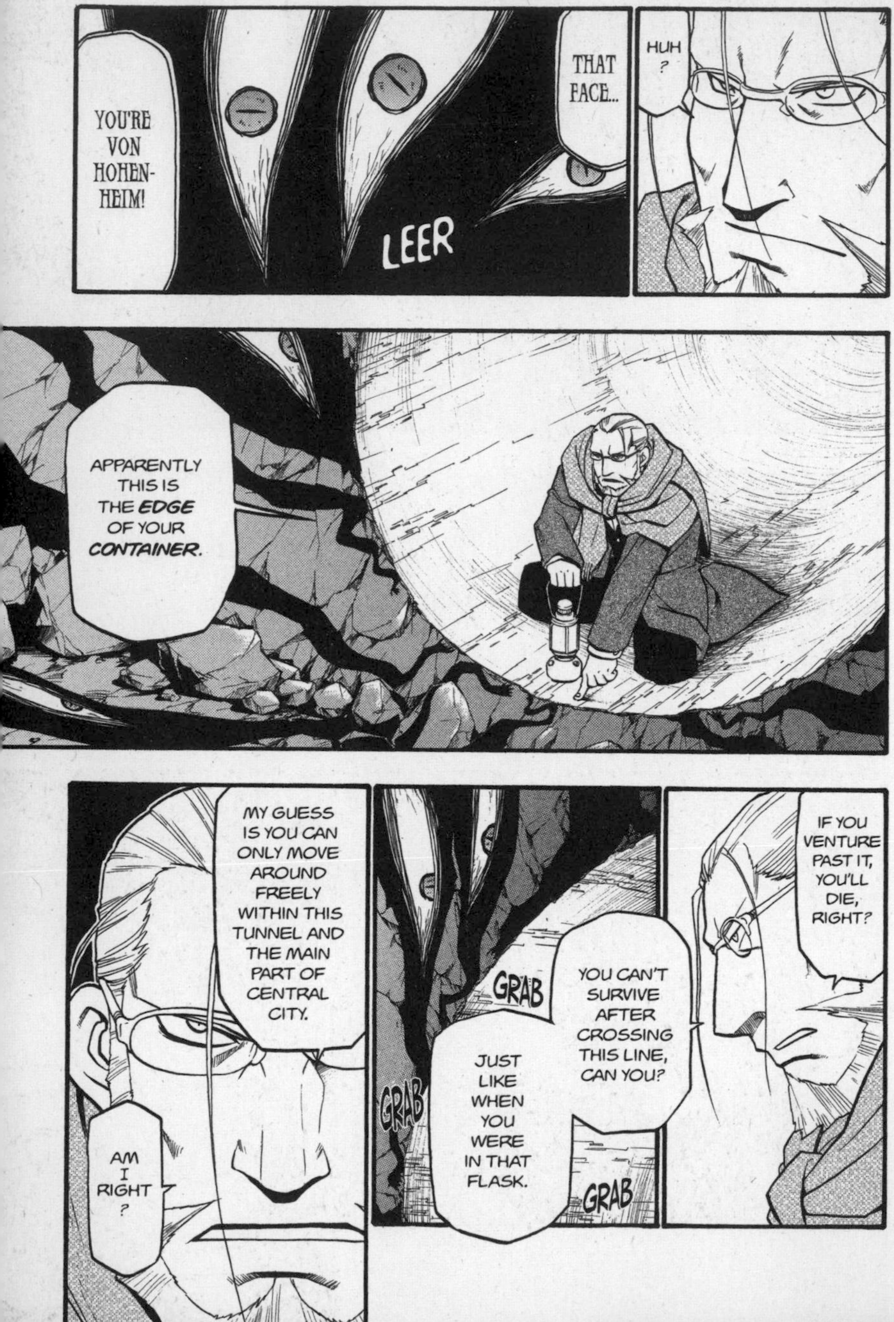
HUH?
THAT FACE...
YOU'RE VON HOHENHEIM!
LEER
APPARENTLY THIS IS THE EDGE OF YOUR CONTAINER.
IF YOU VENTURE PAST IT, YOU'LL DIE, RIGHT?
YOU CAN'T SURVIVE AFTER CROSSING THIS LINE, CAN YOU?
GRAB
JUST LIKE WHEN YOU WERE IN THAT FLASK.
GRAB
GRAB
MY GUESS IS YOU CAN ONLY MOVE AROUND FREELY WITHIN THIS TUNNEL AND THE MAIN PART OF CENTRAL CITY.
AM I RIGHT?

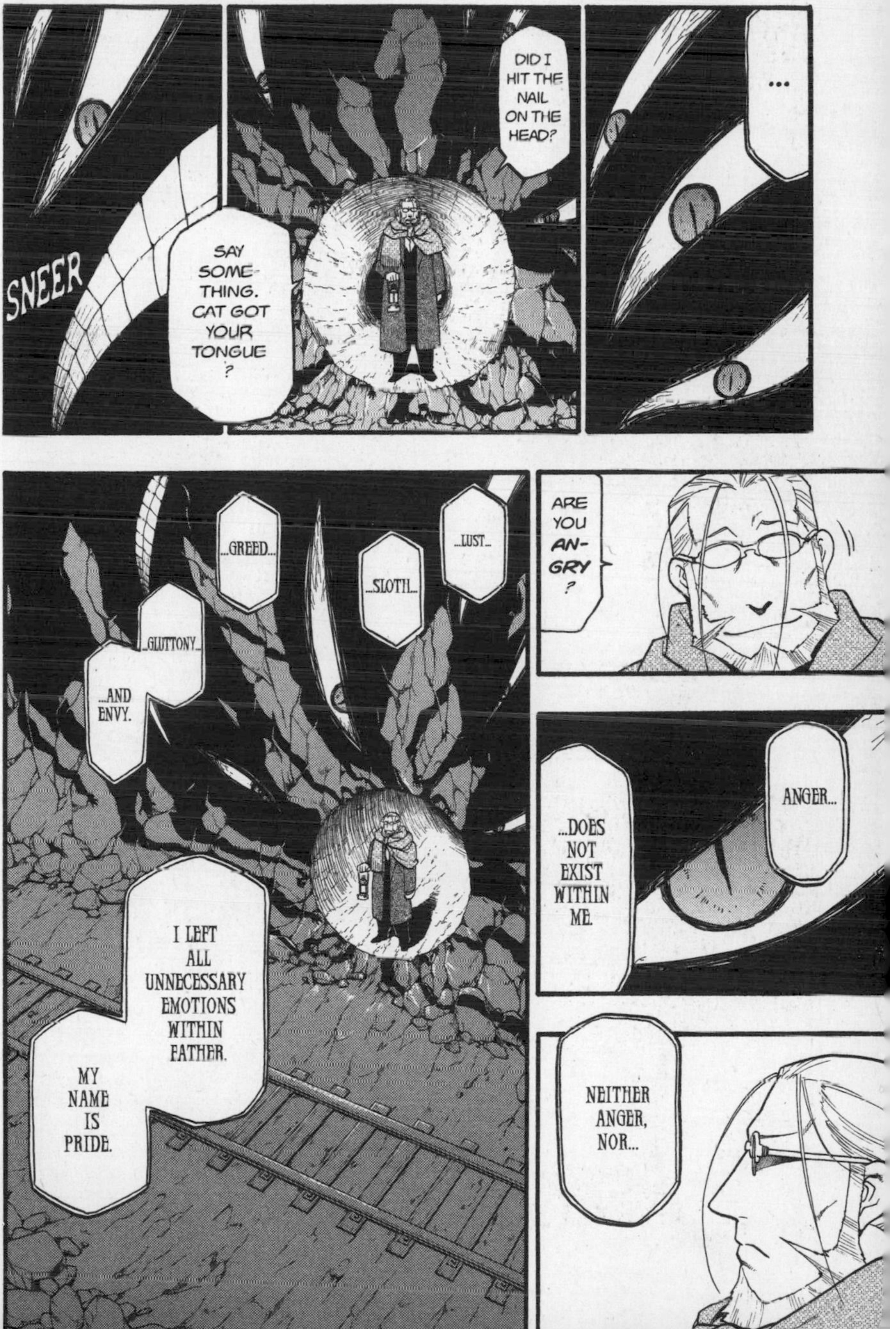
...
DID I HIT THE NAIL ON THE HEAD?
SAY SOMETHING. CAT GOT YOUR TONGUE?
SNEER
ARE YOU ANGRY?
ANGER...
...DOES NOT EXIST WITHIN ME.
NEITHER ANGER, NOR...
...LUST...
...SLOTH...
...GREED...
...GLUTTONY...
...AND ENVY.
I LEFT ALL UNNECESSARY EMOTIONS WITHIN FATHER.
MY NAME IS PRIDE.

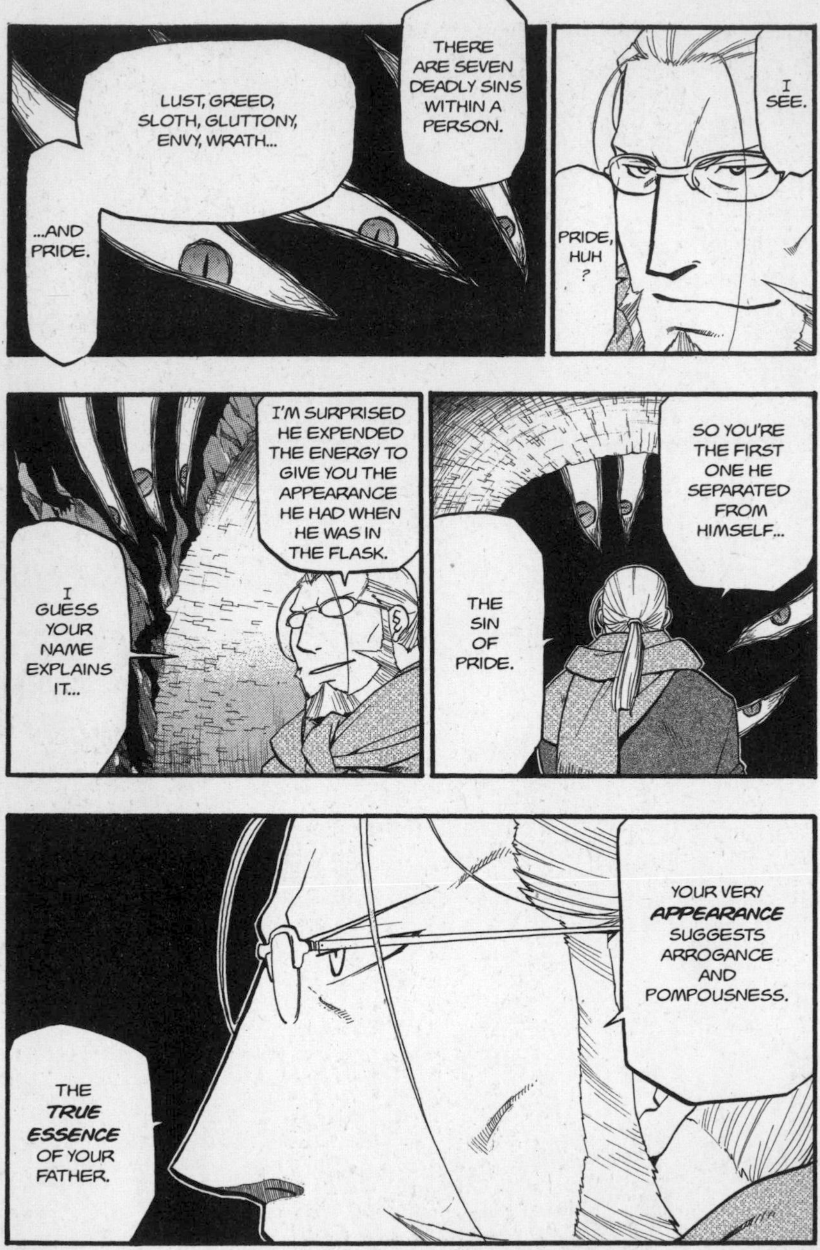
I SEE.
PRIDE, HUH?
THERE ARE SEVEN DEADLY SINS WITHIN A PERSON.
LUST, GREED, SLOTH, GLUTTONY, ENVY, WRATH...
...AND PRIDE.
SO YOU'RE THE FIRST ONE HE SEPARATED FROM HIMSELF...
THE SIN OF PRIDE.
I'M SURPRISED HE EXPENDED THE ENERGY TO GIVE YOU THE APPEARANCE HE HAD WHEN HE WAS IN THE FLASK.
I GUESS YOUR NAME EXPLAINS IT...
YOUR VERY **APPEARANCE** SUGGESTS ARROGANCE AND POMPOUSNESS.
THE **TRUE ESSENCE** OF YOUR FATHER.

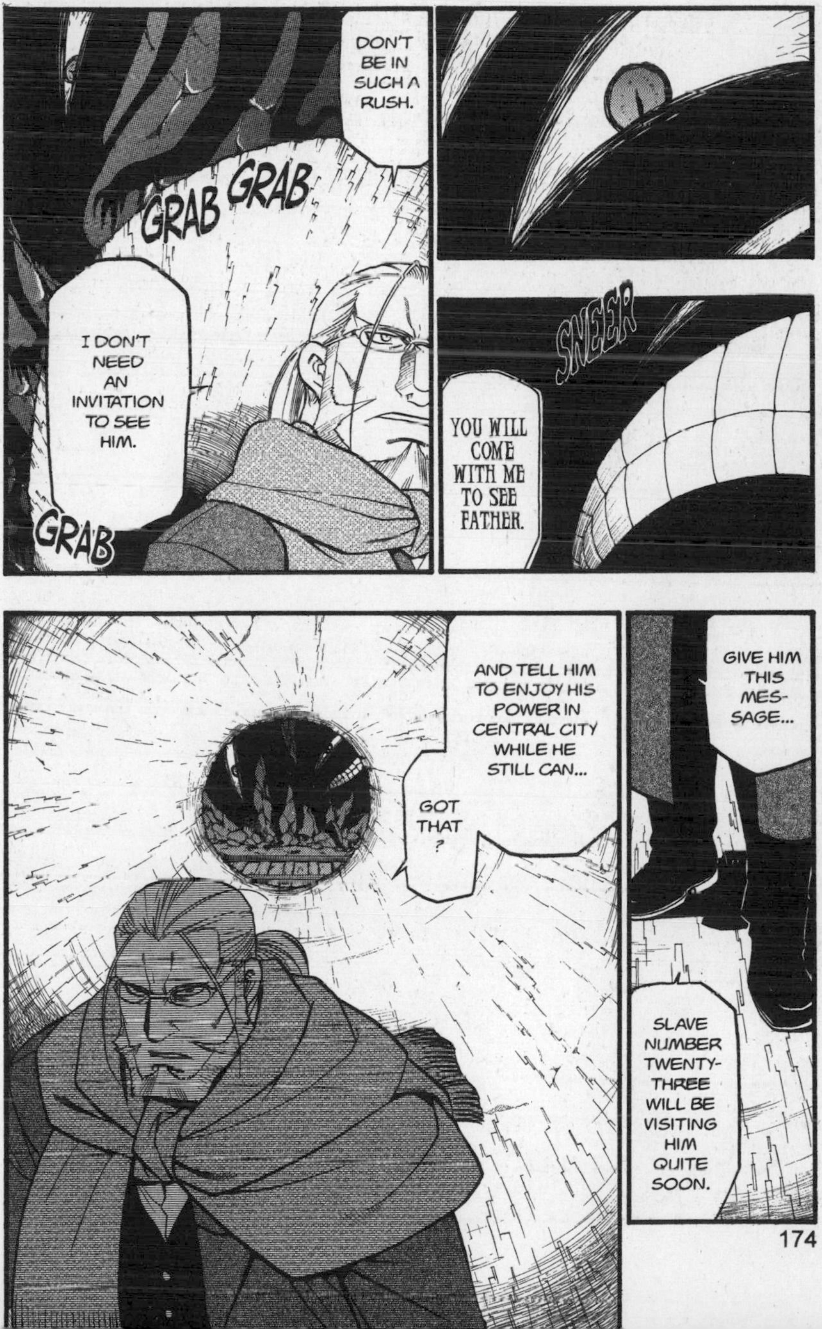
SNEER
YOU WILL COME WITH ME TO SEE FATHER.
DON'T BE IN SUCH A RUSH.
GRAB GRAB
I DON'T NEED AN INVITATION TO SEE HIM.
GRAB
GIVE HIM THIS MESSAGE...
SLAVE NUMBER TWENTY-THREE WILL BE VISITING HIM QUITE SOON.
AND TELL HIM TO ENJOY HIS POWER IN CENTRAL CITY WHILE HE STILL CAN...
GOT THAT?

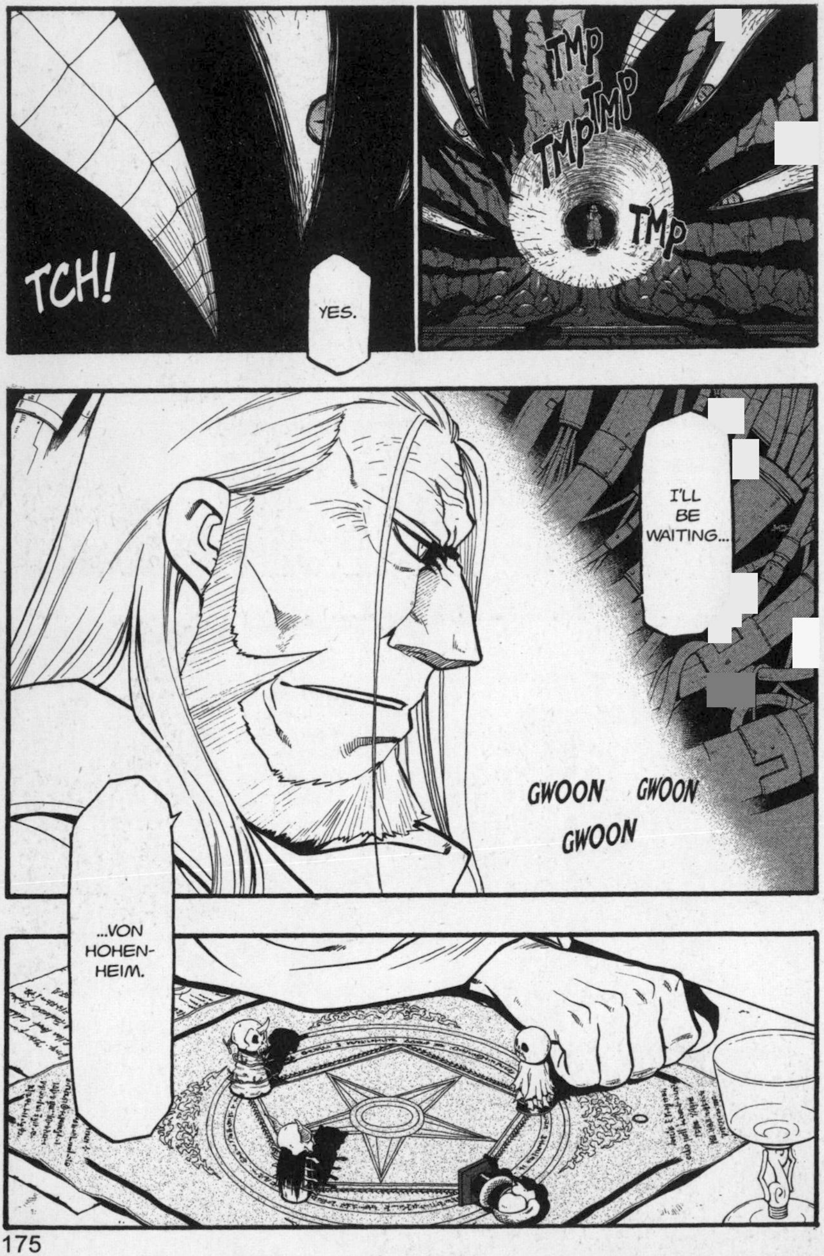
TMP
TMP
TMP
TMP
TMP
YES.
TCH!
I'LL BE WAITING...
GWOON GWOON
GWOON
...VON HOHEN-HEIM.

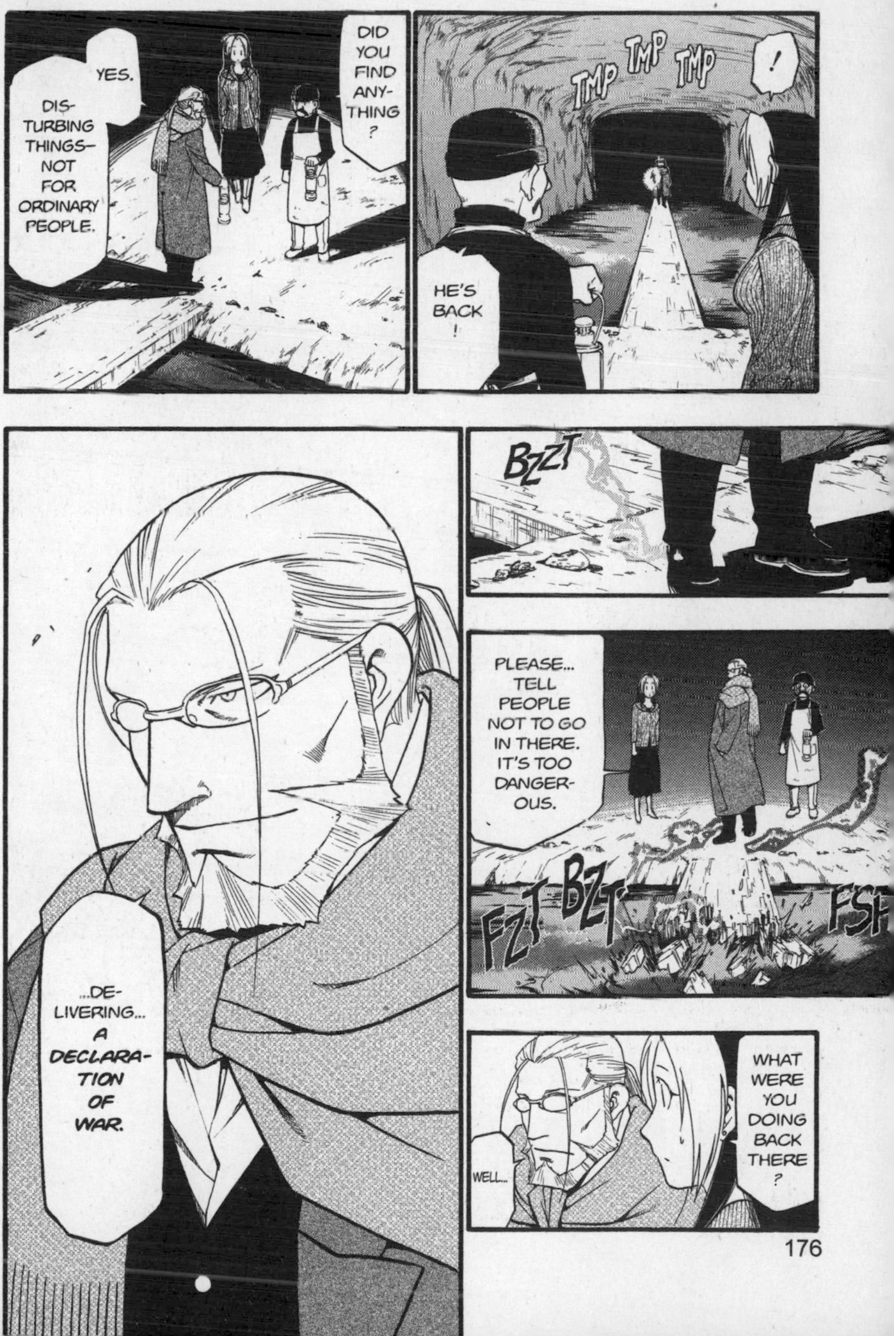
TMP TMP TMP
!
HE'S BACK!
DID YOU FIND ANYTHING?
YES.
DISTURBING THINGS—NOT FOR ORDINARY PEOPLE.
BZZT
PLEASE... TELL PEOPLE NOT TO GO IN THERE. IT'S TOO DANGEROUS.
FZT BZT
WHAT WERE YOU DOING BACK THERE?
WELL...
...DELIVERING... A DECLARATION OF WAR.

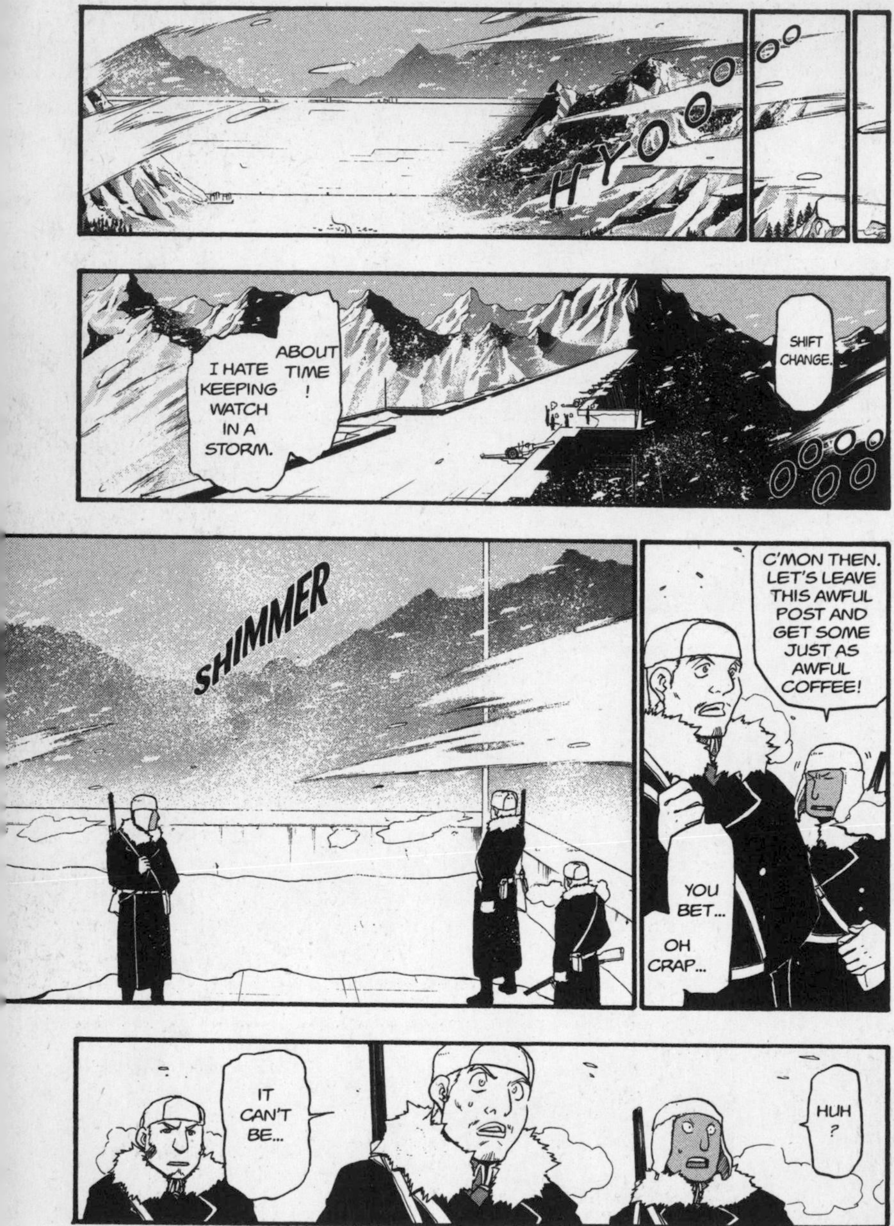
HYOOOOOO
SHIFT CHANGE.
ABOUT TIME! I HATE KEEPING WATCH IN A STORM.
C'MON THEN. LET'S LEAVE THIS AWFUL POST AND GET SOME JUST AS AWFUL COFFEE!
YOU BET...
OH CRAP...
SHIMMER
HUH?
IT CAN'T BE...

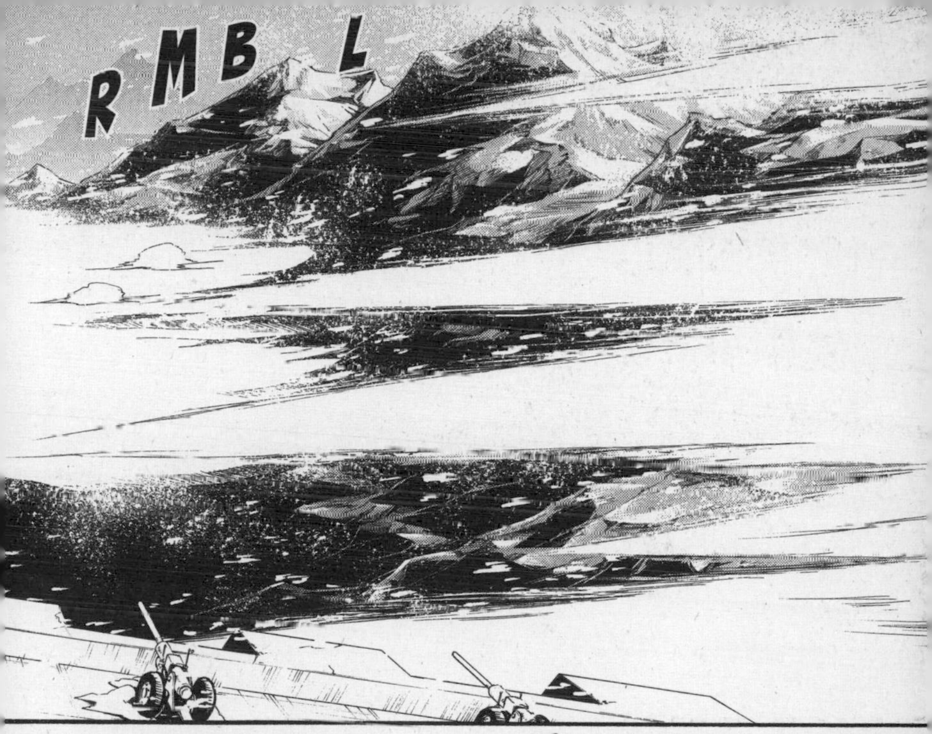
RMBL
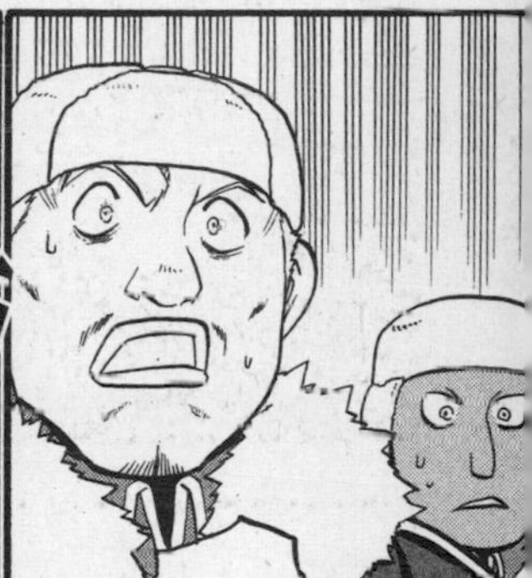
D-D...
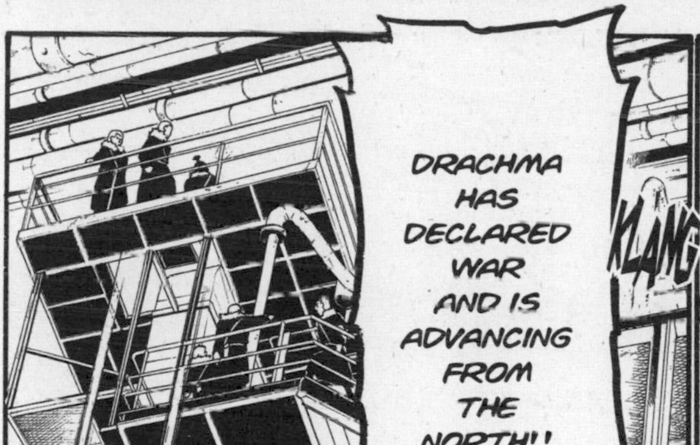
KLANG
DRACHMA HAS DECLARED WAR AND IS ADVANCING FROM THE NORTH!!
KLANG
KLANG

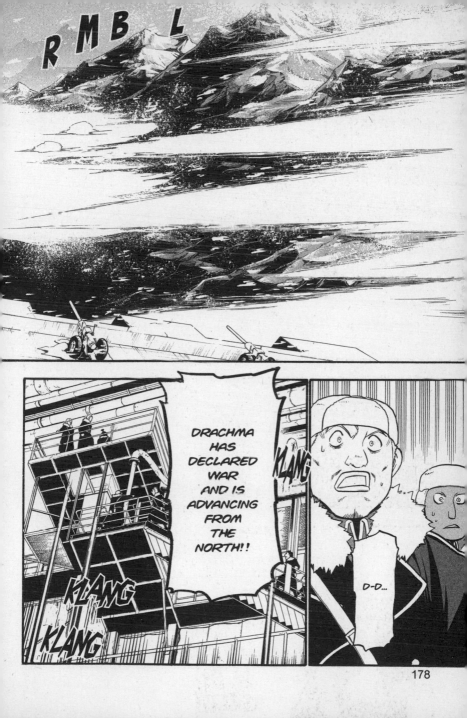

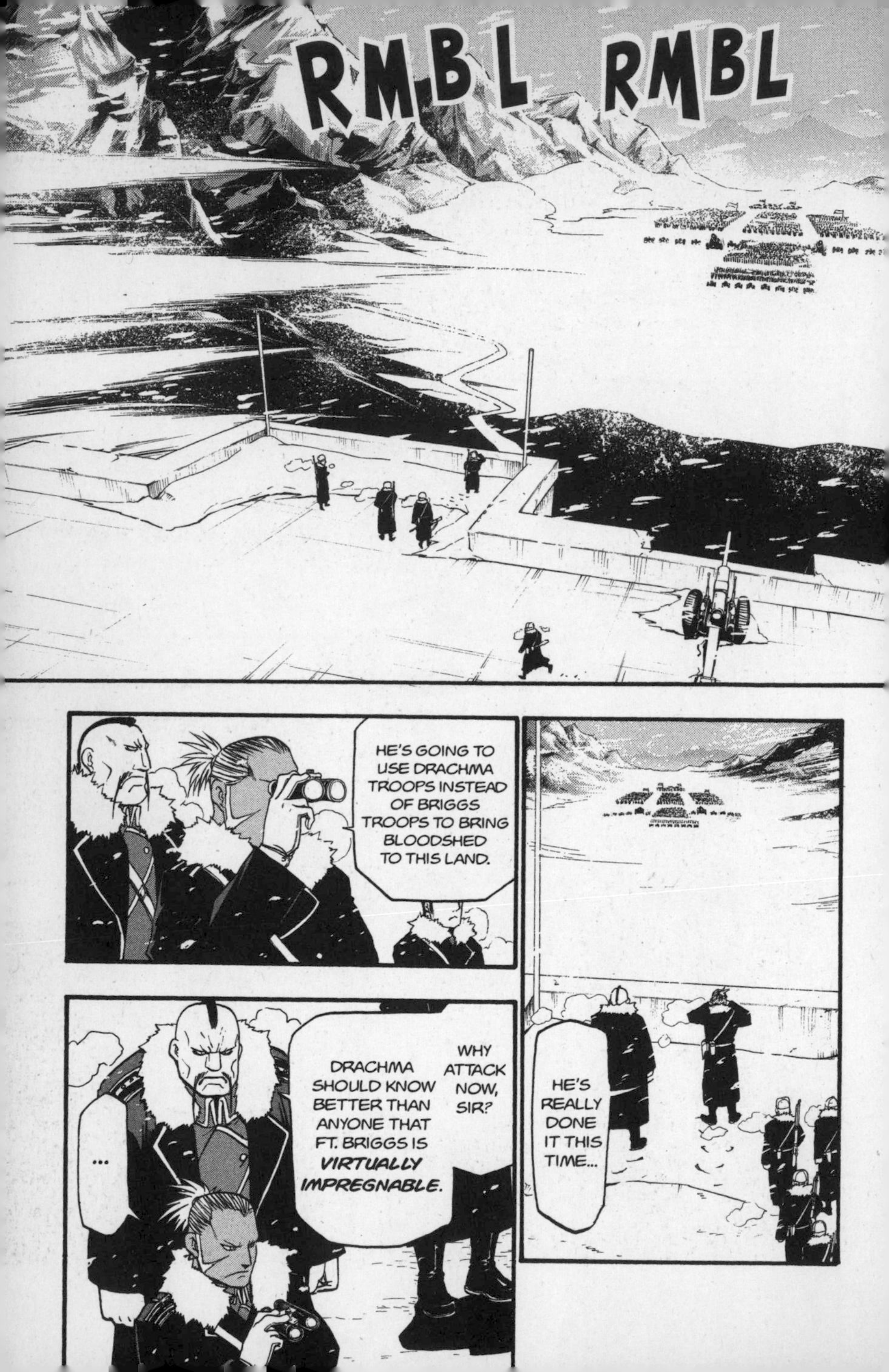
RMBL RMBL
HE'S REALLY DONE IT THIS TIME...
HE'S GOING TO USE DRACHMA TROOPS INSTEAD OF BRIGGS TROOPS TO BRING BLOODSHED TO THIS LAND.
WHY ATTACK NOW, SIR?
DRACHMA SHOULD KNOW BETTER THAN ANYONE THAT FT. BRIGGS IS ***VIRTUALLY IMPREGNABLE***.
...

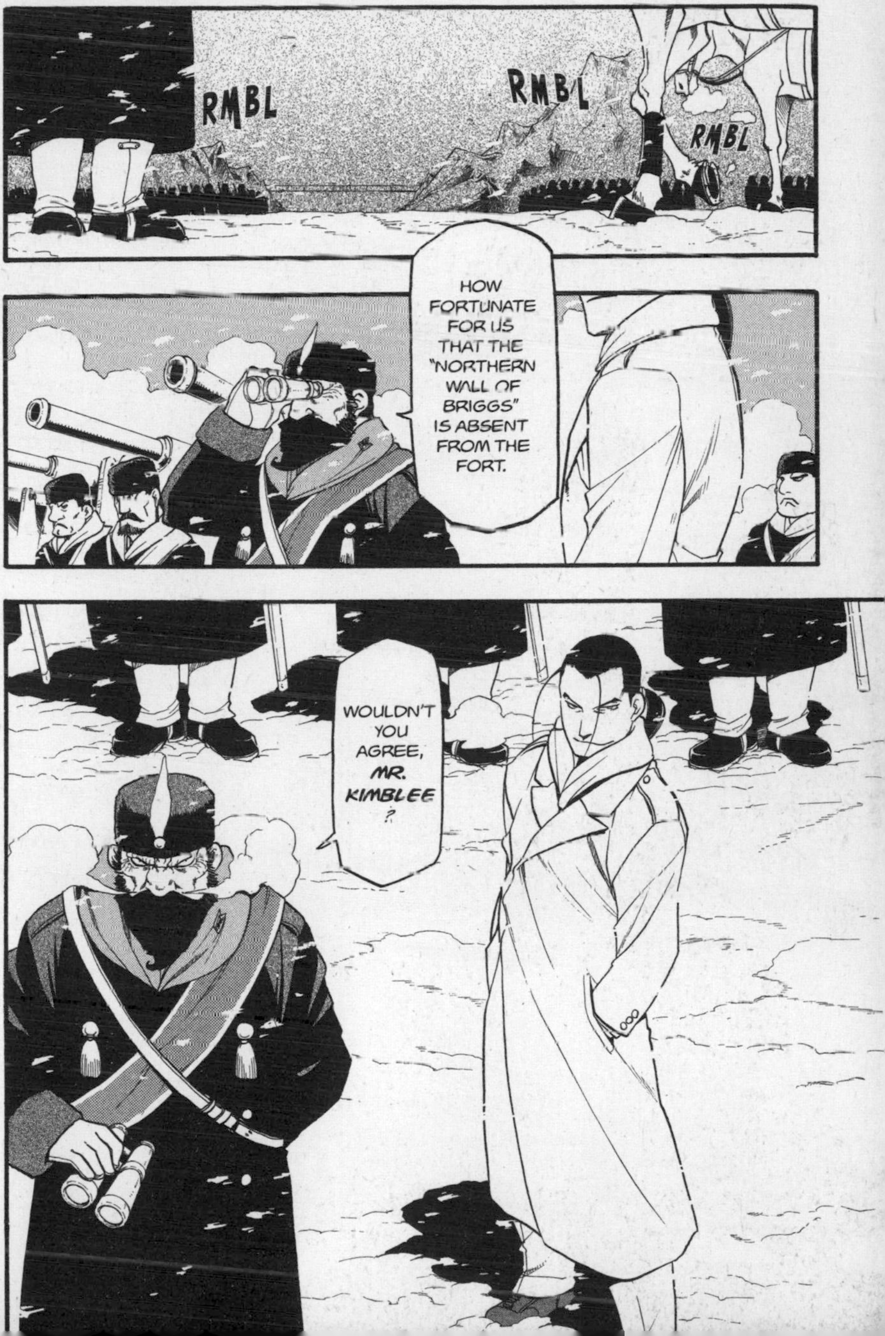
RMBL
RMBL
RMBL
HOW FORTUNATE FOR US THAT THE "NORTHERN WALL OF BRIGGS" IS ABSENT FROM THE FORT.
WOULDN'T YOU AGREE, MR. KIMBLEE?

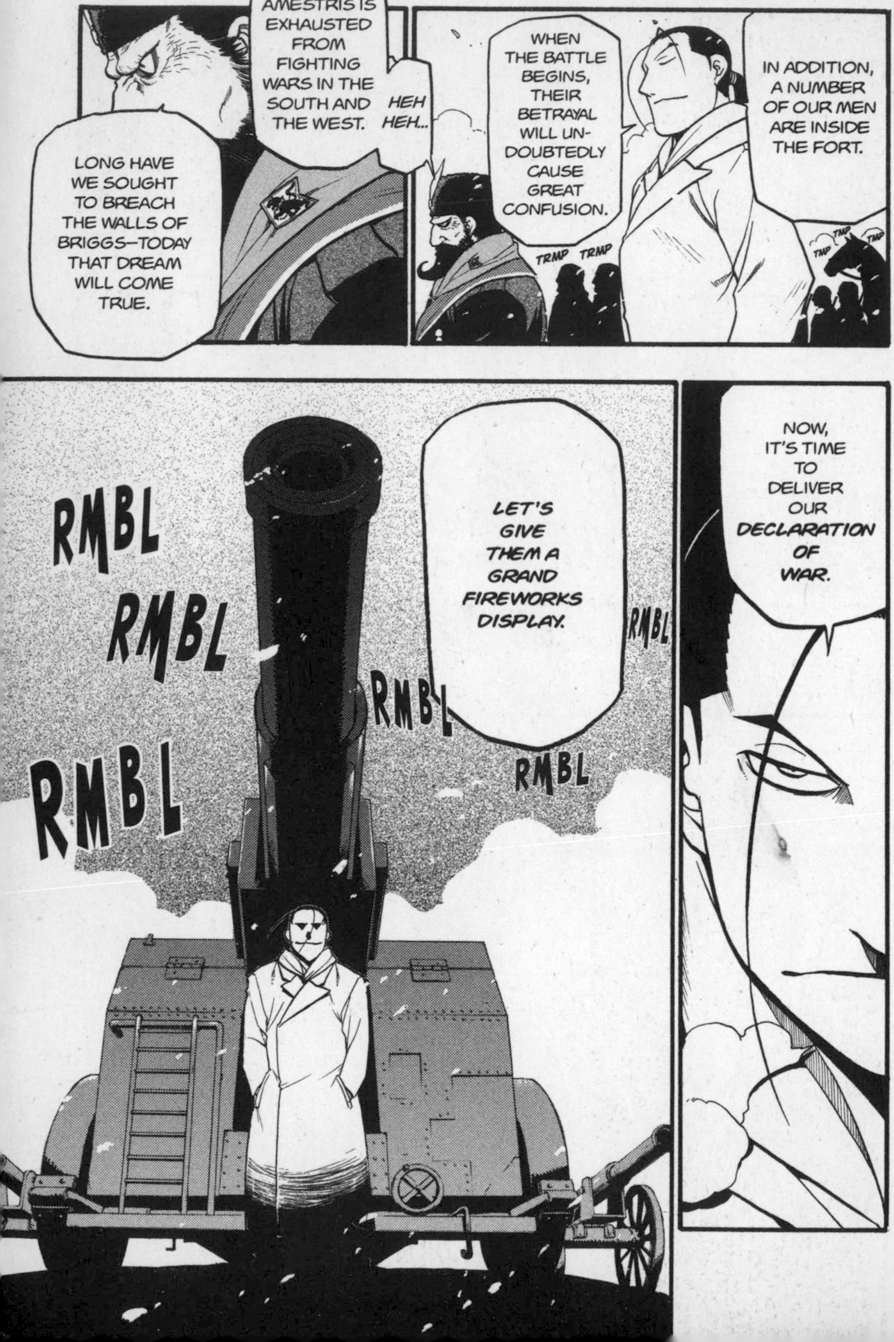
IN ADDITION, A NUMBER OF OUR MEN ARE INSIDE THE FORT.
TMP TMP TMP TMP
WHEN THE BATTLE BEGINS, THEIR BETRAYAL WILL UNDOUBTEDLY CAUSE GREAT CONFUSION.
TRMP TRMP
HEH HEH...
AMESTRIS IS EXHAUSTED FROM FIGHTING WARS IN THE SOUTH AND THE WEST.
LONG HAVE WE SOUGHT TO BREACH THE WALLS OF BRIGGS—TODAY THAT DREAM WILL COME TRUE.
NOW, IT'S TIME TO DELIVER OUR *DECLARATION OF WAR.*
RMBL
LET'S GIVE THEM A GRAND FIREWORKS DISPLAY.
RMBL
RMBL
RMBL
RMBL
RMBL

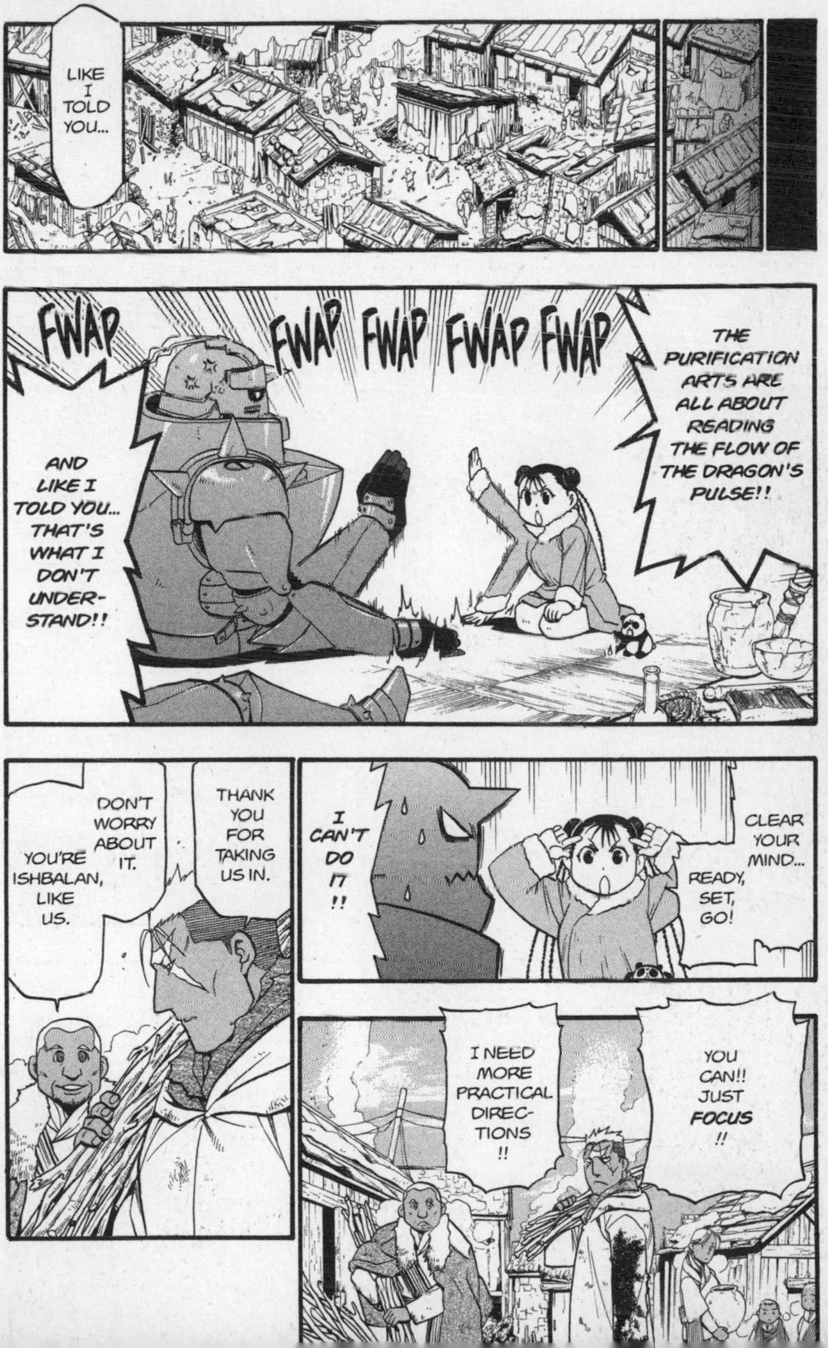
LIKE I TOLD YOU...
THE PURIFICATION ARTS ARE ALL ABOUT READING THE FLOW OF THE DRAGON'S PULSE!!
FWAP FWAP FWAP FWAP
FWAP
AND LIKE I TOLD YOU... THAT'S WHAT I DON'T UNDER-STAND!!
CLEAR YOUR MIND... READY, SET, GO!
I CAN'T DO IT!!
YOU CAN!! JUST FOCUS!!
I NEED MORE PRACTICAL DIREC-TIONS!!
THANK YOU FOR TAKING US IN.
DON'T WORRY ABOUT IT.
YOU'RE ISHBALAN, LIKE US.

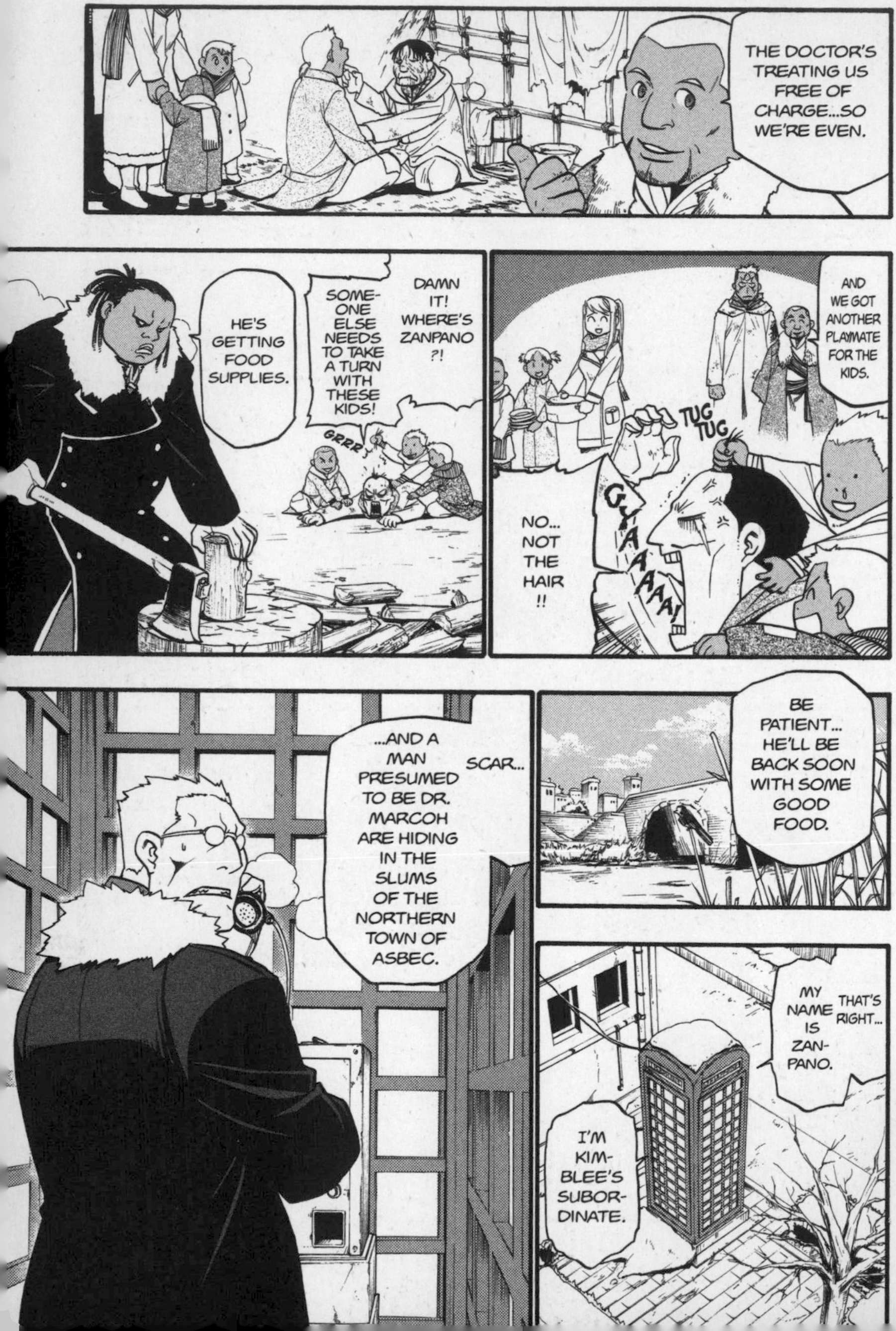
THE DOCTOR'S TREATING US FREE OF CHARGE...SO WE'RE EVEN.
AND WE GOT ANOTHER PLAYMATE FOR THE KIDS.
TUG TUG
GYAAAAAA!
NO... NOT THE HAIR !!
DAMN IT! WHERE'S ZANPANO ?!
SOME-ONE ELSE NEEDS TO TAKE A TURN WITH THESE KIDS!
GRRR
HE'S GETTING FOOD SUPPLIES.
BE PATIENT... HE'LL BE BACK SOON WITH SOME GOOD FOOD.
THAT'S RIGHT...
MY NAME IS ZAN-PANO.
I'M KIM-BLEE'S SUBOR-DINATE.
SCAR...
...AND A MAN PRESUMED TO BE DR. MARCOH ARE HIDING IN THE SLUMS OF THE NORTHERN TOWN OF ASBEC.

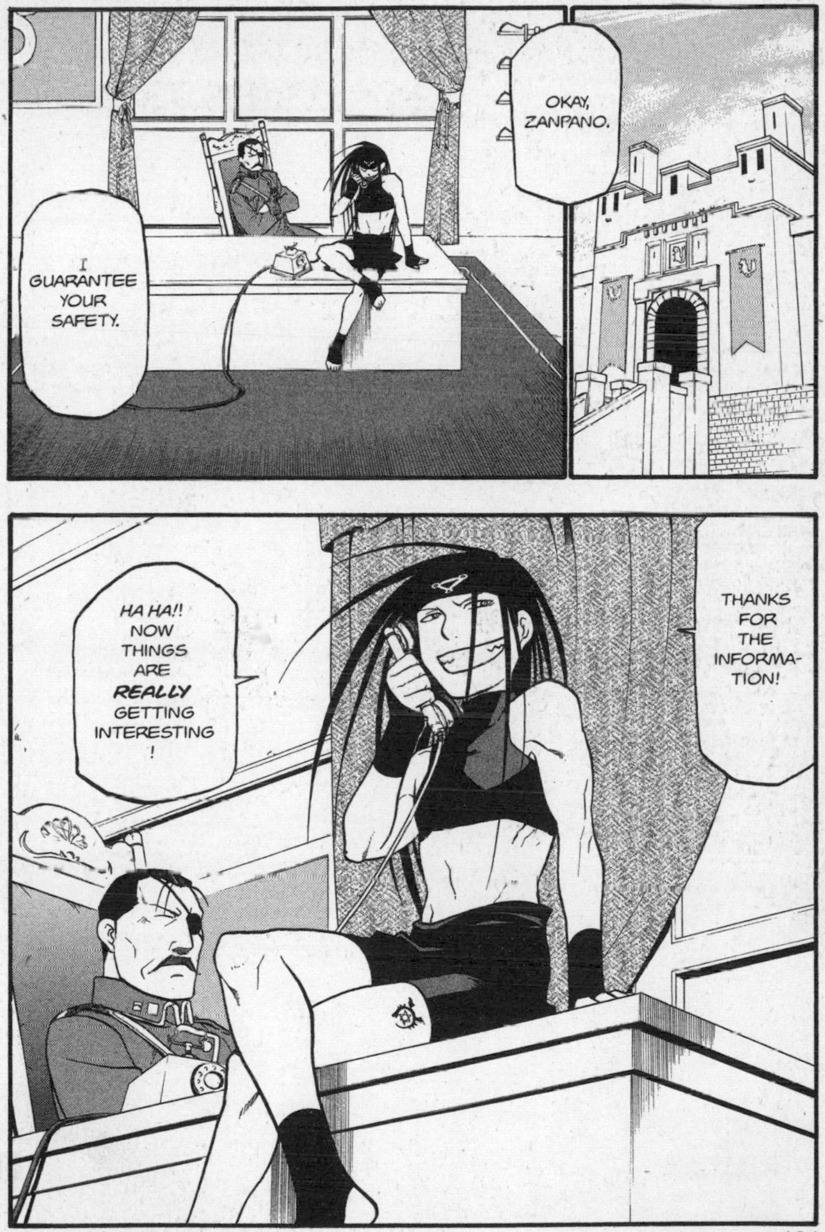
OKAY, ZANPANO.
I GUARANTEE YOUR SAFETY.
THANKS FOR THE INFORMATION!
HA HA!! NOW THINGS ARE *REALLY* GETTING INTERESTING!

To Be Continued in Fullmetal Alchemist Volume 20!

AN ENDANGERED SPECIES

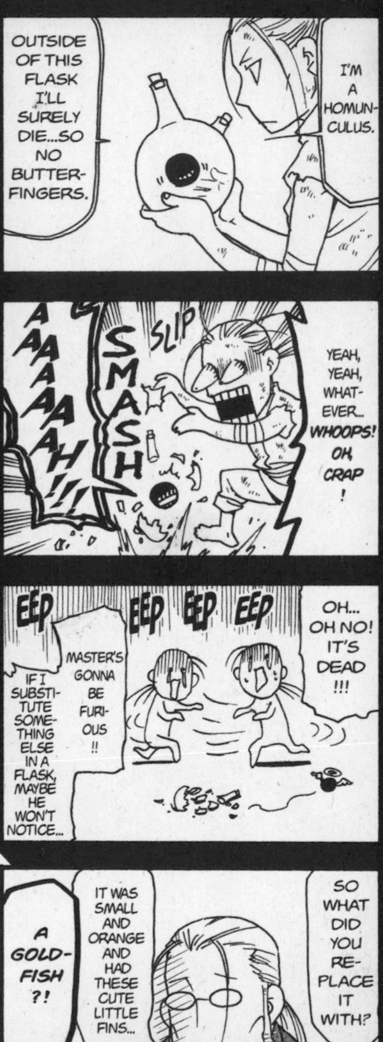
I'M A HOMUNCULUS.
OUTSIDE OF THIS FLASK I'LL SURELY DIE...SO NO BUTTER-FINGERS.
YEAH, YEAH, WHATEVER... WHOOPS! OH, CRAP!
SLIP
SMASH
AAAAAAAH!!!
OH... OH NO! IT'S DEAD!!!
EEP
EEP
EEP
EEP
MASTER'S GONNA BE FURIOUS!!
IF I SUBSTITUTE SOMETHING ELSE IN A FLASK, MAYBE HE WON'T NOTICE...
SO WHAT DID YOU REPLACE IT WITH?
IT WAS SMALL AND ORANGE AND HAD THESE CUTE LITTLE FINS...
A GOLD-FISH?!

FULLMETAL ALCHEMIST 19

SPECIAL THANKS...

JUN TOHKO
NONO
MASASHI MIZUTANI
COUPON
NORIKO TSUBOTA
HARUHI NAKAMURA
MICHIKO SHISHIDO
KEI TAKANAMAZU
YOICHI KAMITONO
My Editor YUICHI SHIMOMURA

AND YOU!!

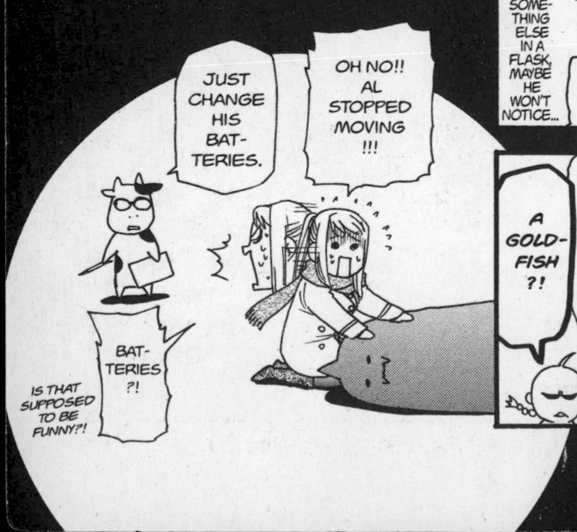
OH NO!! AL STOPPED MOVING!!!
JUST CHANGE HIS BAT-TERIES.
BAT-TERIES?!
IS THAT SUPPOSED TO BE FUNNY?!

A Field Guide to Briggs' Wildlife

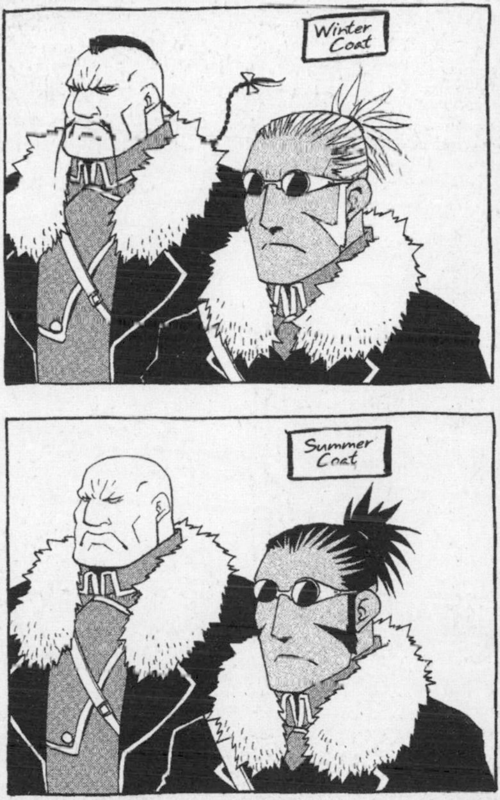
Winter Coat
Summer Coat

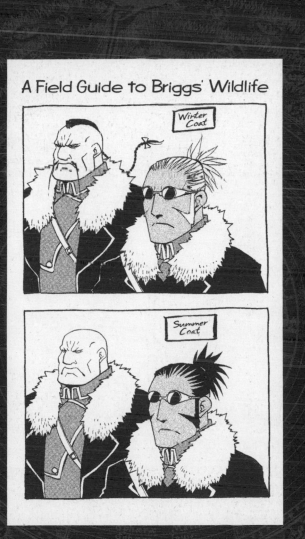

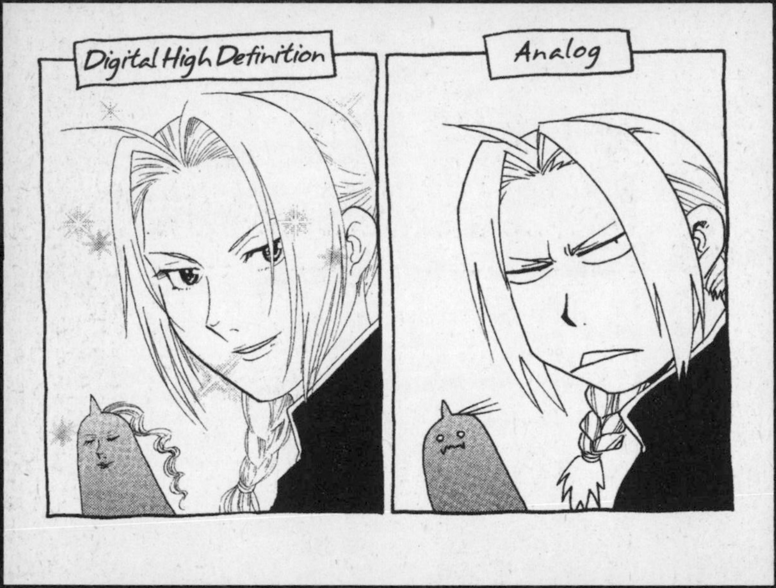
Analog
Digital High Definition

Fullmetal Alchemist Profiles

Get the background story and world history of the manga, plus:

- Character bios
- New, original artwork
- Interview with creator Hiromu Arakawa
- Bonus manga episode only available in this book

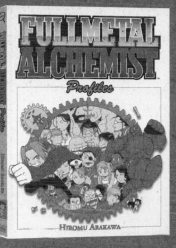

Fullmetal Alchemist Anime Profiles

Stay on top of your favorite episodes and characters with:

- Actual cel artwork from the TV series
- Summaries of all 51 TV episodes
- Definitive cast biographies
- Exclusive poster for your wall

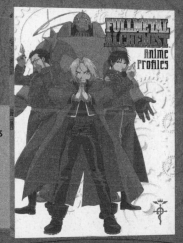

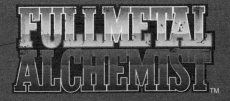

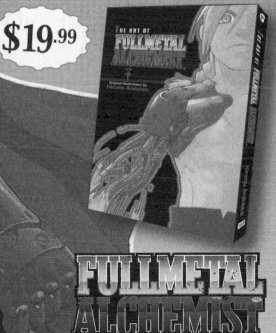

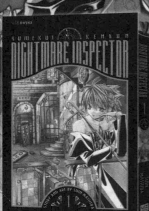

LOVE MANGA? LET US KNOW WHA

OUR MANGA SURVEY IS NOW AVAILABLE ONLINE. PLEASE VISIT: VIZ.COM/MANGASURVEY

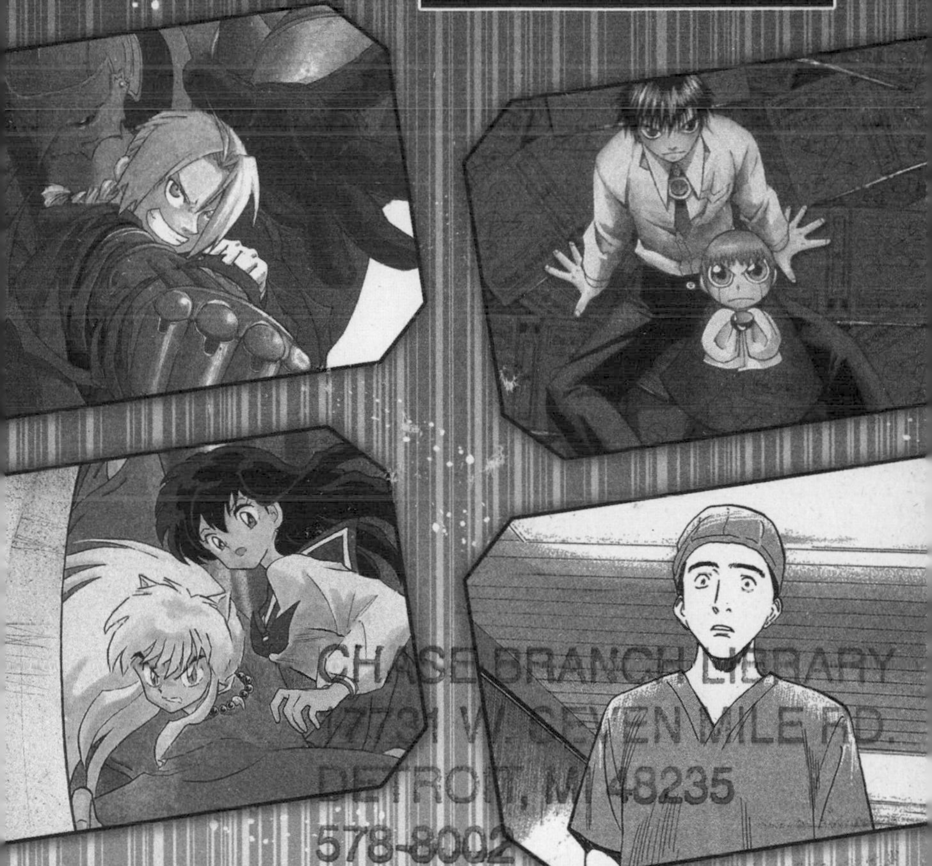

HELP US MAKE THE MANGA YOU LOVE BETTER!